PROJECT/ MATRIX MANAGEMENT POLICY and STRATEGY

Cases and Situations

PROJECT/ MATRIX MANAGEMENT POLICY and STRATEGY

Cases and Situations

Harold Kerzner, Ph.D.
David I. Cleland, Ph.D.

VNR VAN NOSTRAND REINHOLD COMPANY
——————————————— New York

Library of Congress Catalog Card Number: 84–5130
ISBN: 0–442–24719–2

Manufactured in the United States of America

Published by Van Nostrand Reinhold Company Inc.
115 Fifth Avenue
New York, New York 10003

Van Nostrand Reinhold Company Limited
Molly Millars Lane
Wokingham, Berkshire RG11 2PY, England

Van Nostrand Reinhold
480 La Trobe Street
Melbourne, Victoria 3000, Australia

Macmillan of Canada
Division of Canada Publishing Corporation
164 Commander Boulevard
Agincourt, Ontario MIS 3C7, Canada

15 14 13 12 11 10 9 8 7 6 5 4 3 2

Library of Congress Cataloging in Publication Data

Kerzner, Harold.
    Project/matrix management policy and strategy.

    1. Matrix organization.   2. Industrial project
management.   3. Matrix organization—Case studies.
4. Industrial project management—Case studies.
I. Cleland, David I.   II. Title.
HD58.5.K47   1984   658.4′02   84–5130
ISBN 0–442–24719–2

Preface

A kaleidoscope of matrix management systems is emerging in the theory and practice of management today. These systems appear to have one overriding characteristic—a departure from the classical model of management in favor of a multidimensional system of sharing decisions, results, and rewards in an organizational culture characterized by multiple authority-responsibility-accountability relationships. As contemporary organizations become more complex, interdependent, and buffeted by change, the use of extraordinary organizational arrangements to manage their affairs will become more commonplace.

The genesis of modern matrix management is found in the use of project teams organized to deal with a specific, temporary purpose. In the last decade project management has attained a maturity and rightfully takes its place in the theory and practice of management.

The introduction of matrix management starts to change the prevailing culture of the organization. The fluidity of matrix management, where planning, organizing, and control are carried out by mutual adjustment and increased communication and negotiation, creates the need for managers and professionals to work together more than ever. Conflicting directives, uncoordinated activities, territorial battles, professional jealousies, interpersonal strife, role ambiguities, and many more disfunctions are likely to be sensed by the individual in first experiences with matrix management. If this individual has been schooled in the traditional management notion that "one person shall have but one boss," early perceptions of matrix management may create deep feelings of frustration that no one person really is in charge and looking out for the best interests of the individual. If the key managers in the organization have not provided insight, through some form of organizational development, into how the matrix is supposed to operate, matrix management can become the basis for some real human problems. As an executive vice-president stated:

A matrix is hard on people—most seem to find it so. In a recent employee attitude survey at a large industrial complex that was matrixed (or whatever the verb is) 15–20 years ago, the matrix organization drew the least favorable reaction on the whole survey. Analysis of the responses showed that the reaction was pretty much shared by all levels. The concerns were mostly personal, rather than objective—what happens to me and my career, what team do I belong to, how do I identify with the goals and successes of the enterprise, does anybody really know whether I'm doing a good job??? Partly these concerns are geared to "bigness," but the people mostly ascribe them to the matrix and its inherent ambiguities—and so do I. So it becomes top priority for top management, especially top management of a matrix organization, to understand and address the issues in the people dimension.[1]

Much of the concern that the individual has centers on an understanding of the key roles in the matrix. Adequate definition and explanation of these roles is a positive step toward making matrix work.

Matrix Organizational Roles[2]

The cornerstone roles in the matrix organization are depicted in Figure 1. The professional or manager has a reciprocal relationship with the people filling these roles. Although each manager has responsibility for a particular management territory, there must be a sharing of key decisions, results, and rewards. The relative roles of the principals in Figure 1 can be summarized as follows:

General Manager: The chief architect of organizational strategy in the development of objectives and goals against which organizational performance is judged.

Functional Manager: The individual responsible for building and maintaining a base of specialized resources to support organizational objectives and goals.

Project Manager: Responsible for project results, the accomplishment of project objectives on time and within budget.

Work Package Manager: That individual responsible for developing and supporting work packages in the organization.

The Professional: The individual who has assured competence in a particular field or occupation essential to support organizational purposes.

---

[1] "Matrix Management: The General Manager's Perspective," by John W. Stuntz, in *Matrix Management Systems Handbook,* David I. Cleland (editor), Van Nostrand Reinhold Company, New York, 1983. P. 226.

[2] Paraphrased from David I. Cleland, "The Professional in Matrix Management," paper presented at the Project Management Institute Seminar/Symposium, Toronto, Ontario Canada, October 1982. Used by permission.

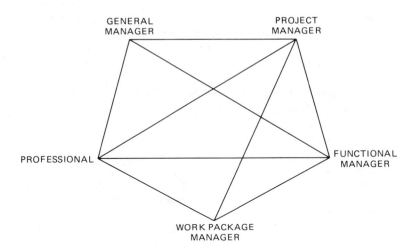

GENERAL MANAGER

PROJECT MANAGER

PROFESSIONAL

FUNCTIONAL MANAGER

WORK PACKAGE MANAGER

Figure 1.   Key Individuals in the Matrix Organization.

New knowledge of the theory and practice of matrix management in its alternative forms is a prerequisite to accepting the change that the matrix environment brings about. A key element of matrix management, which all key people must understand, is the basic dichotomy of the project-driven matrix organization: the project manager who is responsible for *results*—bringing the project in on time, within budget, and satisfying the project objectives—and the functional managers who are responsible for providing the *resources.* A knowledge of the interdependent authority-responsibility-accountability of these managers can do much to understand the two-boss situation that is endemic to matrix management.

Additional knowledge that the individual needs to acquire includes how planning and control are carried out in the matrix environment, how authority-responsibility-accountability patterns evolve, and how motivation and negotiation are critical to successful matrix management.

This casebook is written for use in undergraduate and graduate management programs. Continuing education programs and project/matrix management seminars, symposia, and workshops should find the book appropriate as a text. Certain of the cases and situations have questions at the end to help the students in their analysis. Other cases/situations provide no such guidance, thereby providing the student with a completely unstructured opportunity.

Traditional *cases* and *situations* are included in the book. The case method of instruction has been one of the major distinguishing traditions of management education. We continue that tradition. We introduce the management *situation* as a learning technique. The management *situation* is a combination of management circumstances at a given time that provides a problem or opportunity in matrix management. Such situations occur frequently in the practice of matrix management and are usually unstructured and of an "open-system" nature.

Each of the sections has a current bibliography for the reader who wishes to do further research into matrix management.

The book consists of seven sections, which contain a brief narrative, cases, situations, and bibliography. Briefly the material covered includes the following:

Section 1: Introduction and Implementation of Project/Matrix Management, deals with the design and execution of strategies to launch organizations into the matrix system.

Section 2: The Matrix Organization provides material on the facilitative organizational arrangements required to support the multidimensional authority, responsibility, and accountability patterns of matrix.

Section 3: Staff Selection, Motivation, and Training probes the human dimensions of matrix management.

Section 4: The Execution of Projects presents an overview of the key elements in the project-driven matrix management system to include organizational mission, project, objectives, goals, strategy, organizational structure, project team roles, style, and project resources. This section prescribes the basic elements that must be positioned before the project can be executed.

Section 5: Strategies, Policies, and Procedures lays out the administrative processes required to accomplish matrix management ends.

Section 6: Planning, Scheduling, and Control outlines the information, philosophy, and techniques for thinking through where the project is going and how a consistent pathway for getting there can be maintained.

Section 7: Permanent/International Matrix Management wraps the book up. This section takes the reader into the international and "permanent" context of the matrix form.

Acknowledgments

We acknowledge the participation of Dr. William R. King of the Graduate School of Business of the University of Pittsburgh as a principal in the consulting activities that provide background for certain cases in this book.

We thank Claire Zubritzky and Patricia Ray who supported us with administrative expertise and counsel throughout this project. Many students and clients have provided us with the opportunity and motivation to document the experiences we have had in supporting organizations involved in introducing or improving matrix management systems. Finally, we appreciate the cultural ambience for the generation of knowledge provided by Max Williams, Al Holzman, and Mark Collier, our respective school administrators.

HAROLD KERZNER
DAVID I. CLELAND

Contents

Preface/v
Acknowledgments/ix
 SECTION I. **Introduction and Implementation of Project/Matrix Management/1**

Case Studies:
 1. Project Management at Hyten Corporation/3
 2. Product Management at Costa Pharmaceutical Laboratories/13
 3. Designing and Implementing a Facilitative Matrix Organization/18
 4. A Systems Approach for Evaluating an R&D Project/25
 5. The Beta Construction Company/33
 6. Implementing Project Management— A Communication Problem/42
 7. Implementing a Project Management System in a Research Laboratory/56
 8. Project Firecracker/68
 9. MIS Project Management at First National Bank/73
 10. Webster Industrial Controls/84
 11. Wynn Computer Equipment (WCE)/87
 12. Starr Air Force Base/89
 13. The Evolution of Project Management Concepts from Tools to Realities: Two Case Histories/97
 14. Tennessee Wheelworks, Incorporated/112
 15. The Introduction and Implementation of Matrix Management at Standard Steel/123

Situations:
1. Project Management Image/146
2. Corporate Management Philosophy/152
3. Motivation in the Project-Driven Matrix/158

SECTION II.   The Matrix Organization/163

Case Studies:
16. The Successful Research Pilot Operation—A Case in Support of Dr. McGregor/168
17. Jones and Shephard Accountants, Inc./174
18. Acorn Industries/177

Situations:
4. How Best to Organize for Project Management/182
5. The Cultural Ambience of Matrix Management/190
6. Organizing for Strategic Planning in the Matrix Management Context/191
7. The Line/Staff Organizational Choice/192
8. The Cultural Ambience of the Project-Driven Matrix Organization/194
9. The Plural Executive/196

SECTION III.   Staff Selection, Motivation, and Training/199

Case Studies:
19. The Professional in Matrix Management/203

Situations:
10. Project Manager Candidate Specifications/214
11. Project Management Roles/215
12. Project Management "Magna Carta"/217

SECTION IV.   The Execution of Projects/219

Case Studies:
20. Federal Radar Corporation/225
21. Project Management in the Automotive Industry/239
22. Project Management at Fluor Utah, Inc./248
23. Client Reaction to Ineffective Project Management/263

24. The Case of the Precarious Program/272
25. Thermodyne, Inc., and the *Pegasus* Program/286
26. The Blue Spider Project/297
27. Corwin Corporation/310
28. TRW Systems Group (D)/319
29. TRW Systems Group (E)/328
30. Robert L. Franks & Company/344
31. The Lyle Project/351

Situations:
13. "Advantages/Disadvantages Profile" of Matrix Management/360
14. Perceptions of Matrix Management/364
15. Industrial Systems, Incorporated/367

SECTION V.   Strategies, Policies and Procedures/373

Case Studies:
32. Greyson Corporation/375

Situations:
16. The Reluctant Workers/379
17. Reduction in Work Force/380
18. Project Management Policies/380

SECTION VI.   Planning, Scheduling, and Control/383

Case Studies:
33. Cory Electric/386
34. Spaceage, Inc., (A)/389

Situations:
19. Capital Industries/409
20. Facilities Scheduling at Mayer Manufacturing/411
21. Small-Project Cost-Estimating at Percy Company/413
22. The Marketing Group/413
23. Establishing Planning Priorities/414
24. The Two-Boss Problem/416
25. Development of a Work Breakdown Structure/418
26. Managing the Project Manager's Time/419

SECTION VII. **Permanent/International Matrix Management/421**

Case Studies:
35. The Transnational Corporation/425
36. Bolivia Rural Electrification: A Case Study in Organizational Structure/431
37. The Cargo Ram Project/441
38. Dori International/451
39. The Red Dragon Project/456

Situations:
27. Industry/Construction Projects Division (I/CPD)/461
28. The Cultural Effect of Matrix Management/464
29. Acceleration of an International Matrix Management System/466
30. Responsibility-Sharing in the International Matrix/468
31. The Multinational Corporation/470
32. Implementing International Matrix Management/473

PROJECT/ MATRIX MANAGEMENT POLICY and STRATEGY

Cases and Situations

Section I
Introduction and Implementation of Project/ Matrix Management[1]

A project is a complex system of resources managed to achieve a specific objective within schedule and budget targets. The management of a project usually cuts across organizational lines; projects are unique and usually not repetitive in the same form within an organization.

Project management emerged in an unobtrusive manner, starting in the early 1960s. The term *project,* or *program, management* was used to describe a type of structure that already existed in various forms. No one can claim to have invented project management; its beginnings are often cited as the ballistic missile program of the space program of the United States. The origins of project management can be found in the management of large-scale, ad hoc endeavors, such as the Manhattan Project; large construction projects; and the use of naval task forces.

In the early 1960s we began to recognize project management for what it is. As early as 1961, Fisch, writing in the *Harvard Business Review,* spoke of the obsolescence of the line-staff concept and the growing trend toward the use of a "functional teamwork" approach to organization. In 1961, IBM established system managers with overall responsibility for various computer models across functional divisional lines. In the early 1960s and 1970s, a wide variety of organizations experimented with the use of alternative project-management organization forms. Project management has reached a degree of maturity and has been the precursor of today's matrix management approach. In recent years the term *matrix management* and *matrix organization* have come to be used to describe both project-driven, two-dimensional organizations and organizations that have "permanent" matrix forms. Although the project-driven matrix is the prime focus in this casebook, we shall from

---

[1] Some of the material in this section has been paraphrased from D. I. Cleland and William R. King, *Systems Analysis and Project Management,* 3rd edition, McGraw-Hill Book Co., New York, 1983. Reproduced with permission.

time to time use illustrations of both "temporary" and "permanent" matrix forms.

Understanding the culture of the organization is a prerequisite to introducing project management. An organization's culture reflects the composite management style of its executives, a style that has much to do with the organization's ability to adapt to such a change as the introduction and implementation of a project-management system.

In this section, the case studies and situations deal broadly with the cultural impact of introducing and implementing project management in modern organizations.

RELEVANT BIBLIOGRAPHY

Ackoff, Russell L. *Redesigning the Future—A Systems Approach to Societal Problems.* John Wiley & Sons, New York, 1974.

Anshen, Melvin. "The Management of Ideas." *Harvard Business Review,* July–August 1969.

Bobrowski, Thomas M. "A Basic Philosophy of Project Management." *Journal of Systems Management,* May 1974.

Burck, Charles G. "How GM Turned Itself Around." *Fortune,* January 16, 1978.

Burt, David N. "A Multimatrix Approach to Project Management." *Project Management Quarterly,* September 1980.

Business Week. "How a New Chief is Turning Interbank Inside out." July 14, 1980, pp. 109, 111.

Cleland, David I. "The Cultural Ambience of the Matrix Organization." *Management Review,* November 1981, pp. 24–39.

———. "Defining A Project Management System." *Project Management Quarterly,* December 1977.

———, and William R. King. *Management: A Systems Approach.* McGraw-Hill Book Company, New York, 1972.

———, and William R. King. *Systems Analysis and Project Management,* 3rd edition, McGraw-Hill Book Company, New York, 1983.

Cook, Desmond L. *Educational Project Management.* Charles E. Merrill Publishing Company, Columbus, Ohio, 1971.

Dane, C. W., C. F. Gray, and B. Woodworth. "Successfully Introducing Project Management Techniques into an Organization." *Project Management Quarterly,* December 1981, pp. 23–26.

Davis, Keith. "The Role of Project Management in Scientific Manufacturing." IEE Transactions on Engineering Management, vol. 9, no. 3, 1962.

Davis, S. M., and P. R. Lawrence. *Matrix.* Addison Wesley, Reading, Massachusetts, 1977.

Ellis, L. W. "Effective Use of Temporary Groups for New Product Development." *Research Management,* January 1979.

Fisch, Gerald G. "Line-Staff is Obsolete." *Harvard Business Review,* September 1961.

Fulmer, Robert M. "Product Management: Panacea or Pandora's Box." *California Management Review,* Summer 1965.

George, William W. "Task Teams for Rapid Growth." *Harvard Business Review,* March–April, 1977.

Greiner, Larry E. "Evolution and Revolution as Organizations Grow." *Harvard Business Review,* July–August 1972.

Gullett, C. R. "The Systems Concept Revisited." *SAM Advanced Management Journal,* April 1971.

Kelly, Joe, and Kamran Khozan. "Participative Management: Can It Work?" *Business Horizons,* August 1980.

Kerzner, Harold. *Project Management for Bankers.* Van Nostrand Reinhold Co., New York, 1982.

———. *Project Management for Executives.* Van Nostrand Reinhold Co., New York, 1982.

Levitt, Theodore. "Exploit the Product Life Cycle." *Harvard Business Review,* November–December 1965.

Main, Jeremy. "Work Won't Be the Same Again." *Fortune,* June 28, 1982, pp. 58–65.

Mantell, Leroy H. "The Systems Approach and Good Management." *Business Horizons,* October 1972.

Meads, Donald E. "The Task Force at Work—The New Ad-Hocracy." *Columbia Journal of World Business,* November–December, 1970.

Miles, R. E., and C. C. Snow. *Organizational Strategy, Structure and Process.* McGraw-Hill Book Co., New York, 1978.

O'Brien, James J. "Project Management: An Overview." *Project Management Quarterly,* vol. III, no. 3, September 1977.

Sales, Leonard R., and Margaret K. Chandler. *Managing Large Systems.* Harper & Row, Publishers, Inc., New York, 1971.

Smith, August W. "A Systems View of Project Management." *Industrial Management,* March–April 1976.

Tilles, Seymour. "The Manager's Job: A Systems Approach." *Harvard Business Review,* January–February 1963.

Webber, Ross A. *To Be A Manager—Essentials of Management.* Richard D. Irwin, Inc., Homewood, Illinois, 1981.

Wickesberg, A. K., and T. C. Cronin. "Management by Task Force," *Harvard Business Review,* vol. 40, no. 6, November–December 1962, pp. 111–118.

Williams, Earle C. "Matrix Management Offers Advantages for Professional Services Firms." *Professional Engineer,* February 1978.

CASE STUDY 1: PROJECT MANAGEMENT AT HYTEN CORPORATION

On June 5, 1978, a meeting was held at Hyten between Bill Knapp, Director of Sales, and John Rich, Director of Engineering. The purpose of the meeting was to discuss the development of a new product for a special customer application. The requirements included a very difficult, tight-time schedule. The key to the success of the project would depend on timely completion of individual tasks by various departments.

Knapp: "The Business Development Department was established to provide coordination between departments, but it has not really helped. It just sticks its nose in when things are going good and messes everything up. It has been out to see several customers, giving them information and delivery dates that we can't possibly meet."

Rich: "I have several engineers who have M.B.A. degrees and are pushing hard for better positions within engineering or management. They keep talking that formal project management is what we should have at Hyten. The informal approach we use just doesn't work all the time. But I'm not sure any type of project management will work in our division."

Knapp: "Well, I wonder who Business Development will tap to coordinate this project? It would be better to get the manager from inside the organization instead of hiring someone from outside."

Company Background

Hyten Company was founded in 1922 as a manufacturer of automotive components. In the 1940s the company manufactured electronic components for the military. After the war, Hyten was incorporated and continued to prosper.

Hyten was one of the major component suppliers for the space program, but it did not allow itself to become specialized. When the space program declined, Hyten acquired other product lines, including energy management, building products, and machine tools, to complement its automotive components and electronics fields.

Hyten has been a leader in the development of new products and processes. Annual sales are in excess of $300 million. The Automotive Components Division is one of Hyten's rapidly expanding business areas.

The Automotive Components Division

The management of both the Automotive Components Division and the corporation itself is young and involved. Hyten has enjoyed a period of continuous growth over the past 15 years as a result of careful planning and having the right people in the right positions at the right time. This is emphasized by the fact that within five years of joining Hyten, every major manager and division head has been promoted to more responsibility within the corporation. The management staff of the Automotive Components Division has an average age of 40, and no one is over 50. Most of the middle managers have M.B.A. degrees and a few have Ph.D.s. Currently, the Automotive Components Division has three manufcturing plants at various locations throughout the country. Central offices and most of the nonproduction functions are located at the main plant. There has been some effort by past presidents to give each separate plant some minimal level of purchasing, quality, manufacturing engineering, and personnel functions.

Informal Project Management at Hyten Corporation

The Automotive Components Division of Hyten Corporation has an informal system of project management based on each department handling its own functional area of a given product development or project. Projects have been frequent enough that a sequence of operations has been developed to take a new product from concept to market. Each department knows its responsibilities and what it must contribute to a project.

A manager within the Business Development Department assumes informal project coordination responsibility and calls periodic meetings of the department heads involved. These meetings keep everyone advised of work status, changes to the project, and any problem areas. Budgeting of the project is based on the cost analysis developed after the initial design, and funding is allocated to each functional department based on the degree of its involvement. Funding for the initial design phase is controlled through Business Development. The customer has very little control over the funding, manpower, or work to be done. The customer, however, dictates when the new product design must be available for integration into the vehicle design and when the product must be available in production quantities.

The Business Development Department

The Business Development Department, separate from Marketing/Sales, functions as a steering group for deciding which new products or customer requests are to be pursued and which are to be dropped. Factors they consider in making these decisions are: (1) the company's long- and short-term business plans, (2) current sales forecasts, (3) economic and industry indicators, (4) profit potential, (5) internal capabilities (both volume and technology), and (6) what the customer is willing to pay versus estimated cost.

The duties of Business Development also include coordinating the project or new product from initial design through market availability. In this capacity, the department has no formal authority over either functional managers or functional employees. It acts strictly on an informal basis to keep the project moving and to report on status and potential problems. It is also responsible for selecting the plant that will be used to manufacture the product.

The functions of Business Development were formerly handled as a joint staff function, where all the directors would periodically meet to formulate short-range plans and solve problems associated with new products. The department was formally organized three years ago by the then 38-year old president as a recognition of the need for project management within the Automotive Components Division.

Manpower for the Business Development Department was taken from both outside the company and from within the division. This was done to honor the corporation's commitment to hire people from the outside only after determining that there were no qualified people internally—an area that for years has been a sore spot to the younger managers and engineers.

When the Business Development Department was organized, its authority and responsibility were limited. However, the Department's authority and responsibility have subsequently expanded, though at a slow rate. This was done so as not to alienate the functional managers, who were concerned that project management would undermine their "empires."

Introduction of Formal Project Management at Hyten Corporation

On July 10, 1978, Willbur Donley was hired into the Business Development Department to direct new product development efforts. Prior to joining Hyten, he had worked as project manager with a company that supplied aircraft hardware to the government. He had worked both as an assistant project manager and as a project manager for five years prior to joining Hyten.

Shortly after his arrival, he convinced upper management to examine the idea of expanding the Business Development group and giving it responsibility for formal project management. An outside consulting firm was hired to give an in-depth seminar on project management to all management and supervisory employees in the division.

Prior to the seminar, Donley talked to Frank Harrel, Manager of Quality and Reliability, and George Hub, Manager of Manufacturing Engineering, about their problems and what they thought of project management.

Frank Harrel is 37 years old, has an M.B.A., and has been with Hyten for five years. He was hired as an industrial engineer and three years ago was promoted to Manager of Quality & Reliability. George Hub is 45 years old and has been with Hyten for 12 years as Manager of Manufacturing Engineering.

Donley: "Well, Frank, what do you see as potential problems to the timely completion of projects within the Automotive Components Division?"

Harrel: "The usual material movement problems we always have. We monitor all incoming materials in samples and production quantities, as well as in-process checking of production, and finished goods on a sampling basis. We then move to 100 percent inspection if any discrepancies are found. Marketing and Manufacturing people don't realize how much time is required to obtain either internal or customer deviations. Our current manpower requires that schedules be juggled to accommodate 100 percent inspection levels on 'hot items.' We seem to be getting more and more items at the last minute that must be done on overtime."

Donley: "What you are suggesting is a coordination of effort with Marketing, Purchasing, Production Scheduling, and the Manufacturing function to allow your department to perform its routine work and still be able to accommodate a limited amount of high level work on 'hot' jobs."

Harrel: Precisely, but we have no formal contact with these people. More open lines of communication would be of benefit to everyone."

Donley: "We are going to introduce a more formal type of project management than has been used in the past, so that all departments who are involved will actively participate in the planning cycle of the project. That way, they will remain aware of how they affect the function of other departments and prevent overlapping of work. We should be able to stay on schedule and get better cooperation."

Harrel: "Good, I'll be looking forward to the departure from the usual method of handling a new project. I hope it will work much better and result in fewer problems."

Donley: "How do you feel, George, about improving the coordination of work among various departments through a formal project manager?"

Hub: "Frankly, if it improves communication between departments, I'm all in favor of the change. Under our present system, I am asked to estimate cost and lead times to implement a new product. When the project begins, the Product Design group starts making changes that require new cost figures and lead times. These changes result in cost overrun and not meeting schedule dates. Typically, these changes continue right up to the production start date. Manufacturing appears to be the bad guy for not meeting the scheduled start date. We need someone to coordinate the work of various departments to prevent this continuous redoing of various jobs. We will at least have a chance to meet the schedule, to reduce cost, and improve the attitude of my people."

Personnel Department's View of Project Management

After the seminar on project management, Sue Lyons, Director of Personnel, and Jason Finney, Assistant Director of Personnel, met to discuss changing the organization structure from informal project management to formal project management.

Lyons: "Changing over will not be an easy road. There are several matters to consider."

Finney: "I think we should stop going to outside sources for competent people to manage new projects that are established within Business Development. There are several competent people at Hyten who have M.B.A.s in Systems/Project Management. With their background and familiarity with company operations, it would be to the company's advantage if we selected personnel from within our organization."

Lyons: "Problems will develop whether we choose someone from inside the company or outside."

Finney: "However, if the company continues to hire outsiders into Business Development to head new projects, competent people at Hyten are going to start filtering to places of new employment."

Lyons: "You are right about the filtration. Whoever is chosen to be a project manager must have qualifications that will get the job done. He should not only know the technical aspect behind the project, but he should also be able to work with people and understand their needs. He has to show concern for team members and provide them with work challenge. Project managers must work in a dynamic environment. This often requires the implementation of change. Project managers must be able to live with change and provide necessary leadership to implement the change. It is the project manager's responsibility to develop an atmosphere to allow people to adapt to the changing work environment.

"In our department alone the changes to be made will be very crucial to the happiness of the employees and the success of projects. Employees must feel they are being given a square deal, especially in the evaluation procedure. Who will do the evaluation? Will the functional manager be solely responsible for the evaluation, when in fact he might never see the functional employee for the duration of a project? He could not possibly keep tabs on all his functional employees who are working on different projects."

Finney: "Then the functional manager will have to ask the project managers for evaluation information."

Lyons: "I can see that could result in many unwanted situations. To begin with, say the project manager and the functional manager don't see eye to eye on things. Granted both should be at the same grade level and neither should have authority over the other. But let's say there is a situation where the two of them disagree as to either direction or quality of work. That puts the functional employee in an awkward position. He will tend to bend toward the individual who signs his promotion and evaluation form. This can influence the project manager into recommending an evaluation below par regardless of how the functional employee performs. There is also the situation where the employee is on the project for only a couple of weeks. He spends most of his time working by himself and does not get a chance to know the project manager. The project manager gives the functional employee an average rating even though the employee has done an excellent job. This results from very little contact. Then what do you do when the project manager allows personal feelings to influence his evaluation of the functional employee? If the project manager knows the functional employee personally, he might be tempted to give a strong or weak recommendation, regardless of performance."

Finney: "You seem to be aware of many difficulties that project management might bring."

Lyons: "Not really, but I've been doing a lot of homework since I attended that seminar on project management. It was a good seminar, and because there is not much written on the topic, I've been making a few phone calls to colleagues for their opinions on project management."

Finney: "What have you learned from these phone calls?"

Lyons: "That there are more personnel problems involved. What do you do in this situation: The project manager makes an excellent recommendation to the functional manager. The functional employee is aware of the appraisal and feels he should be given an above-average pay increase to match the excellent job appraisal, but the functional manager fails to do so. One personnel manager from another company incorporating project management ran into problems when the project manager gave an employee of one grade level responsibilities of a higher grade level. The employee did an outstanding job taking on the responsibilities of a higher grade level and expected a large salary increase or a promotion."

Finney: "Well that's fair isn't it?"

Lyons: "Yes it seems fair enough, but that's not what happened. The functional manager gave an average evaluation and argued that the project manager had no business giving the functional employee added responsibility without first checking with him. So then what you have is a disgruntled employee ready to seek employment elsewhere. Also, there are some functional managers who will give above-average pay increases only to those employees who stay in their departments and make them look good."

Finney: "So how does this leave our organization with respect to implementing formal project management?"

Lyons: "Right now I can see several changes that would take place. The first major change would have to be attitudes toward formal project management and hiring procedures. We do have project management here at Hyten, but on an informal basis. If we could administer it formally, I feel we could do the company a great service. If we seek project managers from within, we could save time and money. I could devote more time and effort to wage and salary grades and job descriptions. We would need to revise our evaluation forms—the present ones are not adequate. Maybe we should develop more than one evaluation form: one for the project manager to fill out and give to the functional manager, and a second form to be completed by the functional manager for submission to Personnel."

Finney: "That might cause a few problems. Should the project manager fill out his evaluation during or after project completion?"

Lyons: "It would have to be after project completion. That way the employee would not feel tempted to screw up the project if he felt he had not been evaluated fairly. If he felt he wasn't justly evaluated, he could decide not to show up for a few days—these few days of absence could be most crucial for timely project completion."

Finney: "How will you handle evaluation of employees who work on several projects at the same time? This could be a problem if employees are really enthusiastic about one project over another. They could do a terrific job on the project they are interested in and slack off on other projects. You could also have functional people working on departmental jobs who would charge to the project overhead. Don't we have exempt and nonexempt people charging to projects?"

Lyons: "See what I mean? We can't just jump into project management and expect a bed of roses. There will have to be changes. We can't put the cart before the horse."

Finney: "I realize that, Sue, but we do have several M.B.A. people working here at Hyten who have been exposed to project management. I think that if we start putting our heads together and take a systematic approach to this matter, we will be able to pull this project together nicely."

Lyons: "Well Jason, I'm glad to see that you are for formal project management. We will have to approach top management on the topic. I would like you to help coordinate an equitable way of evaluating our people and to help develop the appropriate evaluation forms."

Product Management as Seen by the Various Departments

The General Manager arranged, through the Personnel Department, to interview various managers confidentially. The purpose of the interview was to evaluate the overall acceptance of the concept of formal project management. The answers to the question, "How will project management affect your department?" were as follows:

Frank Harrel, Quality & Reliability Manager

"Project management is the actual coordination of the resources of functional departments to achieve the time, cost, and performance goals of the project. As a consequence, personnel interfacing is an important component of the success of the project. In terms of quality control, it means less of the attitude of the structured workplace where quality is viewed as having the function of finding defects and, as a result, is looked upon as a hindrance to production. It means that the attitude toward quality control will change to one of interacting with other departments to minimize manufacturing problems. Project management reduces suboptimization among functional areas and induces cooperation. Both company and department goals can be achieved. It puts an end to the can't-see-the-forest-for-the-trees syndrome."

Harold Grimes, Plant Manager

"I think that formal project management will give us more work than long-term benefits. History indicates that we hire more outside men for new positions than we promote from within. Who will be hired into these new project management jobs? We are experiencing a lot of backlash from people who are required to teach new people the ropes. In my opinion, we should assign inside M.B.A. graduates with project management training to head up projects and not hire an outsider as a formal project manager. Our present system would work fine if inside people were made the new managers in the Business Development Department."

Herman Hall, Director of M.I.S.

"I have no objections to the implementation of formal project management in our company. I do not believe, however, that it will be possible to provide the reports needed by this management structure for several years. This is because most of my staff are deeply involved in current projects. We are currently working on the installation of minicomputers and on-line terminals throughout the plant. These projects have been delayed by the late arrival of new equipment, employee sabotage, and various startup problems. As a result of these problems, one group admits to being 6 months behind schedule and the other group, although on schedule, is 18 months from its scheduled completion date. The rest of the staff currently assigned to maintenance projects consists of two systems analysts who are nearing retirement and two relatively inexperienced programmers. So as you can readily see, unless we break up the current project teams and let those projects fall further behind schedule, it will be difficult at this time to put together another project team.

"The second problem is that even if I could put together a staff for the project, it might take up to 2 years to complete an adequate information system. Problems arise from the fact that it will take time to design a system that will draw data from all the functional areas. This design work will have to be done before the actual programming and testing can be accomplished. Finally, there would be a debugging period, when we receive feedback from the user on any flaws in the system or enhancements that he needs. We could not provide computer support to an 'overnight' change to project management."

Bob Gustwell, Scheduling Manager

"I am happy with the idea of formal project management, but I do see some problems implementing it. Some people around here like the way we do things now. It is a natural reaction for employees to fight against any changes in management style.

"But don't worry about the Scheduling Department—my people will like the change to formal project management. I see this form of management as a way to minimize if not eliminate schedule changes. Better planning on the part of both department and project managers will be required, and the priorities will be set at corporate level. You can count on our support, because I'm tired of being caught between Production and Sales."

John Rich, Director of Engineering

"It seems to me that project management will only mess things up. We now have a good flowing chain of command in our organization. This new matrix will only create problems. The Engineering Department, being very technical, just can't take direction from anyone outside the department. The project office will start to skimp on specifications just to save time and dollars. Our products are too technical to allow schedules and project costs to affect engineering results.

"Bringing in someone from the outside to be the project manager will make things worse. I feel that formal project management should not be implemented at Hyten. Engineering has always directed the projects, and we should keep it that way. We shouldn't change a winning combination."

Fred Kuncl, Plant Engineering

"I've thought about the tradeoffs involved in implementing formal project management at Hyten and feel that Plant Engineering cannot live with them. Our departmental activities are centered around highly unpredictable circumstances that sometimes involve rapidly changing priorities related to the production function. We in Plant Engineering must be able to respond quickly and appropriately to maintenance activities directly related to manufacturing activities. Plant Engineering is also responsible for carrying out critical preventive maintenance and plant construction projects.

"Project management would hinder our activities because project management responsibilities would burden our manpower with additional tasks. I am against project management because I feel that it is not in the best interest of Hyten. Project management would weaken our department's functional specialization, because it would require cross utilization of resources, manpower, and negotiation for the services critical to Plant Engineering."

Bill Knapp, Director of Marketing

"I feel that the seminar on formal project management was a good one. Formal project management could benefit Hyten. Our organization needs to focus in more than one direction at all times. To be successful in today's market, we must concentrate on giving all our products sharp focus. Formal project management could be a good way of placing individual emphasis on each of the products of our company. Project management would be especially advantageous to us because of our highly diversified product lines. The organization needs to efficiently allocate resources to projects, products, and markets. We cannot afford to have expensive resources sitting idle. Cross-utilization and the consequent need for negotiation ensure that resources are used efficiently and in the organization's best overall interest.

"We can't afford to continue to carry on informal project management in our business. We are so diversified that all our products can't be treated alike. Each product has different needs. Besides, the nature of a team effort would strengthen our organization."

Stanley Grant, Comptroller

"In my opinion, formal project management can be profitably applied in our organization. Management should not, however, expect that project management would gain instant acceptance by the functional managers and functional employees, including the Finance Department personnel.

"The implementation of formal project management in our organization would have an impact on our cost control system and internal control system, as well.

"In the area of cost control, project cost control techniques have to be formalized and installed. This would require the accounting staff to: (1) break comprehensive cost summaries into work packages, (2) prepare commitment reports for "technical decision makers," (3) approximate report data, and (4) concentrate talent on major problems and opportunities. In project management, cost commitments on a project are made when various functional departments, such as Engineering, Manufacturing, and Marketing, make technical decisions to take some kind of action. Conventional accounting reports do not show the cost effects of these technical decisions until it is too late to reconsider. We would need to provide the project manager with cost commitment reports at each decision state to enable him to judge when costs are getting out of control. With timely cost commitment reports, he could take needed corrective actions and be able to approximate the cost affect of each technical decision. All these would require additional personnel and expertise in our department.

"In addition, I feel that the implementation of formal project management would increase our responsibilities in the Finance Department. We would need to conduct project audits, prepare periodic comparisons of actual versus projected costs and actual versus programmed manpower allocation, update projection reports and funding schedules, and sponsor cost improvement programs.

"In the area of internal control, we will need to review and modify our existing internal control system to effectively meet our organization's goals related to project management. A careful and proper study and evaluation of existing internal control procedures should be conducted to determine the extent of the tests to which our internal auditing procedures are to be restricted. A thorough understanding of each project we undertake must be required at all times.

"I'm all in favor of formal project management, provided management would allocate more resources to our department so we could maintain the personnel necessary for the added duties, responsibilities, and expertise required."

After the interviews, Sue Lyons talked to Wilbur Donley about the possibility of adopting formal project management.

Lyons: "You realize that regardless of how much support there is for formal project management, the General Manager will probably not allow us to implement it for fear it will affect the performance of the Automotive Components Division."

CASE STUDY 2: PRODUCT MANAGEMENT AT COSTA PHARMACEUTICAL LABORATORIES

The pharmaceutical industry is considered to be one of the most highly competitive industries in business today. Numerous companies, both major and minor, compete to gain a share of the billions of dollars spent worldwide on health care services.

Costa Laboratories, headquartered in Chicago, Illinois, is one of the 10 largest pharmaceutical houses in the world. The corporation consists of eight divisions employing in excess of 25,000 people and having 1977 sales of $1.5 billion.

The Pharmaceutical Products Division of Costa is the third largest division, with sales of $250 million. Primary products of the division consist of antianxiety agents, antihypertensive agents for controlling blood pressure, antiepileptic drugs, hematinics, and vitamins.

In June 1978, the division underwent a reorganization that affected various marketing and promotion functions within the division. Previously, the various functions of pricing, product management, advertising, market research, and sample promotion existed as separate service centers, with staff members reporting to their respective department heads. Though the system worked efficiently in terms of each function, management felt it lacked one element for truly multidisciplined strategic planning: cohesion. The resources of each of these service departments were not always equally or immediately available to a particular business unit.

Inevitably, this tended to create problems of competing priorities. With the budgets of each of the service centers under separate control, there were natural inhibitions on transferring or allocating resources across functional boundaries as needs arose. Simply stated, there was no common accountability for the activities or objectives of the various service units.

Thus, basic to the reorganization, was the formation of new business planning units called *strategic planning centers.* The purpose of each center was to undertake and assume responsibility for the strategic business and promotional planning of an assigned group of products. The strategic planning center, utilizing the concept of zero-based budgeting, was designed to give each center both authority and responsibility for allocation of resources to strategies and media that would best accomplish the center's profit goal. It was the responsibility of the planning center to analyze the various strategies and develop action plans based on the current realities of the marketplace.

The reorganization of the key elements of the division also had the effect of broadening the authority and responsibility of the product manager, now referred to as a *Business Unit Manager.*

Under the previous system, the product manager lacked the authority to coordinate the activities of supporting departments in order to direct them toward his established objective of effective product promotion. Instead he was faced with a chain-of-command-type situation. The essential departments of market research, advertising, manufacturing, distribution, and sample promotion were reached only through their respective managers or vice-presidents who weighted requests in terms of priorities and, most specifically, budget expenditures to complete the requested projects.

Resulting factors of the system often led to such situations as incomplete and late marketing research data, due to communication problems over the type and amount needed; advertising that projected the wrong theme or used improper advertising copy, which created regulatory problems with the Food and Drug Administration; manufacturing and distribution problems, which resulted in a new product being sold to retailers by the sales force with no stock available in the distribution centers to be shipped to them; and the failure to send drug samples out to the sales force for promotion to the medical community. Such factors and those of competing departmental priorities tended to further develop a system that supported frustration and the inability of departments to view an objective, in the framework of the systems approach, in terms of the whole objective, rather than just their specific departmental contribution to that objective.

The reorganization of the divisional structure was intended to broaden the authority of the product manager under the business unit concept.

Under the new concept, the organizational structure was as follows within the strategic planning center:

1. Director of strategic planning
2. Business unit manager (product manager)
3. Promotion manager
4. Pricing assistant
5. Marketing research assistant
6. Medical liaison
7. Manufacturing liaison
8. Sales liaison

Within this framework, the business unit manager reports to the director of strategic planning for all activities conducted within the unit itself. The unit or product manager coordinates the activities of advertising under the promotion manager, pricing under the pricing assistant, marketing research under the auspices of the market research assistant, medical under the director of the medical department, and contact with the sales department under a sales liaison.

Specifically, the relationship to the various departments within the business unit exists as follows:

1. Pricing—Within the framework of pricing, the role of the business unit manager is severalfold. He is responsible for determining and updating factory costs of products; he is responsible for monitoring profit margins and adjusting retail prices when factory costs threaten to reduce the margin; he must monitor competitive product pricing so as to maintain near parity with highly competitive products; and he is responsible

for segmentation of pricing between retail, wholesale, and government customers. The product manager not only works closely with the pricing assistant for the above requirements, but he also maintains active communication with pricing in regard to competitive bidding situations. With the intense competition becoming keener daily, many large-volume pharmaceuticals are being placed up for bid by hospital (nonprofit) and government customers. It is the role of the unit manager and the pricing assistant to accept or reject bids in the context of profit potential in terms of factory cost versus dollars realized from the bid, potential for retail sales as a result of a patient obtaining a refilled prescription for a drug that was first given in a hospital, etc. In addition, they must analyze when the drug was sold on bid, the type and size of the customer requesting the bid, and the status of competition in regard to who they are and what prices they are offering. Primary responsibility in pricing belongs to the pricing assistant, but all efforts are coordinated by the unit manager, who accepts or rejects pricing recommendations. In turn, many decisions of a pricing nature, i.e., acceptance of a large-volume bid, have an effect on manufacturing, specifically product planning. Often these effects are changes in product forecasts and necessitate changes in product priorities. This requires involvement between the unit manager and manufacturing to reset those priorities.

Normally, a business unit manager interfaces with manufacturing only in terms of unit forecasts that control production schedules, product specifications and quality assurance, inventory control, and production capacity questions. However, the manufacturing liaison also works closely with the unit manager to handle any sudden manufacturing problems that might arise, such as equipment problems that could significantly affect product throughput. The business manager provides essential manufacturing cost information when the unit manager is considering early factors of a new product or line extension.

2. Advertising—Within the framework of advertising, the unit manager works closely with the advertising promotion manager. The promotion manager is responsible for aspects of product promotion dealing with advertising, most often of the medical journal type, and creating sales aids used by the sales force. The promotion manager, often a creative artist, uses ideas suggested by the unit manager, along with his own, to create effective advertising that will convey a sales message to the medical community in an ethical and acceptable manner designed to reinforce the message communicated by the field sales force. In addition, the promotion manager creates sales aids or detail booklets, which contain medical product information, for use by the sales force with the medical community. Last, the promotion manager has the responsibility of coordinating the promotional budget with the business unit manager for all assigned products. Twice yearly the managers draw up and review promotional budgets to ensure that proper expenditures are being carried out according to the promotional plan and to readjust any factors of advertising, etc., that are not falling within the scope of the market plan. Final coordination and control of advertising and promotion rest with the business unit manager.

3. Marketing Research—This department is extremely important to the unit manager in terms of usable information. To formulate, implement, and receive feedback from a marketing plan, the unit manager relies heavily on data obtained by market research. Foremost among the many roles that the business unit manager plays is

the maintenance and improvement of his products' share of market. He constantly strives for better methods to increase market share, and for usable information he relies heavily on market research. Market research uses a variety of tools; for example, surveys of physicians on a particular product. This type of information can allow the unit manager fo judge the efficacy of his promotional theme in terms of physician recall from sales force calls and journal advertising. Other information provided by market research provides a handle on competitive activity concerning efficacy and depth of promotion as far as increases or decreases of sales force calls, sample mailings, and plain mailings, along with an esimate of total dollars spent on each category. Other areas essential to the unit manager and provided by market research include a statistical picture of the manager's product category, specifically the increase or decrease of a pharmaceutical category; for example, the antibiotic market. It also can portray how his particular product is faring against competition in terms of increase or decrease of market share; the number of new prescriptions written for a particular product, including his own and competition; and the segmentation of a product category into retail and hospital markets.

Last, marketing research can provide valuable information to the unit manager in terms of consideration of new products or line extensions. In early stages, a prime consideration for a new product is the state of the product category, increasing or decreasing, and the conclusion that a new product can gain a good share of market and be profitable. Marketing research can provide the essential information so the unit manager can begin to make an informed decision.

Because of the importance of market research, a prime role in its operation must be played by the product manager in order to concentrate its efforts to gain the most accurate information.

4. Medical Department—The purpose of interfacing with the medical department is twofold: (1) all printed material of a promotional nature must be approved by the medical department for authenticity, accuracy, and compliance with FDA standards; (2) all requests for documentation and information from the medical community on a variety of medical subjects are the responsibility of the medical department. The business unit manager must have all promotional material he has developed approved by the medical department before it can be sent to the sales force. This material is reviewed for content accuracy under generally accepted medical guidelines enforced by the FDA. The medical department will either approve promotional material or return it for restructuring, with appropriate comments. In addition, the product manager relies on the medical department to handle complex medical questions from the medical community and often uses these as a benchmark for judging physician interest in his promotional message. Last, the medical department and the product manager interface strongly during clinical studies of a new product. The progress or failure of a drug during clinical studies can be the basis for either committing large sums of money to formulating a new product marketing plan or scrapping a potential new product.

In the medical department the unit manager has the ability to coordinate efforts, but he cannot exercise direct authority because of the lack of in-depth medical knowledge and the independent nature of the physicians and scientists he is working with.

5. Regulatory Affairs—This particular department is concerned primarily with

compliance of company products and promotional efforts with the enforced standards of the Food and Drug Administration. For the safety of consumers, the FDA maintains rigid standards over all aspects of pharmaceutical company operations from manufacturing to sales. The product manager is primarily concerned with Regulatory affairs over the correctness and accuracy of promotional materials, i.e., advertising and sales force promotional aids. The Regulatory Department reviews all such material and must give written approval before it can be released for general usage. In addition, the department monitors the medical package inserts required for all drugs for correctness and adherence to FDA standards.

The involvement of the product manager with the Regulatory Department is not that extensive, but, due to the very sensitive nature of strict compliance with FDA regulations, the manager must constantly be aware of the actions, if any, that Regulatory is taking to maintain full compliance with FDA regulations.

6. Sales—This department can be referred to as the object of the product managers affection or disgust. It is a department that he interfaces with most strongly. This department represents the action that is the culmination of all efforts by the product manager and all other supportive departments. It is here that the forecasts are won or lost on the success or failure of a product. It is here that all promotional efforts are exerted to produce sales. It is also here that product management and sales management can clash over promotional themes, sizes or samples, pricing, bids, stock situations, and promotional priorities.

The primary effort expended by the product manager with regard to the sales department is one of motivation. In essence the product manager must sell his promotional program to the managers of the sales department. Usually it involves the discussion of the program by product and sales management and, if disagreement arises, compromising. Promotional efforts are a mutual effort between product and sales management.

In dealing with the sales department, the product manager interfaces with a variety of individuals. He works with a vice-president of sales, a director of sales, numerous regional and district managers, the salesmen themselves, and sales training. He is truly one individual who must be able to motivate many. The old saying "give us the tools to sell with" is in proper context here. The product manager does provide the tools to sell with, in that he provides everything from promotional materials up to the design of sales samples. He remains in constant touch with sales to obtain feedback on programs. He must be prepared to alter ineffective programs, react quickly to competition, and always maintain a consistency in materials and ideas that are usable by the sales force, for the result of all this effort by the product manager is successful programs that lead to sales increases.

Thus, the role of the product manager is manifold. Initially he formulates the market plans for all his assigned products, utilizing the skills and resources of support departments. The market plans serve as a baseline from which to formulate promotional ideas and contain important areas, such as the status of a particular pharmaceutical product category in terms of growth potential, competitive activity and methodology for coping with it, descriptions of key customers, the final promotional budget, a complete layout of planned promotional activities, and expected results based on short- and long-range forecasting.

The product manager also plays a key role in forecasting long- and short-range goals. Utilizing the support departments of market research, manufacturing, and pricing, he is responsible for setting objectives both of a tactical and a long-range nature. These objectives consist of forecasting gross dollar sales, percentage of market, unit sales and percentage of market served in relation to market share. These forecasts in turn are used for corporate long-range planning in terms of gross dollar sales, capital expenditure requests by manufacturing to meet demand for increased unit sales, and formulating specific dollar budgets for use by various departments based on total percentage of sales.

One of the most important roles of the product manager is the creation of new product ideas. Often in his surveillance of the market, the manager recognizes a need for a specific product. Utilizing support departments he formulates preliminary information on market potential, competitive products, estimated gain of market share with his product, based on price parity or price undercut, manufacturing costs with profit margin, new product requirements of the FDA, and time periods required to market the product.

He brings together his ideas and those of others into a cohesive goal-seeking action plan.

To reiterate, the role of the product manager is manifold. A product manager is first an innovator bringing new product and promotional ideas into reality. The product manager is a planner. It is he who formulates long-and short-range forecasts and market plans and then monitors them constantly for accuracy. The product manager is a coordinator. It is he who coordinates the various departments toward a specific objective within the bounds of a given budget. These departments range from research and development to sales, and the product manager must have the ability to converse on all these levels. Last, the product manager is a motivator and a trainer. It is he who maintains a clear view of the objective and must often clear away the confusion created by meshing the efforts of unrelated departments. He must communicate the objective, clarify its purpose, and then motivate others to help him reach it. Often he must train those individuals to work effectively toward the objective, and these individuals can range from research and development to first-year salesmen.

CASE STUDY 3: DESIGNING AND IMPLEMENTING A FACILITATIVE MATRIX ORGANIZATION[1]

Introduction

This case will describe some of the major forces and factors encountered when an industrial organization in the energy systems market converted from a traditional functional organization to the matrix form.[2]

---

[1] D. I. Cleland, "Designing and Implementing a Facilitative Matrix Organization: A Case History," paper presented at the Project Management Institute Seminar/Symposium, Anaheim, Calif., October 1978.

[2] The organization will be designated as Company X in this case.

The energy crisis in 1974 stimulated an already strong market demand for energy systems in the public utility sector. Public utility customers began to seek vendors for such systems to be developed and placed in an operational mode in as short a time as possible. Development of the software and hardware for these systems required that Company X form teams in different disciplines to do the job. Customers insisted that the vendors establish a single focal point for management of each project. Company X rushed into a matrix organizational form to satisfy the customer requirements for such a focal point. Company X failed to prepare the people involved for the cultural and organizational changes that the matrix organization fostered.

Customer Dissatisfactions

It did not take long for customer dissatisfactions to signal that things were not going as expected. Customer unhappiness with the management of the project became evident through such problems as these:

- Although the organizational charts provided to the customer reflected a focal point to manage the project, the project manager did not have authority to commit Company X on the project.
- Emerging technical problems on the project were not being evaluated at any central location in Company X's organization.
- Customer requests for information or assistance were being passed around in Company X without overall coordination being carried out by a central individual. In some situations the customer's people got involved coordinating matters within Company X in order to get the answers needed!
- Project development schedules began to slip, cost overruns appeared highly probable, and the technical performance goals appeared to be seriously threatened.

Customer dissatisfactions reached a vociferous stage in a meeting between the public utility's chief executive and the president of Company X; the customer threatened to cancel the contract and institute legal proceedings unless some remedial action was taken.

Within Company X there was considerable uneasiness; the project manager had frequently expressed his lack of leverage to make things happen in managing the project. Functional managers felt threatened by the project manager's attempts to obtain resource support from their professional groups. An alarming number of professional and managerial people had resigned or had transferred to collateral positions elsewhere in the company. Professional people working on the project were not sure who was their boss. In one situation a senior programmer resigned from Company X. Not knowing who his immediate supervisor was, he dropped his letter of resignation in the mail to the company president!

Clearly, the matrix organization was not working in Company X! It was at this time that the author was brought in to consult with the managers of Company X on "how to get the project back on track!"

Gathering the Data

After the author was given a general orientation into Company X and the project, he conducted a series of in-depth interviews with the following officials: executive vice-president, senior functional managers, project manager, deputy project manager, key project engineers, and small groups of software and hardware professionals.

In addition, several days were spent interviewing key customer executives to get a flavor of the customer's viewpoint. All the interviews were conducted in the context of "diplomatic immunity," with the results not identified with any individual. This "diplomatic immunity" was necessary to ensure candid evaluations and comments. On balance, all the people being interviewed cooperated, to various degrees, in providing relevant information and opinions on the development and management of the project. When it became clear that there would be no report cards on individuals submitted as a result of the interviews, everyone tended "to let it all hang out."

The interviews confirmed what had been suspected by people concerning the efficacy with which the project was being managed:

1. The formal authority and responsibility of the project manager vis-à-vis the functional managers had been neither established nor communicated to the key participants.
2. Although the organizational charts reflected a focal point for the management of the project, the project manager had failed to function as a single point of management and accountability for the project. This failure was more organizational than personal.
3. Individual professionals in the technical communities of Company X were in an identity crisis, not knowing for whom they really worked. A corollary of this was the lack of a strong superior-subordinate relationship in these technical communities. Career counseling, merit performance administration, and a subordinate's need for "someone I can talk to" were being seriously neglected.
4. The lack of effective organizational interfacing among the project manager and the functional managers hampered the operation of a "work package assignment" a process in which the work packages could be assigned and followed as work was performed. The inability to monitor and control these work packages made meaningful project review impossible.
5. With only two exceptions, the people interviewed in Company X believed that the project could not be brought in on time and within budget. Those interviewees, who were members of the technical community, felt that there was a low probability of the project attaining the state of the art that had been promised to the customer. Although this was not a direct matrix organization problem, the nebulous nature of the matrix organizational reporting lines and processes *may* have contributed to the failure to have such perceptions communicated to key managers who could have done something about the situation.
6. There was considerable discomfort with the two-boss syndrome of the matrix organization. People sensed that they were doing something wrong in their working relationships, but were not able to put a finger on what was wrong.
7. People in the functional areas were not committed to support the project. The

project manager failed to sense his role in motivating the key people on the project. No team building had been undertaken by the project manager; indeed, it was difficult to identify the members of the team on the project.

8. It was abundantly evident that the key executives of Company X neither understood the theoretical underpinnings of the matrix organization nor understood the cultural changes that type of organization would bring to the company.

After the data bases developed from the interviews had been analyzed and presented to top management of Company X, a remedial strategy was suggested to correct some of the problems uncovered during the interviews. The first remedial action undertaken was a series of workshops, "Project Management and the Matrix Organization," conducted for key managers, project engineers, and key professional members of the technical community. The material presented at these workshops consisted of lectures on the theory and practice of project management and small peer group discussion sessions for the participants. The theory of project management centered on the alternative organizational forms of project management and the systems nature of project management. The lectures were structured to present a conceptual framework of how the matrix organization is supposed to work. Many examples of how other companies had reorganized along matrix lines were presented, along with a description of some of the problems that a company typically encounters when it tries the matrix organization. A presentation of these problems helped the participants understand that their problems with the matrix organization were not unique—or unsolvable.

The small peer group discussions were unstructured, the better to foster dialogue on the material presented in the formal lectures and to seek some insight into the question: "What implications does project management have for us?" Each small peer group was presented a series of other pertinent questions or discussion suggestions gleaned from the data bases developed from the interviews. Such questions as the following helped to stimulate the discussions:

- What does Company X seem to be doing right about project management? Wrong?
- How effective is our current organizational approach to project management?
- How might project management be improved in our company?
- How might the customer perceive our approach to project management?

Questions of this sort helped to provide insight into how Company X might again reorganize into a matrix form—a reorganization that was subsequently undertaken.

The Reorganization

The second reorganization of the company along the lines of a matrix structure was accomplished over a period of several months. To initiate the reorganization, a tentative structure was announced along the approach indicated in Figure 1. Eight functional areas and a project (program) management area were selected to represent the basic structure of the company. From the eight functional areas, many subfunctional areas evolved to accommodate the professional specialization and management span of control required to support company objectives.

Figure 1 highlights the organizational complexities of such a structure: several characteristics of this structure are worth noting. There were 18 major formal program-functional interfaces that the program managers had to deal with. "Systems integrators" in the engineering department were appointed to coordinate the integration of the hardware and software. Table 1 contains a description of the studies of the "systems engineering integrator"; such people performed a sort of deputy program manager role in providing technical leadership to the projects.

Figure 1 highlights the importance of the program work packages in the organizational schema of Company X. The complementary role of the program manager and the functional manager gained a specificity through the work package—a model of the work to be accomplished on the program.

Table 2 was developed to specify the formal authority and responsibility relationships of the program-functional interface of Company X. The specification of this interface evolved over a period of time through a series of workshops that afforded people the opportunity to get used to the new organizational approach.

Side Problems and Opportunities

The reorganization was not accomplished without some negative results. Several managers found the organizational complexities of program management not to their liking and left the company. Some professionals in the engineering community saw the role of program manager as an opportunity to gain general manager-type experience before assuming a general manager role. The in-depth analysis carried out in reorganizing the company along the matrix structure brought other problems and opportunities to the surface. Some of these would have eventually surfaced, but the participation of the people in the workshops provided a cultural ambience that encouraged candor on the part of the participants and helped to facilitate the emergence of problems

Table 1. Systems Engineering Integrator Energy Systems.

Provides technical leadership to achieve program compliance with specifications integrating hardware and software in support of program objectives.

- Interprets the technical requirements of the program.
- Verifies that the design and implementation of the system software and hardware perform the functions specified at the level of performance stipulated in the program objectives.
- Works with appropriate technical director or representative to provide technical guidance in specifying update work packages for accomplishing technical parameters of the program.
- Participates as a member of the program team.
- Provides focal point for integration of software and hardware into system capable of providing performance required.
- Works closely with the program manager in supporting total program objectives.
- Reports to systems engineering manager.

dling any political situations that came up, in decision making, and in opening doors to top management when higher level decisions were necessary.

First Project

The project management expert's previous experience had convinced him that the choice of the first project was very critical, for it could rapidly indicate whether project management really works. Two months after he joined the bank, a decision was made to start the implementation process and to start with a single project and evaluate its progress. The project was large enough to be a good test of project management and to provide top management with a convincing case for continuing to use project management.

The project management expert carried out the broad functions of the communications expediter and assumed the responsibility of project director on the first project to ensure its success. After two months the project was well under way and it was evident to all that the project was going to be very successful. Since it was then proposed to put other projects under project management, the projects were organized as a matrix with the existing functional disciplines at the bank.

The initial 30-day study phase of the project was completed within cost and budget. Top management was extremely satisfied with the project and considered it to be highly successful. The project saved the bank approximately $5 million per year. It also proved to be a good selling tool for the bank, and top management makes a big point in its writing and other presentations that the bank operates under project management. The bank now has eight projects under project management, and any new project where there is considerable risk involved is a candidate for project management.

Problems Encountered

The only serious problems encountered in implementing project management at the bank were concerned with convincing the various levels of management that project management was the way to go. As previously indicated, there were few problems encountered in obtaining the full support of top management; however, middle management was a different story. It took approximately two years of concentrated effort to eliminate the last areas of resistance.

During this implementation period, there were a number of instances of conflict characterized by foot-dragging and haggling over authority. This conflict was almost entirely due to the unfamiliarity of the line/functional managers with the matrix and their failure to accept the multiboss situation. The conflict was accentuated when the functional manager and the project manager were on the same level and sometimes led to a power struggle over who really controlled the efforts of the project personnel. Project management insisted that project personnel live by tight schedule, budget, and performance deadlines, which functional managers were not used to.

Another problem encountered, and one that still remains somewhat of a problem, is caused by the high visibility inherent in major projects under project management. This proved to be a major problem at the bank, because they were not used to high visibility in their organizational units. High visibility was particularly disturbing to project personnel, as they could not longer hide in anonymity or blame others for project failure. An occasional problem resulted from the appointment of a project manager who turned out to be very weak. The project would have been doomed had the project director not been strong and willing to make decisions.

The final problem in the bank environment involved getting people to be project managers, project directors, and full-time project personnel. Accepting a project management job in addition to a regular full-time position was not appealing to a vice-president. For project personnel, there were (and are) few incentives and no rewards for serving on a project team. In fact, there were the usual disincentives such as (1) loss of "permanent home" for project personnel to return to and (2) the uncertainty as to who makes project team member performance evaluations. The problem of a bonus or other incentives for project personnel is still a topic of discussion at the bank.

A Public Utility Tries Project Management

The second case history involves a major west coast power-generating electrical utility. It is involved in the design, development, construction, and contracting for the construction of fossil-fueled power plants and, more recently, nuclear power plants. It is also involved in hydroelectric power generation, high-voltage power transmission, extrahigh-voltage power transmission (EHV), and such new energy alternatives as solar power.

Until its original initiation of project management in 1972, the utility was a typical line/discipline organization. This organization evolved through the years, but always had a power supply department (responsible for operation) and always had an engineering department. The manpower levels in engineering went up and down with business cycles; however, just prior to the reorganization they had a very strong engineering department organized by discipline. The major divisions were mechanical engineering, civil engineering, electrical engineering, and the new addition, nuclear engineering. Each division of the line organization had its own supervisor, who reported to the manager of engineering.

The utility had some very significant projects during the 1950s and 1960s, prior to the implementation of project management. The largest of these were fossil-fueled steam power plants, which were handled by a lead-discipline management concept. This concept had some of the functions of project management, but without the responsibility and authority and without even title or recognition. For example, a lead-discipline engineer would come to Civil Engineering and indicate what he needed. A man would be assigned to the project, but this man had other jobs to do and did not always accomplish the project work on time. And if he didn't do the work, the lead-discipline engineer had no recourse to mandate that the work be done. If he received no response, the work didn't get done, and he had no ability or power to go to top management; all he could do was complain to his immediate supervisor who sometimes could negotiate with the other disciplines.

The lead-discipline concept worked; however, many problems were encountered. Many of the projects were primarily coordinated with an engineer-constructor who did the actual work. On other projects, usually smaller, but sometimes very significant, the utility did its own design. These kinds of projects were particularly troublesome.

Power generation plants, particularly coal and nuclear, were becoming bigger and far more complex, particularly in the involvement with regulatory agencies. These factors were greatly affecting the utility's ability to manage projects within cost and schedule, and management was coming to the realization that there must be a better way.

The Reorganization Process

Management at all levels at the utility realized as early as the middle 1960s that it needed something different. Top management started to look for a better way to organize, because it recognized that there were duplication problems, budget and schedule overruns, interdepartmental squabbles, and project overlaps and gaps.

The problems came to a head in 1972, when engineering management decided that it was not properly organized to get its job done and that it needed to improve working relationships with the other major company division—power supply (operations). Engineering management formed a task force of key people (not management) who were to work with a consultant and outline his work. A consultant was hired, and his first task was to interview key people and gather sufficient data on which to base a reorganization proposal. He pinpointed the real conflicts and eliminated the unjustifiable complaints. He then held a number of meetings with middle management, which resulted in a report containing a proposed reorganization that was eventually approved by top management.

Objections immediately surfaced from middle management; the proposed reorganization did not really solve the problems. The consultant had been specifically asked—how should they reorganize? He was not asked how they should handle projects, and he did not address this problem in his report. He was looking only at the problem of fragmented disciplines, and there was considerable realignment of disciplines after his report was implemented. Instead of further centralizing disciplines, there was some decentralization to get disciplines closer to the activity.

The need for better management of projects was not recognized by either management or the consultant. However, when the consultant's report was received, the utility was just getting into a major nuclear project. A member of middle management, the Chief of Nuclear Engineering, was perceptive enough to see that something major was missing, and that was the project management concept. He read the report and pointed out to his management, department head vice-presidents, that this element was really missing here and that the consultant had not addressed this important point. As a result the consultant returned, the projects and prospective project managers were identified, and the implementation of project management was put in motion. Top management approved the action with a wait-and-see attitude, indicating that it wanted to see how it worked out.

The Implementation of Project Management

The utility found that the consultant was of little help in implementing the process, either because project management was not within his scope or he did not have the expertise to advise on the implementation—he had not provided management with a game plan for getting the ball rolling. They realized that they had the ball and had to come up with their own game plan. Under the leadership of the Chief Nuclear Engineer, who later became manager of projects or manager of project managers, a staff group was formed to develop a game plan. The initial implementation was not companywide, for the problems of being recognized by the other departments still existed. The game plan was adapted primarily for the engineering department, and the reorganization affected only two departments—power generation and engineering. Implementation of project management on a companywide scale came much later, after it had been thoroughly accepted in the engineering department and its advantages had been demonstrated.

The game plan provided for the implementation of the following actions:

To convert all projects in the engineering department to project management in the matrix mode and assign project managers. There were nine active projects at this time.

To orient top management on the advantages of project management and to obtain its commitment and firm support for the concept.

To give the involved people, i.e., engineering personnel and management, an understanding of what project management was all about, so as to obtain their firm support.

To provide for the preparation of project charters, revised organization charts, new jurisdiction statements and job descriptions, and project manager salary levels.

The effort to implement project management was directed by the Chief Nuclear Engineer with help from the previously mentioned staff group. The Chief Nuclear Engineer became the communications expediter and served as a forcing function, in that he personally kept up the momentum and pushed for the rapid implementation of project management. He recognized that help was needed in obtaining the unqualified support of all people who would be involved in project management. Therefore, a training organization was given a contract to carry out the effort.

It was recognized that the function of the educational or training effort would be to adjust the attitudes of management and project personnel. Next it was recognized that the place to start was with top management, because the rest of the job is much easier if an unqualified top management commitment has been obtained. Top management had to understand what project management means and that it now must depend much less on line management for information and for assignment of responsibility. Top management must also relinquish some of its authority and decision making prerogatives. As is often the case, top management was very receptive to the training consultant's arguments and firm top management support was obtained.

The utility staff group then worked with the training team to develop an orientation program for the rest of the organization. The training was to be conducted at two levels: (1) the line managers and supervisors along with the project managers, (2) the workers who would be involved with projects. Because of the help of the outside training organization, this orientation period was relatively short, and the project organization in a matrix mode was set up.

Problems Encountered

The major types of problems encountered at the utility during the implementation of project management were: (1) resolving conflict between managers, (2) achieving acceptance of the two-boss situation, (3) picking project managers, (4) providing project managers with a career path, and (5) picking project management tools.

The critical problems occurred during the process of "selling" middle management and working out the operational details. Many bittter battles occurred during the long conferences involving middle management and the Chief Nuclear Engineer and his staff. Some middle-line managers proved to be completely intractable and had to be put into positions where they were not involved in the project matrix. Others became project managers where they had to completely reorient their line of thinking and their management approach. During the implementation period there were a few power struggles, primarily between project and line managers over who was really in control of some aspect of the project. Some of the line managers felt that they had been deserted by top management and that the rug had been pulled from under them. Top management's strong support of the project managers was necessary during this implementation phase, but did cause some difficulties and animosities.

The problem of how do you pick project managers was not faced early in the implementation process. Utility management felt that the best people to lead a project were the same people who had been doing it all along. Therefore, most project managers were picked from the ranks of line managers. This procedure caused some problems at first, but for the most part those preferring to be line managers returned to the line and people that liked project work gravitated to the project office. Some of the best project managers who have remained in project work were coordinators before the implementation of project management.

The major problem encountered during the implementation phase with project management tools involved the search for adequate reporting techniques. The original manager of projects wanted a consistent format for reporting, i.e., the same format for the reports from each project, providing him with sufficient visibility to take corrective action. He wanted to know how well his project managers were functioning as well as communicating information. The staff group was assigned to develop a format that originally required a rather large report. However, once the project management concept had achieved companywide acceptance, it became a one-page report, and today it has practically disappeared. The need for a common format disappeared once other lines of communication were opened, and the project managers developed their own reporting styles.

Another problem that developed during the implementation phase was the utilization of planning and scheduling techniques. A consistent format again proved to be unnecessary, and the tools utilized differed widely depending on the project. Small projects required only simple bar charts, and larger projects utilized critical path scheduling, although usually computerized. It was not until approximately two years after the initial implementation of project management that computerized methods were in general use.

Case History Conclusions

Project management has been accepted as a way of life at both the bank and at the utility. All projects are planned and controlled by project managers utilizing a matrix mode in the overall organization. Project managers function either for a single large project or as a multiproject manager for small, uncomplicated projects. A program manager or a manager of projects serves as a coordinator of all projects, a manager of priorities, and an allocator of resources.

Looking back on these two examples of the implementation of project management, a number of conclusions are apparent. These conclusions can be used as criteria for the successful implementation of project management. Project management is most likely to succeed if all or most of the following criteria are met:

1. There is a great need in the organization for a better way of handling complex jobs.
2. The need is recognized by top management, even if it does not know what to do about it.
3. The jobs are multidisciplinary or multidepartmental.
4. Both top management and line or functional management are thoroughly sold on the need for project management and are ready for it before it is implemented.
5. The process of implementing project management is carefully planned and carried out according to plan.
6. The first project is chosen with great care, because it must be successful; if the first project is a failure, project management is doomed.
7. There is one dedicated person (or more) who is a firm believer in project management and will shepherd it through the critical implementation phase.

The first criterion is met whenever an organization finds that it is not able to cope with complex, multidisciplinary jobs. The need for "a better way" must then be recognized by some member of management and ultimately by top management (Criterion 2). A job may be complex and still not require project management. Project management is called for when the job is not only complex, but is also multidisciplinary or multidepartmental. The basic need for project management occurs because of the necessity to coordinate across organizational boundaries to integrate the job (Criteron 3).

The fourth criterion states that all levels of management must be in favor of project management. It is very important that top management be 100 percent supportive of project management, but it is equally important or even more important that lower levels of management be sold. This is particularly important with the operating levels, the users of the results of the project. If the user is not on the side of project management, the project management concept is dead. The operating levels can be very difficult to sell unless all presentations are made in their operating language.

The fifth criterion indicates that every project must have a complete and workable project plan. However, every project plan must be designed specifically for each particular project. A standard planning format is a good place to start, but the actual elements of the plan should be carefully chosen for relevancy to the needs of each particular project. An important portion of the project plan should be the decisions leading to a workable control system, whatever existing control systems the organization may use or modify for project use. However, each project has its own unique control problems, and it is essential that each project be individually evaluated. Each project will have individual control problems and will need its own control system, specifically designed for project needs. For example, if PERT is not needed, it shouldn't be forced on the project. The project control system should be kept as simple as possible.

The first project must be an outstanding success (Criterion 6). Everyone in the organization from top management to the operating levels has his or her fingers crossed until that first project is a success. At this point everyone jumps on the bandwagon and fully supports project management, but if the first project fails, project management is doomed.

The two case histories indicate that the last of the seven criteria for the implementation of project management is by far the most important. There must be a single dedicated person who serves as a focal point for promoting project management. He must be a firm believer in project management and have the ability and the authority to shepherd it through the critical implementation phase. He must ensure that the other six criteria are met, with particular emphasis on selling the project management concept to all levels of management. The actions taken by this communications expediter in the implementation process are discussed in the following sections of this paper.

The Implementation Process

The conclusions drawn from the two case histories suggest that the implementation of project management can be laid out as a rational process as shown in Figure 5. The process begins when a company or organization acquires one or more very complex multidisciplinary jobs. The organization usually finds that it cannot handle the new jobs within capabilities of its existing organization. There are no provisions for carrying out jobs that cross many organizational boundaries. In addition, management discovers that the new jobs have created havoc with the existing management structure.

The first critical step involves some member of the organization recognizing that there is a critical need for a better way to carry out such complex jobs.

This recognition of a need may come from any level in the organization. Usually the need is recognized by top management, as it was in the two case histories. Although top management may recognize a need, it may not know what to do about it. The recognition that project management is the best answer to the problem usually comes from a lower level in the organization. The person advocating project management in the organization, whether in management or not, has had previous experience with project management or has attended a seminar on it. Thus the concept of project

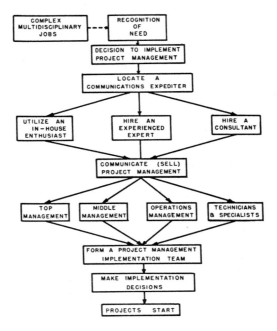

Figure 5.   The Implementation Process.

management is introduced into the organization. A considerable period of time for discussing project management and its alternatives usually results.

The next critical step is the decision by top management to implement project management. This decision may have been the result of careful consideration by top management, by the advice of a consultant, or by the successful efforts of enthusiasts within the organization selling top management.

It is at this point that a mistake is often made. Top management, in its enthusiasm for the new concept, jumps in with both feet. Top management issues a directive indicating that the organization now has project management, and having made the decision, it assumes that its job is done. It then turns to other matters, fully expecting project management to automatically work without further executive attention. Unfortunately a critical step has been ignored. The entire organization has not been prepared to accept the new concept. The chances are that the rest of the organization, particularly middle and operations management, will reject project management, and it will fail. This failure of a worthwhile concept is not limited to project management. It occurs frequently with other worthwhile concepts, such as long-range planning and management by objectives (MBO). Failure to adequately prepare the organization for a radically new concept almost inevitably results in failure.

How is an organization adequately prepared for a radically new concept? Top management must first recognize that the new concept cannot be forced down the throats of its management team. Next it must realize that adequate time must be provided to prepare the organization for this new concept and that there must be one or more dedicated people to direct this effort. The key to success depends upon the correct choice of this dedicated individual or individuals.

How are dedicated individuals located? Top management has three alternatives:

1. Utilize an in-house enthusiast in project management.
2. Hire an experienced expert in project management from another organization.
3. Hire a management consultant.

The first alternative is usually the most satisfactory, because someone within the organization is most familiar with the people with whom he or she must communicate and with the idiosyncrasies of the organization. If there is no one in the organization who has the specific requirements needed for the important job of communications expediter, top management must fall back on one of the other two alternatives. Hiring an outside expert in project management can work very well if he or she is given sufficient time to learn the workings of the organization. The outside expert should be from another similiar organization, preferably in the same kind of business, and should have gone through the job of implementing project management with a good track record. Hiring a management consultant on a temporary basis is somewhat more risky. A management consultant may or may not have extensive experience in project management. In addition, a consultant has no personal career interest at stake, not normally staying in the organization long enough to see how everything works out. Neither of these alternatives is quite as good as utilizing a home-grown enthusiast; however, these two alternatives must be considered in the absence of local talent. Of course, there are a number of variations and combinations of the three alternatives just discussed.

The first case history (the bank) is an example of an organization that recognized that it needed help and that it had no in-house project management enthusiast; so it hired an expert and gave him the specific job of implementing project management. This approach worked very well, because the expert took the time and made the effort to become thoroughly knowledgeable about the organization of the management team he was joining. He was also careful not to throw his weight around and make any large waves until he was certain that he had the complete support and confidence of all levels of management. The implementation process then went very smoothly, and the first project was outstandingly successful. As a result, project management is now a permanent part of the bank's management tools. Implementation of project management at the bank went very smoothly because there was a definite communications expediter appointed by top management and charged with doing that specific job.

The second case history (the utility) is also an example of an organization that recognized that it needed a better way to conduct large complex projects. It took the approach of utilizing a consultant, and engineering management formed a task force of key people who were to work with the consultant and to outline and direct his work. However, the consultant proved to be relatively ineffective and limited in his knowledge of implementing project management. His principal contribution was a series of recommendations for reorganization of the utility's Engineering Department.

Fortunately, the organization proved to have an in-house enthusiast for project management. This member of middle management effectively and enthusiastically promoted the use of project management long after the consultant had disappeared. Due almost entirely to the middle manager's efforts, the resistance to project management disappeared, and the concept was sold first in the Engineering Department and later throughout the organization.

The actions taken by this dedicated individual must be carefully planned to assure the success of project management. In analyzing the actions taken, it is apparent that the primary job is that of communications expediter. In the role of communications expediter, he or she carries out a number of communication functions:

- Ensures that all members of the organization understand the principles of project management.
- Informs all members in the organization of the advantages of project management.
- Informs the members of management and the project team of the personal gains they can derive from project management.
- Sells all levels of management on the need for project management and on the value of its successful utilization.
- Ensures that all levels of management and specialists on the prospective project team are communicating with each other.

The communications expediter will find that his selling effort must cover all levels in the organization. The selling effort must start with top management to ensure that all company executives are 100 percent behind the concept. Even when the need for project management originated with top management, the communications expediter must conduct a selling effort to ensure that he or she has reached all members of top management. Unless top management is fully supportive, the effort to sell the rest of the organization will probably fail.

It is then important that the concept be sold to middle and operations management. These managers, particularly those who are directly in charge of operations, must be sold on the concept, because they are the ones who will actually conduct the project. Operations management can make the project a success or failure. The operations manager must ensure that project work receives its fair share of the effort. An operations manager cannot over emphasize his discipline and neglect the project, particularly in a matrix organization.

In many organizations there are technicians and specialists whose roles are so important to the success of the project that they too must be sold on the concept. The work of the specialists may be the very heart of a technical project. There is always the danger that technicians and specialists will overemphasize their disciplinary interests over project work unless they are in full accord with project management.

The next critical step is the formation of a project management implementation team. The purpose of the formation of this team is to provide a decision making body that will be charged with making the critical implementation decisions. In some cases, i.e., the bank case history, the implementation team may not be necessary because the job of this team has been assigned to some specific individual. In many cases the job will be given to the communications expediter. If it is felt that a team is necessary, the members should represent all levels of management and technical specialists, with particular emphasis on operations management.

There are many critical decisions that must be made prior to the actual implementation of project management. The most important of these decisions are:

- How will projects be organized?
- Who will be the first project manager?
- What will be the first project?

Only after these questions have been completely resolved should a project charter be written and the first project started.

The Communications Expediter

As previously indicated, the successful implementation of project management is very dependent on the efforts of the communications expediter. It makes little difference to his effectiveness whether the communications expediter is specially chosen by top management or whether he just happens to be at the right spot at the right time. In either case he should have certain personal characteristics, primarily enthusiasm for the project management concept and the ability to sell it to others in the organization. Management experience and abilities are not of primary importance, because he may or may not at a later date become a project manager. His primary job is to prepare the organization for project management; therefore, his ability as a salesman is his most important characteristic. He must be able to convey the project management story with enthusiasm and conviction.

Assuming that the communications expediter is a full-time employee, either an in-house enthusiast or hired as a project management expert, at what organizational level should he or she be? It makes very little difference, although the higher the organizational level, the more effective the individual should be. It would perhaps be ideal if this single dedicated person were a member of top management, since he or she would have sufficient clout to see that their plans and ideas were carried out. However, as previously indicated, a concept such as project management can seldom be rammed down the throat of an organization.

Fortunately, almost invariably this single dedicated person is a member of middle management. It is at this managerial level that the prerequisite imagination, practical experience, and personal drive are most likely to be found. Middle management is usually the most receptive to new ideas. In addition, middle management has the authority, i.e., the power, to try out new ideas. It also has the accessibility to and the influence with top management to get its ideas implemented. Lower levels of management are quite likely to run into just too many obstacles to be successful in functioning as the communications expediter.

Conclusions

There is a tremendous hurdle between the decision to implement project management and the actual process of implementation. The job of the communications expediter is to get the organization over this hurdle successfully with a minimum of conflict and trauma. The efforts of the communications expediter serve to prepare the organization for project management and ensure that it will work when implemented.

CASE STUDY 7: IMPLEMENTING A PROJECT MANAGEMENT SYSTEM IN A RESEARCH LABORATORY[1]

Introduction

Battelle, Pacific Northwest Laboratories is a division of Battelle Memorial Institute, corporate headquarters located in Columbus, Ohio. The Pacific Northwest Division, called Battelle-Northwest, or BNW, and established in 1965, is headquartered in Richland, Washington.

A major thrust of BNW is to do research work for the U.S. Department of Energy on a project or task basis within the framework of a long-term major contract. Other research work is done for industrial and government sponsors on individual contracts for separate projects. Sponsors of such projects include both U.S. and international organizations worldwide. This represents a major change from the laboratory of 15 years ago that was largely dedicated to providing technical support to the Atomic Energy Commission's Hanford plant.

BNW has a total staff of about 2,700 persons with widely diversified capabilities representing most of the technology-oriented disciplines and, in recent years, many of the social sciences. Unique applications of scientific expertise are the rule rather than the exception. One example is the highly experienced metallurgist who solves materials problems for the nuclear industry and works secondarily on the development of intrauterine devices.

In addition to a very broad range of scientific and engineering capabilities directed to service a wide variety of customers, the size and complexity of projects range from the small, single-discipline type to the large (multimillion dollar), multidisciplinary project.

Although there continues to be funding of research to investigate or explore fundamental scientific areas that contribute to the fund of knowledge, a trend in government-financed research has been toward specific, goal-oriented efforts geared to short-term commercialization or results. There has also been a trend toward larger, more complex projects, such as full-scale technology demonstrations.[2]

As these changes in BNW's research business evolved, the less structured, or less formal, approach to managing projects began to break down, and instances of problems and sponsor concern or criticism increased. In the early 1970s BNW manage-

---

[1] By Miles A. Patrick, Battelle, Pacific Northwest Laboratories, Richland, Washington. *1979 Proceedings of the Project Management Institute,* 11th Annual Seminar Symposium, Atlanta, Georgia, October 1979, The Project Management Institute, Drexel Hill, Pennsylvania. Used by permisison.
[2] E. B. Roberts and A. L. Frohman, "Strategies for Improving Research Utilization," *Technology Review,* March/April 1978.

ment instituted a review of project management activities. Good work was produced, but did not bring about significant changes. By 1975 a consulting firm had been engaged by BNW, and an internal committee was working on a computerized project information system. However, this system and the consultant were used only in a few isolated instances.

A first major step was taken when top management attacked the problem with specific actions. One of the actions was the task of developing a Research Project Management System (RPMS). The fact that an experienced project manager was selected for this task rather than an administrative or "systems" type was the second major step in eventually gaining system implementation in the laboratory.

The objective of the RPMS was to improve effectiveness in managing research projects by establishing uniform requirements and procedures, simultaneously retaining flexibility needed for a wide variety of research and sponsors. In addition, the RPMS was designed not to inhibit the highly creative environment necessary for good research.

System Requirements

A requirement for designing the RPMS was that the system had to be flexible enough to accommodate BNW's wide range of research projects, sponsors, and clients. It was also required that the appropriate level of uniform, disciplined project management be achieved throughout the laboratory, while maintaining a creative environment for good research work. A creative environment is vital in a research laboratory, and some level of freedom to investigate and explore is very important for (1) maintaining an atmosphere that encourages the generation of innovative, new ideas, and (2) retaining a large staff of highly trained, specialized scientists and engineers.

In such working environments relatively few changes and policies are implemented by authoritative direction from upper management. Therefore, to gain implementation of the RPMS, a high degree of participation at all levels in developing the system was considered essential. Further, the Director of Research wanted the initial thrust of the system to be directed toward small to medium-sized projects, those funded up to $3 to 5 million per year.

The RPMS has been implemented without changing BNW's organization structure. Project managers at BNW usually report to section managers. This is the "first line," or lowest level, in the management structure with respect to the professional staff. However, project managers may be assigned at any level in the structure. The overall structure as it applies to the research groups is shown in Figure 6.

Although Figure 6 would be described as a "functional" organization, it frequently operates across organizational lines, which, from the project managers' perspective, resembles a "matrix" form.[3] This situation occurs because many of BNW's projects require the use of several different scientific or engineering specialties represented by researchers in several different organization components. For example, a project might need a chemical engineer, a biologist, a statistician, an economist, an ecologist,

---

[3] R. Youker, "Organization Alternatives for Project Managers," presented at the Eighth Annual Symposium, Project Management Institute, Montreal, Canada, October 6–8, 1976.

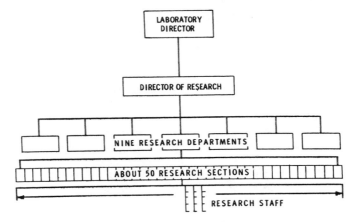

Figure 6.   BNW Research Organization.

and a social scientist, all located in different components, one of whom is designated project manager.

System Design Process

The data collection phase in the development of the system consisted of interviews with BNW research project managers from several departments and review of some of the extensive material on the subject of project management published in the past 10 to 12 years. The results of the data collection, literature survey, and early drafts of a system description were reviewed with a senior management group that included the Director of Research, Director of Programs, Director of Projects, Director of Operations and Services, and Director of Human Resources. This group also reviewed the work of a task force separately appointed to address the process and formats for the project managers' reports on project status to functional line managers.

Following these reviews, a revised draft of the system was further reviewed by all the Research and Development Department managers. The reactions of these managers were received in a workshop, at which time a consensus was reached as to the final direction of the review process. This workshop was led by the Director of Research, and was in the context that the decision had been made that BNW would have a RPMS. Therefore, the purpose of the review process was to shape it into a system appropriate and helpful for use at BNW.

Each department manager then appointed a project manager and a section manager as his representative on task forces to work out the details of the system. The third draft of the system, now in manual form, provided the starting point for the work of task forces. Each task force member had an opportunity to review the material privately, and then the two task forces met independently, but nearly concurrently, in workshops with the author to shape and define the system.

Both task forces devoted concentrated efforts to these independent workshops and then met jointly to review a fourth draft and to resolve a few remaining differences. A very important element in the success of these workshops was the participation of the Director of Human Resources who served as a highly skilled facilitator.

Comments were also received from two project management consultants to Battelle, who independently reviewed the manual.

A fifth draft had a final review by the research department managers and the Director of Research. A manual entitled *Research Project Management System* was then distributed throughout the laboratory with a directive from the Director of Research that the system be used. This directive also requested that each department prepare its own plan for implementing the system on its projects.

Next, workshops were held with each of the nine research departments. Participants included all the functional line managers, administrative staff, and key project managers. The objective for each workshop was to outline the plan and schedule for implementing the system, which, of course, necessitated becoming familiar with the system requirements. One constraint was noted, i.e., that the system had been extensively reviewed, was officially in place, and was not, at that time, subject to further critique or change. However, revisions were certainly expected, and they would result from further analysis based on actual experiences in using the system.

Implementation plans varied considerably. Some departments chose to begin with only a few selected projects, whereas others decided to exclude only a few of their projects. Individual departments were permitted considerable latitude in this regard. Gaining acceptance and willing implementation was considered much more important than compliance for the sake of compliance. BNW management viewed reluctant compliance as "cosmetic," since such compliance is not only artificial, but is counterproductive, requiring diversion of effort and energy that detracts from getting the research work done and contributes little or nothing to effective project management. Even after the extensive review process used, it was only through actual, on-the-job application that management could determine if the system was appropriate for general use in the laboratory.

The portion of the system that established project status reports from project managers to line managers was implemented on a pilot basis in one department for about six months before the manual was issued for general use. After initial resistance was overcome in this pilot effort, the reporting process functioned quite smoothly. This success was attributed to the following:

- Staff response to a particularly effective department manager, highly respected, who insisted, "Let's at least give it a try."
- Once past the fairly difficult task of preparing the first reports, the staff found that updating the reports was less onerous and required less time than had been anticipated.
- The reports were found to be useful and helpful.
- Actions by functional line managers resulting from reviewing the reports were visible to the staff.

One must always expect resistance to change as natural and even desirable. Even though stability is also important, progress requires change. To facilitate bringing about change to a relatively uniform system for managing research projects, it is necessary that those affected be able to see change as progress that will help them. With a staff of research scientists and engineers, such change cannot be accomplished by authoritative direction from any level of management.

For Battelle-Northwest this view is essential in maintaining the kind of work environment conducive to creative, innovative output expected from researchers. It is extremely rare for good results to come from a management directive requesting a new idea or invention by next Tuesday. The system must be responsive to researchers' needs, including the uncertainties involved in this kind of work. The elements of the RPMS have been formulated accordingly.

The System

The RPMS, as applied at Battelle-Northwest, includes the following major elements:

- Project planning process
- Review and approval procedures
- Change control
- Information to project managers
- Information to functional line managers

The process of preparing proposals and establishing contracts is an important part of managing projects. However, this process is not addressed in the RPMS, since the process has been long established and functions well. The RPMS has added a requirement to the proposal process that a project plan document (PPD) be prepared. This can be done either before or after a proposal is prepared, but is usually done after the work has been authorized. Sometimes this is called *project replanning*.

Because both the proposal and the PPD cover the same subjects, i.e., objectives, work statements, responsibility assignments, and schedule and cost estimates, the question "What is the difference between them?" is frequently asked. Major differences are their levels of detail and their purposes. The proposal is directed to a potential customer, and is, therefore, a selling document primarily for the benefit of the sponsor. It is meant to provide the potential customer with information needed to reach a decision.

The PPD, on the other hand, is meant to establish a BNW project manager's plans for the work in enough detail that a good basis for managing or controlling the project is established. The PPD is also meant to communicate these plans and the project manager's needs for resources to functional line management. In short, the PPD is primarily for the internal benefit and use of BNW, although the PPD is frequently shared with the sponsor.

Figure 7 indicates the usual process flow and the interrelationships of the major elements in the RPMS. The item "Line Management Communication Sponsor(s)" is considered very important in the system, but is separate from the direct flow of the RPMS process. This is included to assure that BNW project managers understand that these additional communication channels do not replace or dilute the required,

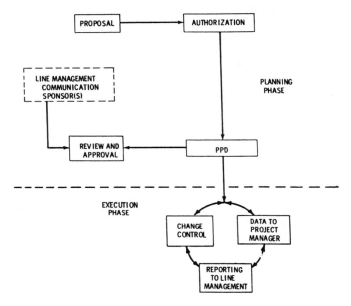

Figure 7.   Research Project Management System.

direct communications between the project manager and his contact in the sponsor's organization.

For several reasons, it is considered necessary that these supplementary communication channels be established between comparable management levels. These communications are not intended for detailed reviews of projects, but are usually informal contacts to check on the perceptions of the sponsor's management about how things are going. When more detailed reviews with the sponsor are needed, then appropriate knowledgeable staff are involved.

The review and approval of PPDs is considered a key element in assuring that project planning is done well. Internal project reviews are also conducted at selected times when judged to be appropriate by any level of management.

Also indicated in Figure 7 is the expected interaction of the three elements of the execution phase of a project: "information to the project manager," "information to functional line management," and "change control."

The basic procedural requirements of the RPMS and options to provide flexibility relative to all the system elements are shown in Table 3.

Many of the requirements shown in Table 3 reflect considerable interaction between project managers and functional line managers. BNW management considers this situation consistent with the concept of shared responsibility for projects, which is fundamental to BNW and to the design of the RPMS.

The RPMS information flow and how it relates to various management actions

Table 3.   BNW RPMS Requirements/Options.

System Elements	System Requirements	System Options

Project Planning	• (Line management-sponsor communications). The specific level of management will be defined in each instance by the lead department manager (in consultation with the project manager and section manager); the designated Battelle line manager will instigate action to establish such lines of communication.
	• Three key documents will result from the planning phase of a project and are to be completed prior to initiating the execution phase:
	  • Proposal
	  • Contract or work authorization
	  • Project plan document (for each project over $100,000 Total Cost)
		• Who will establish communications
		• Frequency of contact with Sponsor
		• PPD format
		• Schedule method or technique
		• Extent of work breakdown
		• How tasks are structured

Review and Approval Procedures	• The lead department manager will establish the levels of line management required for review and approvals. • When the project manager is satisfied with the written statement of the project objectives, this will be reviewed at least informally with the immediate manager. • The scope will be reviewed with the line management to assure adequacy, clarity, propriety, and completeness. • The task descriptions will be reviewed with organizational line management primarily to gain commitment of identified staff, equipment, and facilities to the project. • The project manager will review the cost estimate and the schedule to assess the level of uncertainty.	• Specific review process is open • Who will approve • What is to be reviewed with the sponsor • Specific participants in reviews

Table 3 (cont.)

System Elements	System Requirements	System Options
	• The control schedule and control estimate with the total PPD will be reviewed with organizational line management and will be approved by both the project manager and the designated line management.	
Change Control	• In order to increase the level of consciousness in deciding on changes, each will be documented. The "Record Change" form will be completed and processed. This will also provide for appropriate approvals. The approvals required will be established by information contact with the lead line manager. • Any change that requires a revision of the project plan document will be processed through the same approvals obtained on the original plan.	• Specifically when to document changes • Who is to approve various changes • Distribution of "Record of Change" forms
Information to Project Managers	• The project manager will specify participants reporting for each project, i.e., weekly, biweekly, or monthly.	• Report format • Report content • Reporting frequency • Who will provide reports
Information to Functional Line Managers	• The project manager is responsible for the periodic submission of a progress/variance report (specific format) to the lead line manager. The frequency of these reports will be consistent with the frequency of reporting to department managers. • Each section manager will add an appropriate supplement or contents and forward monthly progress/	• Reporting frequency variable • Choice of long or short forms • Selection of project categories • Report content

Table 3 (cont.)

System Elements	System Requirements	System Options

	variance reports to the department manager for a face-to-face monthly review. Exceptions to this monthly frequency, for specific projects, can be established with concurrence of the department manager and the director of research. For this review, the section manager will categorize all projects in his/her responsibility.
	• Monthly, the department manager will pass on the project progress/variance reports for the following categories with any additional comments to the director of research:
	  • Major potential problem projects
	  • High visibility/significance projects
	• The director of research will schedule a monthly face-to-face review of projects with department managers.
	• The lead line manager will decide which form (long or short) is applicable.	

relative to BNW's projects is shown in Figure 8. The monthly project review meetings shown between section management, department management, and the Director of Research do not imply a detailed review of each and every project. These are highly summarized reviews of the status of all projects, with concentration on those with reported exceptions or significant variances from plan. More detailed reviews of selected projects involve the project manager and staff.

In the initial phases of implementing the RPMS, some project managers expressed concern that their authorities would be further diluted by the significant review and approval procedures by line management. However, as experience was gained in actually using the system, many project managers indicated a feeling that their authorities had been increased. They felt that the balance of power had shifted in their favor relative to line management. Two factors seem to contribute to this: (1) clarification

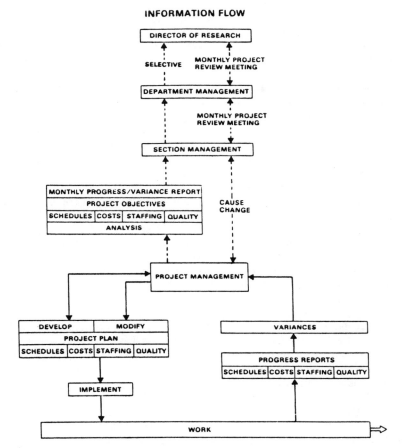

Figure 8.   Information Flow.

of roles in assignments and expectations; (2) improved project planning and line management approvals strengthen commitment of resources to project manager.

System Implementation Followup

After the RPMS manual was issued and the departmental implementation plans were developed, several activities were initiated that reinforce the use of the system.

The Director of Research has included the status of RPMS implementation in his monthly management reviews with each department manager. This is in addition to periodic reviews of selected projects.

After about a year into the implementation phase, a senior staff member was selected to conduct an independent review throughout the laboratory to determine how the system was working. The review sought to establish how the RPMS was really being used as compared with filed documentation of compliance.

Although differentiating between real application and "cosmetic compliance" is difficult, this independent appraisal has provided important and valuable feedback on the implementation status.

Following the early phases of implementation, BNW initiated an internal course in project management based on the RPMS. The course addresses how to use the system, the concepts of project management interpersonal relationships, and available support services. Each class meets in a seminar mode for a total of 32 hours. In addition to serving as lead instructor for this course, the author has participated in project reviews and has provided advice and assistance to project managers and others in applying the RPMS.

During the second year of implementation, the project cost-reporting system was completely revised. No changes had been made in cost reporting in the basic RPMS. The focus of the new cost system is the overall process described in the RPMS.

The original task forces of research project managers and line managers involved in developing the RPMS were reactivated to work with the finance systems staff in modifying the cost reports. Totally new report formats resulted from this work designed to reference costs to the project work breakdown structures. The experiences with the RPMS were very valuable in enabling the research staff to better communicate needs to the finance system staff.

Communicating these needs seemed to have been a significant problem in the past and was the principal reason that revising the cost-reporting system was not attempted until after RPMS had been implemented. A basic question was whether to implement two major changes simultaneously or in separate, successive steps. There is probably no right answer to this question, but BNW believes that the course chosen had some advantages:

- Better definition of cost-reporting needs
- Reiteration of the laboratories' commitment to the RPMS
- Reinforcement of the RPMS implementation process in its second year of general application.

The RPMS was intended for small to medium-sized projects, that is, those from $50,000 or $100,000 up to a few million dollars each. BNW usually has 200 to 300 such projects active at any given time. For larger, demonstration kinds of projects that usually involve new facilities, a separate manual entitled *Major Projects Management System and Procedures* has been prepared and issued. The number of projects considered to be major that are active at any given time is quite small, i.e., three or four. Although the principles are the same, this major projects system is somewhat more rigid and formalized than the RPMS. It also incorporates an earned-value system for project control.

BNW chose to use two separate systems rather than one, with selective alternate features to reduce the potential for confusion among a large number of project managers leading small to medium-sized projects. The level of project management experience varies considerably within the laboratory. On the other hand, those managing major projects are usually senior people, with extensive experience, capable of interfacing or merging the two systems when necessary.

Summary

In general, BNW is satisfied that good progress has been made in implementing the RPMS in its laboratory without unduly upsetting the environment for doing highly creative research. After about three years of effort, which includes about two years of general application, internal reviews indicate that progress has been as good as hoped. BNW has found that the RPMS is being applied on 80 to 90 percent of the projects over $100,000 in value and on many of the smaller ones. As was expected, acceptance has been reached much sooner in sections that are more engineering-oriented than in those that are more scientific in thrust. In the first year, slightly over half of the section managers in engineering components had accepted RPMS and were positively inclined toward it. Well into the second year, the reactions among the more scientifically oriented section managers were found to be one-third favorable, one-third neutral, and one-third negative. In contrast, a sampling of project managers in the scientific areas indicated two-thirds were positive and one-third negative in their reactions.

With the continuation of the internal course and accumulation of successful projects, including favorable sponsor reaction, BNW believes that the acceptance level and actual use have increased beyond these earlier indicators. After about three years, BNW noted that a year had passed with no projects in serious trouble.

In retrospect, the key factors in the success of the RPMS seem to have been:

- Top management gave support and commitment to the system.
- BNW developed its own system for its own use.
- The lead assignment in the development of the system was given to an experienced, senior project manager.
- Extensive involvement of project managers and section managers was obtained in developing the system.
- A high degree of flexibility was built into the RPMS.
- The use of BNW's own internal education program, taught by knowledgeable, senior people, helped implement the system.

Much of the resistance to the change to a functioning, relatively uniform RPMS has centered on a reluctance on the part of research staff to have their project plans and actions visible, particularly to higher management. We have heard all the reactions to planning so clearly identified several years ago by Russell Archibald:[4]

- " 'You can't schedule creativity.' "
- " 'I don't have time to plan—I have to get some work done.' "

---

[4] R.D. Archibald, "Planning, Scheduling, and Controlling the Efforts of Knowledge Workers," *1969 Proceedings of the Project Management Institute,* Georgia Tech., Atlanta, Georgia, October 9–10, 1969.

- " 'Too much paperwork.' "
- " 'Good idea for all the others, but not for me; I'm different.' "
- " 'You don't understand our problems.' "
- "[Planning] is difficult, creative work. It is revealing, and most people don't like to lay their technical or business souls bare to be seen and abused by others. I am afraid that if I produce a plan, I will be irrevocably committed to it, and will lose my professional freedom of action. I believe that planning will somehow eliminate my ability to create, invent, and leave my mark on the effort."

Overcoming this resistance requires diligent, careful attention over a long period of time. Acceptance by the staff is absolutely essential and can be gained, slowly, by the process discussed here and is attained only when the researchers perceive that the system is worthwhile and contributes to their success.

We know good progress has been made when the manager of a major life sciences department tells the Director of Research, "You know, this PPD thing is really turning out to be helpful to us."

CASE STUDY 8:   PROJECT FIRECRACKER

"Don, project management is the only way to handle this type of project. With $40 million at stake we can't afford not to use this approach."

"Listen, Jeff, your problem is you take seminars given by these ivory tower professors, and you think you're an expert. I've been in this business for 40 years and I know how to handle this job—and it isn't through project management."

History and Background

Jeff Pankoff, a registered professional engineer, came to work for National Incorporated after receiving a mechanical engineering degree. After he arrived at National he was assigned to the engineering department. Soon thereafter, Jeff realized that he needed to know more about statistics and he enrolled in the graduate school of a local university. When he was close to completing his M.S., National transferred Jeff to one of its subsidiaries in Ireland to set up an engineering department. After a successful three years, Jeff returned to National's home office and was promoted to chief engineer. Jeff's department increased to 80 engineers and technicians. Spending a considerable time in administration, Jeff decided an M.B.A. would be useful, so he enrolled in a program at a nearby university. At the time this project began, Jeff was near the end of the M.B.A. program.

National Corporation, a large international corporation with annual sales of about $600 million employs 8,000 people worldwide and is a specialty machine, component, and tool producer catering to the automotive and aircraft manufacturers. The company is over a hundred years old and has a successful and profitable record.

National is organized in divisions according to machine, component, and tool production facilities. Each division is operated as a profit center. (See Figure 9.) Jeff was assigned to the Tool Division.

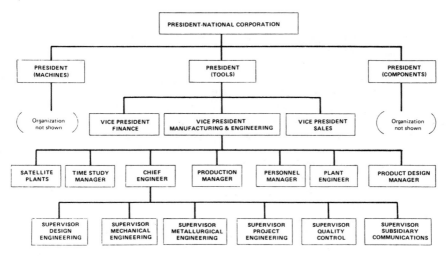

Figure 9.

National's Tool Division produces a broad line of regular tools as well as specials. Specials amounted to only about 10 percent of the regular business, but over the last five years had increased about 5 percent to the current 10 percent. Only specials that were similar to the regular tools were accepted as orders.

National sells all its products through about 3,000 industrial distributors located throughout the United States. In addition, National employs 200 sales representatives who work with the various distributors to provide product seminars.

The traditional approach to project assignments is used. The engineering department, headed by Jeff, is basically responsible for the purchase of capital equipment and the selection of production methods used in the manufacture of the product. Project assignments to evaluate and purchase a new machine tool or to determine the production routing for a new product are assigned to the engineering department. Jeff assigns the project to the appropriate section, and, under the direction of a project engineer, the project is completed.

The project engineer works with all the departments reporting to the vice-president, including production, personnel, plant engineering, product design (the project engineer's link to sales), and time study. As an example of the working relationship, the project engineer selects the location of the new machine and devises instructions for its operation with production. With personnel the engineer establishes the job description for the new job as well as for the selection of people to work on the new machine. The project engineer works with plant engineering on the moving of the machine to the proper location and instructs plant engineering on the installation and services required (air, water, electricity, gas, etc.). It is very important that the project engineer work very closely with the product design department, which develops the design of the product to be sold. Many times the product designed is too ambitious an undertaking or cannot be economically produced. Interaction between departments is essential in working out such problems.

After the new machine is installed, an operator is selected, and the machine is ready for production. Time study, with the project engineer's help, then establishes the incentive system for the job.

Often a customer requests certain tolerances that cannot be adhered to by manufacturing. In such a case, the project engineer contacts the product design department, which contacts the sales department, which in turn contacts the customer. The communication process is then reversed, and the project engineer gets an answer. Based upon the number of questions, the total process may take four to five weeks.

As the company is set up, the engineering department has no authority over time study, production, product design, etc. The only way that the project engineer can get these departments to make commitments is through persuasion or through the chief engineer, who could go to the vice-president of manufacturing and engineering. If the engineer is convincing, the vice-president will dictate to the appropriate manager what must be done.

Salaries in all departments of the company are a closely guarded secret. Only the vice-president, the appropriate department manager, and the individual know the exact salary. Don Wolinski, the vice-president of manufacturing and engineering, pointed out that this approach was the "professional way" and an essential aspect of smooth business operations.

The Ill-Fated Project

Jeff Pankoff, the chief engineer for National, flew to Southern California to one of National's (tool) plants. Ben Ehlke, manager of the Southern California plant (SCP), wanted to purchase a computer-numerical-controlled (CNC) machining center for $250,000. When the request came to Jeff for approval, he had many questions and wanted some face-to-face communication.

The Southern California plant supplied the aircraft industry, and one airplane company provided 90 percent of SCP's sales. Jeff was mainly concerned about the sales projections used by Ehlke in the justification of the machining center. Ehlke pointed out that this was based on what the airplane company had told him they expected to buy over the next five years. Because this estimate was crucial to the justification, Jeff suggested that a meeting be arranged with the appropriate people at the airplane company to explore these projections. Since the local National sales representative was ill, the distributor salesman, Jack White, accompanied Jeff and Ben. While at the airplane company (APC), the chief tool buyer of APC, Tom Kelly, was informed that Jeff was there. Jeff received a message from the receptionist that Tom Kelly wanted to see Jeff before he left the building. After the sales projections were reviewed and Jeff was convinced that they were as accurate and as reliable as they possibly could be, he asked the receptionist to set up an appointment with Tom Kelly.

When Jeff walked into Kelly's office the fireworks began. He was greeted with, "What's wrong with National? They refused to quote on this special part. We sent them a print and asked National for their price and delivery, indicating it could turn into a sizable order. They turned me down flat saying that they were not tooled up for this business. Now I know that National is tops in the field and that National can provide this part. What's wrong with your sales department?"

All this came as a complete surprise to Jeff. The distributor salesman knew about it, but never thought to mention it to him. Jeff looked at the part print and asked, "What kind of business are you talking about?" Kelly said, without batting an eye, "Forty million dollars per year."

Jeff realized that National had the expertise to produce the part and would require only one added machine (a special press costing $20,000) to have the total manufacturing capability. Jeff also realized he was in an awkward situation. The National sales representative was not there and he certainly could not speak for sales. However, a $40 million order could not be passed over lightly. Kelly indicated that he would like to see National get 90 percent of the order if they would only quote on the job. Jeff told Kelly that he would take the information back and discuss it with the vice-presidents of sales, manufacturing and engineering and that most likely the sales vice-president would contact him next.

On the return flight, Jeff reviewed in his mind his meeting with Kelly. Why did Bob Jones, National's sales vice-president, refuse to quote? Did he know about the possible $40-million order? Although Jeff wasn't in sales, he decided that he would do whatever possible to land this order for National. That evening Jack White called from California. Jack said he had talked to Kelly after Jeff left and told Kelly that if anybody could make this project work, it would be Jeff Pankoff. Jeff suggested that Jack White call Bob Jones with future reports concerning this project.

The next morning, before Jeff had a chance to review his mail, Bob Jones came storming into his office. "Who do you think you are committing National to accept an order on your own without even a sales representative present? You know that all communication with a customer is through sales."

Jeff replied, "Let me explain what happened."

After Jeff's explanation, Jones said, "Jeff, I hear what you're saying, but no matter what the circumstances, all communications with any customer must go through proper channels."

Following the meeting with Jones, Jeff went to see Wolinski, his boss. He filled Wolinski in on what had happened. Then he said, "Don, I've given this project considerable thought. Jones is agreeable to quoting this job. However, if we follow our normal channels, we will experience too many time delays and problems. Through the various stages of this project, the customer will have many questions and changes, and will require continuous updating. Our current system will not allow this to happen. It will take work from all departments to implement this project, and unless all departments work under the same priority system, we won't have a chance. What we need, Don, is project management. Without this approach where one man heads the project with authority from the top, we just can't make it work."

Wolinski looked out the window and said, "We have been successful for many years using our conventional approach to project work. I grant you that we have not had an order of this magnitude to worry about, but I see no reason why we should change even if the order were for 100 million dollars."

"Don, project management is the only way to handle this type of project. With forty million dollars at stake we can't afford not to use this approach."

"Listen Jeff, your problem is you take seminars given by these ivory tower professors, and you think you're an expert. I've been in this business for forty years and I know how to handle this job—and it isn't through project management. I'll call a meeting of all concerned department managers so we can get started on quoting this job."

That afternoon, Jeff and the other five department managers were summoned to a meeting in Wolinski's office. Wolinski summarized the situation and informed the assembled group that Jeff would be responsible for the determination of the methods of manufacture and the associated manufacturing costs that would be used in the quotation. The method of manufacture, of course, would be based upon the design of the part provided by product design. Wolinski appointed Jeff and Waldo Novak, manager of product design, as coheads of the project. He further advised that the normal channels of communication with sales through the product design manager would continue as usual on this project.

The project began. Jeff spent considerable time requesting clarification of the drawings submitted by the customer. All these communications went through Waldo. Before the manufacturing routing could be established for quotation purposes, questions concerning the drawing had to be answered. The customer was getting anxious to receive the quotation because its management had to select a supplier within eight weeks. One week was already lost due to communication delay. Wolinski decided that to speed up the quoting process he would send Jeff and Waldo along with Jones, the sales vice-president to see the customer. This meeting at APC helped clarify many questions. After Jeff returned, he began laying out the alternative routing for the parts. He assigned two of his most creative technicians and an engineer to run isolated tests on the various methods of manufacturing. From the results he would then finalize the routing that would be used for quoting. Two weeks of the eight were gone, but Jeff was generally pleased until the phone rang. It was Waldo.

"Say Jeff, I think if we change the design on the back side of the part, it will add to its strength. In fact, I've assigned one of my men to review this and make this change and it looks good."

While this conversation was going on, Wolinski popped into Jeff's office and said that sales had promised that National would ship APC a test order of 100 pieces in two weeks. Jeff was irate. Product design was changing the product. Sales was promising delivery of a test order no one could even describe yet.

Needless to say, the next few days were long and difficult. It took three days for Jeff and Waldo to resolve the design routing problem. Wolinski stayed in the background and would not make any position statement except he wanted everything "yesterday." By the end of the third week the design problem was resolved, and the quotation was prepared and sent out to the customer. The quotation was acceptable to APC pending the performance of the 100 test parts.

At the start of the fourth week, Jeff, with the routing in hand, went to Charlie Henry, the production manager, and said he needed 100 parts by Friday. Charlie looked at the routing and said, "The best I can do is a two-week delivery."

After discussing the subject for an hour, the two men agreed to see Wolinski. Wolinski said he'd check with sales and attempt to get an extension of one week. Sales asked the distributor salesman to request an extension. Jack White was sure it would be okay so he replied to Bob Jones without checking that the added week was in fact acceptable.

The 100 pieces went out in three weeks rather than two. That meant the project was at the end of the sixth week and only two remained. Inspection received the test pieces on Monday of the seventh week and immediately reported them not to be in specification. Kelly was upset. He was counting heavily on National to provide these parts. Kelly had received four other quotations and test orders from National's competitors. The prices were similar and the test parts were to specification. However, National's parts, although out of specification, looked better than their competitors'. Kelly reminded Jones that the customer now had only nine days left before the contract would be let. That meant the 100 test parts had to be made in nine days. Jones immediately called Wolinski who agreed to talk to his people to try to accomplish this.

The tools were shipped in 11 days, 2 days after the customer had awarded orders to three of National's competitors. Kelly was disappointed in National's performance but told Jones that National would be considered for next year's contract, at least a part of it.

Jeff, hearing from Waldo that National lost the order, returned to his office, shut the door and thought of the hours, nearly round the clock, that were spent on this job. Hours that were wasted because of poor communications, nonuniform priorities, and because there was no project manager. "I wonder if Wolinski learned his lesson; probably not. This one cost the company at least six million dollars in profits, all because project management was not used." Jeff concluded that his work was really cut out for him. He decided that he must convince Wolinski and others of the advantages of using project management. Although Wolinski had attended a one-day seminar of project management two years ago, Jeff decided that one of his objectives during the coming year would be to get Wolinski to the point where he would, on his own, suggest becoming more knowledgeable concerning project management. Jeff's thought was that if the company were to continue to be profitable it must use project management.

The phone rang, it was Wolinski. He said, "Jeff, do you have a moment to come down to my office? I'd like to talk about the possibility of using, on a trial basis, this project management concept you mentioned to me a few months ago."

CASE STUDY 9:   MIS PROJECT MANAGEMENT AT FIRST NATIONAL BANK

During the last five years, First National Bank (FNB) has been one of the fastest growing banks in the Midwest. The holding company of the bank has been actively involved in purchasing small banks throughout the state of Ohio. This expansion and the resulting increase of operations has been attended by considerable growth in numbers of employees and in the complexity of the organizational structure. In five years the staff of the bank has increased by 35 percent, and total assets have grown by 70 percent. FNB management is eagerly looking forward to a change in the Ohio banking laws that will allow statewide branch banking.

ISD History

Data processing at FNB has grown at a much faster pace than the rest of the bank. The systems and programming staff grew from 12 in 1970 to over 75 during the first part of 1977. Because of several future projects, the staff is expected to increase by 50 percent during the next two years.

Prior to 1972, the information services department reported to the executive vice-president of the Consumer Banking and Operations Division. As a result, the first banking applications to be computerized were in demand deposit, savings, and consumer credit. The computer was seen as a tool to speed up the processing of consumer transactions. Little effort was expended to meet the informational requirements of the rest of the bank. This caused a high-level conflict, since each major operating organization of the bank did not have equal access to systems and programming resources. The management of FNB became increasingly aware of the benefits that could accrue from a realignment of the bank's organization into one that would be better attuned to the total information requirements of the corporation.

In 1972 the Information Services Division (ISD) was created. ISD was removed from the Consumer Banking Operations Division to become a separate division reporting directly to the president. An organization chart depicting the Information Services Division is shown in Figure 10.

Priorities Committee

During 1972 the Priorities Committee was formed. It consists of the chief executive officer of each of the major operating organizations whose activities are directly affected by the need for new or revised information systems. The Priorities Committee was

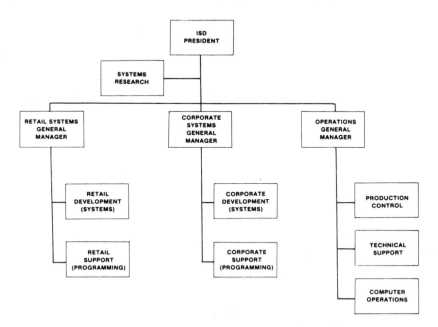

Figure 10.   Information Services Division Organization Chart.

established to ensure that the resources of systems and programming personnel and computer hardware would be used only on those information systems that could best be cost-justified. Divisions represented on the committee are included in Figure 11.

The Priorities Committee meets monthly to reaffirm previously set priorities and rank new projects introduced since the last meeting. Bank policy states that the only way to obtain funds for an information development project is to submit a request to the Priorities Committee and have it approved and ranked in overall priority order for the bank. Placing potential projects in ranked sequence is done by the senior executives. The primary document used for Priorities Committee review is called the project proposal.

The Project Proposal Life Cycle

When a user department determines a need for the development or enhancement of an information system, it is required to prepare a draft containing a statement of the problem from its functional perspective. The problem statement is sent to the president of ISD, who authorizes systems research (Figure 10) to prepare an impact statement. This impact statement will include a general overview from ISD's perspective of:

- Project feasibility
- Project complexity
- Conformity with long-range ISD plans

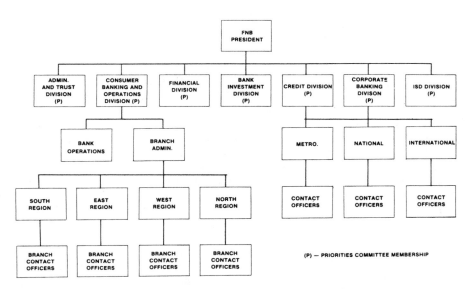

Figure 11. First National Bank Organization Chart.

- Estimated ISD resource commitment
- Review of similar requests
- Unique characteristics/problems
- Broad estimate of total costs

The problem and impact statements are then presented to the members of the Priorities Committee for their review. The proposals are preliminary in nature, but they permit the broad concept, with a very approximate cost attached to it, to be reviewed by the executive group to see if there is serious interest in pursuing the idea. If the interest level of the committee is low, then the idea is rejected. However, if the Priorities Committee feels the concept has merit, it authorizes the systems research group of ISD to prepare a full-scale project proposal that contains:

- A detailed statement of the problem
- Identification of alternative solutions
- Impact of request on:
- User division
- ISD
- Other operating divisions
- Estimated costs of solutions
- Schedule of approximate task duration
- Cost/benefit analysis of solutions
- Long-range implications
- Recommended course of action

After the project proposal is prepared by systems research, the user sponsor must review the proposal and appear at the next Priorities Committee meeting to speak in favor of the approval and priority level of the proposed work. The project proposal is evaluated by the committee and either dropped, tabled for further review, or assigned a priority relative to ongoing projects and available resources.

The final output of a Priorities Committee meeting is an updated list of project proposals in priority order with an accompanying milestone schedule that indicates the approximate time span required to implement each of the proposed projects.

The net result of this process is that the priority setting for systems development is done by a cross section of executive management; it does not revert by default to data processing management. Priority setting, if done by data processing, can lead to misunderstanding and dissatisfaction by sponsors of the projects that did not get ranked high enough to be funded in the near future. The project proposal cycle at FNB is included in Figure 12. Once a project has risen to the top of the ranked priority list, it is assigned to the appropriate systems group for systems definition, system design and development, and system implementation.

The time spent by systems research in producing impact statements and project proposals is considered to be overhead by ISD. No systems research time is directly charged to the development of information systems.

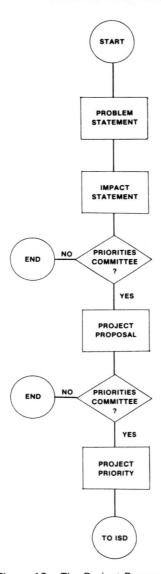

Figure 12. The Project Proposal Cycle.

Project Life Cycle

As noted before, the systems and programming staff of ISD has increased in size rapidly and is expected to expand 50 percent during the next two years. As a rule, most new employees have previous data processing experience and training in various systems methodologies. ISD management recently implemented a project management system that was dedicated to providing a uniform step-by-step methodology for the development of management information systems. All project work is covered by tasks that make up the information project development life cycle at FNB. The subphases used by ISD in the project life cycle are:

1. Systems definition
   a. Project plan
   b. User requirements
   c. Systems definition
   d. Advisability study
2. Systems design and development
   a. Preliminary systems design
   b. Subsystems design
   c. Program design
   d. Programming and testing
3. System implementation
   a. System implementation
   b. System test
   c. Production control turnover
   d. User training
   e. System acceptance

Project Estimating

The project management system contains a list of all normal tasks and subtasks (over 400) to be performed during the life cycle of a development project. The project manager must examine all the tasks to determine if they apply to his project. He must insert additional tasks if required and delete tasks that do not apply. The project manager next estimates the amount of time, in hours, to complete each task of each subphase of the project life cycle.

The estimating process of the project management system uses a "moving window" concept. ISD management feels that detailed cost estimating and time schedules are meaningful only for the next subphase of a project, where the visibility of the tasks to be performed is quite clear. Beyond that subphase, a more summary method of estimating is relied upon. As the project progresses, new segments of the project gain visibility. Detailed estimates are made for the next major portion of the project, and summary estimates are done beyond that until the end of the project.

Estimates are performed at five intervals during the project life cycle. When the project is first initiated, the funding is based on the original estimates, which are derived from the list of normal tasks and subtasks. At this time, the subphases through the advisability study are estimated in detail, and summary estimates are prepared for the rest of the tasks in the project. Once the project has progressed through the advisability study, the preliminary systems design is estimated in detail, and the balance of the project is estimated in a more summary fashion. Estimates are conducted in this manner until the systems implementation plan is completed and the scope of the remaining subphases of the project is known. This multiple estimating process is used because it is almost impossible at the beginning of many projects to be certain of what the magnitude of effort will be later on in the project life cycle.

Funding of Projects

The project plan is the official document for securing funding from the sponsor in the user organization. The project plan must be completed and approved by the project manager before activity can begin on the user requirements subphase (1b). An initial stage in developing a project plan includes the drawing of a network that identifies each of the tasks to be done in the appropriate sequence for their execution. The project plan must include a milestone schedule, a cost estimate, and a budget request. It is submitted to the appropriate general manager of systems and programming for review, so that an understanding can be reached of how the estimates were prepared and why the costs and schedules are as shown. At this time the general manager can get an idea of the quantity of systems and programming resources required by the project. The general manager next sets up a meeting with the project manager and the user sponsor to review the project plan and obtain funding from the user organization.

The initial project funding is based on an estimate that includes a number of assumptions concerning the scope of the project. Once certain key milestones in the project have been achieved, the visibility on the balance of the project becomes much clearer, and reestimates are performed. The reestimates may result in refunding if there has been a significant change in the project. The normal milestone refunding points are as follows:

1. After the advisability study (1d)
2. After the preliminary systems design (2a)
3. After the program design (2c)
4. After system implementation (3a)

The refunding process is similar to the initial funding with the exception that progress information is presented on the status of the work and reasons are given to explain deviations from project expenditure projections. A revised project plan is prepared for each milestone refunding meeting.

During the systems design and development stage, design freezes are issued by the project manager to users announcing that no additional changes will be accepted to the project beyond that point. The presence of these design freezes are outlined at the beginning of the project. Following the design freeze, no additional changes will be accepted unless the project is reestimated at a new level and approved by the user sponsor.

System Quality Reviews

The key element in ensuring user involvement in the new system is the conducting of quality reviews. In the normal system cycles at FNB, there are 10 quality reviews,

7 of which are participated in jointly by users and data processing personnel, and 3 of which are technical reviews by data processing personnel only. An important side benefit of this review process is that users of a new system are forced to become involved in and are permitted to make a contribution to the systems design.

Each of the quality review points coincides with the end of a subphase in the project life cycle. The review must be held at the completion of one subphase to obtain authorization to begin work on the tasks of the next subphase of the project.

All tasks and subtasks assigned to members of the project team should end in some "deliverable" for the project documentation. The first step in conducting a quality review is to assemble the documentation produced during the subphase for distribution to the Quality Review Board. The Quality Review Board consists of between two and eight people who are appointed by the project manager with the approval of the project sponsor and the general manager of systems and programming. The minutes of the quality review meeting are written either to express "concurrence" with the subsystem quality or to recommend changes to the system that must be completed before the next subphase can be started. By this process the system is fine-tuned to the requirements of the members of the review group at the end of each subphase in the system. The members of the Quality Review Board charge their time to the project budget.

Quality review points and review board make-up are as follows:

Review	*Review Board*
User requirements	User oriented
Systems definition	User oriented
Advisability study	User oriented
Preliminary systems design	User oriented
Subsystems design	Users and D.P.
Program design	D.P.
Programming and testing	D.P.
System implementation	User oriented
System test	User oriented
Production control turnover	D.P.

To summarize, the quality review evaluates the quality of project subphase results, including design adequacy and proof of accomplishment in meeting project objectives. The review board authorizes work to progress based upon its detailed knowledge that all required tasks and subtasks of each suphase have been successfully completed and documented.

Project Team Staffing

Once a project has risen to the top of the priority list, the appropriate manager of systems development appoints a project manager from his staff of analysts. The project manager has a short time to review the project proposal created by systems research before developing a project plan. The project plan must be approved by the general manager of systems and programming and the user sponsor before the project can be funded and work started on the user requirements subphase.

The project manager is "free" to spend as much time as required in reviewing the project proposal and creating the project plan; however, his time is charged to the project at a rate of $26 per hour. The project manager must negotiate with his "supervisor," the manager of systems development, to obtain the required systems analysts for the project, starting with the user requirements subphase. The project manager must obtain programming resources from the manager of systems support. Schedule delays caused by a lack of systems or programming resources are to be communicated to the general manager by the project manager. All ISD personnel working on a project charge their time at a rate of $26 per hour. All computer time is billed at a rate of $64 per hour.

There are no user personnel on the project team; all team members are from ISD.

Corporate Data Base

John Hart had for several years seen the need to use the computer to support the corporate marketing effort of the bank. Although the majority of the bank's profits were from corporate customers, most information systems effort was directed at speeding up transactions handling for small unprofitable accounts.

Mr. Hart had extensive experience in the Corporate Banking Division of the bank. He realized the need to consolidate information about corporate customers from many areas of the bank into one corporate data base. From this information, corporate banking services could be developed not only to better serve the corporate customers, but also to contribute heavily to the profit structure of the bank through repricing of services.

The absence of a corporate data base meant that no one individual knew what total banking services a corporate customer was using, because corporate services are provided by many banking departments. It was also impossible to determine how profitable a corporate customer was to the bank. Contact officers did not have regularly scheduled calls. They serviced corporate customers almost on a hit-and-miss basis. Unfortunately, many customers were "sold" on a service because they walked in the door and requested it. Mr. Hart felt that there was a vast market of uptapped corporate customers in Ohio who would purchase services from the bank if they were contacted and "sold" in a professional manner. A corporate data base could be used to develop corporate profiles to help contact officers sell likely services to corporations.

Mr. Hart knew that data about corporate customers were being processed in many departments of the bank, but mainly in the following divisions:

- Corporate Banking
- Corporate Trust
- Consumer Banking

He also realized that much of the information was processed in manual systems, some was processed by time-sharing at various vendors, and other information was computerized in many internal information systems.

The upper management of FNB must have agreed with Mr. Hart, because in

December of 1976, the Corporate Marketing Division was formed with John Hart as its executive vice-president. Mr. Hart was due to retire within the year, but was honored to be selected for the new position. He agreed to stay with the bank until "his" new system was "off the ground." He immediately composed a problem statement and sent it to the ISD. Systems research compiled a preliminary impact statement. At the next Priorities Committee meeting, a project proposal was authorized to be done by systems research.

The project proposal was completed by systems research in record time. Most information was obtained from Mr. Hart. He had been thinking about the systems requirements for years and possessed vast experience in almost all areas of the bank. Other user divisions and departments were often "too busy" when approached for information. A common reply to a request for information was "the project is John's baby; he knows what we need."

The project proposal, as prepared by systems research, recommended the following:

- Interfaces should be designed to extract information from existing computerized systems for the corporate data base (CDB).
- Time-sharing systems should be brought in-house to be interfaced with the CDB.
- Information should be collected from manual systems to be integrated into the CDB on a temporary basis.
- Manual systems should be consolidated and computerized, potentially causing a reorganization of some departments.
- Information analysis and flow for all departments and divisions having contact with corporate customers should be coordinated by the Corporate Marketing Division.
- All corporate data base analysis should be done by the Corporate Marketing Division staff, using either a user-controlled report writer or interactive inquiry.

The project proposal was presented at the next Priorities Committee meeting, where it was approved and rated as the highest priority MIS development project in the bank. Mr. Hart became the user sponsor for the CDB project.

The project proposal was sent to the manager of corporate development, who appointed Jim Gunn as project manager from the staff of analysts in corporate development. Jim Gunn was the most experienced project manager available. His prior experience consisted of successful projects in the Financial Division of the bank.

Jim reviewed the project proposal and started to work on his project plan. He was aware that the corporate analyst group was then understaffed, but was assured by his manager, the manager of corporate development, that resources would be available for the user requirements subphase. He had many questions concerning the scope of the project and the interrelationship between the Corporate Marketing Division and the other users of corporate marketing data. But each meeting with Mr. Hart ended with the same comment: "This is a waste of time. I've already been over this with systems research. Let's get moving." Jim also was receiving pressure from the general manager to "hurry up" with the project plan. Jim therefore quickly prepared his project plan, which included a general milestone schedule for subphase completion, a general cost estimate, and a request for funding. The project plan was reviewed by the general manager and signed by Mr. Hart.

Jim Gunn anticipated the need to have four analysts assigned to the project and went to his manager to see who was available. He was told that two junior analysts were available now and another analyst should be free next week. No senior analysts were available. Jim notified the general manager that the CDB schedule would probably be delayed because of a lack of resources, but received no response.

Jim assigned tasks to the members of the team and explained the assignments and the schedule. Since the project was understaffed, Jim assigned a heavy load of tasks to himself.

During the next two weeks the majority of the meetings set up to document user requirements were cancelled by the user departments. Jim notified Mr. Hart of the problem and was assured that steps would be taken to correct the problem. Subsequent meetings with the users in the Consumer Banking and Corporate Banking Divisions became very hostile. Jim soon discovered that many individuals in these divisions did not see the need for the corporate data base. They resented spending their time in meetings documenting the CDB requirements. They were afraid that the CDB project would lead to a shift of many of their responsibilities and functions to the Corporate Marketing Division.

Mr. Hart was also unhappy. The CDB team was spending more time than was budgeted in documenting user requirements. If this trend continued, a revised budget would have to be submitted to the Priorities Committee for approval. He was also growing tired of ordering individuals in the user departments to keep appointments with the CDB team. Mr. Hart could not understand the resistance to his project.

Jim Gunn kept trying to obtain analysts for his project, but was told by his manager that none were available. Jim explained that the quality of work done by the junior analysts was not up to par due to lack of experience. Jim complained that he could not adequately supervise the work quality, because he was forced to complete many of the analysis tasks himself. he also noted that the quality review of the user requirements subphase was scheduled for next month, making it extremely critical that experienced analysts be assigned to the project. No new personnel were assigned to the project. Jim thought about contacting the general manager again to explain his need for more experienced analysts, but did not. He was due for a semi-yearly evaluation from his manager in two weeks.

Even though he knew the quality of the work was below standards, Jim was determined to get the project done on schedule with the resources available to him. He drove both himself and the team very hard during the next few weeks. The quality review of the user requirements subphase was held on schedule. Over 90 percent of the assigned tasks had to be redone before the Quality Review Board would sign-off on the review. Jim Gunn was "removed" as project manager.

Three senior analysts and a new project manager were assigned to the CDB project. The project received additional funding from the Priorities Committee. The user requirements subphase was completely redone despite vigorous protests from the Consumer Banking and Corporate Banking Divisions.

Within the next three months the following events happened:

- The new project manager resigned to accept a position with another firm.
- John Hart took early retirement.
- The CDB project was "tabled."

CASE STUDY 10:   WEBSTER INDUSTRIAL CONTROLS[1]

Webster Industrial Controls (WIC) is a 32-year-old company that manufactures quality industrial control systems for aerospace, defense, construction, electronics, and nuclear components. In 1975, WIC incorporated formal project management, by decree. On December 19, 1978, the case writer visited WIC to ascertain some of the major problem areas that affected successful project management operations. Several of WIC's personnel were interviewed. All the questions discussed revolved about three major areas of concern:

- What are the major problems with current WIC operations?
- What are the major weaknesses with the current organizational structure, the project managers, and the functional managers?
- What kind of training would you like to see developed here at WIC to help you perform your job better and to improve your working relationships with other project management personnel?

Below are the responses to these questions. The responses have been somewhat edited for conciseness and clarity of thought.

Q. What are the major problems with current WIC operations?

A. *Scheduling:* "Many people, both in project management and production, do not understand why we have such a terrible problem in scheduling activities. Sure, our people understand the necessity for getting the order out as fast as possible in order to meet customer requirements, but there are severe environmental factors. The government has tied our hands with requirements on qualified customer vendors.

"Qualifying a vendor, means qualifying with respect to safety. This leads us to other questions. Does our vendor have design control? Has the vendor made these parts obsolete? How do we get vendor commitment? We spend $25 to 50 thousand per product before we can call it qualified.

"All vendors who have input also have changing situations. We have to write test procedure acceptance criteria, often under adverse conditions. If the control system is all right, then the point of release to manufacturing will be six months to a year. That's after three to four years in design. Also, how do we incorporate information on aging to show that the theoretical life of a nuclear control system is 40 years? I wish I knew?"

---

[1] Disguised case.

A. *Priorities:* "There is lack of communication about how and why priorities can continuously shift. Manufacturing has the greatest concern. Priorities in manufacturing are related to the dollar value of the contract, usually through the marketing group and the project manager. Although there are several reasons for establishing a priority, the most common cause is with penalty or liquidated damages (i.e., failure to perform on a given date because the customer has people waiting to work and the equipment is not yet available).

"We have good channels to the upper levels of the organization for priority-setting. But this doesn't resolve our problem. How do we keep people motivated with a shifting priority environment? Maybe we can't help it in our environment, but at least explaining the rationale to our people might ease some of the tension."

A. *Conflicting Instructions to Manufacturing:* "This creates real havoc in our organization and results from a lack of information, untimely information, wrong data, or engineering not complete. The result is that manufacturing blames engineering, stating that it is engineering's fault (possibly because of incorrect drawings and wrong parts), whereas engineering charges that manufacturing made it wrong and didn't order the parts in time.

"When this occurs, we usually just get our heads together and hash it out. If penalty clauses are included as part of the contract or any other clause that may require special attention, the usual result is weekly team meetings. Now time management becomes a problem. Perhaps there are better ways to handle this.

"We have a very poor monitoring and control system. Not only are we tied down with too much paperwork, but the value of this paperwork always forces me to ask whether or not it is necessary. Less than 50 percent of our orders go out without final push. Here we are designing industrial control systems, and we have no system that functions on its own.

"Fortunately we've been successful because we have an easy access to upper-level management. They usually get totally involved and try to give us immediate resolution.

"Planning is poor, at best. Sometimes, marketing provides a very, very poor forecast, and everyone has to live with it. This becomes a problem when our new project managers are at a low level on the learning curve. Manufacturing sometimes doesn't know the status of a piece of equipment until it physically appears in that department.

"We cannot control resources unless we have planning and know what's coming. I don't know what's coming until I see it on the floor. What happened to proper planning?"

Q. What are the major weaknesses with the current organizational structure, the project managers, and the functional managers?

A. "I've been here several years, and I have no idea about how project management is supposed to work. Who has what authority, responsibility, how, when, . . . ?

"Project managers cannot be successful unless they know the total picture, especially manufacturing operations. Perhaps they should spend some time there. Project engineers are not allowed to track activities in the production area. I'm not sure this is the way the project management system is supposed to work. There must be a better way to get total control of resources.

"We have an extremely weak information system and poor feedback. Manufacturing does not want the project engineer in its domain to get feedback. It claims that the project manager prevents people from working. The system shouldn't work this way. We have to get these people together to iron out their differences.

"I've often wondered if there's a better way to control our paperwork, especially engineering change notices (ECNs). These ECNs are very, very unmanageable. Who is responsible for chairing configuration management? What are the requirements? Nobody seems to know."

Q. What kind of training would you like to see developed here at WIC to help you perform your job better and to improve your working relationships with other project management personnel?

A. "What is project management? I don't know. Why do the project engineers report to marketing, but have little authority in manufacturing? Is this the way the system should work?

"Section supervisors and group leaders now act as interface agents between department managers and project personnel. If they have to supervise more than five or six people, the system may break down. Is there a better way?

"Once a system is shipped, in effect, parts distribution becomes the customer interface. Aren't we therefore project managers? We should also be trained in project management.

"Project management has a pecking order—not enough pull. Are there better ways of establishing authority and responsibility relationships?

"There is a lack of communications. Much information is not said or understood. How well do we listen? Perhaps people don't listen or just have a parochial view.

"We must understand priorities and conflict resolution, as well as why urgency is needed.

"Interpersonal skills, from A to Z. Can this and attitude problems be taught or do they come with OJT? How do we keep a cool head in stress situations? Can we teach professionalism and positive reaction?

"What is project management? I don't know. I lost track about two years ago. We've made too many changes and nobody knows what's going on.

"I want to know the flow of paperwork. It's very difficult to become dedicated if you're kept in the dark.

"The biggest problem is paperwork. We overcomplicate things by doing it serially instead of in parallel. Perhaps this is why we can't ship as fast as the customer would like.

"Project managers are not technical specialists. Our project managers need formal training in project management. As far as I know, they've had none.

"How can I do my job if I don't know who the players are?

"There is logic to decisions, but people just don't listen. They build up roadblocks.

"What is a cost control system? A project manager does not know where he stands costwise on a project? That shouldn't be. We need help.

"Should our project managers be customer- or cost-oriented? When should we compromise? Most project managers are at the extremes. The best ones know when to give and take. Can this be taught.

"We in engineering are instructed to keep out of manufacturing. So, we have less information as to how manufacturing works.

"Project managers do not understand the operation of each department. That's a mistake in project management. Also, they are very weak in planning and do not close the feedback loops. The result is scramble time. We need better planning and control of our resources. We need a cadet indoctrination program for ongoing people. Our people can read black and white, but not gray. They have strong tunnel vision. I'm not sure if this is good or bad.

"We've had project management training programs in the past where everyone walked out saying that it was a fine program. Unfortunately, it was a failure because our people could not relate the information to their everyday jobs. Don't you make the same mistake."

CASE STUDY 11:   WYNN COMPUTER EQUIPMENT (WCE)

In 1965, Joseph Wynn began building computer equipment in a small garage behind his house. By 1982, WCE was a $1 billion a year manufacturing organization employing 900 people. WCE's major success has been attributed to the nondegreed workers who have stayed with WCE over the past 15 years. The nondegreed personnel account for 80 percent of the organization. Both the salary structure and fringe benefit packages are well above the industry average.

CEO Presentation

In February 1982, the new vice-president and general manager made a presentation to his executive staff outlining the strategies he wished to see implemented to improve productivity.

"Our objective for the next 12 months is to initiate a planning system with the focus on strategic, developmental, and operational plans that will assure continued success of WCE and support for our broad objectives. Our strategy is a four-step process:

- Better clarification of expectations and responsibility.
- Establish cross-functional goals and objectives.
- Provide feedback and performance results to all employees in each level of management.
- Develop participation through teamwork.

"The senior staff will act merely as a catalyst in developing long- and short-term objectives. Furthermore, the senior staff will participate and provide direction and leadership in formulating an integrated manufacturing strategy that is both technology- and human-resources-driven. The final result should be an integrated project plan that will:

- Push decision making down.
- Trust the decision of peers and people in each organization.
- Eliminate committee decisions.

"Emphasis should be on communications that will build and convey ownership in the organization and a *we* approach to surfacing issues and solving problems."

In April 1982, a team of consultants interviewed a cross section of Wynn personnel to determine the pulse of the organization. The following information was provided:

- "We have a terrible problem in telling our personnel (both project and functional) exactly what is expected on the project. It is embarrassing to say that we are a computer manufacturer and we do not have any computerized planning and control tools."
- "Our functional groups are very poor planners. We, in the project office, must do the planning for them. They appear to have more confidence in and pay more attention to our project office schedules than to their own."
- "We have recently purchased a $65,000 computerized package for planning and controlling. It is going to take us quite a while to educate our people. To interface with the computer package, we must use a work breakdown structure. This is an entirely new concept for our people."
- "We have a lack of team spirit in the organization. I'm not sure if it is simply the result of poor communications. I think it goes further than that. Our priorities get shifted on a weekly basis, and this produces a demoralizing effect. As a result, we cannot get our people to live up to either their old or new commitments."
- "We have a very strong mix of degreed and nondegreed personnel. All new, degreed personnel must prove themselves before being officially accepted by the nondegreed personnel. We seem to be splitting the organization down the middle. Technology has become more important than loyalty and tradition, and, as a result, the nondegreed personnel, who believe themselves to be the backbone of the organization, now feel cheated. What is a proper balance between experience and new blood?"
- "The emphasis on education shifts with each new executive. Our nondegreed personnel obviously are paying the price. I wish I knew what direction the storm is coming from."
- "My department does not have a data base to use for estimating. Therefore, we have to rely heavily upon the project office for good estimating. Anyway, the project office never gives us sufficient time for good estimating, so we have to ask other groups to do our scheduling for us."
- "As line manager, I am caught between a rock and a hard spot. Quite often,

I have to act as the project manager and line manager at the same time. When I act as the project manager I have trouble spending enough time with my people. In addition, my duties also include supervising outside vendors at the same time."

- "My departmental personnel have a continuous time management problem, because they are never full time on any one project, and all of our projects never have 100 percent of the resources they need. How can our people ever claim ownership?"

- "We have trouble in conducting upfront feasibility studies to see if we have a viable product. Our manufacturing personnel have a poor interfacing with advanced design.

- "If we accept full project management, I'm not sure where the project managers should report. Should we have one group of project managers for new processes and products and a second group for continuous (or old) processes and products? Can both groups report to the same person"

CASE STUDY 12:   STARR AIR FORCE BASE (SAFB)

"You have to remember when looking at SAFB that we have a military structure superimposed on a government structure that, in turn, is superimposed on a civilian traditional structure. In addition, we have some sort of project management structure on top of everything. Military personnel get rotated through this maze of interrelationships every two or three years, but the civilian population have to endure it forever. Living with it isn't the problem as long as we understand it and how it should work. I've been here at SAFB for over 15 years and I don't think that I fully understand the organization."

History

From its inception in the late 1940s, Starr Air Force Base has historically been a leader in high-technology, electronic R&D activities. The majority of the base's military and technical civilian personnel have advanced degrees in technical disciplines. The working atmosphere at SAFB appears to be much more cordial than at other installations, because engineers notoriously are interested more in work challenge than in organizational structures, empire-building, and internal politics.

Observations

In the summer of 1981, several employees (GS-9 through GS-15) were interviewed concerning their views of project management at SAFB. The following indicate their feelings.[1]

"We must realize that project management here at SAFB is different from private

---

[1] Several of these comments have been modified for clarity.

industry. Industry, especially in project-driven organizations, has profits as its primary concern. SAFB is somewhere between a project-driven and nonproject-driven organization, with emphasis on efficiency, productivity, visibility, and mobility rather than profits."

"There are also major differences in the work flow and project size. Most of our projects are in the $200 to $300 thousand range, with very few over $1 million. We use project management (with horizontal work flow) primarily to develop an RFP. After the RFP is developed, we seem to have functional control of the project, where a line employee acts as the project monitor. Actually, we are more likely to appear as contract monitors than project managers."

"The biggest frustration here appears to be authority. Authority rests with the division managers, especially for the distribution of funds. The branch is responsible for task performance, and section chiefs have responsibility for work units. Although we do have some projects that operate on a horizontal line, most of our projects are controlled at the section level, especially after the RFP is prepared."

"Perhaps the biggest source of frustration in authority is in the civilian-military interface. It is pretty obvious that all the authority rests with the military, regardless of the reporting level of the civilian project manager. Military personnel sit on the top of our organization, and we have a well-established staircase of management from the bottom up. Unfortunately, the staircase does not work from the top down, because many of our military personnel (especially at the top) believe themselves to be the true project managers and meddle in the lower levels of the organization. It is a shame that these senior military types don't realize the damage they inflict with their meddling and violating of the civilian structures. Sometimes, I believe that the best qualifications for a military leader at SAFB would be a degree in some discipline other than engineering."

"We occasionally have projects that are large enough to support a project office. The project offices generally report to division heads. However, there are projects where the project office fell under the control of a technical advisor."

"Another serious problem is the promotion policy and cycle. Our lower-level people are frustrated with the basic system, but the upper-level personnel are frustrated by the promotion systems. Technical expertise does not appear to be a criterion for promotion. Visibility appears to be most important. Many of our employees are volunteering for project management and project engineering positions, so that they can become more visible to top management. The idea is simple; if you continuously make briefings to top management concerning the status of your project, then the executive staff will get to know you on a first-name basis, and your chances for promotion may be greater."

"I wish I knew how industry manages its projects. I would like nothing better than to be able to assist them in time of trouble. Unfortunately, I do not know when, where, or how to interface properly, especially when tradeoffs are necessary. Sometimes the person I interface with in industry sits pretty low in the organization and needs upper-level management approval for decisions. This creates additional frustration."

"Industry seems to have us between a rock and a hard spot once we award the contract. We do not appear to have any kind of forward financing to keep the contractors honest. We must expend all the funds or lose them. As a result, when the contractor says he has expended all of the hours or money, work stops, and perhaps there will be no final report. We also have no effective way to evaluate the past performance of contractors who are now bidding."

"Many of our people are technical experts in some engineering discipline, but lack ability or training in other pertinent areas, such as cost analysis or proposal preparation. This holds true for proposal evaluation as well as proposal preparation. We place too much emphasis on dollars rather than on performance. We continuously avoid looking at the procurement cycle. Sometimes we have just two weeks to evaluate six-month proposals. Some of our own people have developed a laziness syndrome in detailing information and communications. We consistently look for the easiest way to estimate, and this forces us to make a linear burn rate assumption rather than to look at history. I simply don't understand why we aren't using some sort of data base."

"Our system has an inherent weakness in that we have bottom-up planning rather than top-down planning. As a result, we (especially top military personnel) shuffle priorities without a strong technical base. Our priority system appears to be directly related to the quantity of paperwork. Since many of our people simply track projects, we spend a lot of time and effort on paperwork. I'm not sure how much tracking is professional. It will take strong leadership to back away from all this paper work."

"I don't think we actually have people here who are project managers, at least not according to industrial definitions. Some of our engineers are program element managers, but do not evaluate. They simply monitor (and sometimes control) funds. Some of our engineers act as consultants to other labs while acting as project element managers."

"My boss gets no feedback from the project office or lead engineer as to my performance on the project. Some people get absolutely no rewards or recognition for work done well. We need recognition ('fill in the squares') for promotion. Also, if we were to go to some kind of merit system based upon performance, we'll still need horizontal as well as vertical performance evaluation."

"Our strength here is our technological base. I'm not sure that we can be pushed into project without sacrificing technology."

"Many of our projects are in virgin territory and even our line managers lack the necessary information. How do we break into new areas or ground? How do we perform risk assessment here? How do we find the right projects and put manpower on the right work? Many of our best ideas originate in the depths of the working area, but still require upper-level approval."

"I would like to see project management at SAFB where project managers could be equivalent to division heads or at least a GS-14. That would eliminate some of the log jam that we have in the GS-12 through GS-14 slots. Under this type of arrangement we can train people to become professional project managers by creating a separate line function for perhaps up to 10 full-time project managers. If an employee wants a vertical rather than horizontal career, he can go back to a line function or position for vertical promotion."

"This concept of creating a line group of project managers has an interesting application. Within industry, project management is an ideal way to give people exposure to the operation of the entire company. Perhaps we can employ that concept here at SAFB. Any person aspiring to become a branch or division manager must first have a tour of duty in project management before fulfilling this position. Therefore, branch and division managers will become knowledgeable in total SAFB operations, rather than their own line group. This type of training would be invaluable for military personnel as well as civilian personnel and would be compatible with the SPO training provided at Wright-Patterson Air Force Base."

"If we try to implement any change like this at SAFB, will we need approval at the AFSC level? Will this change have to be made at all agencies of AFSC?"

"Conflicts cannot be resolved at the lower levels of management. By decree, any issue must go upstairs, and we end up getting help that we don't want or need."

"If we go to project management, we'll have trouble with the military, because it also must be visible for promotion. Military personnel will probably take the key project management slots and leave the crumbs for us. Lately, military officers have taken over some of the key (branch and division) positions formerly held by civilians. This creates frustration for civilians because it limits their career progression."

"Most industrial companies have three career paths; technical, line management, and project management. Here, at SAFB, we recognize only the first two, with the third one being implied."

"Can we set up project management as though it is a mini-SPO?"

Table 4.   Results of the Project Management Course Questionnaire.

Rank	Topic	Total Points
1	Managing total resources	220
2	Program scheduling	209
3	Project management bottlenecks	203
4	Planning and organizing work	196
5	Communications	187
6	Human resources management	182
7	Pricing: the final phase of planning	179
8	Preparing proposals and bids	179
9	Expectations and interface	175
10	Cost control	173
11	Project management concepts	171
12	The evaluation process	171
13	The selection process	170
14	Total interface relationships	169
15	Negotiations	168
16	Definitions and job descriptions	165
17	Network scheduling	164
18	Conflicts	164
19	Computerized project planning	159
20	Organizational structures	153
21	Case studies	152

"How can we prevent micromanagement by our senior personnel?"

"Sometimes I have been given a direct order by military officers not to report any bad news on projects, because the officers are fearful that bad news on projects may have a serious impact on their evaluation for promotion. So we conceal the bad news until the officer gets rotated to another assignment, and then the replacement gets greeted with a surprise."

Inhouse Training

Two hundred hours of in-house training programs on project management were scheduled for 1981-82 to introduce both military and civilian personnel to the discipline of project management. Prior to the seminar, 48 employees were asked to rank the 21 topics to be covered during the seminars on a scale of 1 through 5 (top). The results are shown in Table 4.

Job Descriptions

One of the major difficulties in going to a project management line organization is in developing job descriptions for the various GS grade levels. Tables 5 through 8 show the current job descriptions of various GS grades for electronics engineers.

Table 5.   GS-7 Electronics Engineer.

I. DUTIES AND RESPONSIBILITIES:

1. Designs electronic equipment of moderate complexity that forms a part of a system. Uses higher mathematics, such as algebra and calculus, in establishing design characteristics and parameters.

2. Makes comprehensive studies of existing techniques and equipment in use and by a search and study of pertinent engineering data and technical reports for possible application to assignments.

3. Makes evaluations and prepares reports on findings involving design, construction, and final performance of a specific task. Makes recommendations and decisions that affect the program with regard to evaluation of new equipment and new developments.

4. Evaluates equipment in relation to other portions of overall task by devising test procedures and compiling and evaluating test data. Makes engineering modifications of assigned equipment or of associated equipment as a result of analysis of test results.

5. Constructs breadboard models of circuitry for use in investigation and analyses of circuits. Selects types and layout of chassis for best electrical and mechanical effect. Exercises initiative in obtaining design criteria from existing literature. Uses judgment in selecting circuit best suited for the particular need.

6. Meets engineers within the laboratory to explain work accomplished.

7. Receives classroom and on-the-job training related to assigned field of work.

II. CONTROLS OVER WORK:

Works under close guidance and instruction from supervisor, who gives oral or written instructions pertaining to work assignments. Work is reviewed often for technical adequacy and accuracy through discussion on written progress reports.

Table 6.   GS-9 Electronics Engineer.

I. DUTIES AND RESPONSIBILITIES:

1. Analyzes problems, studies technical literature and existing technology, and discusses with supervisor or other personnel having experience in assigned area to obtain information pertaining to problem area.

2. Compiles basic technical data for the preparation of necessary specifications, exhibits, and exhibit revisions, stating technical requirements, tests, and test procedures required in accordance with AFSC directives.

3. Evaluates bid proposals of prospective contractors to determine contractor best qualified to accomplish work. Recommends contractor most suitable for the particular contract, taking into consideration proposed approach to problem, personnel, and facilities to be expended. Attends bidders' conferences to explain the requirements of the contract and to answer questions pertaining thereto.

4. Administers engineering aspects of contract by evaluating suitability of techniques and components proposed by contractor and proposed deviations from specification requirements. Evaluates and reports on contractor's progress and recommends major changes or authorized minor changes.

5. Designs and constructs breadboard models and runs tests in validating engineering or scientific concepts applicable to assignment. Analyzes test data and recommends changes in approach to supervisor. These recommendations may influence the design of equipment/techniques in the experimental stages.

6. Attends test runs and evaluates test data before recommending acceptance of equipment/techniques. Writes or approves technical manual outlining operating techniques of equipment.

7. Attends meetings with representatives of SAFB and other centers, contractors and universities in gathering and dispensing technical information for application to assigned area.

8. Receives classroom and on-the-job training related to assigned field of work.

II. CONTROLS OVER WORK:

Receives work assignments from supervisor or higher grade employee, who provides guidance on problems arising and determines effectiveness of results in meeting requirements. Receives on-the-job training, including instruction and guided practice in performing duty assignments. Classroom training is evaluated through discussion/written progress reports. Guidelines are in the form of technical pamphlets, articles, text books, techniques, and advances in the field.

The difficulty is in creating job descriptions for various levels of project management and project engineering. Using Tables 5 through 8 as the basis, how can we create meaningful job descriptions that distinguish between the responsibilities of various project management pay grades?

Table 7.   GS-11 Electronics Engineer.

I. DUTIES AND RESPONSIBILITIES:

1. Exercises initiative and originality in analyzing requirements, determining problem areas, and establishing approaches for solution to engineering problems. Investigates and analyzes all possible sources of data in assigned field to determine the feasibility, utility, and accuracy of these sources as related to assigned problems. Researches technical literature for new or existing equipment and/or techniques to determine possible application to assignments or recommends modifications of the techniques that can be applied. Makes recommendations and decisions as a result of analysis and investigations on techniques and/or equipment that can be utilized as developed to meet AF requirements. Uses initiative and originality in analyzing requirements and determining problems.

2. Determines contractor services required to develop equipment/techniques as assigned. Writes engineering exhibits for the work to be performed on contract; reviews and evaluates technical proposals received from interested contractors; recommends those qualified to perform work based on their technical capabilities. Administers technical portion of contract by monitoring work performed at contractor's plant. This entails observing experiments being conducted, discussing methods being utilized, and/or determining alternative methods to alleviate unsatisfactory progress. Evaluates progress reports and final engineering report prepared by the contractor to ensure that contractual requirements are met. Plans and conducts acceptance test; approves or disapproves contractual effort on the basis of equipment performance and compliance with contractual requirements.

3. Submits budget estimates to supervisor for future work to be accomplished in accordance with known requirements. Prepares documentation, including technical plans and estimates of funds, manpower, and facilities to accomplish the programs, using the AFSC Program Management instruction guidelines.

4. Attends conferences with personnel of universities, operational commands, other center and government agencies to discuss present and contemplated applied research efforts in assigned area, present results of experimentation, and obtain and/or exchange information for application to problems.

5. Writes technical memoranda, reports, and papers outlining development of techniques and/or equipment to resolve technical problems; specifies approaches taken, results achieved, test administered, data accumulated, correlations and evaluations made, and conclusions reached. Makes specific recommendations based on peculiar test data that are unexplainable and should be investigated.

II. CONTROLS OVER WORK:

Receives general work assignments from supervisor. Objectives, time limitations, priorities, and unusual problems are discussed and resolved by supervisor. Work is reviewed upon completion for compliance with overall objectives and conformances to established engineering practices and branch policy. Guidelines are established policies, precedents, engineering techniques, and standard and technical reports and textbooks.

III. OTHER SIGNIFICANT FACTS:

Requires a thorough understanding of engineering techniques and theory gained through four years of engineering training in a recognized college or university or training equivalent in type, scope, and thoroughness. Travel by military aircraft is required in accomplishment of assignments.

Table 8.   GS-14 Electronics Engineer.

I. DUTIES AND RESPONSIBILITIES:

1. Serves as the SAFB technical focal point and lead engineer for the development of a secure, efficient system. Conceives, plans, formulates, and guides applied research, techniques, and analysis studies. This involves the development of advanced/improved components. Resolve problem areas, represent significant advances in the state of the art, and pave the way for extensive related developments and/or eventually result in a new technique or practical device.

2. Conducts detailed scientific studies and investigations on exceptionally difficult scientific problems. Assumes complete technical responsibility for formulating plans and hypotheses, interpreting findings, and carrying them through to completion. Serves as group leader in generating ideas and studies to be pursued by personnel within the section.

3. Writes technical papers of new and complex techniques and devices specifying analysis and evaluation from an advanced technological point of view. These papers are of considerable interest to the professional community in that the contributed inventions, designs, or techniques involved are of material significance in the solution of critical problems for application to R&D programs. Outlines development or design problems, approaches taken, results achieved, tests performed, data accumulated, correlations and evaluations made, and conclusions reached. Exercises considerable scientific skill and authoritative knowledge of conventional and unconventional techniques.

4. Provides technical guidance and advisory services in assigned areas to SAFB personnel, other centers, and other military and civil agencies, engaged in similar or related technical areas; specifies techniques and design criteria to be used to maximize the efficiency of new and novel strategic command and control systems/techniques.

5. Serves as Air Force representative on mission analysis studies, technical committees, and teams of service and interservice high-level personnel for the purposes of evaluating technical approaches, guiding and/or recommending most optimum technology as required. Analyzes reports or literature emanating from studies, techniques, investigations, and systems design in association with keeping abreast of other technological source documentation to ascertain a well-directed, continuous technological flow toward immediate and long-range goals. Identifies areas and initiates action where redirection is deemed advisable.

6. Studies and evaluates scientific and engineering proposals submitted by contractor personnel containing radically new or novel approaches, criteria, techniques, and engineering design. Renders scientific judgments; recommends modifications and alterations, and/or determines feasibility of approaches and design features and the desirability and acceptability of such proposals.

7. Visits contractors' plants and universities to discuss technical requirements and objectives of research and development projects and to review progress of contractual work. Provides technical guidance and instructs contractors to vary the emphasis being placed on different phases of the program; establishes trends to be followed on controversial programs; resolves technical differences and makes decisions when modifications or selection of different modes of approach are required to meet desired objective. These decisions are often precedent-setting and are the basis upon which planning of future research and development is based.

8. Attends symposia in professional engineering fields of interest to branch to exchange information on work performed. Conducts studies on specific programs that may arise from general requirements placed on the division to meet new requirements or resulting from changing field operational concepts. Recognizes problems needing solution and recommends possible method of solution.

9. Represents the center at conferences with personnel of other centers.

10. Maintains continuous review and analysis of applicable research and development pro-

Table 8 (cont.)

grams of SAFB, other centers, Department of Defense, and civilian agencies and the operational requirements received from higher headquarters to determine research and development effort required and ensure that latest state of the art is reflected in the SAFB effort to meet Air Force operational requirements.

11. Serves as group leader and exercises technical control over personnel engaged in in-house and contractual efforts to develop new and novel concepts necessary for the successful exploitation of strategic command and control.

II. CONTROLS OVER WORK:

Works under general administrative supervision of section chief. Briefs superior on the status of planning and plan accomplishments. Work is reviewed for conformance with broad directives and policy; technical findings and recommendations are accepted as authoritative and conclusive. Although precedents are practically nonexistent for the major portion of assignments, guidelines are available in the form of broad requirements and policy statements received from higher headquarters.

III. OTHER SIGNIFICANT FACTS:

Requires a thorough understanding of engineering/scientific techniques and methods gained through four years of engineering/scientific training in a recognized college or university or training equivalent in type, scope, and thoroughness.

CASE STUDY 13:   THE EVOLUTION OF PROJECT MANAGEMENT CONCEPTS FROM TOOLS TO REALITIES: TWO CASE HISTORIES[1]

This paper encompasses the activities of a consulting firm, Creative Management Group, Inc., as it applies its consulting engagement by two specific utilities, one being very successful, the other being totally unsuccessful.

Lawrence J. Renas, Vice-President of Construction Management, Dayton Power & Light, is assisting in presenting this paper as the representative of a successful implementation of project management. Due to professional ethics, the second utility—in which an unsuccessful implementation had occurred—is not being mentioned. But it is one of the major utilities in the country.

There are certain premises that must be established before a complete examination of project management can be discussed. The most important condition of implementing a successful project management approach must be the environment of the organization where the implementation and application of project management techniques are to be instituted. The environment is controlled by:

[1] By Alan J. Shepherd, Creative Management Group, Inc., Southfield, Michigan. *1975 Proceedings of the Project Management Institute,* 7th Annual Seminar Symposium, San Francisco, California, October 1975, The Project Management Institute, Drexel Hill, Pennsylvania. Used by permission.

- Personnel
- Corporate political situation
- Limitations of the existing organization structure
- Corporate direction and procedures in the instituting of project management being defined and communicated
- Definition and evaluation of quantitative goals and objectives throughout the transition from functional management to project management

By definition of project management, it is assumed throughout this paper that the project for which this concept is implemented has complete autonomy from the balance of the functional organization within the corporate entity. Autonomy does not necessarily mean that it will not use the corporate entity's existing functional organization, but there would be a clear distinction between the existing corporate functions and the role of the project management team. In all cases, the project management team has discretionary use of capabilities of the normal organization functions.

The limitation to implementation of the project management approach, when applied to utilities, is that though they are dynamic, capital-intensive organizations, utilities tend to be quasi-public institutions and become static and entrenched, operating in a manner to which they have become accustomed. Coupled with this, a quasi-public institution as an entity "is not subject to the profit incentives of a normal corporation." Therefore, its goals and policies relative to the maintenance of the status quo, in relationship to personnel, provide no incentive for performance criteria as a method of evaluation. Corporations must measure success not only from a balance sheet, but from the aggressiveness and capability of their personnel, especially in management roles. If it is assumed that personnel are the limiting factor within a utility (as in any corporation), and since built-in profit is structured within a utility, utilities are defeating the incentive to run their projects within the limitations of cost effectiveness, cost control, schedule control, and, last but not least, operational control, by providing a static, noncreative management team of job secure personnel.

This background on utilities serves the purpose of stating that within Dayton Power & Light (DP&L), this environment was not the case. The DP&L Stuart Plant construction project was of a completely autonomous environment. The personnel in this project management task group not only felt loyalty to their corporate organization, but even greater loyalty to the project organization. In addition, the most important aspect is that there were no political or corporate influences on the activities of these personnel.

The J. M. Stuart Generating Station, consists of four, supercritical, 600 megawatt generating facilities. Construction started in June 1966. Unit II, which was the first unit to start construction, was complete; Unit I, which was the second unit, was approximately 90 percent complete, with only one year left to complete to commercial status; Unit III was just starting erection of the boiler (had just completed erection of the steel); and Unit IV was just in the foundation stages, when Creative Management Group, Inc., was engaged to provide scheduling and project management consultation to the DP&L project management team in March 1971.

The objective of the DP&L project management team in bringing in a scheduling effort was that it felt remarkable progress had been made in progress of the project from a totally disorganized, out-of-control situation to an under-control, organized, planned operation. But equally important, it recognized that a mangement tool was needed to provide for the maintenance of the original budget and schedule.

Historically, Unit II was originally awarded to a construction manager who, in effect, was to be the project manager. The engineering consultant was not assigned field responsibility for coordination and quality control and had no site supervision. During the first 3¼ years of the project, an amount in excess of $94 million of a budget of $58 million was spent on the first unit (Unit II) only, which initiated DP&L to revise its direction and management organization for construction. This provided the environment for DP&L's entrance onto the project as an active management function, since it was unknown when Unit II was going to be complete and at what cost. DP&L project management called in the engineer-consultant to provide some form of information relative to schedule and the cost to complete. These were the initial tools that DP&L had to complete Unit II into an operational facility. Within six months, with no formal scheduling, cost reporting, or manpower control, the project management task force had Unit II under control enough to feel that the unit could be completed and that the amount of dollars was known and would be well spent.

The attack relative to Unit I was more effective. Unit I progress to completion had not been that much different from Unit II, except that more work was accomplished with less scrambling. The work was delineated into work packages by the DP&L project management team and, as a result, was brought in well within the original budget and time parameters.

At that point, the DP&L project management task force wanted to know how and what could be done to gain efficiency. It was satisfied with its organization and goals, but knew it had to find a better way to schedule and control the project. It felt the information relative to schedule and productivity could be quantified in its present condition and, if there was a manner in which to quantify it, it knew its effect could be much greater.

In March 1971, the DP&L project management task force engaged Creative Management Group to develop a schedule for the balance of work on Unit III and for Unit IV in its entirety. The assignment was twofold; not only to come up with the scheduling and other related project management techniques required, but to come up with a training program so that organization could educate itself for the tools on Unit III. By the time Unit IV was ready for scheduling, personnel could not only use the tools, but would become masters of the tools of project management.

Using this approach, Creative Management Group brought to the site a task force of its own, comprising five technical personnel knowledgeable in power plant construction and in CPM scheduling. In a 6½-week effort, working with the foremen, general foreman, and superintendents of the DP&L project task force and project contractors, Creative Management Group developed a schedule for the balance of work for Unit III. The most important technique used by Creative Management Group was the establishment of separate meetings with individual contractors and representatives of the DP&L task force. Out of these meetings, individual work plans for the contractors were documented by Creative Management Group consultants. The amount of detail supplied by each contractor, to say the least, was general in nature and nonquantitative, but more of a qualitative nature. For example, the boiler erector indicated in 30 items the effort to erect the boiler, which he defined would be an 18- to 24-month procedure. This time/sequence relationship for erection, as a result of manual network computations, turned out to cover a time span of only 11 months. Creative Management Group then had a general meeting with all the contractors, after documenting each one of the work plans into rough CPM networks. Using ploys known as "question and answer" and "peer equality," Creative Management Group consultants asked each individual contractor to tell them how to tie the work plans together. This was the turning point.

When questioned, a contractor would define in detail and quantify what the requirements were to do his work tasks as outlined in his work plan. It so happened that these details were not on the preceding contractor's work plan and, as such, could not be tied to the gross general item for which the questions arose. Typical to an inventory explosion, the details started coming out of the woodwork. As a net result, what originally was a project general work plan of from 600 to 800 items, turned out to be a 5,000 plus detailed network for the balance of work on Unit III.

Having successfully delivered the work plans, and having communicated with the contractors, it was now the responsibility of the DP&L project task force and Creative Management Group to come up with scheduling information in a format that would represent the project plan. The scheduling information had to be transmitted to the lowest level of management of each participating group within the organization, not only to the task force, but to each and every contractor on the project.

One of the major tools in making sure that the information was disseminated to the appropriate personnel, and in a form they could use, is included as Table 9. This information is in the form of a 6-week "to do" list of all the items in a weekly status that are supposed to start and finish. Each report was separated and packaged for each individual contractor, as well as each individual construction function, and for the DP&L project management personnel. This weekly schedule report was, in effect, the lubricant that was used to provide the information of a rather complex system.

Is is not known to the authors to what degree the individual foremen accepted the schedule, but we do know that it was used in the weekly coordination meeting and that, without exception, every trade foreman had it on a clipboard that he used to communicate with his working crew. The schedule was prepared in such a manner that not only was the logic relative to construction implemented, but restraints relative to crew availability and crew size were also indicated. On Unit III there was no quantification as to what resources were required. Only the logical restraint between the crew movement was indicated. This provided a good enough check on the limitation of resource management (manpower requirements were calculated manually) as the first attempt in providing for a realistic schedule.

The net result of the scheduling effort on Unit III was a 25 percent reduction in labor cost of these items remaining for construction at the time of the inclusion of the scheduling within that unit's completion. Table 10 below indicates those actual savings in man hours and dollars.

The difference relative to "learning curve" versus "increase in productivity" was a question that had to be answered in order to attribute the savings to the scheduling effort. As such, Creative Management Group was further engaged by the DP&L project management task force to come up with a system by which productivity and man-hours, unit and dollar control could be achieved. The effort was based upon the following premise; a detailed chart of accounts had to be developed for which the following criteria were used:

- Was the information retrievable?
- Was the information consistent with existing data requirements relative to plant accounting, Federal Power Commission accounting, the joint accounting between Dayton Power & Light and the two other owning utilities, and for Continuing Property Record accounting?

Based upon the above criteria used in detailing the accounts, a system criterion was defined in what was to be the "Construction Management System." The system design of this working tool required considerable effort by DP&L personnel in explaining to the consultant how they, in the field, retrieved and were able to enter data into a manual system concerning man-hour and unit installation information. The retrieval of dollars was no problem, for the present accounting function could retrieve the dollar relationship with no additional effort. Special attention was paid to the manner in which DP&L people were able to project man-hours and determine physical percentage completion. Both methods are rather simple and based upon accepted practices. The projection on man-hours is based upon productivity to date after mobilization has occurred on any individual item, while computation of a physical percentage of completion is based on a statistical weighted average concept for developing the value of each unit in place.

The end result was a data management system entitled "Construction Management System" (CMS). This system is a rather complex system in terms of the data base and data manipulation requirements, but is an easy system for data input and for report request and report format options. Use of a three-level output reporting scheme with summary, intermediate, and detail reporting capabilities; in addition, report retrieval on as many as 10 user codes is available, which facilitates the use of selective and exception reporting schemes. As a result of having the CMS available to all levels of management from field to corporate management, they have at their disposal figures on unit count, man-hour expenditures, dollar expenditures, productivity, and evaluation as to physical percent complete by any grouping of the items within the plant, as well as the total plant in construction. In addition, the proper accounting function could be done with considerable savings in man-day effort upon the closing of the project. Examples of the type of reports contained with the CMS are shown in Tables 11, 12, and 13.

Unit IV not only had the inclusion of the CMS but, more important, an application of resource management was added to the existing CPM schedule. Each item in the CPM network was delineated relative to crew size, crew requirement relative to specific trade, and any other resource limitation. Using an existing resource leveling

Table 9.

THE FOLLOWING REPORT IS BASED ON THE UPDATED COMPUTER RUNS, DATA DATED 07 MAY 1973 AND REFLECTS THE CPN SCHEDULE OF PROGRESS FOR THE PERIOD THROUGH 29 JUNE 1973.

THIS REPORT SHOULD BE USED AS A CHECK IN THE WEEK TO WEEK PROGRESS BUT AT NO TIME, WORK THAT CAN BE PERFORMED NOW, SHOULD BE DELAYED UNTIL LATER BECAUSE OF THE SCHEDULE.

WEEK OF	WORK ITEM	DESCRIPTION	DURTN	START	FINISH
7MAY73		START			
	26025	I/S LUBE OIL PIPE HNGRS - TG	15	7MAY73	
	34060	INST HANGERS MS & HR ABOVE EL 708	15	7MAY73	
	34065	I/S HANGERS MS & HR EL 708 TO DEAER RF	12	7MAY73	
	34180	BOILER START-UP PIPING ELEV. 532-577	35	7MAY73	
	34185	INST BFPT EXHAUST DUCT EL 332	40	7MAY73	
	34215	INST PPG HP HTR AREA EL 532-0 - 577-0	102	7MAY73	
	34225	INST PPG BE TWN BFPTCHP HTR COLS 65-70W SIDE	54	7MAY73	
	34270	INST HANGER CR.&HR. EL 577-0 TO GRND FLR	15	7MAY73	
	34322	INST BSU PPG EL 708-0 TO DEARATOR RF	30	7MAY73	
	34325	HANG PPG CR 3-7,4-1,2,3,4,5,EL 640-0 CR 5-1	24	7MAY73	
7MAY73		FINISH			
14MAY73		START			
14MAY73		FINISH			
21MAY73		START			
	34195	I/S PPG BFPT AREA COLS 81-89,G-F EL 532,552	100	21MAY73	
	34324	INSTALL BS, SU VENTS, BV	40	23MAY73	
21MAY73		FINISH			
	34065	I/S HANGERS MS C HR EL 708 TO DEAER PF	12		22MAY73
	26025	I/S LUBE OIL PIPE HNGRS - TG	15		25MAY73
	34060	INST HANGERS MS & HR ABOVE EL 708	15		25MAY73
	34270	INST HANGER CR.&HR. EL 577-0 TO GRND FLR	15		25MAY73

Date	No.	Activity	Qty		
20MAY73		**START**			
	26005	I/S STEAM SEAL PIPE HANGERS MAIN TURBINE	8	29MAY73	7JUN73
	34200	INST PPG MAIN TURBINE OIL TANK TIE EL 532	16	29MAY73	8JUN73
20MAY73		**FINISH**			
?JUNE73		**START**			
	34070	HANG PIPING MS 162,HR 162,EL 726-EL 663	24	5JUNE73	
4JUN73		**FINISH**			
11JUN73		**START**			
	26005	I/S STEAM SEAL PIPE HANGERS MAIN TURBINE	8	11JUN73	
	34325	HANG PPG CR 3-7,4-1,2,3,4,5,EL 640-0 CR 5-1	24	11JUN73	
		START			
	34075	INST HANGERS MS, HR., ELEB 663-577	8	15JUN73	
	34140	I/S PIPING COILS 94-96 CG-B EL 5326552 RIVER	20		
	26000	I/S GLAND STM EXHAUSTER	3		
11JUN73		**FINISH**			
18JUN73		**START**			
	26010	I/S STEAM SEAL PIPING MAIN TURBINE	90	20JUN73	
	26035	I/S HYDROGEN DETAINING TANK - TG	3	21JUN73	
	26030	I/S AIR DETAINING TANK - TG	4	22JUN73	
18JUN73		**FINISH**			
	34322	INST BSU PPG EL 708-0 TO DEARATOR RF	30		18JUN73
	26000	I/S GLAND STM EXHAUSTER	3		19JUN73
	34200	INST PPG MAIN TURBINE OIL TANK TIE EL 932	16		19JUN73
	34085	INST HANGERS MS, HR., ELEB 663-577	8		20JUN73
25JUN73		**START**			
	34280	HANG PPG CR CHR I/S DE SPRHTR-I/S VALVE V300-1	30	26JUN73	
	34440	INST ASH SLUICE WTR PPG SLUICE PUMP AREA	100	28JUN73	
25JUN73		**FINISH**			
	26035	I/S HYDROGEN DETAINING TANK - TG	3		25JUN73
	34180	BOILER START-UP PIPING ELEV. 532-577	35		25JUN73
	26030	I/S AIR DETAINING TANK - TG	4	27JUN73	

Table 10.

Unit 3 vs. Unit 1 Man-Hours & Dollar Savings

Item[a]	Man-Hours			Dollar per Man-Hour	Savings	
	Unit 1	Unit 3	Difference		Dollars	Percent of Unit 1
Piping	384,600	269,300	115,300	10.719	1,235,900	30.0
Insulation-Boiler	98,005	73,847	24,158	12.324	297,720	24.7
Insulation-Other	83,438	64,455	18,983	10.035	190,490	22.8
Electrical	356,405	284,400	72,005	10.719	770,450	20.2
Subtotal	922,448	692,002	230,446		2,494,560	25.0

[a] Listing only items affected in their entirety by the use of CPM scheduling.

technique through the solution of the CPM network, it was able to forecast a leveled schedule based upon the availability of resources and project what the future resources would be to maintain a project schedule.

The following scheme was utilized: on monthly updates, the resource allocated would be used for only a 60-day period. The resulting schedules would then be the project schedule for the 60-day period. This would basically involve a redefinition of the early start data of the network solution and a recomputation of the float available for that individual item or group of items. Therefore, the project schedule required only the following input requirements to ensure a valid working schedule:

- Status of the project to date properly reflected in the network, as well as a valid projected network for the balance of work.
- The resources that were going to be utilized on individual work items to transpire over the next 60 working days had to be reanalyzed and reevaluated.
- The availability of resources had to be very well defined for the next 60 working days.

It is important to note here that, although the working schedule for the construction job site was the result of a leveled network solution relative to resource restraints, the management of DP&L also received a nonleveled schedule showing the additional items that were available to do work, but due to limitations of resources were not scheduled. It was then up to management of DP&L to have options available that it could use to schedule the work in a day-to-day situation based on the objective schedule as a result of the CPM approach. It was determined that the day-to-day schedule requirements were the decision of the superintendents of the jobsite, and that the CPM scheduling reports issued were to be used only as a check in the day-to-day progress and for planning future schedules. For this reason it is imperative now to understand that the working schedule by no means was a bible. It was a

Table 11.

Dayton Power and Light Company
Construction Management System • • • • Work Progress & Status Report

Reporting Level - Detail Project 000000	Report Period 38 01Sep74 To 30Nov74
Report Is Sorted By Contractor-Code DC1910	Pun Date 18Feb75 Page 395

J. M. Stuart Station Number 4
Schriber Sheet Metal & Roofers, Inc.
Totals and Variances for This Contractor.

1.Original Estimated Manhours.	550.00	4.To Date Manhours.	709.00	7.Projected Total Manhours.	2,500.00
2.Original Estimated Units....	N/A	5.To Date Units....	N/A	8.Projected Total Units....	N/A
3.Original Estimated Production Rate	N/A	6.To Date Production Rate	N/A	9.Projected Total Production Rate	N/A

Variance In Projections

13.Percent To Date (Manhours)....	28.36	10.This Period Manhours.	.00	19.Manhours To Date.	1,950.00
14.Percent To Date (Units).......	N/A	11.This Period Units....	N/A	20.Manhours Period..	.00
15.Percent To Date (Physical)....	16.70	12.This Period Production Rate	N/A	21.Units To Date....	N/A
16.Percent This Period (Manhours)	.00	Unit Definition (Each	)	22.Units This Period	N/A
17.Percent This Period (Units).	N/A				
18.Percent This Period (Physical)	.00				

Account Description / Code / Reference •Unit Code Definition•	Manhours Est. (Proj. 1/7)	Manhours To Date (Period 4/10)	Units Est. (Proj. 2/8)	Units To Date (Period 5/11)	Production Rate Est. (Proj. 3/9)	Production Rate To Date (Period 6/12)	Percent Manhr To Date (Period 13/16)	Percent Units To Date (Period 14/17)	Variance Manhour To Date (Period 19/20)	Variance Units To Date (Period 21/22)
All Others Itemp. Struct.I	0	307	.00	.00	.00	.00	.0	.0	0	.00
J101008. Contr. 4 •Per Cent	0	0	.00	.00	.00	.00	.0	.0	0	.00
Schriber Sheet Metal & Roofers (Misc.)	50	0	1.00	1.00	50.00	.00	.0	100.0	0	.00
01089019 Contr. 1 •Each	50	0	1.00	.00	50.00	.00	.0	.0	0	.00
Roof Deck, Metal	0	11	.00	30.00	.00	.38	.0	.0	0	.00
03210001 Contr. 2 •Per Cent	0	0	.00	.00	.00	.00	.0	.0	0	.00
Roofing (Incl Flashing)	500	367	100.00	15.00	5.00	24.50	15.0	15.0	1,950	.00
03212001 Contr. 1 •Per Cent	2,450	0	100.00	.00	24.50	.00	.0	.0	0	.00
Frames, Steel (Structural)	0	22	.00	.00	.00	.00	.0	.0	0	.00
03232001 Contr. 4 •Ton	0	0	.00	.00	.00	.00	.0	.0	0	.00
Totals	550	709	N/A	N/A	N/A	N/A	28.3	N/A	1,950	N/A
	2,500	0	N/A	N/A	N/A	N/A	.0	N/A	0	N/A

Table 12.

Dayton Power and Light Company

Construction Management System • • • • Work Progress & Status Report

Reporting Level - Account	Project 000000	J. M. Stuart Station Number 4		Report Period 38 01Sep74 To 30Nov74	
Report Is Sorted By Construction Code	100102	Weld-Main Stream Pipe		Run Date 10Feb75 Page 211	

Totals and Variances For This Construction

1.Original Estimated Manhours.	5,974.00	4.To Date Manhours.	9,739.50	7.Projected Total Manhours.	9,739.50
2.Original Estimated Units....	78.00	5.To Date Units....	78.00	8.Projected Total Units....	78.00
3.Original Estimated Production Rate	76.58	6.To Date Production Rate	124.86	9.Projected Total Production Rate	124.86
13.Percent to Date (Manhours)....	100.00	10.This Period Manhours.	.00		Variance in Projections
14.Percent to Date (Units).......	100.00	11.This Period Units....	.00	19.Manhours to Date.	3,765.50
15.Percent to Date (Physical)....	100.00	12.This Period Production Rate	.00	20.Manhours Period..	.00
16.Percent This Period (Manhours)	.00			21.Units to Date....	.00
17.Percent This Period (Units)...	.00	Unit Definition (Each	)	22.Units This Period	.00
18.Percent This Period (Physical)	.00				

| Construction Description | | Manhours | | Units | | Production Rate | | Percent | | Variance | |
| | | Est. | To Date | Est. | To Date | Est. | To Date | Manhr | Units | Manhour | Units |
Code	Reference •Unit Code Definition•	Proj. 1/7	Period 4/10	Proj. 2/6	Period 5/11	Proj. 3/9	Period 6/12	To Date Period 13/16	To Date 14/17	To Date Period 19/20	To Date Period 21/22
4MS-1 Weld Sec Sh Outlet Branch		770	1,549	10.00	10.00	77.00	154.95	100.0	100.0	779	.00
100102 04450002 •Each	•	1,549	0	10.00	.00	154.95	.00	.0	.0	0	.00
4MS-2 Weld Sec. Sh Outlet Branch		755	1,449	10.00	10.00	75.50	144.95	100.0	100.0	694	.00
100102 04450005 •Each	•	1,449	0	10.00	.00	144.95	.00	.0	.0	0	.00
4MS-3 Weld Main Steam Header		1,945	4,513	14.00	14.00	138.92	322.35	100.0	100.0	2,568	.00
100102 04450008 •Each	•	4,513	0	14.00	.00	322.35	.00	.0	.0	0	.00
4MS-4 Weld Turbine Inlet - Branch		330	877	4.00	4.00	82.50	219.37	100.0	100.0	547	.00
100102 04450011 •Each	•	877	0	4.00	.00	219.17	.00	.0	.0	0	.00
4MS-5 Weld Turbine Inlet Branch		262	813	4.00	4.00	65.50	203.25	100.0	100.0	551	.00
100102 04450014 •Each	•	813	0	4.00	.00	203.25	.00	.0	.0	0	.00
4MS-7 Weld Boiler Fu Pump Turbine Sup		958	267	16.00	16.00	59.87	16.68	100.0	100.0	691—	.00
100102 04450017 •Each	•	267	0	16.00	.00	16.68	.00	.0	.0	0	.00
4MS-8 Weld Ia Bf Pump Turbine Inlet		421	168	8.00	8.00	52.62	21.00	100.0	100.0	253—	.00
100102 04450020 •Each	•	168	0	8.00	.00	21.00	.00	.0	.0	0	.00
4MS-9 Weld Ib Bf Pump Turbine Inlet		533	102	12.00	12.00	44.41	8.50	100.0	100.0	431—	.00
100102 04450023 •Each	•	102	0	12.00	.60	8.50	.00	.0	.0	0	.00
Totals		5,974	9,739	78.00	78.00	76.58	124.86	100.0	100.0	3.765	.00
		9,739	0	78.00	.00	124.86	.00	.0	.0	0	.00

Table 13.

Dayton Power and Light Company

Construction Management System • • Accounting Status & Progress Report

Reporting Level - Intermediate   Project 000000   J. M. Stuart Station Number 4   Report Period 038 01Sep74 to 30Nov74

Report is Sorted By Contractor Code   000175   American Bridge Division   Run Date 10Feb75   Page 59

Totals For This Contractor Code

1.Company Labor to Date....... .00	5.Material to Date............. 1,861,897.23
2.Company Labor This Period... .00	6.Material This Period......... .00
3.Contract Labor to Date....... 851,187.48	7.Equipment Usage to Date...... 12,006.82
4.Contract Labor This Period.. .00	8.Equipment Usage This Period.. .00

9.Other to Date...... .00	11.Total to Date...... 2,725,091.53
10.Other This Period.. .00	12.Total This Period.. .00

Account Code	(CCD)	(FPC)	Page Ref.	Company Labor to Date	This Period 1/2	Contract Labor to Date	This Period 3/4	Material to Date	This Period 5/6	Equipment Usage to Date	This Period 7/8	Other to Date	This Period 9/10	Total to Date	This Period 11/12
Frames, Steel (Structural)															
03232001	61004251	000311	•	.00	.00	762,152.85	.00	1,361,897.23	.00	12,006.82	.00	.00	.00	2,156,056.90	.00
Frames, Structural Steel (Cont.)															
03232004	61004251	000311		.00	.00	.00	.00	500,000.00	.00	.00	.00	.00	.00	500,000.00	.00
Conveyor 45															
04310011	19004001	000312		.00	.00	463.63	.00	.00	.00	.00	.00	.00	.00	463.63	.00
Boiler Steel Supports															
04354001	16004001	000312		.00	.00	60,582.00	.00	.00	.00	.00	.00	.00	.00	60,582.00	.00
Deaerator															
04424001	27004002	000312		.00	.00	7,989.00	.00	.00	.00	.00	.00	.00	.00	7,989.00	.00
				.00	.00	851,187.48	.00	1,861,897.23	.00	12,006.82	.00	.00	.00	2,725,091.53	.00

guideline. Since the guideline had to demonstrate many options, but identify the best option and some of the alternatives, it is clear that the leveled schedule was the best option, with the unleveled schedule reflecting the options.

In addition, every 6 months we ran the entire schedule under a resource leveling module (which was never distributed to other than those associated with management planning and scheduling from the total project viewpoint) to evaluate the total project resource requirements. Whenever the manpower and other influencing resource restraints indicated an unleveled solution or a higher than normal probability of nonsuccess of the completion date, logic was revised, as well as manpower requirements, to bring in the project within the mandatory completion date. It was then this revised network, which was run on a 6-month interval, was used as the premise for the network for the working schedule, which was updated and recalculated on a 3- to 4-week basis.

In effect, the same network was used for both long-range and short-range scheduling, but different applications of type of solution were used to take advantage of the time/cost/effectiveness relationship of network based planning and scheduling systems.

Now it becomes my unpleasant task to go into the failure aspect of implementation and application of network and resource based scheduling. The premise used for this assignment was very similar to the case of Dayton Power & Light.

Creative Management Group was retained by a major utility to develop this utility's capability in the field of construction scheduling. Another consultant was retained to develop the utility's capabilities in the field of construction cost control. Both consultants worked for a special task group designated as Construction Cost Control and Scheduling, with one person named as a manager of this task group. This task group recruited its men from within the utility organization. In all cases, these personnel had little or no construction experience, but were all degreed engineers and accountants and were considered by the utility to be competent and highly potential management personnel. As a point of fact, the initial make-up was of people who had been in the construction operation for less than three to five years, but were on recent jobsites in such capacities as project auditor or contact liason engineer between the construction jobsite and the corporate engineering facility. As additional people were brought into the project, there was less evidence of their construction experience.

Creative Management Group initially went into the field on one project to devleop a schedule with the contractor and representatives of the utility. Due to impending political problems between the construction organization and construction cost control and scheduling organization, very little cooperation existed. As a point of concern, the scheduling group's mandate was to work with the field, but to work out of the corporate offices. Unfortunately, this was the first major breakdown in the communication line. The resulting schedule of this first effort was quite detailed (in our opinion overdetailed), but due to the lack of information available, there was no other way to isolate the information so it could be of use.

To add to the problems of implementing a schedule, there were personality conflicts no only between the client's construction forces and the client's scheduling group, but between the client's scheduling and construction personnel and representatives of Creative Management Group. Unfortunately, CMG was not given the opportunity of working with the construction forces to sell them on the concept of how this was going to help them. Therefore, much resistance between Creative Management Group's effort and the construction field personnel started to grow.

Also charged with the responsibility of developing an engineering schedule that was tied to the construction schedule, Creative Management Group and the client's scheduling group retrieved a great deal of information from the client's engineering organization and the client's engineering consultant. There was considerable cooperation by the client's engineering consultants. The client's scheduling group for the first time realized the complexity of the engineering information, related to the construction process. They diligently worked through the amount of information and developed conceptually sound network models of the engineering process. The problem now was to retrieve the timing information relative to these networks and, in effect, to try to get the engineering personnel to discipline themselves to commit certain information within limitation of time parameters. This was an almost impossible task, an unrealistic approach where the timing information was given to us after the fact. Engineering supplied timing projections in generalized and gross statements. This led to the burdensome effort by our consultants, as well as the client's staff, of trying to come up with a working schedule for the engineering function within an eight-month period. This was never accomplished. To the dismay of our staff, the client's staff became quite complacent with not having a realistic schedule and was satisfied with massive data (and to go through the data processing effort to produce large amounts of useless paper data) that was of little use to management of the engineering function. The total engineering schedule for this project had now degenerated into a summary schedule, not by specific items, very, very poorly maintained relative to projection, but very successfully maintained relative to history.

The construction schedule also fell completely apart in the field, since there was minimum communication between the scheduling group, the field construction personnel, and the contractors and never was utilized by the site construction personnel; only to be used as a whipping post as far as their attitudes toward construction scheduling.

Approximatley five months after Creative Management Group's engagement by this client on one facility, it was decided to try the same approach on a second facility. On this second facility, there was much more cooperation between the field personnel and scheduling group. The construction networks that were developed were more readily accepted by the construction contractors and the client's construction management. The engineering aspect was much more complex, because the first facility, being a fossil-fired unit, did not require the regulatory engineering effort and did not therefore demand quality control, quality assurance, etc., being integrated into the schedule. This second project, which was a nuclear facility, became very complex in the engineering aspect because of these regulatory and licensing requirements. The engineering aspect of this nuclear facility, from my understanding, has never been fully integrated into a project schedule, while the construction schedule has been degraded now to basically a management summary type schedule and, as such, has no application in the field.

I have briefly summarized this 18-month assignment because going into detail would only point fingers at the many areas of failure. I feel the following dissertation on "what" would be more appreciated than specific instances being discussed, allowing one to reach his own conclusion as to the "why."

My personal evaluation of the major cause of the failure of this effort was due to it being controlled out of an office environment with people not readily accepted by both the field and engineering organization. For any form of management tool to work, it is mandatory that management be located within the area being managed. In the case of our engagement, we were placed in a corner to work with client personnel who were not realistically suited to their positions. "People" is the name of the game in management.

Successful project management requires being able to provide information to people who are not only knowledgeable in the technical end, but also in the application (must have practical experience) end. Often construction management, being a new concept, encounters a resistance to change. It is then the management function to sell this concept, so that those affected by the change feel comfortable. No attempt was made by the client's personnel to gain the confidence of the user group. The corporation's attitude on having this new scheduling and cost control group as a task force, rather than an operational department, did not institute a sense of credibility to the scheduling group's personnel nor to the engineering and construction organizations within the client's organization. The facts that there were two consultants and that both the engineering and construction people had to work with two different philosophies using the same information provided an additional avenue of resistance.

The third and most important area of resistance occurred in the scheduling and cost control group being an office function rather than a field-oriented function. This was not only communicated by the construction personnel, because even though in their ivory tower they were well aware that for any schedule to be meaningful, it had to come through the field. Even if the scheduling function was within the engineering group which was an office function, it would have been closer to the field rather than in its own isolated ivory tower.

Midway through our engagement (approximately the ninth month), the cost control scheduling group was formally organized into an operating department under the vice-president of construction, rather than its initial task force status. This did help the credibility, but, once again, the roles at this point were well-established and the resistance of the previous nine months continued to create more barriers.

A slight digression is now worth pursuing to one of the other missions of Creative Management Group on this assignment. It was our function for this client to develop a very powerful scheduling network computer program. Much of this program had previously been documented in systems design. Since this client had approximately five major power plants scheduled for construction during the next five years, it was appropriate to consider an effort to continue the development of this system into an operational scheduling and resource management program. It turned out to be even a greater failure than the construction scheduling or the engineering scheduling. Once again, head-on combat ensued between our consulting staff and the client's computer organization (operations and programming).

This engagement of Creative Management Group turned out to be a total fiasco and was terminated by mutal consent some time ago. As a result, Creative Management Group took a hard look at our effort and found fault not only with the client's

organization but with us. Creative Management Group's objective was to make a
workable and valuable installation within the client's organization. Due to personality
conflicts, Creative Management Group became a lot more emotional and a lot less
objective, allowing the emotion to overcome its objectivity. We became ineffective
in trying to assist a client in developing its capabilities. The confession related to
this is being used only . . . not for the moral value but for the professional value.
We now feel that an implementation program could have been achieved if Creative
Management Group would have performed the following preliminary services prior
to its involvement with direct project scheduling:

- Work with the client's organization to develop the environment for implementation prior to immediate implementation.
- Work with the client in the development of the personnel.
- Proceeded with a slower rate of progress for a more thorough implementation on one project, rather than a shotgun approach on two projects.

The client, too, had some clean-up to do. It should have communicated to the
organization that project scheduling and cost control were mandatory requirements
to gain effective control of the construction projects, facilitating optimization of our
efforts. The selection of personnel should have been more thoroughly controlled,
being more conducive to instituting the objectives of management's direction, not
only from a standpoint of technical transmission of the information, but from requiring
the personnel to react, report, and have accountability for the information.

In the case of Dayton Power & Light, Creative Management Group is still working
with it on another facility, as well as providing over-the-shoulder consultation on
its continual improvement of the management information system. DP&L has just
installed a minicomputer with communication systems at its new construction jobsite
and at its home construction base in Dayton. This will allow for daily input of
labor information, as well as for the normal business of providing payroll and other
construction management information.

These two case studies, though diverse, were excellent experiences for the author
in approaching the management function of dealing with project management. It
not only showed that there can be varying degrees of success or failure, but that
the true value of project management lies not only in producing information but in
the client's utilization, attitude, and organizational communication of the information.

CASE STUDY 14: TENNESSEE WHEELWORKS, INCORPORATED[1]

Tennessee Wheelworks, Incorporated—better known as TWI—exemplified the American economic dream. From its origins as a small backyard operation in the 1920s,
it was the country's major supplier of suspension systems for medium- and luxury-

[1] Reprinted, by permission of the publisher, from *Getting Results with Matrix Management* by
Grant E. Mayberry, pp. 83–88. © 1980 by Education for Management, Inc. Published by
AMACOM, a division of American Management Associations, New York. All rights reserved.

size passenger cars by the 1970s. In the late 1970s, booked orders from the three major automobile manufacturers seemed to assure continued growth.

In addition to suspension systems for passenger cars, TWI also produced heavy-duty suspension systems for trucks of all sizes, off-the-road vehicles, and tracked vehicles, ranging in size from farm tractors to combat vehicles (including amphibious assault and landing craft, which were scheduled for full production in the 1980s).

Organizationally, TWI comprised a corporate office that linked two separate divisions. Each division was a profit center headed by a corporate vice-president. AutoSysParts Division designed, manufactured, and marketed automobile suspension systems and replacement parts. The HDSysParts Division performed the same operations for vehicles requiring heavy-duty suspension systems and replacement parts.

Each division was organized along lines established by the respective vice-presidents. Tim Richards, who headed AutoSysParts, had found the classical functional structure satisfactory. His organization is shown in Figure 13. The head of HDSysParts, Peter Grant, favored a project-oriented operation. The organization chart for HDSysParts is shown in Figure 14.

How the Divisions Were Formed and Structured

Prior to World War II, the outputs of suspension systems by TWI for passenger cars and for heavy-duty vehicles had been about equal. The company was small enough so that there was no need to have a separate division for each of the two major product lines. During the war years, passenger-car production ceased, and the automotive industry was mobilized to meet the needs of the military. The transition had little impact on TWI because of its small, flexible structure.

In 1950, the company established the two divisions in response to the boom production of passenger cars. From the beginning, AutoSysParts had accounted for the higher earnings. Its functional organization structure, which the division had from the outset, proved adequate. Its product line remained essentially static in terms of basic manufacturing and marketing operations. Plant and equipment modernization followed industry patterns, and additional personnel were hired as needed to maintain the division's high level of labor productivity.

While AutoSysParts was growing at an increasingly rapid rate, HDSysParts had to scratch and claw merely to show its slight profit. The division was definitely the corporation's poor relation.

In 1965, Peter Grant was appointed director of HDSysParts. He knew that a reorganization was necessary. Although AutoSysParts was able to perform profitably with a classic functional organization structure, Grant realized immediately that HDSysParts could not. His division had few resources, a smaller share of its market, and more aggressive competitors, because the marketplace itself was specialized and therefore limited. Any growth in competitive strength would have to come by means of innovation—in terms of management *and* product design and marketing.

After much consultation with his staff and personal study of the alternatives available, Grant realized that he had to prune much deadwood from the organizational structure and concentrate the resources of the division where they would be most effective. This he did by establishing two project offices, which were responsible for

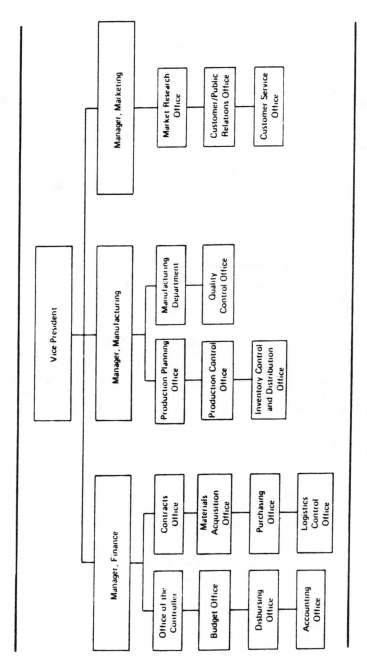

Figure 13.   Organization Chart for AutoSysParts.

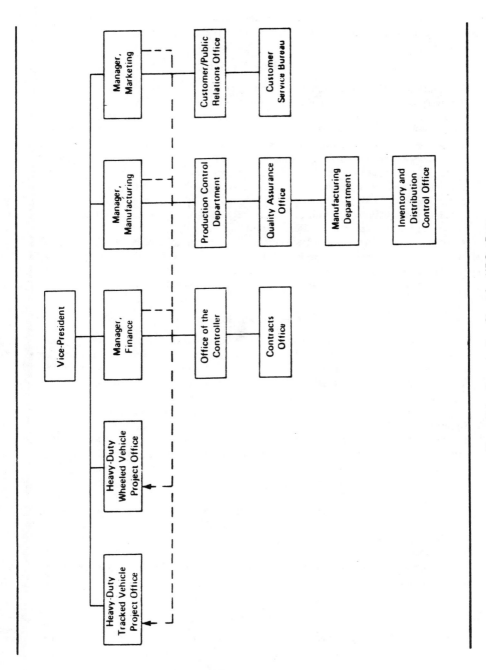

Figure 14. Organization Chart for HDSysParts.

115

planning and research. This step freed line managers to devote full-time to their responsibilities of managing the resources under their direction.

The Tide Turned

Going into the 1970s, AutoSysParts was fat and sassy. Times were booming; it seemed that every driver in the United States—and there appeared to be no end to them—demanded cars that weighed at least 3,500 pounds or more. Tim Richards's division could barely keep up with the demand for its suspension systems. When the bubble burst, it seemed to Richards that there were two causes: fuel economy standards were established by the federal government, and gasoline became an almost endangered substance. At about this time, the automotive industry decided that it had to drastically reduce the weight of passenger cars, and the driving public almost frantically switched its preference to small foreign cars.

While AutoSysParts ran into difficulties, HDSysParts began to grow. The innovative management techniques of Peter Grant had caught hold. World conditions increased military demand for tracked vehicles. Perhaps the gains of HDSysParts seemed significant only because of the decline of the earnings of AutoSysParts—but the disparity between the two divisions' earnings was becoming more narrow. Corporate headquarters began to be alarmed about the situation AutoSysParts was in.

What Richards Did

Tim Richards established a management task force composed of managers immediately under his supervision. The task force's objective was to formulate a strategy for cutting into the losses that were resulting from a shrinking market. However, the group was unable to come up with any practical solution—each manager saw the problem not as his or her own but as that of the other managers. The solution proposed by the manager of finance—that the size of on-hand inventory be limited—was met with heated argument from the manager of marketing, who claimed that this would result in fewer sales, because it would hinder service to customers who needed parts in a hurry. When the manager of manufacturing wanted to replace inefficient plant equipment with a computer-assisted design and production system, the manager of finance did not agree that it would be cost-effective given its initial expense. And so it went.

Richards finally saw that these task force meetings were dividing the departments at a time when everyone should be working together. He dissolved the task force and hired a management consulting firm. But the ideas the consultants proposed could not be implemented without too drastic an overhaul of the division, and Richards did not want this. Almost at the end of his sanity, he decided to meet Peter Grant and ask for advice.

Grant's Advice

In response to Richard's cry for help, Peter Grant studied the problem AutoSysParts had and suggested that one viable solution would be to alter the division's structure, if only temporarily. And after reviewing the structure of HDSysParts, Richards saw that a project-oriented approach had possibilities for his division. He realized that the functional structure that had characterized AutoSysParts from its inception was too inflexible to allow for practical responses to problems. At the same time, he felt that the approach used by HDSysParts was not the answer, because it was designed to meet a series of repetitive problems, which called for a permanent subsystem. The problems faced by AutoSysParts were more acute in nature and required even greater flexibility for prompt decision making. Richards thought that some type of a matrix overlay could be the answer.

Tim Richards listed AutoSysParts's problems and discovered that what he needed was a substructure that could draw on talent already available within his division, and that the substructure selected should indeed be temporary. The perfect substructure for AutoSysParts would provide a short channel of communication between the operating groups, so that they could arrive at a decision or a series of decisions that could be quickly implemented. This would not require a major divisional reorganization, which would have been expensive and time-consuming.

Time Runs Out

Alice Anthony, the daughter of one of the founders of Tennessee Wheelworks, Incorporated, and current president of the company, was regarded in the trade as a very sharp businesswoman. Her standing in the economic community was so high that her male counterparts in other companies held her in awe. She spoke with authority, and she expected her employees—from the bottom to the top of the organization—to do, without question, as she directed. She would, however, listen to opposing arguments before she made decisions.

AutoSysParts and its falling earnings were the subjects of the monthly meeting she held with Richards and Grant. Tim Richards knew that he had to produce or look for other employment. He also knew that Alice Anthony had already thought of removing him in favor of Peter Grant. She was interested most in results, not in his years of service with the company.

The meeting among the three resulted in Richards standing alone. Anthony favored retaining the organizational structure of AutoSysParts, because it had a proven record of success. Grant favored merging AutoSysParts with his own division. Anthony gave Richards until the next month's meeting to come up with a solution.

After the meeting with Anthony and Grant, Richards returned to his office and called his senior staff members together. He told them about the meeting and gave them one week to present him with ideas for a matrix overlay that could deal with the critical issues. As he saw them, the critical issues were:

- AutoSysParts had to improve its product line immediately.
- Additional resources were not available.
- The change in demand was essentially simple and could be met by technology readily available within AutoSysParts.
- The substructure should be temporary.

The Solution

The senior staff members' suggestions resulted in the matrix format shown in Figure 15. At the next meeting with Anthony and Grant, Richards introduced the solution. He explained that organizational rigidity was causing AutoSysParts to fail. What the division needed was flexibility to respond to the changing market conditions. Anthony received the idea of an overlay coolly, but Richards was given a chance to explain how it would work.

This structural alteration, Richards explained to Anthony and Grant, would provide a drastically shortened communication loop, which would permit input from the three departments to flow to him through the matrix office. The benefit of this communication loop would be that Richards would receive data that were a composite of the individual departments' input and that were unencumbered by the departments' parochial viewpoints. The structure would be staffed by personnel drawn from the functional departments as needed, so that specific expertise would be available without disrupting the ongoing efforts of the departments involved. Finally, the manager of the matrix would be an impartial judge of the input furnished and could separate the impractical from the practical while assuring that the final data presented to the vice-president (Tim Richards) would be acceptable to each of the departments. Any internal bargaining would have taken place before the recommendations were made to Richards—and before he instructed implementation.

Finally, once the design for a new suspension system was achieved, the matrix office could be dissolved easily, and the division could move forward, in a better position to recover its lost share of the market.

Grant agreed that a temporary overlay could indeed be the solution to Richards's immediate dilemma. With Grant's support, Richards was able to convince Anthony that the overlay be tried.

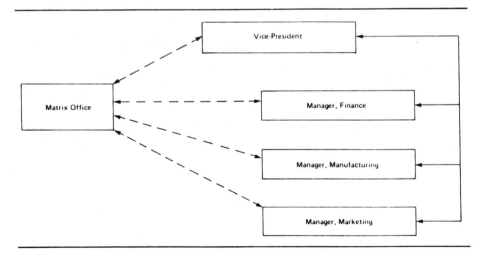

Figure 15. The Matrix Overlay for AutoSysParts.

The Challenge

Alone in his office, waiting for his three line managers to arrive, Tim Richards, director of AutoSysParts, thought over the meeting he'd had with Alice Anthony, president of TWI, and Peter Grant, director of HDSysParts—the other division of TWI. Richards's proposal to insert a matrix substructure crossing interdivisional lines of responsibility had been endorsed. He was even assured that the corporate office would not interfere in the matter. But there was one catch: he had six months to change the financial position of AutoSysParts.

Actually, AutoSysParts was still in the black. But new orders were off by some 25 percent. The projection was that this downward trend would continue unless something was done immediately. One thing was certain: New orders would increase *if* AutoSysParts could produce a suspension system suitable for passenger cars weighing between 1,000 and 2,500 pounds. Providing such a system *rapidly* was the problem.

As soon as his three managers arrived, Tim knew that difficulties lay ahead. He could feel the tension they brought with them. They had less confidence in the usefulness of a matrix overlay than Richards had. The senior staff had worked as a good management team in other times of crisis; now each manager seemed to be interested only in defending the efficiency of his or her own operation against the operations of the other two. Richards knew that the matrix manager's job would be impossible unless this anxiety could be reduced.

Refining the Matrix

Richards reviewed the meeting he had had with Alice Anthony and Peter Grant. The three managers listened without interrupting. Fred Brown, the manager of marketing, spoke first: "What's the first step—filling in the blanks in the matrix or appointing a matrix manager and leaving the job to him?"

"Who is going to be the manager?" asked Jenny Wright, manager of finance.

Richards answered that he intended to appoint the person he felt was the most qualified. But, he added, before he appointed a matrix manager, their first step was to flesh out the too sketchy outline of the substructure. The matrix manager could fill in other blank spaces later.

Each of the line managers had ideas about how the structure should be fashioned. After several hours of discussion, the matrix began to take form, and all agreed that it should be structured as shown in Figure 16. As the figure shows, with this overlay:

1. The matrix office would be on the same management level as the three line managers.
2. Each line department would provide personnel with the particular expertise that would be required to support the matrix office.
3. The matrix manager would have direct access to the vice-president.

Selecting the Matrix Manager

Richards listed the qualities the matrix manager would have to have: management expertise, engineering and design skills, the capability to handle financial matters,

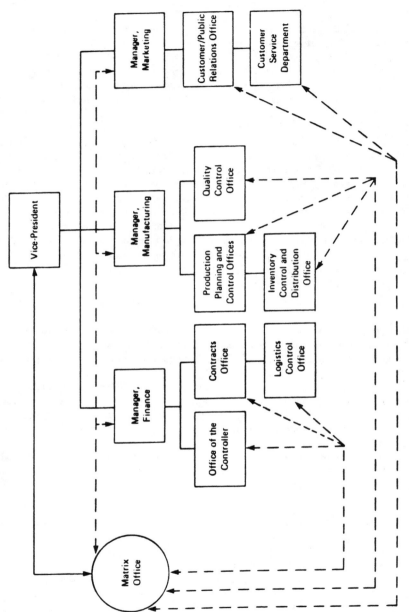

Figure 16.   The Refined Matrix for AutoSysParts.

experience in diagnosing customer needs, and the ability to deal with constant pressure, which could be expected from all the line managers. Perhaps most important, the matrix manager would have to regard the matrix as his or her own enterprise and be able to locate and utilize available resources quickly and effectively.

Logic suggested that many potential problems could be eliminated if the three managers and Richards could come to an agreement about who would head the matrix. So, Richards privately asked each of the managers to give him a list of four names of people within the AutoSysParts Division who would be acceptable as matrix manager. He stipulated that the names be submitted in a sealed envelope by the close of business the next day. He also stated two conditions: (1) each manager should designate one of his or her four candidates as the most qualified and should provide a statement supporting the designation. The person the manager chooses as most qualified could be a member of his or her own department or could be in another department in the division; (2) of the other three candidates, one could be currently employed in the manager's own functional area, but the other two must be employed in the other departments.

Richards was curious about how the submissions would turn out. He had a fair idea who each manager would name as most qualified; the other choices would be interesting.

When he opened the envelopes, Richards couldn't help but feel pleased with his understanding of the three members of his senior staff. As he had expected, they had all selected themselves as the most qualified, and they had defended their choices by saying that the major problems to be faced by the matrix manager were within their own areas of expertise. Tim had to admit that he understood why they had all chosen themselves: No manager wants to be considered unable to manage something within his or her capacity.

There was one name that appeared on all three lists: Oliver Porteus, who headed the office of customer and public relations in the marketing department. Porteus was a capable manager, and he did know what customers liked and disliked about the division's product line. When the managers found out that they had all listed Porteus as a candidate, they were surprised. They all thought him a good worker, but they indicated that if one of them did not get the job, it should go to someone in manufacturing. However, the more Richards thought about Porteus as a choice, the more he became convinced that Oliver Porteus was the right person to head the matrix.

Delegating Authority to the Matrix Manager

In just a few days, the basic outline of the matrix subsystem had been refined, and the matrix manager had been selected. The next step was to provide Porteus with sufficient authority to carry out his responsibilities—hopefully with as few problems as possible.

The charter of authority Richards drew up appointed Oliver Porteus as matrix manager for a period of six months. During this time, Porteus would be responsible for staffing and operation of the matrix office. He was empowered to divert employees from any organizational unit below the level of department manager to serve in the matrix office for as long as his or her services were necessary. However, the charter also stated that employees engaged in a matter designated as critical by the department manager were not to be used in the matrix.

Porteus realized that he had a broad endorsement from the director of AutoSys-Parts. He also realized that much was not defined by the charter. Early on, he decided that he would provide a weekly briefing for Tim Richards and a twice-monthly briefing for the three line managers. He was determined to cooperate as much as possible with the line managers, but he was also determined to achieve the goals of the matrix within the stipulated time.

Conflicts Arise

Porteus learned very quickly that he needed a small permanent staff to handle daily office routine. Secretarial and clerical employees could handle most of this work. Porteus also wanted someone to serve as his deputy, who would be responsible for designing a sequential planning network, such as PERT (Program Evaluation and Review Technique). For this critical position, he thought immediately of Martha Henney. Martha worked in the controller's office and was generally recognized as one of the best program and financial analysts at AutoSysParts.

When Porteus asked Jenny Wright, manager of finance, to release Martha to work on the matrix for a period of six months, the entire plant heard the resounding "Not on your life!" Wright did not want the matrix to interfere with the running of her department. Needless to say, Porteus had a real problem. He needed Martha Henney, and even though he had the backing of the division director to obtain whatever personnel he required, Jenny Wright would not cooperate.

Porteus also began to notice that those people who did report when requested were reluctant to take any meaningful action that could be seen as even slightly detrimental to their home offices. In a nutshell, after one week on the job, Porteus was sinking in the quicksand of interoffice politics. If he wanted to meet his deadline, he had to get the problems resolved quickly.

Lonely Is the Captain

Porteus was disillusioned and in need of a friendly word. Also, he was scheduled to make his first weekly progress report to Tim Richards. He knew that he must maintain an upbeat posture, and he reminded himself that this was only the end of the first week—he still had many more weeks to go. When he changed his outlook, he was able to report to Richards on his successes and his setbacks (never "failures") honestly and without apology.

By the end of the second week, Porteus had secured Martha Henney for the deputy position. And he was enjoying an increasing degree of cooperation from his staff. By the end of the first month, it was apparent that Porteus was on the right track. The matrix substructure seemed destined for success, much to the surprise and pleasure of everyone. "How did Porteus do it?" they all wondered.

CASE STUDY 15   THE INTRODUCTION AND IMPLEMENTATION OF MATRIX MANAGEMENT AT STANDARD STEEL[1]

This case will focus on the development of the matrix form of organization at one company—Standard Steel, Burnham, Pennsylvania, a Division of Titanium Metals Corporation of America. Standard Steel's reasons for selecting this approach will be explored in conjunction with the known advantages and disadvantages of a matraix system. The case will also examine whether the company's initial expectations have been accomplished and whether the matrix management approach should be continued.

Introduction

Standard Steel began operation in 1811 as Freedom Forge, along the banks of the Kishacoquillas Creek, approximately 60 miles northwest of Harrisburg, Pennsylvania. From native ore, iron was smelted and forged into bars, rods, and sheets for blacksmiths, wagon makers and shipwrights. For much of its history, Standard Steel has been associated with the railroad industry. That association started with the opening of the first wrought iron railroad tire mill in the United States in 1856. Approximately 2,000 tires were produced that first year. Today, the company produces 4,000 forged wheels per week. For the first 150 years, the sales volume increased to $20 million. However, during the next 20 years, it grew to nearly $200 million. In addition, its product diversification increased substantially, and a second plant located in Latrobe, Pennsylvania, was added to the organization. Currently, Standard Steel is one of the country's most completely integrated and largest suppliers of specialty steel forged products in the world. Critical parts for missiles, rocket booster engines, jet engines, nuclear reactor vessels, heavy construction equipment, as well as many other high-stress, high-temperature applications, are made by the two plant operations. From the modest two-man operation that existed in 1811, the company now employs approximately 2,600 and has an annual payroll in excess of $50 million.[2]

At the end of 1980, the company manufactured 16 percent of the country's railroad wheels and 27 percent of the railroad axles. However, as further indication of the product diversification that has taken place over the company's long history, it also supplies 22 percent of the rings for the construction equipment, jet engine, mining, and bearing industries. In addition, Standard Steel is a major supplier of open die forgings and heavy shafting for marine and nuclear reactor applications.[3]

Standard Steel has grown rapidly in volume and diversification of its product line, especially in the past 20 years. In addition, the company faced a variety of other business challenges. In 1977, the year before the matrix management approach was adopted, the return on investment was relatively poor. Had the market prices

---

[1] This case was prepared by Gary L. Heimbach, Director of Personnel Administration at the Standard Steel Co., Burnham, Pennsylvania 17009.
[2] *Years of Change and Progress at Standard Steel,* a brochure prepared by John Wright Associates.
[3] Paul Cathey, "How Metals Industry Uses Management Tools," *Iron Age,* vol. 221, no. 46, November 1978, pp. 38–41.

been a little lower or product costs a little higher, the company would have lost money. Through substantial cost reduction, increased productivity, and product innovation, approximately $7 million in cost reduction was realized in 1978. However, increases in labor, material, and energy costs totally wiped out those savings. During 1977, the company realized only a 50 percent delivery credibility rating. In other words, only 50 percent of the railroad wheel and axle, open die forging, and ring products were being delivered on time. This was a strong indication that the old management structure was not able to deal with the company's dramatic growth rate. The old standby of increasing productivity and reducing costs was not enough to get the company back on track. The business activities had become so complex at Standard Steel that the system became overloaded. Top managers had time only to put out fires, rather than plan for the long-range future of the company. These shortcomings were not due to individual incompetence, but the inadequacies of the organizational structure. The new approach selected was matrix management.[4]

Why Matrix Management?

The establishment of a matrix approach comes about through an evolutionary process that, in all probability, would not be the same for every organization. In general, the first stage of development is the temporary task force brought together to solve a particular problem or complete a project. The need to share resources is evident. Normally, the project is not large enough to warrant its own resources. Support can come from a variety of sources, including functional units within the organization, outside consultants, and subcontractors. The project is also normally complex and temporary, with decision making channeled through a project or task leader. The second stage is when the task force becomes permanent. A typical example is a brand manager. At Standard Steel, business committees, each concerned with a product line and consisting of participants from different function areas, represent permanent teams and are currently at this stage in the evolution. The third stage is when a permanent product or project manager is appointed to coordinate the activities and input of the team or committee assignments. The distinguishing feature is a balance of power between functional and project managers. The manager embedded in the core definitely has two bosses.

Although, in stages 2 and 3, the structure becomes permanent, the deployment of people throughout the matrix may change constantly. Matrix, however, is not necessarily an ultimate form of organization. There seems to be a tendency to revert toward stage 1, assuming the evolution continues. But the matrix behavior and culture continue.[5]

Matrix allows for the coexistence of a centralized and decentralized organization. The product or project team can make all the critical tradeoffs relevant to its independent activity, while calling upon the centralized organization for technical proficiency.

---

[4] John E. Fogarty, "Managing with Matrix at Standard Steel," speech delivered to Susquehanna University in November 1979.

[5] Don Hellriegel and John H. Slocum, Jr., *Organizational Behavior,* 2nd edition. West Publishing Co., St. Paul, Minn., 1979, p. 125.

A matrix management approach assumes upper management cannot make optimizing decisions, considering the complexities and uncertainties of the modern organization. The frequency of exceptional cases and unpredictability of the timing requires experts involved in lateral interactions capable of negotiating tradeoffs as the need for decisions proliferates. Matrix is introduced to cope with the conflict between specialization verus the need for coordination, which occurs with such frequency that the up-the-line approach of the functional organization cannot handle the load.[6] In a projection of General Electric's organization for the next 10 years, the company's Organization Planning Bulletin of September 1976 states:

> We've highlighted matrix organization . . . not because it's a bandwagon that we want you all to jump on, but rather is a complex, difficult and sometimes frustrating form of organization to live with. It's also, however, a bellwether of things to come. . . . And all of us are going to have to learn how to utilize organization to prepare managers to increasingly deal with the high levels of complexity and ambiguity in situations where they have to get results from people and components, not under their direct control . . . where so many complex, conflicting interests must be balanced.[7]

As the above quote implies, the matrix is intended to focus on more than one essential organizational task at the same time and provide for human processing of a great deal of complex information. While the traditional organization is shaped like a pyramid, the diamond-shaped organization shown in Figure 17 is one author's attempt to clarify how the matrix induces the above characteristics. At the top of the diamond, as with the traditional pyramid organization, is top management, whose role it is to perform the following.

1. Support and provide enthusiasm for the matrix to those involved in it.
2. Develop and maintain a balance of power between the functional and product sides of the matrix. This can be done through performance evaluations, pay levels, and access to top management.
3. Manage the decision process. Bring conflicts out into the open, and discuss conflicting positions in an open and supportive manner.
4. Provide direction and set performance standards.

At the left side of the diamond is the functional unit, or input side, of the organization. The functional manager's role is different in a matrix in the following ways:

1. Decisions may have to be shared with product managers, especially in a fully developed matrix, in areas of performance appraisal, pay increases, and employment decisions, including the selection of employees.

---

[6] Leonard R. Sayles, "Matrix Management—The Structure with a Future," *Organizational Dynamics,* vol. 5, no. 2, Autumn 1976, pp. 2–17.
[7] Stanley M. Davis and Paul R. Lawrence, "The Matrix Diamond," *The Wharton Magazine,* vol. 2, no. 2, Winter 1978, pp. 19–27.

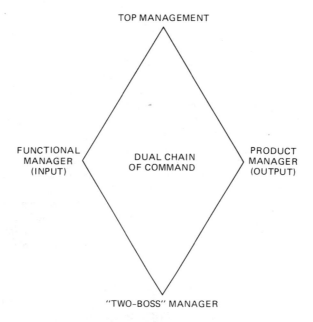

Figure 17. The Matrix Diamond.

2. Anticipate training needs for the product units and provide administrative support for staff and physical resources required by product units.
3. Develop a product orientation as well as functional.

At the right side is the product manager who adopts the following roles:

1. Exert influence on functional managers through knowledge and constant preparation and by responding quickly to requests for information.
2. Search for imaginative ways to share scarce resources. Be aware that shortages may occur, and react with reason.
3. Establish a balanced orientation for all functional units. Prevent bias toward any one unit.

At the bottom of the diamond is the subordinate manager with two bosses. His new role creates problems of dual group membership, new demands for communication, and a variety of uncertainties. He must adopt a more generalist orientation than required in a functional organization.[8]

It should be noted that, even in a full matrix, only a small percentage of the

---

[8] John H. Slocum, Jr., "Problems of Matrix Organization—Roles of Key Individuals," material used during management training program at Standard Steel, Burnham, Pa., January 1978.

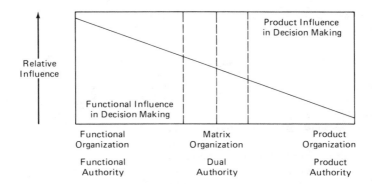

Figure 18.   Choosing the Organizational Design (Jay R. Galbraith, "Matrix Organization Design," *Business Horizons*, February 1971).

managers are actually involved in the matrix directly. At Standard Steel, 30 managers out of 350 are involved in the business committees.

Many companies, including Standard Steel, recognizing that a change was necessary, asked what was the best organizational design. The alternatives may be described as a continuum, as shown in Figure 18. Recognizing that not all organizations need a full matrix, a choice can be made based on relative influence of the functional side or product side. The direction a company moves in will depend on the nature of its current organizational structure. If the current organization is represented by the left side of the continuum, the addition of task teams, for example, would move the organization more to the right. Other influencing factors include: budget approvals, design changes, location and size of offices, and salaries. Factors that would influence choice or organizational design would be diversity of product line, rate of change of product line, interdependency among subunits, level of technology, presence of economies of scale, and organizational size. The greater the diversity of product lines and the greater the rate of change, the more pressure there will be to move toward a product structure. The large amount of knowledge to be maintained by functional managers exceeds their capacity to absorb it. Interdependencies among subunits refers to the idea that a problem in one unit can have a direct impact on goal accomplishment in another. If a rapid response to market changes is required, then scheduled activities are squeezed, a greater number of joint decisions are required, and a need for product influence develops. The pressure, therefore, exists to move to the right in Figure 18. The use of new technologies requires expertise in the technical specialties. If the organization is to make effective use of the expertise, the functional form of organization is superior, and, therefore, there will be a tendency for the organization to move toward the left. The reliance on expensive equipment in manufacturing, test facilities in engineering, and warehousing facilities in marketing are factors involved in economies of scale considerations. The greater the economies of scale, the greater the pressure to move to the functional side. The size of the organization serves only to moderate the influence of economies of scale and expertise. The greater the size, the smaller the cost of lost specialization and lost economies of scale when the product form is adopted.[9]

Advantages of the Matrix Design

In general, matrix is especially effective when numerous complex factors are involved in decision making and when the environment is dynamic. Matrix organizations can react quickly. General management skills, such as negotiating, balancing, and trading off among various costs and benefits, can be developed more widely and at lower organizational levels in a matrix organization. The personal rewards, motivation, and excitement for participants can be high. Since the backgrounds of the participants are diverse, the quality of decisions and ease of implementation are improved.[10] In referring to the flexibility of a matrix structure, Standard Steel's president stated, in an article written in the October 15, 1979 issue of *Iron Age,* that the coordinators of their business committees can be changed depending on the problems and issues the product line faces:

> For example . . . when the matrix managing system began operating, we were in the process of improving our Ring Mill facilities to speed up and increase production by installing the latest ring-making technology. Therefore it seemed clear the Manager of Ring Mill Manufacturing should be the coordinator of that Committee. For a year and-a-half as we worked to improve productivity in the new facilities, increase yield, reduce rejects, and coordinate our raw material scheduling with the Melt Shop, this worked beautifully. Then we reached a point where these matters were under control. Now we want to concentrate on financial control of that operation, optimize our costs, find ways to effect cost reductions. So the manufacturing man, while still a member of that matrix team, has been replaced as coordinator by the financial man. Eventually, it's conceivable the marketing man will assume that role.[11]

Matrix enables a company to push decision making farther down the organization than the functional structure. One resultant advantage of this is to permit top management to concentrate on the future rather than the crisis of the minute. In another article written in the November 20, 1978 issue of *Iron Age,* Standard Steel's president stated:

> In today's highly complex business world, top managers have got to have time to think about the future—anticipating the problems that may develop, conceiving the strategies that will lead to continued growth. They've got to have time to recognize change and deal with it.[12]

---

[9] Jay R. Galbraith, "Matrix Organization Design," *Business Horizons,* February 1971, pp. 29–40.

[10] Hellriegel and Slocum, *Organizational Behavior,* p. 125.

[11] Paul Cathey, "Make Profit Centers Work Through Matrix Managing," *Iron Age,* vol. 222, no. 39, October 1979, pp. 45–48.

[12] Cathey, "How Metals Industry Uses Management Tools," p. 39.

A second advantage of lower level decision making is that it helps develop middle managers into top managers. They are required to function more like business managers than functional specialists. They also gain an appreciation for the responsibilities and concerns of the various functions.

Interestingly enough, one of the main advantages of a matrix is that the traditional functional structure is permitted to remain intact. The functional organization allows for a degree of stability and security. Team members can be moved on to new tasks or even new teams expeditiously. Without the functional organization, it would be possible for temporary task teams to become permanent and, thereby, result in higher costs, loss of creativity, and inability to respond to changes. The functional organization also provides for the acquisition and development of technical specialists. Compared to a pure product or project form of organization, the matrix makes better use of available human resources because of the existence of the functional units. As an illustration, if a product unit has two projects, each requiring one electromechanical engineer and one electronics engineer—but only on a half-time basis, it would have to hire four engineers and incur duplicate costs or hire electrical engineers and lose specialization.[13]

There is another advantage of the matrix approach that also relates to the area of management development. At Standard Steel, the members of the business committees deal with every phase of their product line, including profit and loss. This broad picture of the company's business activities and the frequent exposure to other functional responsibilities has had a positive effect on their performance. The following statement was made by Standard Steel's president in a speech to a class at Susquehanna University: ". . . a profoundly positive feature revealed itself; that being a matrix team member helped each man to perform his functional responsibilities more astutely, more confidently and more aggressively."[14]

Disadvantages of the Matrix Design

Every form of organization has advantages and disadvantages. If the functional structure is chosen, the technologies are developed, but the projects fall behind due to lack of effective coordination. If the project organization is chosen, good cost and schedule performance is realized, but the technologies are not developed as well.

The matrix attempts to adopt the best of both organizations. However, there are disadvantages associated with the matrix structure as well. The following describes the conditions a matrix may create that could inhibit overall organizational effectiveness:[15]

1. *Anarchy*—This represents a formless state of confusion where the managers functioning within the matrix do not recognize a boss to whom they feel responsible. This will occur if arrangements for decision making are not made explicit.

---

[13] Jay R. Galbraith, "Matrix Organization Design," pp. 29–30.
[14] John E. Fogarty, "Managing with Matrix at Standard Steel."
[15] Stanley M. Davis and Paul R. Lawrence, "Problems with Matrix Organizations," *Harvard Business Review*, vol. 56, no. 3, May/June 1978, pp. 131–142.

2. *Groupitis*—This problem stems from the mistaken belief that matrix management is the same as group decision making. Though some group decisions are reasonable, in many circumstances the problem becomes acute when the practice is followed where all decisions must be made in group meetings, even though some decisions involve matters of which only one or two team members are knowledgeable. "Groupitis" occurs in most cases because of the lack of a serious educational effort to clarify, in the minds of all participants, what a matrix is and is not.

3. *Excessive Overhead*—During the initial stages of implementing a matrix structure, overhead costs rise. Limited research in this area indicates that, as the matrix matures, there is a tendency for productivity gains to offset those additional costs. Better decisions and reduction of featherbedding contribute to the increase in productivity. There being no place to hide in a matrix, managers will tend to produce.

4. *Decision Strangulation*—This problem can occur when constant clearing of decisions is necessary. The manager in the matrix feels he or she must get approval from his or her functional manager. As a result, decision making requires several meetings. This type of problem occurs because of improper delegation, rather than the matrix concept itself. Another form of decision stangulation refers to the strong temptation to pass on, to higher management, conflicts that appear unresolvable. This problem is aggravated when the higher managers fail to send the problem back to their subordinates for resolution. A third problem area occurs when a unilateral decision making style is present. Managers exercising this style of decision making are very frustrated with a system that subjects their decisions to carefully reasoned debates before being accepted by the team.

5. *Sinking*—A matrix organization has difficulty surviving at high levels in a company and, therefore, tends to sink to lower levels where it thrives. If the matrix is seeking its appropriate place in the organization, sinking is not a problem. However, a problem does exist if the sinking occurred because senior management did not understand or had not been able to implement the concept. Sinking that occurs for this reason is probably due to other pathologies, especially power struggles.

6. *Power Struggles*—The essence of a matrix structure is the dual authority aspect between functional and product groups. However, there is a constant tendency for this power to shift in one direction or another. While a matrix encourages friendly competition, all-out combat must be prevented! Power struggles develop when the proper balance between the functional and product dimensions is not maintained.

7. *Navel Gazing*—Because a matrix requires considerable interdependence of people and tasks, there is a tendency for those involved to get absorbed in internal relations at the expense of paying attention to the outside world, especially customers. The process of curing other pathologies draws attention inward and serves to increase the probability that navel gazing will occur.

Another disadvantage is illustrated by Standard Steel's experience.

Because matrix management was a relatively new approach, there was not a great deal of information available that might have helped the company in adopting the new approach. This is especially true for small to medium organizations. Standard Steel was one of the first metalworking companies to adopt matrix and one of the few to get so deeply involved. The lack of information gained through experience of similar companies required a trial-and-error approach. Standard Steel initiated its matrix during the fall of 1977 and, after three years, the system is still being fine-tuned. To develop fully the matrix culture that encourages cooperative relationships and the matrix behavior that minimizes conflicts, the trial-and-error period will last two to three years for most companies. Standard Steel experienced substantial difficulties initially in attempting to convert functional specialists with many years of experience into business managers required to function to a substantial extent in a group setting. The managers directly involved in the business committees were being asked to change their approach and orientation to decision making. They were now team members working with managers from other disciplines in a peer group situation, rather than through the disciplined environment of the traditional pyramid structure. The organizational development (OD) effort that Standard Steel used, which is generally considered essential for any company making the transition to the matrix, may also be considered a disadvantage. In general, the objective of the OD is to reorient the managers to their new role and provide the tools necessary to deal with peer group relationships and the dual authority structure.

Team Building to Facilitate Transition

The organizational development activities engaged in by Standard Steel should not be different in substance from what would be appropriate for any company making the transition from a functional to a matrix structure. As with most organizational development training, the services of an expert from outside the company were used. A five-man team, made up of Pennsylvania State University faculty members from the College of Business Administration, was called upon to conduct the training. The faculty team was headed by Dr. John W. Slocum, Jr., then Professor of Organizational Behavior and now at Southern Methodist University. Dr. Slocum had worked closely with Standard Steel on a variety of projects for approximately 10 years and was, therefore, very familiar with the company's management personnel. A memorandum from Standard Steel's president to members of the business committees, announcing the training program, gives some indication why the OD training was considered necessary. The memorandum identifies the peer group aspect of matrix management, as well as the dual authority feature. There was expressed concern for the possibility of individuals feeling split or isolated from their functional unit. Emphasized was the difference between management development and OD. The president stated that it is the committees that need training, not the individual manager. As a committee, new and more effective ways of problem solving, decision making, coordination, integrating resources, sharing information, and dealing with problem situations that arise must be learned.

The training program was conducted one day per week for 10 weeks. The first 9 weeks were consecutive and the 10th occurred one month later. The one-month lag between the 9th and 10th sessions provided participants the opportunity to absorb the concentration of information and evaluate its use in actual practice. The sessions were held at the company's social club facility, which is a few miles from the plant. Each session was scheduled for approximately seven hours and conducted by one of the five members of the faculty team. The material covered in each session was as follows:

Session 1:   Discuss and examine the nature of a matrix organization. The relationships of dual authority and responsibility, the need to establish vertical information channels, and the role of the managerial integrator will be stressed.

Session 2:   Explore the basis of group dynamics and how groups can avoid group-think. The concept of synergy as it relates to outcomes of group decision making will be discussed.

Session 3:   Reducing intergroup and interpersonal conflicts in teams.

Session 4:   Discuss how to run a successful meeting and lead group discussions.

Session 5:   The role of leadership in small group decision making settings. Each manager will be able to examine his own patterns of influence.

Session 6:   Discuss the motivational techniques that will integrate the goals of employees with those of the organization.

Session 7:   Explore goals and design options in team development.

Session 8:   Dramatize the advantages of both competition and collaborative models in intergoup relations.

Session 9:   Explore each member's role in the team and how roles must be integrated to form an effective team.

Session 10:   The management of group performance.

The training program began very much like many management-oriented programs. The junior managers were at least moderately enthusiastic, while some of the "old-timers" grumbled that they'd had all this before. By the end of the fourth session, all the frustrations created by the new matrix structure had come to a head. Over the two to three-month period since the business committees had been formed, the frustrations with dual authority and responsibility, plus the uncertainty of their mission, lay just below the surface. Concerns and complaints were verbalized, but primarily only in private conversations. However, during the fourth session, the faculty team member asked all teams to list what they felt their business committee's responsibilities were. The request was made because the faculty team and top management suspected that the business committees were drifting off target. The results confirmed their suspicion. However, the responsibility issue served to open the door on all pent up frustrations and concerns. Some team members now openly questioned the matrix approach. Concern was expressed by others that the new approach would not work. Possibly, the most common complaint was that the team members did not fully understand the role of their committee or the extent of its authority. The president of Standard Steel and the faculty team leader called a special session, which was attended by the president, all vice-presidents and the business committees, to resolve the issues. In retrospect, the identification of the problem by the faculty team and the quick corrective action taken by the company's president were a major turning point in the successful evolution of the matrix structure during those early stages.

The Functional Organization at Standard Steel

Once the business committees were formed at Standard Steel, they integrated into the overall organizational structure. The functional organization at Standard Steel did not change as a result of the integration of the business committees. Figure 19 shows the upper levels of the functional organization. A brief description of the primary activities of each department follows:

Commercial. Product responsibility is divided into transportation products and general industrial products; the latter is divided further into east and west regions. Field sales offices are placed in strategic locations throughout the country. In addition to the external sales organization, there is an inside sales unit that processes inquiries and orders and serves as a communication link between the sales force, customers and the plants.

Marketing. The small staff is organized by product responsibility. Its primary activities are in the area of pricing and forecasting.

Metallurgical engineering. The major activities of this department are technical services, quality assurance, and process metallurgy. Technical services metallurgists service customer claims and investigate product failures. The quality assurance effort is extensive at Standard Steel due, in part, to the high potential for product liability. Quality assurance includes product and process inspection, physical testing, nondestructive testing, and chemical analysis. The process metallurgy units are organized by product, with an additional unit having responsibility for melting practices. Each process unit provides substantial input as to what manufacturing steps must be taken to give the product the metallurgical properties required by the customer.

Operations. Plant maintenance, manufacturing, and melting are the areas of responsibilities of the operations department. The plant facilities at Burnham and Latrobe utilize extensive amounts of equipment to produce and transport the products. The installation, repair, and servicing of this equipment is the principal activity of the plant maintenance section. The manufacturing activities are divided along product lines, each section having total responsibility for the manufacturing processes required to make the diversity of products that are grouped into that product line. The plant manager of the Latrobe plant reports to the vice-president of operations, and the managers of the staff functions at that facility report to their respective functional vice-presidents.

Manufacturing services. The overall responsibility of this department is to support the operations function. Much of the support is in the areas of industrial engineering

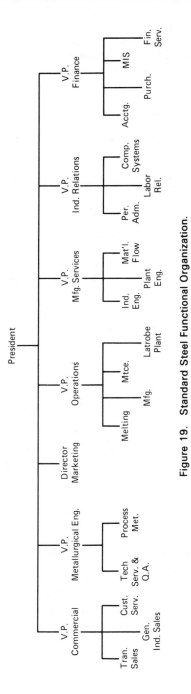

Figure 19.   Standard Steel Functional Organization.

and plant engineering. The industrial engineering section is primarily involved in activities designed to improve the efficiency and reduce the costs through methods engineering, facilities planning, and coordination of cost reduction programs. Equipment modification, development of specifications, and design of new equipment and facilities are the primary activities of the plant engineering section. A major section of this department is material flow, which comprises units organized by product line. Within each unit, responsibilities are divided into two areas: production control, which schedules, coordinates, and expedites production; and process engineering, which, in coordination with metallurgical engineering, determines what steps the product must go through and how much it will cost.

Industrial relations. The three major sections of this department are personnel administration, labor relations, and compensation systems. Personnel administration's activities center on the human resource planning of the company. Specific responsibilities include selection of new hires, training and management development, succession planning and career counseling, communications, safety, and health and plant security. The labor relations section negotiates the labor agreements and administers the contract on a daily basis. This section also provides the main communication link with the industrial relations function at the Latrobe plant. All forms of direct and indirect compensation, with the exception of work incentives, are administered through the compensation systems section. This includes wage and salary administration, Workmen's Compensation, pensions, medical benefits, and Thrift Plan.

Finance. The three sections in this department include management information services (MIS), accounting, and purchasing. The MIS section includes data processing and systems development, which are involved in operating the computer hardware and developing better methods of processing and utilizing information. The accounting section performs the traditional accounting functions, including payroll, cost and budgets, tax accounting, receivables, and payables. In addition to buying approximately $55 million in commodities per year, the purchasing section is responsible for stores receiving.

The functional organization at Standard Steel becomes product-oriented below the vice-presidential level. Organizing around product lines provides for a great deal of continuity. For example, the following positions have major functional responsibility for the transportation product line: manager-transportation sales; unit manager-transportation product planning; manufacturing manager-transportation products; and metallurgical manager-transportation products. All four of these positions are also represented on the transportation product business committee, thus providing the incumbent managers both functional and business committee responsibilities for the same product line.

The Business Committees at Standard Steel

In addition to the transportation product committee, there are business committees for ring products, open die products, and melting. Table 14 describes the makeup of the Business Committees. Each member continues to report to his functional boss,

Table 14. Standard Steel's Matrix Organization—Business Committees.

Functional Organization	Transportation Products	Ring Products	Open Die Products	Melting
Metallurgical Engineering	Metallurgical Manager-Transportation Products	Metallurgical Manager-Ring Products	Metallurgical Manager-Open Die Products/Plant Metallurgist-Latrobe	Vice-President-Metallurgical Engineering* and Metallurgical Manager-Melting
Sales/Marketing	Manager-Transportation Product Sales*	Marketing Manager-Ring Products*	Marketing Manager-Open Die Products*	Director-Marketing
Material Flow	Unit Manager-Transportation Products Planning	Unit Manager-Ring Products Planning	Unit Manager-Open Die Products Planning	Unit Manager-Steel Inventory Planning
Industrial Engineering	Manager-Facilities Planning	Manager-Cost Engineering	Supervisor-Industrial Engineering-Latrobe	Manager-Methods Engineering
Manufacturing	Manufacturing Manager-Transportation Products	Manufacturing Manager-Ring Products	Manufacturing Manager-Open Die Products and Plant Manager-Latrobe	Manager-Melting Operations
Finance	Financial Analyst	Financial Analyst	Financial Analyst	Manager-Financial Services and Manager-Purchasing

but each committee as a group reports directly to the president. The intent of this reporting relationship is to demonstrate the full support of top management for the matrix approach and to provide direct access of the committees to the president. One of the primary responsibilities of the business committees is to prepare an annual business plan, including targets for production costs, production inventory, shipping volume and gross profit; monitor actual performance against planned performance; and recommend appropriate interim changes in policy to top management. During the early stages of the matrix development, Standard Steel's president identified committee responsibilities, which were directed toward optimizing profitability, including: question all existing policies and suggest new ones; identify needed changes in systems and procedures; establish manufacturing and marketing goals; provide selective selling guidelines consistent with manufacturing, marketing, and engineering constraints; and identify potential improvement in cost effectiveness.

The business committees meet as often as required to evaluate new developments within their product lines. However, regular meetings are held at least once each month to discuss general manufacturing, marketing, and profit performance. Quarterly, the business committees meet the president. Meetings are also held to prepare the annual business plan.

A coordinator is selected for each business committee by the president. As stated previously, this approach provides for flexibility. For example, during the early stages of the matrix development, production efficiency was most important; therefore, the coordinators were manufacturing managers. Currently, concern for market strategy and product mix is most important, and, therefore, marketing and sales managers are now the coordinators, as indicated by the asterisk in Table 14. Coordinators, rather than chairmen, are used to provide a more equal distribution of authority within each committee.

In analyzing the information in Figure 20, it is obvious that the melting committee is different from the more product-oriented committees. First, the makeup of the committee is represented by two managers from the metallurgical engineering function. The Vice-President of Metallurgical Engineering is the coordinator. Overall, this is a more senior committee in terms of the participant level in the functional organization. Its primary concern is the efficient production of high-quality steel in quantities sufficient to service the company's diverse needs. Keeping up with and, in some cases, advancing the state of the art in steelmaking is an objective that addresses its primary concern. The melting committee is actually an operating committee, rather than a business committee. Another point to be made regarding Figure 20 relates to the open die committee. The committee is heavily represented by managers from the Latrobe facility. This makes sense in light of the fact that much of the open die production has been moved to the Latrobe facility in recent years. As interesting as the matrix organization is from an academic point of view, it must be justified as a viable business action. An objective evaluation of organizational performance must be accomplished to validate the decision to establish the business committees.

Effectiveness of Matrix Management at Standard Steel

The original expectations Standard Steel may have had for the matrix organization were not specifically documented as such. However, in reviewing various sources of internal communication written during the time the product teams were initiated, the following items were extracted and interpreted as top management's expectations of the new approach:

- Improve productivity in each of the product lines (wheels and axles, rings, open die forgings, as well as melting).
- Markedly improve profitability in each of the next three years (1978, 1979, and 1980).
- Improve on-time delivery credibility.
- Generate a nucleus of highly informative and specialized knowledge concerning each product line.
- Reestablish the company's security as a viable business enterprise.
- Provide more time for top management to deal with long-range problems.
- Develop aggressive, confident, and conceptual thinking managers at lower levels in the organization.
- Provide matrix managers with a broader understanding of the company's business activities to enable them to perform their functional responsibilities better.

Certain of the above expectations were primary, and others could be considered by-products inherent in the advantages of a matrix organization. Identifying accomplishments of the original expectations also required investigation of company records and a somewhat piecemeal approach in putting the information together. In evaluating productivity, wheel production has increased approximately 34 percent since the initiation of the transportation product committee. This was accomplished with the same amount of material and human resources. The other major product concern of this committee is axles. The number of axles shipped from 1977 through 1979 increased approximately 14 percent. However, because of major manufacturing changes, other indications of productivity remained basically the same. Within the ring product line, ring production increased approximately 55 percent. At the time the product team was formed, the new ring rolling facility had been in operation only a few months and, therefore, was not at peak production. Though much of the productivity increase would have occurred as the personnel became more proficient with the new equipment and processes, the ring product committee played an important role in developing the new facility's potential. Melting productivity can be measured in two ways: (1) the number of tons of steel has increased nearly 15 percent without adding furnaces; and (2) the number of tons produced per employee increased 18 percent. The open die product line underwent substantial rearrangement of its manufacturing facilities in the past year and has only recently begun to improve productivity.

The on-time delivery credibility at the time the matrix was initiated was poor for all product lines. The progress over the last three years can be summarized as follows, in percentages:

	1977	1978	1979	1980 (YTD)
Axles	75	86	95	99
Wheels	50	96	98	99
Rings	50	74	88	95
Open Die	50	85	90	96

These figures represent the percentage of time Standard Steel was able to deliver a customer's order within two weeks of scheduled shipping date.

Approximately two years into the matrix project, the president of Standard Steel stated, in a speech to a class at Susquehanna University, that the matrix teams had already been successful as a management development tool. The managers involved were definitely developing a broad knowledge of the company's business activities and a greater understanding of the responsibilities and concerns of the other functional areas. The new perspective was helping the matrix managers perform their functional responsibilities more effectively. Because the matrix teams were absorbing more of the day-to-day decision making, members of top management had more time to deal with inflation, foreign competition, government involvement, and other long-range problems.

As an indication of profitability, actual margins as a percentage of net sales increased in absolute terms by 9.8 percent in transportation products, 1.7 percent in open die products, and 5.0 percent in ring products. Operating return on investment increased for all Standard Steel's products by 13.6 percent.

It appears that most of the major objectives have been accomplished or that the foundation has been laid for future improvement. As will become clearer in the next section, the contribution to the accomplishment of the "bottom-line" objectives by the matrix teams was made possible primarily because the matrix has been successful in developing business managers.

Participants' Impressions after Three Years

In addition to analyzing the accomplishment of "bottom-line" objectives, a great deal can be learned of the effectiveness of matrix management at Standard Steel through discussions with matrix participants. One participant from each of the four committees was selected. Three had been involved in the matrix since its initiation, and the fourth for more than two years. The discussions with each participant will be identified by the committee he represents. Basically, the same set of questions was asked of each: What are the positive and negative aspects of working on the committees? How has participation helped your career? In what ways has the committee changed over the past three years? Should Standard Steel continue with matrix management?

Transportation Product Representative

In the area of productivity, the committee's role is primarily one of support to the representative with functional responsibility for production. However, the committee has been very influential in improving profitability. Through improved understanding of the needs and requirements of manufacturing and cost accounting, the sales manager on the committee is able to sell a better mix of products. He now knows what type of orders to avoid and what would require less setup and lower manufacturing costs. The proper product mix will maximize profitability.

The committee has also been effective in new product development. For example, the metallurgical representative identified the need for a railroad wheel made of alloy steel for certain applications. All members of the committee contributed toward the new product's development, manufacture, and sale. Another positive aspect of the matrix approach is that it has given each member a better understanding of the total picture and of the input of each functional area to the accomplishment of the company's overall objectives.

From a negative point of view, counterproductive influences can occur when top management overrules the committee's decisions, which may have come about after considerable analysis. If top management's decision to overrule appears arbitrary or the committee's decisions are overruled too often, the committee will not function as aggressively and may only go through the motions. Also on the negative side, there is some indication that the vice-presidents do not always get as much information concerning committees' activities as they should, either from the committees or the president of the company to whom the committees report. The company's reward systems, such as performance appraisals and merit increases, administered by the functional boss, do not always take into account the committee responsibilities to the degree they should.

The committee is made up of individuals with different personalities as well as functional backgrounds. Though some have stronger personalities and play a somewhat more vocal role, the group is very compatible and effective in achieving objectives. With regard to career influences, the transportation product representative feels he is now better prepared for what could be considered his next career move in the company. This is attributed to the management development advantages of the matrix. He no longer has a myopic view of the organization. This representative also believes the matrix approach should be continued at Standard Steel primarily because of its management development value. But to assure continued improvement, the committees should receive greater latitude in their responsibilities.[16]

Ring Product Representative

In discussing the advantages of the business committees, he emphasized the integration of functions. There is a feeling of solidarity and purpose within the committee that instills a sense of responsibility to each other and the product line. For example, when the manufacturing manager on the committee needs assistance from metallurgical engineering to solve a quality problem, there is a greater probability he will get more effective and timely action from the metallurgical representative of the same committee than if each were acting strictly on a functional basis.

Satisfaction results from having knowledge of the big picture. There is more of a sense of belonging. Instead of merely carrying out orders, you work on solutions to major objectives, many of which the committee develops itself. With this greater involvement by the committee, it appears that the president and vice-presidents enjoy more freedom for long-range activities.

The president plays a very important role in giving the committees direction and clarity of purpose. He provides frequent input through participation in the monthly meetings from time to time, as well as quarterly meetings in which the committees

---

[16] Interview with David Suloff, October 6, 1980, Burnham, Pennsylvania.

present their activities to him. Despite the Committees having received greater responsibility and authority over the past three years, it is still obvious that they are permitted to "run the show" only up to the point where the president disagrees. Another function of the president is to resolve issues involving distribution of limited resources.

Also discussed was the importance of the personalities of the committee's membership. Even though the personality mix in the ring committee includes gamblers and conservatives, there is the compatibility necessary for effective group performance. Any one member, especially the coordinator, should avoid dominating the committee. On the other hand, everyone should be able to defend his position but be able to compromise.

Even though the matrix approach is a demanding one for the participants and includes such negative requirements as numerous meetings, Standard Steel should definitely continue the matrix mainly because of the integration of functions to accomplish common objectives.[17]

Open Die Product Representative

The open die committee has identified new products that will enable the company to better utilize the manufacturing facilities, especially at the Burnham plant. The committee's marketing representative has been instrumental in improving the product mix by expanding participation in markets that provide for increased productivity and, therefore, profit. Another advantage identified was that the participants of the committee have developed a respect for one another and a willingness to help each other on a functional basis.

Committee involvement has provided him with a better feel for the financial and sales end of the business. Despite his many years with the company, it has only been through the committee that he has begun to appreciate the responsibilities of the other functions. In relation to career development, business committee involvement is a practical substitute for being assigned actual responsibilities in the different functional departments.

A difficult aspect of the committees is keeping the functional boss informed of the committee activities that affect his area of responsibility. Sometimes in the enthusiasm of committee activities, he has forgotten to inform his boss until after specific action had already been taken. However, the boss in question recognizes the advantage of having decisions made by those closest to the situation.

The open die committee is now considered to be well balanced regarding its participants. Those participating are in functional positions that are conducive to supporting their committee responsibilities. It is a well-oiled committee that has absorbed increased responsibilities over the last three years. It is felt that the matrix approach should most assuredly be continued at Standard Steel, but not necessarily gravitate toward a full matrix.[18]

---

[17] Interview with William Hile, October 8, 1980, Burnham, Pennsylvania.
[18] Interview with Frank Keller, October 10, 1980, Burnham, Pennsylvania.

Melting Committee Representative

The melting committee is described as an operating committee, rather than a business committee. The overall objective is to make good-quality steel at the lowest possible cost. Because the melting operation is where most of the company's production costs occur, the committee is very concerned with efficiency and costs. Although productivity is the major functional responsibility of the melting manager, the rest of the committee supports him and accepts the challenge as a committee. Failure to achieve a productivity goal may be determined to relate to the selling of products requiring a grade of steel that is difficult and time-consuming to produce. This may be difficult for the melting manager to recognize if he was functioning without the aid of the committee. The committee is also concerned with providing steel to the other committees, rather than a product to a customer. Steel is allocated during times of scarcity based on profitability of the product line.

In summarizing the biggest advantage of the committee, he states that it makes people in responsible positions act as managers. This is accomplished through the total view the individual gets of the company's business activities. We now sell what we can make at a profit, rather than make what we sell regardless of whether it can be made efficiently.

One of the difficult aspects of committee involvement is the time devoted to meetings. However, after three years we have learned to adapt. One way is to form subcommittees that research a specific problem and present it to the whole committee. This saves considerable time. Another problem that can occur is a conflict between functional and committee responsibilities. For example, the committee may decide to sell more product than the marketing representative feels the market can bear. It is necessary that any functional representative on a committee participate from a position of knowledge and functional authority. Otherwise, he will lose credibility.

Despite having one of the most varied functional backgrounds in the company, his committee participation has even further advanced his understanding of the different functions and has improved his ability to transfer this knowledge into action.

Even though the coordinator of the melting committee is a vice-president, all are treated equally when functioning as a committee. There is no hesitation to question and play devil's advocate. Over the three-year period, those not able to contribute or compromise were dropped. Individual performance or lack of it can be readily identified. The committees rid themselves of unproductive or incompatible participants.

In his opinion, the matrix approach should definitely be continued and possibly progress toward a full matrix. There is still opportunity for the committees to absorb greater responsibility, especially for profit.[19]

Summary

Standard Steel, which is nearly 170 years old, grew into a $20 million business during its first 150 years. However, in the next 20 years, the company grew to nearly $200 million. In addition, the company's product diversification increased substantially,

---

[19] Interview with Samuel Boova, October 10, 1980, Burnham, Pennsylvania.

and a second plant was added. Currently, Standard Steel is one of the country's most completely integrated and largest suppliers of specialty steel forged products in the world. The rapid growth in volume and product diversification overburdened the existing functional organization. This fact was reflected by poor return on investment and poor delivery credibility. A new management approach was needed.

A matrix management approach assumes that top management cannot optimize decisions because of the complexities and uncertainties of the organization. The frequency of exceptional cases and unpredictability of the timing requires experts involved in lateral interactions because the up-the-line approach of the functional organization cannot handle the load. By definition, the matrix organization abandons the age-old precept of one man/one boss. The matrix is a multiple-command system that represents a balancing of organizational resources around product lines and functional classifications. The matrix approach is especially effective when numerous complex factors are involved in decision making and when the environment is dynamic. These parameters being present at Standard Steel, the decision was made by the company's president to go with matrix management.

The matrix form of organization has a number of inherent advantages that Standard Steel hoped to realize. Some of these advantages are in the area of management development, more effective decision making and minimizing the need for top management to engage in crisis management. As with any form of organization, matrix has certain inherent disadvantages also. Of primary concern to Standard Steel during the initial stages of development was the possibility of conflict between functional and committee responsibilities, excessive time spent in meetings, and converting managers who have been functional specialists for many years to general business managers with broad responsibilities. However, as was discovered through discussions with participating managers and written statements by the president, many of these anticipated concerns, as well as those previously outlined as inherent disadvantages, never materialized or have been overcome.

In an effort to increase the probability of a successful transition to matrix management, Standard Steel engaged in an organizational development effort. Rather than a management development program for individual managers, the training was directed at the committees. Through a team of Pennsylvania State University faculty members, the subjects of group dynamics, intergroup and interpersonal conflicts, motivation, integration of goals, and the role of the individual in a group setting were covered. The organizational development effort turned out to be a major factor in the successful evolution of Standard Steel's matrix organization during the early stages.

The matrix teams were integrated into the functional organization during the fourth quarter of 1977. The functional organization did not change as a result of the integration. Product committees were formed for each of the three major product lines—ring products, open die products, and transportation products. A committee was also formed for the melting function, which has remained an operating committee, though the product line committees have changed orientation and are now business committees with broader responsibilities. Each committee consists of individuals from the different functional departments who continue to report to their functional boss, but report as a committe to the president of the company. The primary responsibilities of the committees are to prepare an annual business plan; question existing policies and suggest new ones; identify needed changes in systems and procedures; establish manufacturing and marketing goals; provide selective selling guidelines consistent with manufacturing, marketing, and engineering constraints; and identify potential improvement in cost effectiveness. A coordinator is selected by the president for each committee. Coordinators, rather than chairmen, are used to provide a more equal distribution of authority. The coordinators, with their different functional backgrounds, can be easily changed to match any change in direction the committees may take.

Standard Steel's top management had high expectations for the business committees. It was anticipated that the committees would be at least partially influential in accomplishing improvements in productivity, profitability, and on-time delivery. In addition to these bottom-line objectives, it was also anticipated that the committees would develop aggressive, confident, and conceptual thinking managers with a broader understanding of the company's business activities. This broader understanding would enable the matrix managers to perform their functional responsibilities more effectively. With decision making being performed at a lower level in the organization, top management would have more time for long-range planning and problem solving.

It appears that the business committees have been successful in realizing many of the original expectations. Except for the open die product line, there have been good productivity increases since the committees were formed. Profitability has also shown an overall improvement. On-time credibility has substantially improved over the same period. It is difficult to determine to what degree these bottom-line accomplishments would have occurred without the business committees. However, it is generally believed by the participating managers that the committees have been instrumental in these accomplishments, especially profitability and on-time delivery. The president of the company also attributes much of these accomplishments to the committees and has stated that they have been very successful in developing managers with a broader perspective of the company's business. He also stated that decision making is of better quality and has been pushed down into the organization, thus freeing top management to pursue such issues as inflation, overregulation by government, and foreign competition.

Insight into the effectiveness of matrix management at Standard Steel was also acquired through interviews with some of the participating managers. One participating manager from each of the four committees was interviewed. All four were very enthusiastic and strongly recommended continuance of the matrix approach. Though each emphasized certain points, there was a consensus on many of the positive experiences with matrix. Some of these are summarized below:

- Realized increase in profitability through more effective marketing. The marketing representative on the committee now knows what the company can make at a profit and what products to avoid.
- Effective in developing, marketing, and manufacturing new products.
- Provides good management development opportunity. Participants better prepared for next career move.
- Provides for a feeling of solidarity and purpose within each committee.
- Promotes a sense of responsibility to each other and the product line.

- Promotes better understanding of the responsibilities and concerns of the other functions.
- Increases a sense of satisfaction and involvement.
- Requires participants to function like business managers.

Those interviewed were also very pleased with the make up of their committees. After three years, each has realized a compatible mix of personalities and functional backgrounds. The committees, in very subtle and indirect ways, have learned to purge themselves of participants who did not contribute or could not compromise.

Regarding the few negative comments made, there was not as much agreement among those interviewed as with the positive comments. Two of the participants expressed concern that their functional bosses were not always informed of committee activities and decisions that influenced their areas of responsibilities. However, it was generally agreed that top management is very supportive of the committees. Two participants mentioned the additional time spent in meetings, but also stated that, after three years, they have learned to adapt. Other negative comments were made regarding top management overruling the committees' decisions and participants not receiving proper consideration in performance appraisal and merit increases for committee accomplishments.

The case writer made an effort to determine if the matrix approach has been effective at Standard Steel and whether or not it should be continued. It appears that the business committees have been effective to a substantial extent. Quantifiable information, such as productivity, profitability, and on-time delivery percentages, plus the positive remarks of some of the participating managers and the company's president, seems to support that contention. However, the participating managers interviewed are also in agreement that a matrix is a demanding environment and requires considerable effort to develop. At Standard Steel, the development required two years before the committees began to produce expected results and, after three years, it is still being fine-tuned. Initiating the matrix requires determination and a high degree of conviction from top management to overcome the initial problems and almost certain resistance from the participants. Despite the success of the matrix management approach at Standard Steel, it is certainly not for every organization.

Student Assignment

1. Evaluate the strategy used at Standard Steel to introduce and implement matrix management.
2. Describe how the cultural ambience changed at Standard Steel as a result of matrix management.
3. Be prepared to describe the advantages and disadvantages of matrix management from the viewpoint of the organization and the individual.
4. What would you have done differently if you had been a consultant advising this company on a strategy for introducing and implementing matrix management?

SITUATION 1: PROJECT MANAGEMENT IMAGE

The Situation

In the early part of 1974 the Delta Corporation, listed in the Fortune 500, had about 20 percent of its sales in the defense industry. The bulk of its military business consisted of military orders and deliveries for advanced electronic systems in support of U.S. Air Force weaponry. The company's military business had been historically highlighted by production and growth.

The military business in the Delta Corporation was located in the Defense Systems Product Group, one of the major profit centers in the corporation. The military business of the corporation had suffered recent setbacks through the loss of two major military systems contracts. A task force of senior managers and professionals was appointed to try to determine the cause for these two major losses. At the first meeting of the task force, a plan was adopted to begin to develop the data bases that would give some insight into why these two major contracts were lost. At this same meeting it was suggested by the senior marketing manager that the field salesmen had, in recent months, been reporting some evidence of a deteriorating image of the Defense Systems Group's ability to respond effectively to its defense customers' needs.

In the strategy that emerged in the task force, it was decided to hire an outside consulting company to conduct an image assessment of the ability of the Delta Corporation to respond effectively to its defense customers' needs.* This assessment would be added to the data base of other studies being conducted by the task force.

As the consulting firm began to develop the strategy for this assessment, several key ideas of an organization's image and a strategy for its assessments emerged.

The "image" concept. The concept of image is not a simple one. An image exists in the mind of an individual and it is, therefore, difficult to assess. Further, the idea of an image is multidimensional; it has many different aspects in the mind of even a single individual. Moreover, the image that exists at one time can be altered in a variety of ways as time passes.

The importance of an image. Marketing researchers have conclusively demonstrated the significance of an image in the purchasing decisions made in the consumer, industrial, and defense systems markets. Perhaps nowhere is an awareness of one's image so important as in the defense marketing environment; in part because it is probably least well recognized there.

Purchase decisions made by persons on their own behalf and by individuals representing organizations reflect their personal perceptions of products and the company producing them. These personal images are in part determined by the facts as they may exist, *but they are largely made up of subjective factors that are difficult to assess or even define.*

In the defense systems sector, the importance of an overall image—as opposed to the simple facts about a system—may be even more important than in other areas, for even though the purchase decision is the result of a long and careful analysis, it

* Cleland-King, Inc., Pittsburgh, Pa.

is still the decision of human beings. The humans and organizations who make purchase decisions in the defense systems market must live with their decisions and defend them to their various clientele over a long period of time.

First, unstructured interviews were conducted with key personnel both within and outside the Delta Corporation. The purpose of these initial interviews was to define and operationally describe the important dimensions of the product and organizational characteristics that were deemed to be important to the Defense Systems Group's image.

Sixty-one characteristics related to overall image were defined and grouped into nine "key result areas":

- General characteristics
- Personnel image
- Ability to communicate with customers
- Project management skills and capabilities
- Ability to meet normal customer requirements
- Responsiveness to customer's special requirements
- Negotiating skills
- Special capabilities
- Product characteristics

After these elements had been defined and described, a survey instrument was constructed and tested. The survey instrument involved a rating of the Delta Corporation by the respondent in terms of all or a selected subset of the 61 product and organizational characteristics.

The testing of the survey instrument was conducted through interviews with 30 Defense Systems Products Group personnel. The understandings generated by such testing were used to refine the survey instrument for later use with customer personnel. A number of minor modifications in the instrument were made along with one major—the addition of a "product characteristics" category.

The data generated by the 30 internal corporate interviews are incorporated into the body of the final report for comparative purposes. *It should be remembered, however, that the internal corporate data base was rather small and that the interviewing process and survey instrument were in the testing phase when these data were gathered.*

After the survey process and instrument had been tested, evaluated, and refined, personal interviews were conducted nationwide with key customer and government personnel. Individual identifications were not given, because those surveyed were assured that they would not be identified. It was believed that such assurance was essential to achieving candor by survey respondents.

A total of 108 key customer persons were interviewed in a structured fashion using the survey instrument. Respondents were asked to evaluate Delta in terms of 61 dimensions that were described in polar terms. A typical dimension with its associated seven-point descriptive scale is shown in Fig. 20.

In other words, in this illustration, each respondent was asked to describe his perception of the Delta Defense Systems Product-Group in terms of its delivery performance by rating it on a seven-point scale ranging from "Deliver on Time" as "Very

Deliver on time	Very	Quite	Slightly	Neutral	Slightly	Quite	Very	Deliver late

Figure 20.

descriptive" to "Deliver late" as "Very descriptive." As an example, Table 15 shows how the survey instrument for the "key result area" of project management skills and capabilities was structured in the survey instrument.

Two versions of the structured interview were used. One version—for higher-level officials—contained 22 of the most critical characteristics related to the nine key categories. The other version contained all 61 of the characteristics of these nine categories.

After the structured portion of each of the interviews, each interviewee was asked to comment on areas of concern to him. If no comments were volunteered, the interviewer asked specific questions about characteristics that had been evaluated particularly favorably or particularly unfavorably in the structured portion of the interview. This unstructured portion of the interviews generated the narrative data that were integrated into the assessment.

Summary of findings.   This part of the case summarizes the detailed findings of the image assessment conducted by the consulting firm. The summary is in terms of the various "key result areas."

The assessments made are in terms of two respondent groups:

1. customer personnel
2. internal corporate personnel

General characteristics.   Delta has the overall image of a top electronics firm with good technical personnel. However, Delta personnel tend to feel realtively more negative about the overall Delta image than do outside personnel.

The clearest potential problem in this area, as indicated by all groups, is the *lack of aggressiveness of the marketing organization.* The narrative data indicate that the field marketing representatives are well regarded, but that the Defense Systems Group may be *deficient in its customer orientation. The role played by field representatives is also questioned.*

Customer respondents tended to indicate a relatively negative response in the area of *Delta's lack of control of subcontractors.* Delta's personnel did not feel this so acutely.

Personnel image.   The overall competence and businesslike nature of Delta personnel is well regarded. However, the weakest aspect of the Delta personnel image appears to be the *interaction of top management with the customer. Delta top management is not viewed as being in close touch with customers.* Both the quantitative survey data and the narrative responses bear out this perceived inadequacy to a significant degree.

Table 15. Project Management Skills and Capabilities Key Customer Personnel (table entries are percentages).

	Very	Quite	Slightly	Neutral	Slightly	Quite	Very	
They accept the spirit and intent of DOD project management techniques	8	25	42	19	4	2	—	They fight the system with regard to DOD project management techniques
Their project managers have adequate authority and responsibility	9	21	45	18	7	—	—	Their project managers lack enough authority and/or responsibility
Their project managers have their own charters and are virtually free agents	—	14	21	41	24	—	—	Their project managers are constantly tied up in company red tape
Their project managers are professionals	14	38	45	3	—	—	—	Their project managers are inexperienced amateurs
Their project managers control their own project purse strings	3	19	19	38	16	3	—	Project funds are not controlled by their project managers
Their project managers get along nicely with their functional managers	9	39	13	39	—	—	—	Conflict is apparent between their project and functional managers
They are usually helping us with project management techniques	5	14	10	57	14	—	—	We are usually helping them with project management techniques

Moreover, the data indicate that *Delta personnel do not recognize this perception on the part of their customers.* Thus, the customer's image of Delta top management visitation practices does not conform to that internally held.

Field representatives are rated highly for honesty and openness under this key result area, as is the attendance of Delta project managers at project review meetings. In both instances, Delta personnel rate these characteristics more negatively than do customer people.

The narratives in this area showed a *perception of a lack of communication between Delta project managers and top management.* This is especially significant, for it resulted from the unstructured portion of the survey, rather than the structured portion. Additional attention is devoted to this item in summarizing the key result area related to Delta's responsiveness to customer special requirements.

Ability to communicate with customers.   Delta customer personnel indicate a relatively good availability of field representatives. Delta personnel, on the other hand, indicate a relative unawareness of this perception on the part of the customer.

The most negative aspect of customer communications from the customer point of view is that regarding key *Delta personnel changes. Customers do not believe that communications regarding such changes is good.* Delta personnel appear to be divided on the issue of whether such communications are good or not.

A negative attitude toward Delta's practices of providing data for project planning and control is indicated by the data for this area. Indeed, the area of relevant data unavailability and Delta's lack of recognition of the importance of data are brought to the fore by narrative related to a number of different areas. This area will be alluded to in the summary dealing with the "special capabilities" key result area.

Project management skills and capabilities.   Delta project managers are generally regarded as professional and technically expert by Delta clientele. However, *narrative responses associated with his professionalism* and expertise tend to depict him as "too narrow," "too engineering-oriented," "unable to see the whole system" and "spending little time on the flight line."

Delta personnel tend to see their project managers in about the same way as does the customer. They too support the "narrowness" contention in their narratives.

Customers also tend to have a relatively more negative view of the degree of financial control exerted by the project manager than have the internal Delta respondents.

Ability to meet normal customer requirements.   Delta is rated relatively high by customers in terms of providing "positive solutions to problems." However, it is rated relatively low in terms of the cost, time, and performance parameters of Delta projects.

The degree to which these parameters are problems are rated as cost, delivery time, and technical performance, in that order.

Delta personnel perceive themselves as being "best" at technical performance. However, *they see themselves in a much more favorable light than does the customer, so that the difference between Delta perceptions and clientele perceptions is greatest with regard to technical performance.*

Delta technical and cost problems are "explained" in the narratives as being due to poor risk-taking behavior (taking a high risk without an alternative approach) and to buying difficulties (lack of purchasing control). However, there is no further evidence to substantiate these explanations.

Responsiveness to customer's special requirements.   Ratings of Delta's responsiveness are generally good. However, the lack of an efficient system for handling engineering change proposals (ECPs) is singled out for negative evaluation.

This is assessed to be indicative of a lack of a formal, efficient, and effective management information system and a lack of good internal communications among Delta organizations and management personnel.

Delta personnel are well aware of the problems indicated by customer responses. They rate the ECP system even worse than do customers. For example:

Negotiating skills.   The quality of Delta negotiators and their overall performance is rated high by customers and rated relatively low by Delta personnel.

However, customers rate the quality and timeliness of Delta proposals, with particular emphasis on cost proposals, as erratic. Particular attention is paid by customers to the lack of integration, internal conflict, and confusing aspects of Delta proposals.

Special capabilities.   Delta does not rate highly in terms of its special logistics capability or its followup with support equipment and data. Particular reference was made to support data and to deficiencies in handbooks, maintenance data, etc. Specific causes of handbook deficiencies were frequently suggested by respondents, indicating that the negative image is founded on a particularly factual basis in this area.

Product characteristics.   Delta's products are highly regarded for their quality by customers. The two elements indicated as problems in this key result area were "company-provided maintenance data" and "provisioned spare assemblies and parts," thus giving further indications of difficulties in the support and data areas.

Synopsis of assessments.   The 10 assessments made on the basis of the quantitative and qualitative data are:

1. Delta marketing is considered to be a weak spot. Particular negative mention is made of its lack of aggressiveness, its lack of a customer-oriented philosophy, some of its practices, and the role of its field representatives.
2. Delta is not considered to have good control of subcontractors.
3. Delta customers do not feel that Delta top executives interact adequately with the customer.
4. Delta personnel are not adequately aware of their clientele's belief that top management does not interact enough with the customer.
5. Delta customers do not feel that they are kept adequately informed of key personnel changes.
6. Delta is perceived to have relative difficulty in controlling cost, delivery time, and technical performance, in that order.
7. Delta customers do not believe that it has good internal communications or a good formal management information system.

8. Both clientele and Delta personnel recognize special deficiencies in the Delta system for handling ECPs.
9. Delta proposal quality is perceived as erratic by its customers. Particular negative mention is made of the cost elements of the proposals.
10. Delta is not perceived as having good special capabilities in the areas of integrated logistic support, support equipment, and the providing of data to the customer.

At a meeting of the senior executives of the Defense Systems Group, a summary of the detailed findings of the image assessment was presented by the chairman of the task force. A lively discussion followed; finally the vice-president of the firm requested the task force chairman to prepare an evaluation of the image assessment to include, but not necessarily be restricted to, the following:

1. An evaluation of the relative strategic significance of the findings in terms of Delta's defense business
2. A strategy for the correction of deficiencies identified in the image assessment

The senior vice-president of Delta requested that the chairman of the task force present its evaluation and recommendations in four weeks.

Your Task

1. What would you do if you were the chairman of this task force?
2. Is there anything you would have done differently if you had been in charge of the consulting firm doing the image assessment?

SITUATION 2: CORPORATE MANAGEMENT PHILOSOPHY

The Situation

The senior executive of a successful project management company was concerned about the lack of a distinctive management philosophy on the part of key company officials. The company was organized on a line-staff basis, with two product-group profit centers supported by three corporate staff offices: finance and administration, contract management, and strategic planning/marketing.

To encourage the second level managers reporting to him to start thinking about a corporate philosophy of management, this executive put together a "strawman" draft of a philosophy and distributed it to the second level managers for their evaluation. Table 16 contains the letter of transmittal and the draft corporate philosophy of management that were distributed. Please note that this philosophy was broken down into several subcategories.

Table 16.

TO: Second Level Managers

SUBJECT: Draft Corporate Philosophy of Management

I believe it is necessary for us to continue to develop our corporate philosophy of management to complement the work already underway on our linear responsibility charts (LRC). This philosophy can serve as a guide to the way we think about management process in this company. The development of such a philosophy and our subsequent commitment to follow that philosophy should enable us to function more effectively.

Please evaluate, modify, add to, etc., the draft of such a philosophy, which is reflected below.

We will get together in the near future to discuss this philosophy.

Thanks for your continuing help.

Signed: President

We Manage Projects

We manage projects. To support this end, a project manager is appointed to serve as a focal point for the management of each project. Project managers are appointed as close to an "order entry" date as possible and are responsible for planning, organizing, and controlling company resources to be applied to a project. The project manager works with the specialized interest organizational groups in the company to obtain advice, counsel, support, and service to accomplish project objectives on time and within budget.

Mission, Objectives, Goals, Strategies

An organizational mission is the basic purpose of an organization. Our company is in the business of designing and building computer-based systems to control electric power generation and transmission for the electric power industry. An objective is the desired end result of an activity. Each contract in our company has an objective of the delivery of the project on time and within budget. A goal is a milestone that, when accomplished, leads to the attainment of an objective with the desired technical performance capability. Each project in our company will have goals that, when accomplished, move the project toward its desired end result. A strategy is a prescription on how resources will be used to accomplish an organizational mission. Each project and the company is supported by appropriate objectives, goals, and strategies.

Organization Structure

Organization structure is a relationship between certain functions, physical and financial resources, and people. It is based on a grouping of functions and products in acceptance of their similar characteristics and significances. The importance of our organizational structure rests largely on the premise that it complements the corporate strategy and is an instrument through which executive leadership is carried out.

Table 16 (cont.)

Profit Center Decentralization

Profit center decentralization in our company means many things: (1) the organization of the work into distinct profit-responsible *businesses* by product and market segment scope that are distinguishable from each other and other organization components; (2) profit center managers are held responsible for the profit/loss performance of their profit centers; (3) providing decision making responsibility for a particular product line with a single manager commensurate with corporate mission, objectives, goals, and policies; (4) the selection of profit-center objectives, goals, and strategies to complement corporate mission; (5) the separation of segments of the profit-center work, organizing it logically and profitably around certain *functions* and drawing on centralized corporate *functions* that are provided to all organizational units of the corporation; (6) providing a system of corporate leadership in which profit center managers and supporting staff managers define *common* interests, translate these into desired common mission, objectives, goals, policies and procedures and then, *without* being told, accept the responsibility and accountability to make their own decisions in the interests of the overall corporation; and (7) corporate staff managers are held responsible for supporting profit center managers and other corporate officials in accomplishing corporate mission. Profit center managers and corporate staff managers are expected to cooperate as a corporate management team at all times.

Authority

Authority is the legal or rightful power to command or act. *Line* authority is the right, derived from a legitimate source, to act or direct. *Staff* authority is the legal authority of the staff official derived from his appointment as a staff member to assist, advise, counsel, and support the line official to whom he reports. The exercise of staff authority is based on the philosophy of leading within a framework of corporate mission and policy by persuasion rather than by command. *Functional* authority is the legal right to act with respect to specific activities or processes. Authority has two sources: (1) *legal* authority coming from an organizational position (or organizational rank) that an individual occupies; (2) the knowledge, skill, expertise, and personal effectiveness of the individual.

Responsibility is the obligation to act, direct, or command.

Accountability is the condition of being answerable for one's actions—or lack thereof—in a position of authority and responsibility.

Authority, responsibility, and accountability are inseparable parts of the exercise of leadership in a management position and operate through the process of delegation. Delegation is a two-way process *and* is not complete until there is understanding and agreement on the scope of the organizational role and work relationships and the acceptance of accountability between a person and the manager to whom reporting.

Line and Staff *

The following descriptions serve to clarify the differences between line and staff in our company:

* Paraphrased from David I. Cleland and William R. King, *Management: A Systems Approach*, McGraw-Hill Book Co., New York, 1972, pp. 130–131.

Table 16 (cont.)

Line refers to those functions that have a *direct responsibility* for accomplishing the end purpose of the organization.

Line refers to those individuals who are *directly* concerned with producing the good or service offered by the organization.

Line refers to those executives who have *operational* responsibilities.

Line executives tend to be *generalists.*

Line executives *make and execute decisions* related to the attainment of primary organizational objectives.

Line exercises explicit authority as delegated from a higher level manager.

Staff, as contrasted with line, exists to advise and counsel, rather than to command. The following characteristics summarize the nature of staff:

- Staff members perform purely *advisory* functions.

- Each staff member reports to a boss who is appended to the line organization or is a member of the line organization. Therefore, *there is no pure chain of command in staff.*

- Staff members are typically technical *specialists.*

- Staff provides *service and functional* policy formulation, promulgation, and implementation effectiveness through the exercise of functional authority.

- Staff is an extension of the authority of the manager to whom he reports.

- Staff exercises implied authority through counseling, advice, technical expertise, support service, knowledge, etc.

Policies

Policies are general statements or principles that the managers of an organization have agreed upon to guide their thinking in making and implementing decisions and reaching goals, objectives, and missions. Managers are expected to exercise judgment in implementing policy. Policies are the corporate code of conduct and should be established on the highest level of business states. For policies to be most effective they need to be formulated in collaboration with those managers who will be affected principally by such policies. By participating in policy formulation, people cooperate through understanding. Participating in recommending and formulating policies for an organization is of vital importance to the general morale and espirit de corps with which the policies will be carried out. Participation is a basic part of our company's philosophy of management.

Policies should not include detailed rules of procedure. Such rules and details should be incorporated in the procedures, plans, programs, methods, and routines formulated to implement action toward objectives, goals, and missions.

Table 16 (cont.)

Policies provide the key basis for the exercise of authority by a member of the corporate staff through providing the line managers with advice and counsel, specialized assistance, support, and service in accomplishing organizational purposes. Policies are instruments of decentralization.

Procedures

A business procedure prescribed the relationship between functions, physical factors, and people for the purpose of coordinating and facilitating the sequential steps to take in accomplishing a piece of work. Procedures usually do not involve management discretion.

Team Management

Much of the management of our company depends on the effectiveness with which we work together as a team in varied organizational contents:
Management Council, Project Teams, Functional Teams and so forth. A team is a group of individuals who work as a unit. Effective teams are results-oriented and are committed to common objectives, goals, and strategies. Individual team members are strengthened by support from other members and through participative management develop a cultural ambience of openness and commitment. Team members understand their individual and collective roles and constantly seek to strengthen those roles through working together. Conflict of one sort or another invariably arises in the management of our company. The ability to effectively deal with conflict—difference of opinion over a substantive issue—is a key characteristic of a well-functioning team. Effective and timely resolution of conflict is dependent on all manager/professionals to surface the "issues" with peers, subordinates, and superiors as appropriate for timely resolution of the matter.

Business Decision

A business decision is the rational removal of uncertainty with respect to a course of action for an organization that consumes resources. Decision making should be carried out through the use of scientific methods in a systematic way in the solution of organizational problems or the accommodation of organizational opportunities. Decision making involves the evaluation of alternatives through the development of data bases, the assessment of the data bases on each alternative, and the selection of an alternative that best complements organizational strategies. By using a rational approach to decision making, the judgment of the decision maker is sharpened. The final decision is, of course, the prerogative of the manager, vested with the appropriate authority, responsibility, and accountability. Managers are held accountable for their decisions and are expected to be able to explain the rationale for a particular decision. Decision making always includes the design of general strategy on how the decision will be implemented within the framework of corporate mission, objectives, and goals. Managing is a distinct and professional kind of work, which blends thought and action in the making and executing of decisions.

Table 16 (cont.)

Leadership

A manager is a leader. Leadership is a responsibility of all managers. A leader is one who leads others along a way by example, persuasion, or direction as appropriate. A leader accomplishes organizational purposes through other people by influencing the behavior of the people who have a responsibility to do something for the organization. A leader is expected to support the decisions of a higher level manager in the organization structure.

Management Creed

A manager can succeed in the long run only if he sees his work as a whole system—all its people, parts, and environmental impacts and requirements. A manager obtains balanced results through the work of other people who see themselves also acting with initiative and competence through personal efforts and teamwork. Each professional manager is expected to develop an artful management style that reflects an understanding of the value and dignity of the individual as a contributor to organizational purposes. Motivation of an individual is related to the needs of that person. The professional manager must understand the nature of these needs if he is to deal successfully with the challenge of motivating people.

As a focus for our future discussions please evaluate the following management creed, which might help us develop a distinctive management philosophy for this company.

MANAGEMENT CREED (STYLE)

GENERAL PHILOSOPHY

- Will be a profitable, customer-oriented, project-management-driven corporation.
- Will prepare for the future through the development of a system of organizational missions, objectives, goals, and strategies.
- Will maintain leadership in the marketplace.
- Will emphasize decentralized profit center as organizational focus for strategic and operational decision making.
- Will provide superior staff support through the development and monitoring of corporate policy and procedures.
- Will maintain a corporate management council through which corporate policies will be developed.
- Will expect people to be active and supportive of community affairs.

DECISION MAKING

- Will make and implement decisions at the lowest possible level consistent with limits of authority in the corporation.
- Will require a leadership style that demands analytical and timely decisions based on fact.

Table 16 (cont.)

- Will emphasize the relevant decisions that are important for producing superior organizational performance.
- Will support higher level decisions at all times.

INNOVATION

- Will strive to maintain superior products and customer service at lowest competitive cost.
- Will expect innovation in the development, production, marketing, financing, and support of all products and services.
- Will encourage intelligent risk taking.

PERFORMANCE APPRAISAL

- Will evaluate organizational and personnel performance on an ongoing basis.
- Will evaluate organizational and personal performance on basis of objectives and goals developed through employee participation.
- Will expect people to be assertive in the assumption of authority, responsibility, and accountability in their work.

There are several questions we should think about as we evaluate this creed:

1. Will we be committed to support this when and if it is published?
2. Is the creed consistent with profit-driven management?
3. Should we strive for the idealism reflected in the creed?
4. Is our culture ready to accept this sort of Creed?
5. How can we best implement this creed? After implementation, how do we get feedback on whether or not it is working?
6. In what form should the creed be published?
7. How can this creed be worked through other managers/professionals in the company during its development?

Your task

Assume you have been called in as a consultant to assist the executives of this company to improve their management style. Evaluate fully the approach that is currently being taken to accomplish this improvement. Would you recommend that anything different be done? Be prepared to defend your position.

SITUATION 3: MOTIVATION IN THE PROJECT-DRIVEN MATRIX

The Situation

Motivation in the project-driven matrix organization depends on many factors. In many respects the factors that motivate individuals in any organization also motivate them in the matrix organization. But there are some real differences. In the matrix organization the project manager may not have the traditional supervisory relationship with the members of the project team. Consequently he must develop other means to bring out the best in the team members in supporting the objectives, goals, and strategies of the project.

Research has indicated that motivation in the matrix organization depends more on the de facto aspects of authority than on the legal aspects. Negotiating; persuading, and building alliances, trust, loyalty, commitment, communication, and such factors are important in motivating the project team members. Much of the motivation comes from the influence of the peer group and the other clientele with whom the project manager must work.

Table 17. "Factors that Motivate Me to do my Best Work" Survey[a]

Motivation in matrix management depends more on the de facto aspects of authority than the de jure, or legal, aspects. Much of the motivation comes from the influence of the peer group and the other clientele with whom the matrix manager/professional must work.

Please indicate the five items from the list that you believe are the most important in motivating you to do your best work in the matrix organization to which you belong. Are there any additional items you would add to this list?

_____ 1. Steady employment
_____ 2. Respect for me as a person
_____ 3. Good pay
_____ 4. Good physical working conditions
_____ 5. Chance to turn out quality work
_____ 6. Getting along well with others on the job
_____ 7. Chance for promotion
_____ 8. Opportunity to do interesting work
_____ 9. Having "team" services such as office, recreational, and social activities
_____ 10. Not having to work too hard
_____ 11. Knowing what is going on in the organization
_____ 12. Feeling my job is important
_____ 13. Having a written description of the duties in my job
_____ 14. Being told by my boss when I do a good job
_____ 15. Getting a performance rating, so I know how I stand
_____ 16. Attending staff meetings
_____ 17. Agreement with agency's objectives
_____ 18. Large amount of freedom on the job
_____ 19. Opportunity for self-development and improvement
_____ 20. Chance to work not under direct or close supervision
_____ 21. Having an efficient supervisor
_____ 22. Unique contributions
_____ 23. Recognition of peers
_____ 24. Personal satisfaction
_____ 25. Other _____

_____
_____

[a] Source: David I. Cleland and Dundar F. Kocaoglu, *Engineering Management*, McGraw-Hill Book Co., New York, 1981, p. 101.

Over the years of consulting for organizations that are engaged in project/systems work, the case writer has used the survey instrument indicated in Table 17 with professionals in engineering organizations—engineers, scientists, and engineering-scientific managers—involved on project teams as a way of getting them to think about the conditions of motivation in their organizations.

After the people fill out these survey forms, the distribution of the responses is then tabulated for the participants as a group and posted for all to see and to use as a focus for a discussion on the subject: What motivates people in this organization to do their best work? A lively discussion usually follows, as the participants begin to see what motivates them, as well as the peer group with which they are working. In practically all cases a pattern of responses in these project-driven matrix organizations has emerged indicating the items listed in alphabetical order in Table 18 as being the most important in motivating them to do their best work.

Your Task

Assume that you are the project manager of a project in which the managers and professionals supporting that project (the project clientele) have indicated that the most important factors that motivate them are those indicated in Table 18. You believe it would be useful to get these people together to discuss these factors. How would you go about doing this? What are some of the issues that might come up in such a meeting? Some other questions that you might want to ask yourself include:

1. What have I done as a project manager to create an environment on the project team to highlight these factors?
2. Do these factors give me any insight into the interpersonal style that I should strive to develop and practice in dealing with the project clientele?

Table 18. Job Motivational Factors Most Frequent Responses

Chance for promotion

Chance to turn out quality work

Feeling my job is important

Getting along well with others on the job

Good pay

Large amount of freedom on the job

Opportunity for self-development and improvement

Opportunity to do interesting work

Personal satisfaction

Recognition of peers

Respect for me as a person

3. Am I willing to change if these factors indicate that a change is needed in my managerial style?
4. How might I enlist the aid of higher level managers in helping me to provide the kind of environment that these factors indicate is needed in the project?
5. Prof. Michael J. Jucius, in his book *Personnel Management,* published by the Irwin Publishing Co. in 1963, identifies several intangible factors that an individual brings to his job that influence his behavior. According to Jucius, these include: psychological attitudes, physiological condition, political beliefs, moral standards, professional standards, prejudices, and habits. These factors tend to influence how an individual performs his job. Considering this, how might these factors influence the information contained in Table 18?
6. What other issues might be appropriate to discuss relative to the cultural ambience of the project-driven matrix organization?

Section II
The Matrix Organization[1]

The early "principles" of organization set forth various organizing techniques. *Centralization, decentralization, functional, departmental, product, process, and geographical* are the primary patterns and techniques for structuring the organization. Line and staff concepts and the vertical, hierarchical chain-of-command beliefs provided basic points of departure from which to organize activities. In the early 1960s, the emergence of project management precipitated the serious study of the matrix alternative organizational structure. The project-driven matrix structure emerged to satisfy several operating and strategic needs: resource sharing, profit center integrating for large projects, customer requirements, competitive pressures, and serving specific market segments. The growing use of the matrix structure today highlights the old saw that "structure follows strategy."

In a broad context, organizational design includes structure, management systems and processes, formal and informal interpersonal relationships, and motivational patterns. The matrix organizational design is a compromise between a bureaucratic approach that is too rigid and a simple unit structure that is too centralized. The design is fluid: personnel assignments, authority basis, and interpersonal relationships are constantly shifting. It lends a sense of democracy to a bureaucratic context.

From an organizational design viewpoint, the entire organization must be psychologically tuned to the accomplishments within the organization that support higher level organizational objectives, goals, and strategies. The purpose of a matrix design is not only to get the best from its strong project and functional approaches, but to complement these facets with a strong unity of command at the senior level and ensure that the balance of power is maintained in the organization.

---

[1] Portions of the introductory material in this section have been paraphrased from David I. Cleland, "The Cultural Ambience of the Matrix Organization," *Management Review,* November 1981, pp. 24–39.

In some companies only one or, at most, a few divisions may benefit from a realignment to the project-driven matrix form; the others can remain in the pyramidal, hierarchical format. Indeed, a single organizational chart cannot realistically portray the maze of relationships that exist inside a large organization because some units select project management, others opt for the conventional line-staff design, and others choose a hybrid form.

Orientation to Results

Because the matrix design is results-oriented and information-oriented, its very nature implies a need to cut across the line functions, and a compromise results through the bipolarity of functional specialization and project integration. Out of the lateral relationships—direct contact, liaison roles, and integration—comes a faculty to make and implement decisions and to process information without overloading the hierarchical communication channels. It is the need to reduce the hierarchical decision process that motivates establishment of a bilateral design requiring:

- project managers, who are responsible for results
- functional managers, who are responsible for providing resources to attain results

When a matrix design is being implemented in the early stages, a poor harmony will usually exist between the behavioral reality and the structural form. It is at this stage that the process of integration becomes important, and a series of critical actions must be initiated and monitored by senior management.

Superior-subordinate relationships must be modified; individual self-motivation leading to peer acceptance becomes critical. The development of strategies for dealing with conflict, the encouragement of participation techniques, and the delineation of expected authority and responsibility patterns are crucial. The complexity of the resulting organizational design, described by Peter Drucker as "fiendishly difficult," reminds us that the matrix should be used only when there is no suitable alternative. The matrix organizational design is clearly the most complex form of organizational alignment that can be used, and to change an existing design to a fully functioning matrix form takes time—perhaps several years.

Opportunities and Problems

Anyone who has worked in the matrix organizational form will attest to its complexity and difficulty and the opportunities and problems it provides.

Of all the approaches to structuring an organization, the matrix approach requires greatest caution in its design and patience in its implementation. Even in those situations where matrix must be used, as when doing business with the Defense Department, its effective use may be reinforced periodically to assure tht people understand and accept the multiple authority and responsibility patterns that exist.

Matrix, if properly designed and operated, can provide a way of synergizing organizational effort not possible under the more traditional organizational forms. *Business Week* magazine in a recent article described how Hewlett-Packard used matrix techniques to pull together widely scattered divisions into lockstep on a $100 million project.[2] But matrix does not work effectively if it is not properly defined. Bausch & Lomb developed a strategic plan for its Instruments Group that was to be complemented by a matrix-based reorganization where manufacturing responsibility was divided among three new product divisions, with a fourth division to manage sales and services. But, according to *Fortune* magazine, many of the managers remained "confused and demoralized."[3] They could not understand, and they could not accept the matrix structure, and this accounted, at least in part, for the failure of the strategic plan.

The importance of structure was recently illustrated by the experiences of the National Semiconductor Corporation. This company in 1981 had a proliferation of fiercely autonomous profit center product level managers. Half of these managers reported to one group manager, and the other half reported to a different group manager. Certain manufacturing operations were centralized to gain economies of scale, with processing and assembly at several other locations. Coordinating and decision making became difficult, with the structure producing confusion and conflict. Decisions within the product-line profit centers went smoothly, but intergroup decisions had to be pushed all the way up to the chief executive officer (CEO). The same CEO took on the coordination of Intergroup Marketing and International Marketing, which included him in many production and marketing decisions to the point that he ". . . bit off far more than he could chew, much less digest."[4] What happened at National Semiconductor was that the "schizophrenic management structure" contributed to the loss of its top technologist, a key technology team, and a valuable manufacturing man.[5] National Semi-

---

[2] "Can John Young Redesign Hewlett-Packard?" *Business Week,* December 6, 1982, pp. 72-78.
[3] Stratford P. Sherman, "Bausch & Lomb's Lost Opportunity," *Fortune,* January 24, 1983, pp. 104–105.
[4] "Behind the Exodus at National Semiconductor," *Business Week,* September 21, 1981, pp. 95–96.
[5] Ibid., p. 95.

conductor subsequently reorganized to delegate more authority out of the CEO's office.

Texas Instruments, Inc., recently went through an assessment of the strengths and weaknesses of the corporation. It examined its strategies, management systems, organizational structure, planning systems, and each of its businesses. The assessment was initiated by a failure on the part of the corporation to adjust fully to the transition from a $3 billion to a $4 billion company. This failure to adjust affected both the operating and strategic structures of the corporation.

The Product-Customer Center (PCC) is TI's basic operating unit with a focus on creating, making, and marketing products to satisfy customer needs. A PCC manager is expected to be an entrepreneur. However, over time two things happened to reduce the PCC manager's ability to act as an entrepreneur. Within the TI matrix, resources built up in large, centralized support organizations, and, as a result, the decision making of these support units overshadowed that of the PCCs and compromised their control of their businesses. PCC managers were no longer managers of resources; they were negotiators between support organizations. On the strategic management side of TI, things were not going well:

> Strategy management had drifted out of alignment with the PCC management. We had evolved into an almost complete matrix structure of product and technology strategies cutting across many organizations.

> The matrix approach fragmented both people and resources, and diffused authority to the point that managers could not carry out their program responsibilities effectively. With the increasing size and complexity of the matrix, and the accompanying separation of responsibility from resources, the system failed to support effective project teams and program execution suffered.[6]

TI reorganized to strengthen the PCC concept and to provide a new framework for executing key strategic programs. For example, within the semiconductor business, operation has been restructured around seven major PCCs. Each manager of a PCC now controls the resources and operations for that product line from design through development, front-end processing, assembly and test, to product marketing. In addition, within its semiconductors division, TI has created a new advanced development activity where the mode of operation will be to put together project teams under responsible managers for specific periods with defined objectives and adequate resources. These project teams, along with the redefined PCCs, will facilitate the timely execution of these strategies.[7]

Within the matrix organization there is a potential for duplication in staffing. The functional manager who previously was free to manage the organiza-

---

[6] *First Quarter & Stockholders Meeting Report,* Texas Instruments, Inc., May 1982, p. 4.
[7] Ibid., p. 4.

tion relatively unilaterally is forced to act in an environment that places a premium on the integration of resources through a project team consensus. To accomplish project results, he must learn to work with a vocal and demanding horizontal organization.

A cultural characteristic of the matrix design thus causes two key attitudes to emerge: the manager realizes that authority has its limits, and the professional recognizes that authority has its place.

In this section the cases and situations depict applications with accompanying problems and opportunities in the matrix organization.

RELEVANT BIBLIOGRAPHY

Ackoff, R. L. "Toward a System Concepts." *Management Science,* July 1971.

Allen, Louis A. *Charting the Company Organization Structure.* Studies in Personnel Policy, no. 168. National Industrial Conference Board, Inc., New York, 1959.

"An About-Face in TI's Culture." *Business Week,* July 5, 1982, p. 77.

"A Work Revolution in U.S. Industry." *Business Week,* May 16, 1983, pp. 100–110.

Bennis, W. G. "Evolving Organization Obsoleting Pyramid, Etc." *Steel,* April 11, 1966.

Carlisle, Howard M. "Are Functional Organizations Becoming Obsolete?" *Management Review,* January 1969.

"Changing the Company Organization Chart." *Management Record,* November 1959.

Cleland, David I. "The Cultural Ambience of the Matrix Organization." In *Project Management Handbook,* edited by D. I. Cleland and W. R. King. Van Nostrand Reinhold Co., New York, 1983, p. 700.

———. "Understanding Project Authority." *Business Horizons,* Spring, 1966.

———, and Wallace Munsey. "Who Works with Whom." *Harvard Business Review,* September–October 1967.

Davies, C., A. Demb, and R. Espejo. *Organization for Program Management.* John Wiley & Sons, Inc., New York, 1979.

Davis, Stanley M. "Two Models or Organizations: Unity of Command versus Balance of Power." *Sloan Management Review,* no. 1, Fall 1974.

———, and Paul R. Lawrence. "Problems of Matrix Organizations." *Harvard Business Review,* May–June 1978.

Delbecq, Andre L. *Matrix Organization—An Evolution beyond Bureaucracy.* The University of Wisconsin Press, Madison.

Duncan, Robert. "What is the Right Organization Structure?" *Organizational Dynamics,* Winter 1979.

Friesen, E. N. "The Matrix Organization, Another Dimension." *Mechanical Engineering,* October 1982, pp. 84-87.

Galbraith, Jay R. *Organization Design.* Addison-Wesley Publishing Co., Inc., Reading, Massachusetts, 1977.

Goggin, W. C., "How the Multidemensional Structure Works at Dow Corning." *Harvard Business Review,* January–February 1974.

Hollenback, F. A. "The Project Management Organization in Bechtel Power Corporation." In *Project Management Handbook,* edited by D. I. Cleland and W. R. King. Van Nostrand Reinhold Co., New York, 1983, p. 102.

"How Ebasco Makes the Matrix Method Work." *Business Week,* June 15, 1981, pp. 126, 131.

"It's a Stronger Bank that David Rockefeller is Passing to his Successor." *Fortune,* January 14, 1980.

Janger, Allen R. *Matrix Organization of Complex Businesses.* The Conference Board, New York, 1979.

Jermakowicz, Wladyslaw. "Organizational Structures in the R&D Sphere." *R&D Management,* no. 8, Special Issue, 1978.

Kimberley, John R. et al. *The Organizational Life Cycle.* Jossey-Bass Publishers, San Francisco, California, 1980.

Kolodny, Harvey F. "Evolution to a Matrix Organization." *Academy of Management Review,* vol. 4, 1979.

————. "Matrix Organization Designs and New Product Success." *Research Management,* September, 1980.

Kuhns, J. P. "The Matrix Organization." *Program Manager,* January–February 1983, pp. 29-31.

Lombard, George F. "Relativism in Organizations." *Harvard Business Review,* March–April 1972.

Mee, John F. "Ideational Items: Matrix Organization." *Business Horizons,* vol. 7, no. 2, Summer 1964.

————. "Speculation about Human Organization in the 21st Century." *Business Horizons.* February 1971.

Mintzberg, Henry. "Organization Design: Fashion or Fit?" *Harvard Business Reveiw,* January–February 1981.

————. *The Structuring of Organizations.* Prentice-Hall, Inc., Englewood Cliffs, New Jersey 1979.

Paolillo, Joseph G., and Warren B. Brown. "How Organizational Factors Affect R&D Innovation." *Research Management,* March, 1978.

"Putting Excellent into Management." *Business Week,* July 21, 1980, pp. 196-205.

Read, William H. "The Decline of Hierarchy in Industrial Organizations." *Business Horizons,* Fall 1965.

Shannon, Robert E. "Matrix Management Structures." *Industrial Engineering,* vol. 4, March 1972

Shull, Fremont A. *Matrix Structure and Project Authority for Optimizing Organizational Capacity.* Southern Illinois University, Business Research Bureau, Carbondale, October 1965.

Smith, Robert F. *The Variations of Matrix Organization.* Special Study No. 73, The Presidents Association, The Conference Board, New York.

Stuckenbruck, Linn C. "The Integration Function in the Matrix." Paper presented at the PMI Seminar/Symposium, Atlanta, Georgia, October 17-20, 1979.

Williams, Earle C. "Matrix Management Offers Advantages for Professional Services Firms." *Professional Engineer,* February 1978.

CASE STUDY 16:   THE SUCCESSFUL RESEARCH PILOT OPERATION—A CASE IN SUPPORT OF DR. MCGREGOR[1]

Introduction

The purpose of this case study is to relate the parameters of project management in a specific research pilot operation to the six basic tenets of Dr. Douglas McGregor's

---

[1] By David E. Hughes, Manager, Research Engineering Division, and Lawrence R. Cummins, Supervisor, Research Staff Services Division, PPG Industries, Inc., Glass Research Laboratories, Pittsburgh, Pennsylvania. Paper presented at the Project Management Institute Seminar/Symposium, Philadelphia, Pa., October 1972. Used by permission.

Theory Y and to the principle of integration postulated by Dr. McGregor in *The Human Side of Enterprise.*

This study encompasses four major areas relative to this project and other similar projects:

1. History and philosophy of pilot operations at the Glass Research Center of PPG Industries, Inc.
2. The pilot operation: the objectives of the project as perceived by management and staff
3. Organization for project management integration
4. Daily operations related to Theory Y management

The summary includes: the general results of the project, the reasons for success, and the significance for future pilot operations and to project management.

Background: Theory Y

In the decade since the publication of Douglas McGregor's book, *The Human Side of Enterprise,* a style of management known as *Theory Y* has generated considerable debate. This type of management has actually been gaining popularity over the past 30 years. However, in the case of the pilot operation discussed below, it was only in retrospect that the operation became recognizable as Theory Y in action. The pilot program, given only a 25 percent chance of technical success by experts in the field, was organized and run as it was simply because every resource had to be harnessed—and management felt that one of those resources was the enthusiasm and creativity of the pilot personnel. Before discussing the pilot program itself, however, let us take a brief look at the idea behind Theory Y, as McGregor presents it.

The assumptions behind Theory Y management are, in brief: (1) the average individual will naturally exercise self-direction and self-control in the service of objectives to which he is committed; (2) this commitment is largely a function of the rewards associated with achieving the objectives—the most important reward being some type of ego satisfaction; (3) under conditions of repeated ego satisfaction, the individual seeks responsibility and uses his creative potential more fully; and (4) under the conditions of modern industrial life, the individual's creative potential is exercised only partially, if at all.[2]

If these assumptions are valid, then the best way to motivate individuals to complete a task is to create a situation in which achievement of task objectives and personal satisfaction go together. Members of the organization should be able to achieve their own goals best by directing their efforts toward the success of the enterprise. This is what McGregor calls *integration.*

The idea of integration contrasts sharply with the traditional theory that authority is the chief mechanism of motivation. The question is: is McGregor's theory demonstrably valid? As early as 1964, surveys conducted by the Industrial Relations Center of the University of Chicago indicated that the professional research and development

---

[2] Douglas McGregor, *The Human Side of Enterprise,* McGraw-Hill Book Co., New York, pp. 47-48.

employee is job-oriented and is concerned primarily with competent performance in his chosen field.[3] In research and development work, therefore, the opportunity for individual creativity (and not authority alone) should be an effective motivating force. The pilot operation discussed here was, in effect, a laboratory that demonstrated very much the same thing.

The Pilot Operation

Organization.   Pilot operations are nothing new to the glass industry, especially in the developmental aspects of research. The purpose of the pilot operation is to scale up the bench experiment into something large enough to test process parameters and to accommodate a continuous operation. However, it must not be so large that substantial investments are lost in the event of failure. The product is not, in most cases, of any real concern; only the process and its parameters are of immediate consequence.

An examination of previous pilot operations indicated that one of the major roadblocks to success stemmed from difficulties in the communication of objectives. One problem is that management perceives the objectives differently from the technical people, who in turn perceive them differently from those who actually push the buttons on the pilot line. Therefore, before this program began, management, technical, and support personnel met to discuss the overall objectives. Technical difficulties that were anticipated early in the project were also brought out. Thus, the meeting stressed the need for the active support—not merely passive cooperation—of everyone who was to spend the following three months on the project.

The general objective of the pilot operation was to improve the manufacture of a specific glass product, using electric melting technology. The particular objective of management was to provide a new type of manufacturing facility for this glass, within predetermined cost, quality, and throughput constraints. To be successful, the pilot line would have to produce a relatively new product by new methods, using a configuration of equipment that was previously untried. Engineering objectives included collecting data for future use and verifying the accuracy of the mathematical models of the operation.

Several things helped to bring these objectives home to the pilot personnel and to reinforce the atmosphere of cooperation: the type of organization, the way the members of the project team were chosen and grouped into shift crews, and, perhaps most important, the day-to-day exchange of ideas that was built into the program.

At the top of the pilot organization was the project manager, who was actually the head of the department in which the project was being carried out. The project manager was deeply involved in the technical aspects of the pilot operation. He discussed the project at all stages with the personnel at every level of the project organization. The project engineer, who had the pilot operation as his sole responsibility

---

[3] David G. Moore and Richard Renck, "The Professional in Industry," *Administering Research and Development,* C. D. Orth III, et al., editors, Richard D. Irwin, Inc., and the Dorsey Press, 1964, p. 60.

during the period, had the particular function of reinforcing the line of communication between the manager and the rest of the project personnel.

The four shift crews were directly responsible to the project engineer. Each crew was composed of a shift engineer to supervise the entire shift; a shift furnace operator to oversee all furnace-related operations; a shift supervisor to oversee all other operations; and four hourly men, directly responsible to the supervisor, to run batch feeding, rolling, cutting, packing, and other individual operations.

Finally, a team of technical support personnel was on call to help with computer, refractory, electrical, and other problems.

The shift engineers, shift supervisors, and shift furance operators were chosen individually, on the basis of experience with other pilot operations and expertise in critical areas, such as refractories or process control. They were then grouped so that their combined knowledge and experience covered as many as possible of the necessary areas.

The four-man hourly crews were put together in a similar way, from the most experienced of the shop personnel. All had had previous pilot experience.

One other factor was considered before the final list was drawn up for each shift: interpersonal relations. It was felt that success depended largely on communication among the pilot personnel; and effective communication, as Saul W. Gellerman writes, "depends more on the *attitude* of the sender toward the receiver than on the sender's gifts for speaking."[4] With this rationale, the prospective shift engineers, supervisors, and furance operators were asked (privately) whether they could work, free of tension, with the rest of the proposed group for that shift. The hourly crews were put together in a similar way. Finally, staff and hourly crews were matched with the same consideration in mind.

When this organizational structure, represented in Figure 1, was filled, a unique group was ready to run the pilot operation. The overlapping areas of knowledge, plus the spirit of cooperation inherent in the way the total group was put together, created a strong vertical and horizontal interdependence. External motivation for each person on the team came from all sides—not just from above. As evidence of the strength of this kind of motivating force, even though some individuals had expressed the opinion that the operation would never be a success, the prevailing spirit in the group was: "Let's see if we can make it work!"

Daily operation.   Authority, in the traditional sense, seems at first to be lacking. Authority did, in fact, play an important role in the daily operations, but it was used with a nontraditional approach. In daily operation, everything was done to preserve and extend the totally open communication and the spirit of enthusiasm. Daily evaluation meetings were held, and everyone who was not actually required to stay by the pilot line attended. The order of each meeting was: what are the problems; how can we solve them; let's try this solution. One by one, the pilot line problems were discussed. Everyone expressed an opinion. Then, the project manager, who attended all these meetings, made the final decision on a course of action. The

---

[4] Saul W. Gellerman, *Management by Motivation,* American Management Assn., Inc., New York, p. 46.

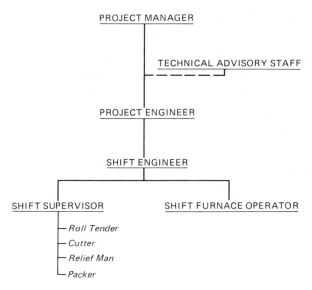

Figure 1. Pilot Facility Organization.

staff members responsible for that area of the pilot line could then leave to implement the decision. This was frequently not necessary, however, because the meetings began early in the morning and were very short. Experience with other pilot operations had shown that discussions that lasted into the middle of the day tended to stifle the desire to start something new—in other words, to dampen the motivation that had been so carefully built up. The lengthy meetings did not, in general, seem to solve more problems, but they did increase frustrations.

The role of the manager's authority is apparent here: the manager had the option to start a solution to some problem in motion, bypassing a long, involved discussion. This use of authority was not strictly one-way, however. When one of the crew had an alternative suggestion, he could talk directly with the manager, who had final authority to implement that suggestion. The entire decision making process was accelerated, while including the maximum number of team members in the formulation of those decisions.

So that all the shifts would be thoroughly familiar with what went on at the meetings, the shift engineer from the daylight shift left detailed notes for the evening shift engineer. The midnight shift engineer stayed on through the early morning meetings. Also, each shift engineer discussed the results of the daily meetings with anyone who had not attended. Reasons behind each decision were discussed. Previous pilot operations had demonstrated that personnel interest and hence motivation were low when the men who actually ran the machinery on the line were merely told to take certain temperatures and change certain variables, without being told what they were accomplishing. As evidence that there was a high degree of personal interest in this program, the project manager never—in three months of operation—had to call anyone from the other shifts when they were needed in an emergency. Those who were needed were, in every case, already there!

In addition to the daily routine, weekly meetings were held with members of the company's research staff to review progress and to discuss possible changes. Communication was thus retained with the main body of company research personnel. (Pilot facility operation is shown in Figure 2.)

Results

Technically, the pilot project was a total success. The product was of salable quality, and the pilot personnel found that the line could actually produce good-quality glass at twice its projected speed. Design and engineering data were obtained for future production operations. The new process, new configuration of equipment, and new product had proved a worthwhile investment. Also, the accuracy of the mathematical models of the operation had been verified.

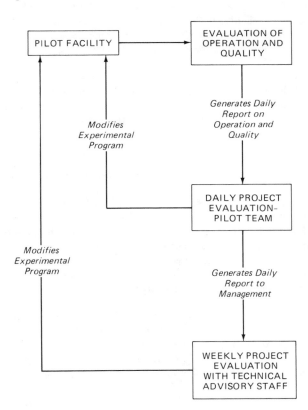

Figure 2.   Pilot Facility Operation.

Perhaps more important for future research, however, was the success of the type of organization used. The success of the project depended, of course, on the expertise of the individuals. However, that expertise might not have been applied so fully, or with such enthusiasm, except for the personal commitment of each member of the group toward the goals of the pilot operation. The fact that each person's opinion was important in decision making meant that each felt a responsibility for operational changes and for their results. Because everyone, including hourly crew members, was in contact with someone who could use considerable authority, each person could see his suggestions being taken into account. This reinforced the individual's personal involvement in the project. In other words, integration of personal and project goals had been achieved. The structure of the organization did not disintegrate to a single level, however; each person still had his responsibility to those above and below him in the project.

The significance to future pilot operations is threefold. First, this pilot project demonstrates the importance of communication and interdependence in a tightly organized research operation. Second, it shows that authority does have an important function in such an operation, but not necessarily the traditional one of producing one-way decisions. Finally, it shows that management, engineers, and other levels of the organization need not remain on separate planes of activity and understanding. Given a personal interest in the success of the operation, the pilot team members did apply themselves more fully and did seek more responsibility than had the personnel of more traditionally run pilot operations. The Theory Y approach, applied unknowingly in this project, produced an unusually high level of motivation that was maintained throughout the entire campaign and gave the project considerably more than the expected 25 percent chance of technical and managerial success.

CASE STUDY 17:   JONES AND SHEPHARD ACCOUNTANTS, INC.

By 1970, Jones and Shephard Accountants, Inc. (J&S) was ranked 18th in size by the American Association of Accountants. To compete with the larger firms, J&S formed an Information Services Division designed primarily for studies and analyses. By 1975, the Information Service Division (ISD) had 15 employees.

In 1977, the ISD purchased three minicomputers. With this increased capacity, J&S expanded its services to help satisfy the needs of outside customers. By September 1978, the internal and external work loads had increased to a point where the ISD now employed over 50 people.

The director of the division was very disappointed in the way that activities were being handled. There was no single person assigned to push through a project, and outside customers did not know who to call to get answers regarding project status. The director found that the majority of his time was being spent on day-to-day activities, such as conflict resolution, instead of strategic planning and policy formulation.

The biggest problems facing the director were the two continuous internal projects (called Project X and Project Y, for simplicity) that required month-end data collation

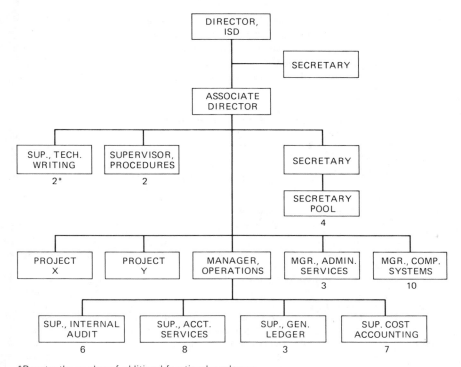

*Denotes the number of additional functional employees

Figure 3. ISD Organizational Chart.

and reporting. The director felt that these two projects were important enough to require a full-time project manager on each effort.

In October 1978, Corporate announced that the ISD director would be reassigned on February 1, 1979, and that the announcement of his replacement would not be made until the middle of January. The same week that the announcement was made, two individuals were hired from outside the company to take charge of Project X and Project Y. Figure 3 shows the organizational structure of the ISD.

Within the next 30 days, rumors spread throughout the organization as to who would become the new director. Most people felt that the position would be filled from within the division and that the most likely candidates would be the two new project managers. In addition, the associate director was due to retire in December, thus creating two openings.

On January 3, 1979, a confidential meeting was held between the ISD director and the systems manager.

ISD Director: "Corporate has approved my request to promote you to division director. Unfortunately, your job will not be an easy one. You're going to have to restructure the organization somehow so that our employees will not have as many conflicts as we are now faced with. My secretary is typing up a confidential memo for you explaining my observations on the problems within our division.

"Remember, your promotion should be held in the strictest confidence until the final announcement later this month. I'm telling you this now so that you can begin planning the restructuring. My memo should help you." (See Table 1 for the memo.)

Table 1.   Confidential Memo.

FROM: ISD Director
  TO: Systems Manager
DATE: January 3, 1979

Congratulations on your promotion to Division Director. I sincerely hope that your tenure will be productive both personally and for Corporate. I have prepared a short list of the major obstacles that you will have to consider when you take over the controls.

1. Both Project X and Project Y managers are highly competent individuals but, in the last four to five days, have appeared to create more conflicts for us than we had previously. This could be my fault for not delegating them sufficient authority or could result from the fact that several of our people consider these two individuals as prime candidates for my position. In addition, the Operations Manager does not like other managers coming into his "empire" and giving direction.
2. I'm not sure that we even need an Associate Director. That decision will be up to you.
3. Corporate has been very displeased with our inability to work with outside customers. You must consider this problem with any organizational structure you choose.
4. The corporate strategic plan for our division contains an increased emphasis on special, internal MIS projects. Corporate wants to limit our external activities for a while until we get our internal affairs in order.
5. I made a mistake of changing our organizational structure on a day-to-day basis. Perhaps it would have been better to design a structure that will satisfy advanced needs, especially one that we can grow into.

The systems manager read the memo and, after due consideration, decided that some form of matrix would be best. To help him structure the organization properly, an outside consultant was hired to help identify the potential problems with changing over to a matrix. The following problem areas were identified by the consultant:

1. The operations manager controls more than 50 percent of the people resources. You might want to break up his empire. This will have to be done very carefully.
2. The secretary pool is placed too high in the organization.
3. The supervisors who now report to the associate director will have to be reassigned lower in the organization if the associate director's position is abolished.
4. One of the major problem areas will be trying to convince corporate management that its change will be beneficial. You'll have to convince management that this change can be accomplished without having to increase division manpower.
5. You might wish to set up a separate department or a separate project for customer relations.

6. Introducing your employees to the matrix will be a problem. Each employee will look at the change differently. Most people have the tendency of looking first at the shift in the balance of power—have I gained or have I lost power and status?

The systems manager evaluated the consultant's comments and then prepared a list of questions to ask the consultant at their next meeting.

1. What should the new organizational structure look like? Where should I put each person, specifically the managers?
2. When should I announce the new organizational change? Should it be at the same time as my appointment or at a later date?
3. Should I invite any of my people to provide input to the organizational restructuring? Can this be used as a technique to ease power plays?
4. Should I provide inside or outside seminars to train my people on the new organizational structure? If yes, how soon should they be held?

CASE STUDY 18:   ACORN INDUSTRIES[1]

Prior to July of 1971, Acorn Industries was a relatively small midwestern corporation dealing with a single product line. The company dealt solely with commercial contracts and rarely, if ever, considered submitting proposals for government contracts. The corporation at that time functioned under a traditional form of organizational structure, although it did possess a somewhat decentralized managerial philosophy within each division. In 1968, upper management decided that the direction of the company must change. To compete with other manufacturers, the company initiated a strong acquisition program whereby smaller firms were bought out and brought into the organization. The company believed that an intensive acquisition program would solidify future growth and development and that the acquisition of other companies would allow it to diversify into other fields, especially within the area of government contracts. However, the company did acknowledge one shortcoming that could possibly hurt its efforts: it never fully implemented any form of project management.

In July of 1971, the company was awarded a major defense contract after four years of research and development and intensive competition from a major defense organization. The company once again relied on its superior technological capabilities, combined with strong marketing efforts, to obtain the contract. According to Christ Banks, the current marketing manager at Acorn Industries, the successful proposal for the government contract was submitted solely through the efforts of the marketing division. Acorn's successful marketing strategy was based on three factors:

---

[1] This case study was prepared by Frank E. Ashcraft under the direction of Dr. Harold Kerzner as a basis for class discussion, rather than to illustrate either effective or ineffective handling of an administrative situation.

1. Know exactly what the customer wants.
2. Know exactly what the market will bear.
3. Know exactly what the competition is doing and where it is going.

The contract awarded in July 1971 led to subsequent successful government contracts, and, in fact, eight more were awarded, amounting to $80 million each. These contracts were to last anywhere from 7 to 10 years, taking the company into early 1981, before expiration would occur. Because of its extensive growth, especially within the area of government contracts as they pertained to weapon systems, the company was forced in 1972 to change general managers. An individual was brought in who had an extensive background in program management and who previously had been involved in research and development.

Problems Facing the General Manager

The problems facing the new general manager were numerous. The company prior to his arrival, was virtually a decentralized manufacturing organization. Each division within the company was somewhat autonomous, and the functional managers operated under a key management incentive program (KMIP). The previous general manager had left it up to each division manager to do what was required. Performance was measured against attainment of goals. If the annual objective was met under the KMIP program, each division manager could expect to receive a year-end bonus. These bonuses were computed as a percentage of the manager's base pay and were directly correlated with the ability to exceed the annual objective. Accordingly, future planning within each division was somewhat stagnant, and most managers did not concern themselves with any aspect of organizational growth other than what was required by the annual objective.

Because the company had previously dealt with a single product line and interacted solely with commercial contractors, little if any production planning had occurred. Interactions between research and develpoment and the production and engineering departments were practically nonexistent. Research and development was either way behind or way ahead of the other departments at any particular time. Because of the effects of KMIP this aspect was likely to continue.

Change within the Organizational Structure

To compound the aforementioned problems the general manager faced the unique task of changing corporate philosophy. Previously, corporate management had been concerned with a single product with a short-term production cycle. Now, however, the corporation faced long-term government contracts, long cycles, and diversified products. Also, considering that the company had almost no individuals who operated under any aspect of program management, the tasks appeared insurmountable.

The goal of the new general manager from 1972 to 1976 was to retain profitability and maximize return on investment. To do this, the general manager decided to maintain the company's commercial product line and operate at full capacity. This decision was made because the company was based on solid financial management, and the commercial product line had been extremely profitable.

According to the general manager, Ken Hawks, "The concept of keeping both commercial and government contracts separate was a necessity. The commercial product line was highly competitive and maintained a good market share. If the adventure into weaponry failed, the company could always fall back on the commercial products. At any rate, the company at this time could not solely rely on the success of government contracts that were due to expire by 1981."

In 1976, Acorn reorganized its organizational structure and created a program management office under the direct auspices of the general manager. (See Figure 4.)

Expansion and Growth

In late 1976, Acorn initiated a major expansion and reorganization within its various divisions. In fact, between 1976 and 1978 the government contracts resulted in the acquiring of three new companies, and the acquisition of a fourth was being considered. As before, the expertise of the marketing department was heavily relied upon. Growth objectives for each division were set by corporate headquarters with the advice and feedback of the division managers. Up to 1976, Acorn's divisions did not have a program director. The program management functions for all divisions were performed by one program manager whose expertise was entirely within the commercial field. This particular program manager was concerned only with profitability and did not closely interact with the various customers. According to Mr. Banks. "The program manager's philosophy was to meet the *minimum* level of performance required by the contract. To attain this he required only adequate performance. As Acorn began to become more involved with government contracts, its position remained that given a choice between high technology and low reliability, the company would always select an acquisition with low technology and high reliability. If we remain somewhere in between, future government contracts should be assured."

At the time, Acorn established a Chicago office headed by a group executive. The office was mainly for monitoring government contracts. Concurrently, an office was established in Washington to monitor the trends within the Department of Defense and to further act as a lobbyist for government contracts. A director of marketing was appointed to interact with the program office on contract proposals. Prior to the establishment of a director of program management in 1977, the marketing division was responsible for contract proposals. Acorn believed that marketing would always, as in the past, set the tone for the company. However, in 1977 and then again in 1978, Acorn underwent further organizational changes (see Figures 5 and 6). A full-

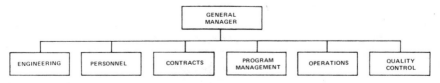

Figure 4.   1976 Organizational Structure.

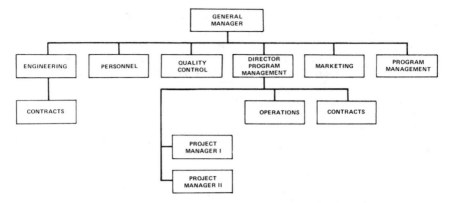

Figure 5.   1977 Organizational Structure.

time director of program management was instituted, along with a program management office, with further subdivisions of project managers responsible for the various
government contracts. It was at this time that Acorn realized the necessity of involving
the program manager more extensively in contract proposals. One faction within
corporate management wanted to keep marketing responsible for contract proposals.
Another decided that a combination of the marketing input and the expertise of
the program director must be utilized. According to Mr. Banks, "We began to realize
that marketing no longer could exclude other factions within the organization when
preparing contract proposals. As program management became a reality we realized
that the project manager must be included in all phases of contract proposals."

Prior to 1976, the marketing department controlled most aspects of contract proposals. With the establishment of the program office, interactions between the marketing
department and the program office began to increase.

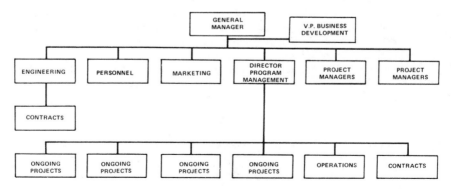

Figure 6.

Responsibilities of the Project Manager

In 1977 Acorn, for the first time, identified a director of program management. This individual reported directly to the general manager and had under his control:

1. The project managers
2. The operations group
3. The contracts group

Under this reorganization the director of program management, along with the project managers, possessed greater responsibility relative to contract proposals. These new responsibilities included:

1. Research and development
2. Preparation of contract proposals
3. Interaction with marketing for submitting proposals
4. Responsibility for all government contracts:
   a. Tradeoff analysis
   b. Cost analysis
5. Interfacing with engineering department to ensure satisfaction of customer's desires

With the expansion of government contracts, Acorn now faces the problem of bringing in new talent to direct ongoing projects. The previous project manager had virtual autonomy over operations and maintained a singular philosophy. Under his tenure many bright individuals left Acorn because future growth and career patterns were questionable. Now that the company is diversifying into other product lines the need for young talent is crucial. Program management is still in the infancy stage.

Acorn's approach to selecting a project manager was dependent upon the size of the contract. If the particular contract was between $2 and $3 billion, the company would go with the most experienced individual. Smaller contracts would be assigned to whomever was available.

Interaction with Functional Departments

Program management being relatively new, few data were available to the company to fully assess whether operations were successful. The project managers were required to negotiate with the functional departments for talent. This aspect has presented some problems because of the long-term cycle of most government contracts. Young talent within the organization saw involvement with projects as an opportunity to move up within the organization. Functional managers, on the other hand, apparently did not want to let go of young talent and were extremely reluctant to lose any form of autonomy.

Performance of individuals assigned to projects was discussed between the project manager and the functional manager. Problems arose, however, due to length of projects. In some instances, if an individual had been assigned longer to the project manager than to the functional manager, the final evaluation of performance rested with the project manager. Further problems thus occurred when performance evaluations were submitted. In some instances adequate performance was rated high in order to maintain an individual within the project scheme. According to some project managers, this procedure was necessary because talented individuals were hard to find.

Current Status

In early 1978, Acorn began to realize that a production shortage relative to government contracts would possibly occur in late 1981 or early 1982. Acorn initiated a three-pronged attack in anticipation of this development.

1. Do what you do best.
2. Look for similar product lines.
3. Look for products that do not require extensive R&D.

To achieve these objectives, each division within the corporation established its own separate marketing department. The prime objective was to seek more federal funds through successful contract proposals and use these funds to increase investment in R&D. The company had finally realized that the success of the corporation from 1972 to 1981 was primarily because of the selection of the proper general manager. However, this had been accomplished at the exclusion of proper control over R&D efforts. A more lasting problem still existed however: program management was still less developed than in most other corporations.

SITUATION 4:   HOW BEST TO ORGANIZE FOR PROJECT MANAGEMENT

The Situation

The chief executive of an industrial systems company recently became concerned about the suitability of the company's organization. This company's mission was to design, build, and install computer-based systems for the electric power industry. These systems control electric power generation and transmission. Advanced energy management systems are under development for several electric utilities in the north-central United States. To motivate the key managers and professionals to give serious thought to the company's organizational design, the chief executive and the vice-president for finance and administration developed a series of memoranda, the essence of which is contained in this case, on the subject of organizational design and distributed them to all the second-level managers in the company, viz., two profit center managers, finance and administration, manufacturing, marketing and strategic planning, and contract management. The company was currently organized on a line-and-staff basis.

The objective of the organizational design study was to examine the alternative organizational structures that might be adopted by the company during the next five years. Implicit in this objective is the need to identify human resource requirements, particularly as they relate to overhead costs.

The strategic plan for 1984 through 1988, in terms of sales and human resource objectives, was as follows:

Year	1984	1985	1986	1987	1988
Sales, billion	$18	$23	$29	$36	$45
Sales/Emp, million	$80	$95	$105	$120	$130
People	225	242	276	300	346

Several organizational design criteria were suggested by the personnel director as a focus for examining the various organizational alignments that the company might evaluate. These criteria were:

1. Structure must support the market strategy.
2. Minimize overhead resource requirements.
3. Structure must support the management of projects.
4. Customers require a focal point, i.e., project managers, for each project.
5. Common resource requirements will be shared as much as possible, but without reducing resources below the critical mass necessary for the product line manager to control his business.
6. Responsibility for results must be coupled with appropriate authority to make decisions necessary to achieve those results.
7. Development of managerial and professional roles; adoption of state-of-the-art support systems; and managerial style and organizational culture will support the organizational structure.
8. Adequate human and nonhuman resources will be provided to support the organization.
9. Organizational change will be evolutionary and will complement effective utilization of all human and nonhuman resources.

To have a common basis for communicating about the various organizational alternatives, it was decided to distribute to everyone a definition of several key terms:

1. *Functional Organization*—A structure that groups responsibilities according to similar types of work to be performed.
2. *Profit Center Organization*—A structure that groups responsibilities into distinct profit-responsible businesses by product and market segment.
3. *Project-Driven Matrix Organization*—A structure in which a project manager acts as a focal point to integrate functional resources to support project objectives.

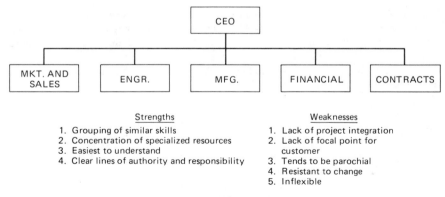

Strengths	Weaknesses
1. Grouping of similar skills	1. Lack of project integration
2. Concentration of specialized resources	2. Lack of focal point for
3. Easiest to understand	customer
4. Clear lines of authority and responsibility	3. Tends to be parochial
	4. Resistant to change
	5. Inflexible

Figure 7. Functional Organization.

4. *Profit Center*—An organizational entity usually comprising product lines for which profit/loss authority and responsibility can be fixed.
5. *Product Line*—A grouping of products having similar characteristics and market segments, normally within a single profit center.
6. *Productivity*—The measure of the ratio of input to output. (For our purpose here, this measure is in sales dollars per employee.)
7. *Project/Program Management*—A discipline that covers the administration of projects from conceptualization to completion, encompassing a set of principles and methods for effective planning, organization, and control with regard to project cost, schedule, and technology.
8. *Work Package*—A clearly distinguishable unit of work at organizational levels where work is performed. Primary responsibility for a work package is assignable to a single organizational element.
9. *Organizational Structure*—The delineation of the relationships between certain functions, physical and financial resources, and human resources based on their characteristics and significances.
10. *Overhead Cost*—A cost that is not directly related to the production, sale, or delivery of goods or services to the customer.
11. *Administrative Cost*—Overhead cost related to the general management and administration of the company.

Three different organizational designs were ultimately selected as the principal ones, around which further study would be done. To facilitate such a study, the following three models of organizational structure, along with some strengths and weaknesses thereof, were distributed (Figures 7, 8, and 9):

1. The functional organization
2. The project-driven matrix organization
3. Hybrid profit center organization

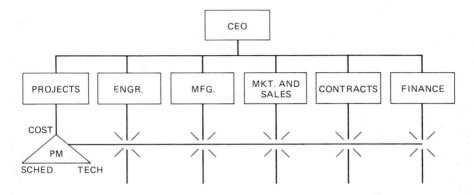

Strengths	Weaknesses
1. Maximum sharing of common resources	1. Difficult to manage
2. Focal point for customer contact	2. Perceived lack of parity of authority and responsibilty
3. Focal point for integration of organizational resources to support projects	3. Creates conflict
4. Provides more flexibility	4. Requires a supportive organizational culture and systems
5. Provides profit center by project	5. Creates additional overhead/ management cost

Figure 8.   Project–Driven Matrix Organization.

During the discussions of the various alternative organizational alignments, the CEO was requested to summarize his corporate philosophy. He responded in the following manner:

- "The focal point of our business is project management. Our very survival and growth depend on successful project management.
- Within our company we will strive to achieve parity of responsibility, authority, and accountability.
- To the extent possible, the 'hierarchy' for control of resources shall be: (1) the project manager; (2) the profit center division; (3) manufacturing and corporate staff. Delegation to the project manager shall be the objective; movement of that control up the organizational hierarchy shall be done only if an increase in efficiency/productivity results.
- We shall operate our company by grouping our projects by market segment, thus creating profit center divisions based on product markets.
- We shall operate our company with the minimum acceptable administrative overhead. We shall not carry slack resources in anticipation of long-term needs.
- The profit center divisions shall be responsible for profit/loss.
- We shall recognize 'dotted line' relationships of functional staff managers.
- We recognize that our most valuable asset is our human resources. The technology of the company rests in their minds. We will support, challenge, and stimulate our employees while providing career growth opportunities.

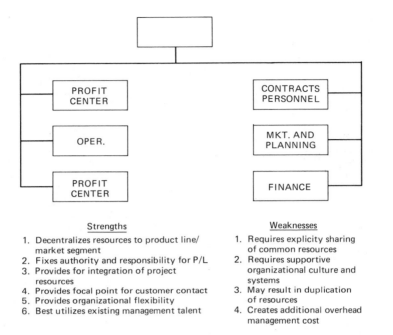

Strengths	Weaknesses
1. Decentralizes resources to product line/ market segment	1. Requires explicity sharing of common resources
2. Fixes authority and responsibility for P/L	2. Requires supportive organizational culture and systems
3. Provides for integration of project resources	
4. Provides focal point for customer contact	3. May result in duplication of resources
5. Provides organizational flexibility	4. Creates additional overhead management cost
6. Best utilizes existing management talent	

Figure 9. Hybrid Profit Center Organization.

- We will reward employees based on their contribution to the achievement of company goals as applicable to the individual. The link between performance and rewards shall be very visible.
- We shall share common resources to the best of our ability."

The corporate philosophy emphasized that the "hierarchy" for control of resources would rest with the project manager, the profit center, corporate manufacturing, and corporate staff, in that order. It was decided that each of the key functions should be evaluated to see where responsibility for that function would best fit in the organization. Accordingly, a functional chart was developed and distributed to all the second-level managers for their assessments. (See Table 2.) Each manager was requested to decide, by placing an X in the appropriate column, where residual responsibility for that function would best fit.

Your Task

Assume you are one of the second-level staff managers in this company:

1. Where would you recommend that the functions be placed?
2. How might your decision be affected if you were:
   a. A project manager?
   b. A profit center manager?
   c. The manufacturing manager?

Table 2. Functional Chart.

Function	Control at					
	Project Manager	Profit Center	Manufac-turing	Finance & Admin.	Mktg. & Strat. Planning	Contract Manage-ment
Develop, manage, report:						
—Project schedules						
—Manage subcontractors (field)						
—Interpretation, resolution of specifications						
—Translate specs. into hardware (H/W)						
—Translate specs. into software (S/W)						
—Write work authorizations, control cost						
—Manage project changes						
—Manage installation, test, & acceptance						
Field						
Factory						
—Manage implementation of H/W & S/W						
—Initiate invoicing						
—Collect invoices (& receivables)						
—Manage customer interface, estimate-to-complete						
—Cost analysis, etc.						
—Develop & manage work breakdown structure						
—Multiple project management						
—Develop technical documentation						
—Customer training						
—On-site purchasing						
—Customer maintenance agreement						
—Field office management						
—Division P/L and balance sheet						

Function	Project Manager	Profit Center	Manufac- turing	Finance & Admin.	Mktg. & Strat. Planning	Contract Manage- ment
—Division contracts management						
—Division financial forecasts						
—Order entry						
—Customer warranty						
—Product catalog & prices						
—OEM Sales						
—Bid & porposal						
—Division strategic planning						
—Inventory levels & flow						
—Division sales & marketing						
—Division sales forecast						
—Division controllership						
—Division staffing						
—Employee training & development						
—H/W manufacturing						
—H/W & S/W R&D						
—Purchasing function						
—Materials control						
—QA/QC						
—Technical publications						
—Facilities management						
—Manage standard cost system						
—Compliance with GAAP						
—Management of budget process						
—Corporate controllership						
—Corporate cost collection & reporting						
—Manage corporate information system						

| | Control at | | | | | |
Function	Project Manager	Profit Center	Manufac-turing	Finance & Admin.	Mktg. & Strat. Planning	Contract Manage-ment
—Tax administration & reporting						
—Financial and business reports to govt.						
—Corporate cash flow analysis & reporting						
—Collection management						
—Preparation of corporate financial statements						
—Corporate financial analysis & reporting						
—Support financial assessment of strategic plans						
—Maintenance of corporate finance & accounting records						
—Maintenance of corporate internal accounting control systems						
—Maintenance of corporate cost accounting						
—Coordinate annual physical inventory						
—Coordinate capital expenditure requests						
—Interface with external accounting & financial institutions						

3. What criteria would you use to make your decisions in questions 1 and 2 above?
4. Do you agree with the strengths and weaknesses of the three organizational models that the company selected for detailed study? Why or why not?
5. How complete were the organizational design criteria suggested by the personnel director?
6. Would you want to add any additional definitions to those already distributed to the managers?
7. Are there any other organizational models this company should consider?
8. If you were the president of this company, is there anything you would have done differently? Is there anything else that should be done?

SITUATION 5: THE CULTURAL AMBIENCE OF MATRIX MANAGEMENT

The Situation

Several forms of matrix management have just been instituted in an industrial firm, e.g., project/program management, task force management, production teams, international management, quality circles, to name a few. It is believed that these forms of matrix management will have a significant influence on the culture of this firm. There is a growing appreciation of the need to assess the characteristics of the *present* and *future* culture of this organization.

For example, one cultural characteristic affected by the matrix approach in modern organizations is the concept of the profit center and the delegation of authority to one manager who is held responsible for producing profitable results. Everything counts at the profit center level, everything is measured there, and people are rewarded accordingly. For those managers who have operated successfully for years in a decentralized profit-center mode, the sharing of decisions and results with some other manager outside the profit center hierarchy can be a cultural shock. There are other cultural characteristics that are found in matrix-oriented organizations.

Your Task

Develop a set of short statements (or phrases) that describe the overall cultural characteristics of a typical industrial organization at the present time and what you would expect those characteristics to be circa 1988. Some things you might wish to factor into these statements or phrases include:

- Profit center concept
- Decision making
- Strategic planning
- Key executive attitudes

- "Operational" versus "strategic management"
- Individual rewards versus group rewards

Prepare a summary briefing of your ideas for presentation.

SITUATION 6:   ORGANIZING FOR STRATEGIC PLANNING IN THE MATRIX MANAGEMENT CONTEXT[1]

The Situation

The International Organization in the XYZ Corporation has existed for several weeks. At a recent management council meeting at corporate headquarters, the newly appointed international president described how the new matrix management system for international operations would be expected to operate. He described four cornerstones of this matrix management system as:

- Shared decision making
- Shared accountability
- Shared financial results

and the fundamental concept that the "country" would be a primary strategic building block of the international organization.

Success in the international marketplace starts with successful strategic planning. The cultural ambience for strategic planning in this company has improved considerably over the past several years. Strategic planning in the international marketplace poses particular challenges to XYZ matrix managers and professionals. The in-country manager will be responsible for the strategic planning encompassing his country.

To get key people in the new international organization to start thinking about strategic planning, the geographic manager for Europe appointed an in-country manager for England. This individual was directed to initiate the development of a strategic plan for England as soon as possible. A tentative mission statement for the corporate operations in England was given: "Develop and implement a corporate multinational strategy for England that provides long-term growth and profitability." To implement this mission statement, a series of tentative objectives were set forth as a point of departure for the strategic planning process. These objectives were:

	($million)
- Financial Objectives	
- Orders entered	252.0
- Sales	221.0
- Operating Profit	21.0
- Corporate IAT	13.0

[1] Adapted in part from D. I. Cleland and W. R. King, *Systems Analysis and Project Management,* 3rd edition, McGraw-Hill Book Co., New York, 1983, p. 58. Used by permission.

- Develop and implement a program to achieve improved productivity of existing plants.
- Increase market coverage in the industrial systems business.
- Establish effective working relationships with key government buying influences.
- Develop an effective system for evaluating the competition in England.
- Establish an effective matrix working relationship with key corporate, product-group, and in-kingdom personnel.
- Expand English export sales opportunities with emphasis on industrial systems project business.

There is a growing appreciation of the need to know how to best organize in-country strategic planning, particularly in the sharing context of matrix management.

Your Task

Assume that you are in the in-country manager of England. Develop an approach of how an in-country manager should best organize resources to accomplish strategic planning. Some items you might wish to consider in developing this organizational approach include:

- A consideration of the strategic planning process
- Use of an organizational design to accomplish strategic planning
- Delineation of authority and responsibility patterns in organizing for strategic planning
- Work breakdown structure for strategic planning

What problems would you expect in strategic planning in the matrix environment? In particular, what do you think will be some of the major problems in planning for a country? What recommendations do you have to help solve (or alleviate) these problems? Prepare a summary briefing of your ideas and conclusions.

SITUATION 7:   THE LINE/STAFF ORGANIZATIONAL CHOICE

The Situation

At a recent meeting of the management council of the Alpha Company, the CEO announced that a realignment of the company's organization structure had been effected. The new organization would be a line and staff relationship within a product-line structure of decentralized division profit centers. Three line organizations were designated: an Industrial Systems Division, a Consumer Products Division, and a Common Operations or Manufacturing Division. Contract Management, Finance and Administration, and Strategic Planning and Marketing were designated as staff organizations. The following additional guidance on the new organization structure was given:

Contract Management.   Each product-line profit center will have an engineer/attorney at each of its major facilities for contract management. This position will report entirely to the product-line manager.

Contract management corporate staff functions will include the following:

- Corporate standards
- Bid/no-bid council, chairman
- Order entry
- Chief legal counsel
- Contract files maintenance
- Contract management audits
- Limits of authority, chairman

Operations.   Operations will be responsible for quality assurance audits in the divisions.

Finance and Administration.   All accounting functions will be done at corporate headquarters.

Sales.   The sales function will be handled by the divisions.

General.   Corporate staff involvement in the divisions is to be coordinated through the division vice-president and general manager.

Concepts of Line and Staff.   The following descriptions serve to clarify the difference between line and staff:*

- *Line* refers to those functions that have a *direct responsibility* for accomplishing the end purpose of the organization.
- *Line* refers to those individuals who are *directly concerned* with producing the good or service offered by the organization.
- *Line* refers to those executives who have *operational* responsibilities.
- Line executives tend to be *generalists.*
- Line executives *make and execute decisions* related to the attainment of primary organizational objectives.
- Line management exercises explicit authority as delegated from the manager to whom he reports.

Staff, as contrasted with line, exists to advise and counsel, rather than to command. The following characteristics summarize the nature of staff:

- Staff members perform purely *advisory* functions.
- Each staff member reports to a boss who is appended to the line organization or is a member of the line organization. Therefore, there is *no pure chain of command in staff.*
- Staff members are typically technical *specialists.*

---

* Paraphrased from D. I. Cleland & W. R. King, *Management: A Systems Approach,* McGraw-Hill Book Co., N.Y., 1972, pp. 130–131.

- Staff *investigates* and supplies information and recommendations to managers who make decisions.
- Staff provides *service and functional* policy formulation, promulgation, and implementation effectiveness through the exercise of functional authority.
- Staff is an extension of the implied authority of the manager to whom he reports.
- Staff exercises implied authority through counsel, advice, etc.

In its Industrial Systems Product Line Division the Alpha Company was in the business of developing, designing, and installing computer-based management information systems for companies engaged in the operation of oil refineries. In the Consumer Products business the Alpha Company manufactured a line of small desk calculators intended primarily for home use. These calculators were distributed through wholesalers to retailers and thence to the consumers.

The nature of the market for the computer-based management information systems business required that there be a designated focal point within the Alpha Company for each contract with a customer. In the recent realignment of the Alpha Company, it was assumed that such focal point would be in the appropriate profit center.

In the concluding remarks to the members of the management council, the president asked each of the members to be prepared to discuss at the next council meeting the implications of the new organizational structure as it might affect their respective operations.

Your Task

Assume that you are one of the members of the management council. What do you think are the implications of the new management structure on your operation?

SITUATION 8:   THE CULTURAL AMBIENCE OF THE PROJECT-DRIVEN MATRIX ORGANIZATION[1]

Introduction

The term *culture* is being used more and more in the lexicon of management to describe the ambience of a business organization. The culture associated with each organization has distinctive characteristics that differentiate the company from others. At IBM the simple precept *IBM means service* sets the tone for the entire organization, infusing all aspects of its environment and generating its distinctive culture. At 3M the simple motto *Never kill a new product idea* creates an organizational atmosphere of inventiveness and creativity. In some large corporations, such as Hewlett-Packard, General Electric, and Johnson & Johnson, the crucial parts of the organization are kept small to encourage a local culture that encourages a personal touch in the context of a motivated entrepreneurial spirit of teamwork.

---

[1] This case has been adapted in part from David I. Cleland, "The Cultural Ambience of the Matrix Organization," *Management Review,* November 1981.

Understanding the culture of the organization is a prerequisite to introducing project management. An organization's culture reflects the composite management style of its executives, a style that has much to do with the organization's ability to adapt to such a change as the introduction of a project management system.

The cultural ambience found in project management influences the skills, knowledge, and value systems of the people who share an interest in the outcome of the project. These people—*The project clientele*—include the managers and professionals who share the authority and responsibility for completing the project on time and within budget. How these people feel and act in their organizational roles determines the nature of the cultural ambience that ultimately emerges.

The Situation

In a mature project-driven matrix organization, the cultural ambience that emerges is likely to have the following characteristics:

- A more open organization
- A participative management style
- Increased human problems
- Consensus decision making
- Two-boss merit evaluation
- Modified wage and salary classification
- Increased management career opportunities
- Socially acceptable adversary roles
- More organizational flexibility
- Productivity improvement
- Increased innovation
- Realignment of company supporting systems
- Development of "general manager" attitudes

Your Task

Evaluate the implications these cultural factors might have in influencing the probable success (or failure) of a firm involved in the project management business. In your evaluation consider at least the following:

1. How might the philosophy of management of the principal manager be affected by these cultural factors?
2. What adjustments, if any, would a key professional have to make upon joining an organization with these cultural factors?
3. What should be the strategy for introducing project management into an organization?
4. Would there be some people who would not fit well into an organization that had these cultural characteristics? Why or why not?
5. A shift to the matrix form is usually easier for a younger organization than for an old established organization. Why?

6. Senior management support and commitment are essential to the success of the matrix organization. Why is this so?

SITUATION 9: THE PLURAL EXECUTIVE

Introduction

The size and complexity of many contemporary organizations have led to a new phenomenon termed the *plural executive*—a permanent, formally established office composed of several individuals who, as a team, perform the functions of top management. The plural executive is a reasonable alternative to the single chief executive and performs as well as the traditional single chief executive approach. This collective style of top management in the plural executive context has many designations, "Office of the President," "Corporate Executive Office," "Management Committee," and is used by such firms as The Bounty Savings Bank, Sears, General Electric, IBM, Bendix, Westinghouse, Dow Corning, and Dupont. Benefits realized from the use of the plural executive include the strength and security of group decisions, more objectivity, continuity of management, and development of personnel. There are problems as well: to name a few—frustration over time required to make decisions, potential compromise to satisfy the team, and conflict arising out of the chemistry of the individual members.

The Situation

A large corporation in the aerospace industry faces the awesome task of managing several large projects across the company's product-group structure. The president suggested a plural executive in the form of a management council to facilitate and coordinate in part the management of these projects. The management council was also to be concerned with the coordination of corporate strategic matters across the profit-center product groups.

The CEO distributed a draft "Management Council Charter" to all senior line and staff managers in the corporation and asked for their comments in writing concerning the suitability of a management council for the corporation. The draft charter follows.

Management Council Charter

The Management Council serves as a plural executive which acts in an advisory role to the President by providing stewardship for the strategic management of the Company. The jurisdiction of the Council includes, but is not necessarily limited to, the following:

- Conducts the affairs of the Company in accordance with established guidelines and objectives as directed by the Company's Board of Directors.
- Participates in the development of a creed expressing a philosophy of manage-

ment by which the Management Council will conduct Company affairs in every area of its influence and action

- Encourages a philosophy of delegating authority to a level that is commensurate with providing most efficiently the organization required, and thereby creating a pool of managers to staff from within the expanding operations of the company.
- Monitors and reviews the development and execution of the Company's mission, objectives, goals, key projects, and key strategies.
- Participates in the management of the Company's operational performance.
- Participates in the development and propogation of a management style compatible with the strategic challenges facing the Company.
- The Council shall consist of officers reporting to the President and others appointed by the President as required. The President will appoint a Deputy Chief Executive Officer to serve as the Council's Chairperson for a period of one year.
- Members of the Management Council shall not delegate their accountability for results or for their stewardship over the affairs of the Company assigned them.

The Council will meet on the last Tuesday of every month unless it falls on a holiday at which time the meeting will be scheduled for the next workday.

Your Task

If you were a senior staff official in this corporation what written comments would you make concerning this management council idea? How would you react if you were a senior line official?

Section III
Staff Selection, Motivation, and Training[1]

The quality and quantity of the human resources support everything else in the matrix organization; organizational structure, professional and managerial roles, leader and follower style, supporting financial and information systems, and the attainment of goals, objectives, and mission of the organization.

The management of a project is a complex undertaking. This complexity is intensified if adequate resources—facilities, material, equipment, money—are not made available on a timely basis.

Without adequate people nothing works well. The quality of the human resources depends on the state of the art of the knowledge, skills, and attitudes of people in the matrix organization. Improving the quality of the human resources can lead to improvements in productivity. Executive and professional development programs and continuing education training courses can be helpful in upgrading the knowledge, skills, and attitudes of managers and professionals.

The rate of obsolescence of today's managers and professionals, due to changes in management practice and technology, can cause a company's pool of people to deteriorate unless strategies and programs are developed to counter the loss of know-how. Maintaining technical excellence is a great challenge for today's professional. Today's matrix managers are equally challenged by the changes in management theory and practice that threaten their current managerial competence. Take for example the burgeoning changes in managerial and follower style.

---

[1] Part of the material in this section has been adapted from an article by Dundar F. Kocaoglu and David I. Cleland, "RIM Process in Participative Management," *Management Review*, October 1983. Used by permission.

Style

Style refers to the distinctive manner of expression and acting of the key matrix managers and professionals that becomes characteristic of the culture of the organization. Managerial and follower style is a reflection of individual and collective knowledge, skills, and attitudes.

The culture of the matrix organization depends on the style followed by the general managers, functional managers, project managers, work package managers, and professionals. Key managers tend to develop and propagate a distinctive manner of expression and acting that becomes characteristic of the organization. Professionals tend to emulate their managers. The collective style of the professionals and managers permeates the organization and gives it a distinctive culture.

Matrix management's culture is a social expression manifest within the organization when it is engaged in managing projects. The culture is likely to have the following characteristics: organizational openness, participation, consensus decision making, acceptable adversary roles, organizational flexibility, the development of general manager attitudes, and managerial roles that are more facilitative than directive. Project management has thoroughly tested traditional managerial styles and has become the forerunner of a powerful management movement in America. A brief look at what is happening in managerial theory and practice gives some insight into the contributions that project management has made in providing a leading edge to a change in management theory.

A new family of managerial/organizational approaches now coming into prominence promises to break with the rigidity and formality of the past. It is difficult to put a single name on what is happening. Some call this movement *quality of life programs;* others call it a *work innovation movement.* Whatever it is called, the end result is a greater degree of manager-employee participation than many old timers can recall. The underlying principle behind this movement is that all employees can truly participate in helping to manage the affairs of the organization. This has been recognized in participative-based strategies, project teams, task force management, and "self-autonomous" production teams for a long time. Today's fascination with these and similar techniques confirms the old saw: *Nothing is more powerful than an idea* whose time has come.

The growing popularity of these participation techniques makes it clear that the managers at all levels will have to discover new ways to become leaders in the facilitation of an environment whereby people can work together with economic and social satisfaction. Those managers who cannot deal with in-depth discussions on their individual and collective roles in the matrix organization in a context of sharing decisions, rewards, and reults will find themselves losing the race between obsolescence and retirement. The impor-tance this can have is illustrated in the statement of one senior corporate executive:

> Many Westinghouse executives will have trouble adapting to this new arrange-ment, [matrix management] which requires considerable interaction and consen-sus decision-making at all levels. Danforth has told the company's top 220 managers that "some of you will adjust and survive, and some of you won't.[2]

Yet many managers (fortunately a diminishing number) still believe their principal job is to exercise "supervision" over the people who "work for" them.

The word *supervision*—the act of overseeing subordinates—is an interesting word. Breaking the word into two parts gives *super* and *vision*. Presumably one who is a supervisor exercises *super vision* over subordinates. In today's complex and dynamic organizations there are limits to the amount of supervi-sion that one can exercise. Each supervisor is dependent on the technical and detailed knowledge of the specialists who are working for him. Though the supervisor is able to judge the effectiveness with which organizational goals and objectives are accomplished, many of the detailed intricacies of how those goals and objectives are accomplished are simply beyond the time and depth of understanding of the manager. In a project-driven matrix system, a manager who knows his limitations in fully exercising "supervision" and his dependence on the people on the project team can develop a broader organizational philosophy in which team members plan and schedule their work, participate in the design of their jobs, and assist in the management of the peer group with which they work to produce results.

From a sociological viewpoint a management culture develops from the social and intellectual patterns within a group of people having a degree of common purpose, goals, language, customs, mores, and traditions. In its organizational context, cultural ambience for project management deals with the social expression manifest in the participants engaged in managing proj-ects. Within such organizations a management style emerges that reflects certain behavioral patterns characteristic of the members of that organization. Such behavioral characteristics influence the attitudes and the modus operandi of the key people. A project management organizational society is made up of many participants in different organizational roles. Superiors, subordi-nates, peers, associates—all working together to bring a project to completion. The management style that ultimately emerges is dependent upon the way participants feel and act within the matrix organizational environment.

---

[2] Hugh D. Menzies, "Westinghouse Takes Aim at the World," *Fortune,* January 14, 1980.

Even if the matrix managers do all these things well, success is not ensured. But if these things are done, the chances for success are greatly enhanced. The development of a cultural ambience that supports participative management requires a long time, perhaps years, to develop. Such a culture is essential to success in project management. Like a favorite rose garden, such a culture requires frequent tending.

The successful introduction and implementation of matrix management into an organization takes patience—time for the people to understand the systems change that has occurred. Some people may never be able to adjust to the unstructured, democratic ambience of the matrix culture. A strong educational effort is needed to acquaint key managers and professionals with the theory and practice of matrix management. Time should be taken to do this right at the start, using the existing culture as a point of departure.

The project manager plays many roles; a key role is as a team leader and motivator. A project manager works through and for others as he performs his managerial role. Consequently he needs to understand the forces that motivate the individual in the workplace. To motivate members of the project team is to stimulate them to action. Team members are motivated by a wide variety of stimuli. There are some factors that seem to have an influence in motivating project team members to action and thought—to do something in support of the project objectives, goals, and strategies.

Finally, staffing in matrix needs tends to vary; both the quantity and quality of personnel needed in the organization are difficult to estimate because of the varying needs of the ongoing projects, as these projects go through their life cycle.

The following cases and situations deal with the human resource side of matrix management.

RELEVANT BIBLIOGRAPHY

Adams, John R., and Stephen E. Barndt. "Behavioral Implications of the Project Life Cycle." In *Project Management Handbook,* edited by D. I. Cleland and W. R. King. Van Nostrand Reinhold Co., New York, 1983, p. 222.

———, and Nicki S. Kirchof. "A Training Technique For Developing Project Managers," *Project Management Quarterly,* March 1983, pp. 81-89.

Butler, Arthur G., Jr. "Behavioral Implications for Professional Employees of Structural Conflict Associated with Project Management in Functional Organizations." University of Florida, 1969, *Business Administration.*

Cooper, M. R., B. S. Morgan, P. M. Foley, and L. B. Kaplan. "Changing Employee Values: Deepending Discontent." *Harvard Business Review,* January–February 1979.

Dunne, Edward J., Jr., Michael J. Stahl, and Leonard J. Melhart, Jr. "Influence Sources of Project and Functional Managers in Matrix Organizations." *Academy of Management Journal,* March, 1978, pp. 135-140.

Gunz, Hugh P., and Alan Pearson. "How to Manage Control Conflicts in Project Based Organizations." *Research Management,* vol. 22, March 1979.

Hammerton, James C. "Management and Motivation." *California Management Review,* vol. XIII, no. 2, Winter 1970.

Hanan, Mack. "Make Way for the New Organization Man." *Harvard Business Review,* July–August 1971.

Hill, Raymond E. "Managing the Human Side of Project Teams." In *Project Management Handbook,* edited by D. I. Cleland and W. R. King. Van Nostrand Reinhold Co., New York, 1983, p. 581.

Hodgetts, Richard M. "Leadership Techniques in the Project Organization." *Academy of Management Journal,* June 1968.

Hollingsworth, A. T., Bruce M. Meglino, and Michael C. Shaner. "Copies with Team Trauma." *Management Review,* August 1979.

Labovitz, George H. "Managing Conflict." *Business Horizons,* June 1980.

Lee, James A. "Behavioral Theory versus Reality." *Harvard Business Review,* March–April 1971.

McGregor, Douglas. *The Human Side of Enterprise.* McGraw-Hill Book Co., New York, 1960.

Mills, D. Q. "Human Resources in the 1980s." *Harvard Business Review,* July–August 1979.

Reeser, Clayton. "Some Potential Human Problems of the Project Form of Organization." *Academy of Management Journal,* vol. 12, December 1979.

Sashkin, Marshall. *A Manager's Guide to Participative Management.* American Management Association, New York, 1982.

Slevin, Dennis P. "Motivation and the Project Manager," In *Project Management Handbook,* edited by D. I. Cleland and W. R. King. Van Nostrand Reinhold Co., New York, 1983, p. 552.

———. "Leadership and the Project Manager." In *Project Management Handbook,* edited by D. I. Cleland and W. R. King. Van Nostrand Reinhold Co., New York, 1983, p. 567.

Thamhain, Hans J., and Gary R. Gemmill. "Influence Styles of Project Managers: Some Project Performance Correlates." *Academy of Management Journal,* vol. 17, no. 2, June 1974.

———, and David L. Wilemon. "Leadership, Conflict, and Program Management Effectiveness." *Sloan Management Review,* Fall, 1977.

Thornbery, Neal E., and Joseph R. Weintraub. "The Project Manager: What It Takes To Be A Good One." *Project Management Quarterly,* March 1983, pp. 73-76

CASE STUDY 19:   THE PROFESSIONAL IN MATRIX MANAGEMENT[1]

Introduction

The introduction of matrix management starts to change the prevailing culture of an organization. One of the first changes perceived by the discerning professional is the multiple authority-responsibility-accountability relationships that evolve. Such patterns cause the professional to be concerned about the following:

- Who's my boss?
- Who rates me?
- Who's responsible for my professional development?

[1] Adapted from David I. Cleland, "The Professional in Matrix Management," paper presented at Project Management Institute 14th Annual Seminar/Symposium, October 4-6, 1982, Toronto, Ontario, Canada, and from Dundar F. Kocaoglu and David I. Cleland, "RIM Process in Participative Management," *Management Review,* October 1983.

- Who's my administrator?
- Who provides me with logistical support?
- What will matrix management do to my career?

When an individual has the first contact with matrix management, early frustrations can result. The fluidity of matrix management where planning, organizing, and control are carried out by mutual adjustment and informal communication, creates a need for the professionals to work together more than ever. Conflicting directives, uncoordinated activities, territorial battles, professional jealousies, interpersonal strife, role ambiguities, and many more dysfunctions are likely to be perceived by the professional in first perceptions of matrix management. If this professional has been schooled in the traditional management notion that "one person shall have but one boss" early perceptions of matrix management may create deep feelings of frustration that no person really is in charge and looking out for the best interests of the individual. If the key managers in the organization have not provided insight, through some form of organizational development, as to how the matrix is supposed to operate, matrix management can become the basis for some real human problems. As an executive vice president stated:

> A matrix is hard on people—most seem to find it so. In a recent employee attitude survey at a large industrial complex that was matrixed (or whatever the verb is) 15-20 years ago, the matrix organization drew the least favorable reaction on the whole survey. Analysis of the responses showed that the reaction was pretty much shared by all levels. The concerns were mostly personal, rather than objective—what happens to me and my career, what team do I belong to, how do I identify with the goals and successes of the enterprise, does anybody really know whether I'm doing a good job??? Partly these concerns are geared to "bigness," but the people mostly ascribe them to the matrix and its inherent ambiguities—and so do I. So it becomes top priority for top management, especially top management of a matrix organization, to understand and address the issues in the people dimension.[2]

Much of the concern that the professional has centers on an understanding of the key roles in the matrix.

Matrix Organizational Roles

The cornerstone managerial roles in the matrix organization are depicted in Figure 1. The professional has a reciprocal relationship with the people filling these roles. Although each manager has responsibility for a particular management territory, there must be a sharing of key decisions, results, and rewards. The relative roles of the principals in Figure 1 can be summarized as follows:

---

[2] "Matrix Management: The General Manager's Perspective," by John W. Stuntz, in *Matrix Management Systems Handbook,* David I. Cleland (editor), Van Nostrand Reinhold Co., New York, 1982.

General Manager: The chief architect of organizational strategy in the development of objectives and goals against which organizational performance is judged.

Functional Manager: The individual responsible for building and maintaining a base of specialized resources to support organizational objectives and goals.

Project Manager: Responsible for project results, the accomplishment of project objectives on time and within budget.

Work Package Manager: That individual responsible for developing and supporting work packages in the organization.

The Professional: The individual who has assured competence in a particular field or occupation essential to support organizational purposes.

Given that these overall organizational roles have been established, what personal changes does the professional need to be concerned about to work effectively in matrix management?

Personal Changes

The individual working in matrix management will find it necessary to develop new *knowledge, skills,* and *attitudes.*

New knowledge of the theory and practice of matrix management in its alternative forms is a prerequisite to accepting the change that the matrix environment brings about. A key element of matrix management that the professional must understand is the basic dichotomy of the matrix organization: the project manager who is responsible for *results*—bringing the project in on time, within budget, and satisfying the project objectives—and the functional managers who are responsible for providing

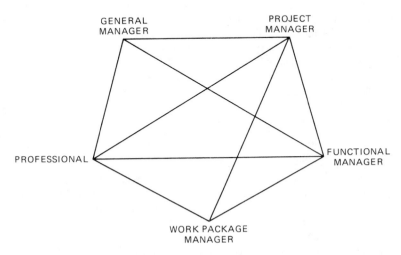

Figure 1.   Key Individuals in the Matrix Organization.

the *resources*. A knowledge of the interdependent authority-responsibility-accountability of these managers can do much to understand the two-boss situation that is endemic to matrix management.

Additional knowledge that the individual needs to acquire includes how planning and control are carried out in the matrix environment, how authority-responsibility-accountability patterns evolve, and how motivation and negotiation are critical to successful matrix management.

New skills are required—the greatest of all is the ability to develop and maintain interpersonal competence. Things happen in matrix management more by the strength of the individual's personality than by the formal, delegated authority of the office the individual holds. No one person has exclusive rights to leadership in matrix management. The leadership role is fluid—the professional has the opportunity to lead when a particular competence is needed to make or to facilitate the making of decisions. When the individual takes advantage of the many opportunities to provide temporary leadership in matrix management, that person is undergoing excellent on-the-job training for general or functional management. The temporary leader can test leadership knowledge and skills without making a commitment to a key management role before being ready.

The development and maintenance of a set of attitudes supportive of matrix management may be the most important attribute for the professional to acquire. A description of these attitudes rings much of "motherhood," yet that is the real world of matrix. Trust and confidence within the community of managers and professionals who work together as a team is characteristic of effective matrix organizations. A professional soon learns that a commitment to the project objectives and strategies through the project team is a personal thing that has nothing to do with organizational charts, policies, and procedures. Only the individual can make that commitment. A state of mind that recognizes the legitimacy and rationale of the matrix way of doing things is essential to successful project management. People work together so closely in matrix that it is impossible to hide anything. A professional's poor performance is soon evident for all to see. The peer group demands disciplined performance. The professional who lacks integrity, who malingers, who is not a team member, or who just cannot handle the job will simply be forced out of the matrix team.

The development of the new knowledge, skills, and attitudes on the part of the professional is greatly facilitated if individual and collective roles in the organization are properly developed and understood. The use of linear responsibility charting (LRC) can provide a methodology for defining such roles.

Linear Responsibility Charting*

If a manager were to coach a football team, he would doubtlessly take great care to define the role of each player. After a player's role was defined, then the coach would work with the team to develop supportive roles among the players to facilitate the group strategy necessary to win. The roles would be built around specific territories that each player would cover. Each member of the team would expect to practice until he fully understood his role and he was committed to that role. If a role was not fully understood or if a player was not committed to a particular role, more

---

* See pp. 222–224 for a discussion of the LRC in the context of a project team.

practice would be required until the degree of understanding and commitment necessary to develop a winning team existed.

No coach would think of putting a football team on the field without definition and much practice. Yet many managers put a matrix management team on the field with inadequate role definitions. I believe most managers do this because they do not have or do not use an available hands-on pragmatic methodology for defining individual and reciprocal roles.

The use of a position description to describe what a professional does is useful—and usually necessary for wage and salary classification. Unfortunately job descriptions by themselves too often are written only to give a professional responsibility for a specific area of work. Such a description does not describe how the professional is to work in supporting other roles in the organization. As the position description emphasizes only the jurisdiction of authority and responsibility, it is all too often interpreted to imply property rights over a specific territory of the organization. Frequently this property right is exercised as a fiefdom right by the professional. Protection of the territory of the fiefdom becomes more important than working as a member of a matrix management team. Overprotection leads to the development of shortcomings in how the professionals work together as a supportive team.

These shortcomings can be alleviated by the use of linear responsibility charting (LRC)—a methodology for developing individual and collective managerial roles in carrying out the work of an organization. Six key elements make up the form and process of an LRC:

- An organizational position
- An element of work—a *work package*—that must be accomplished to support organizational objectives, goals, and strategies
- An organizational interface point—a common boundary of action between an organizational position and a work package
- A legend for describing the specificity of the organizational interface
- A procedure for designing, developing, and operating LRCs for an organization
- A commitment and dedication on the part of the members of the organization to make the LRC process work

Table 1 portrays the first four elements of an LRC. These elements are described below.

1. The organizational position on the LRC is simply a position taken from the traditional organizational chart and put into the columns of the LRC. In Table 1 these positions are:

- Operations center
- Contract management
- Finance & administration
- Profit centers (divisions)
- Marketing & strategic planning
- Management council (the plural executive composed of the key managers in the organization. This plural executive deals with key strategic and operational matters in the organization)

Table 1. Linear Responsibility Chart.

(2) Work Packages	(1) Operations Center	(1) Contract Management	(1) Finance & Admin.	(1) Profit Center Division	(1) Profit Center Division	(1) Marketing & Strat. Plan.	(1) Management Council
	(3)	(3)	(3)	(3)	(3)	(3)	(3)
	etc.	etc.	etc.	etc.	etc.	etc.	etc.

(1) Organizational Positions (Functions)

(2) Work Packages

(3) Interface Points—the heart of the LRC and the organization

2. The work package reflected on the lines of the LRC is an element of work the accomplishment of which involves the utilization of resources (time, materials, funds, etc.) and leads to the accomplishment of a mission, objective, or goal in the organization. Work packages exist vertically (within a functional specialty) and horizontally, i.e., between functional specialities. The total work in the organization is continually broken down into smaller and smaller units until the level of the lowest definable individual task is reached. The concept of the work package is consistent with authority and responsibility principles, in that authority should be delegated to the lowest level in the organization with someone responsible for the organizational matter that has been delegated.

Through the use of a work package an individual can be held accountable for a specific matter in the organization as that matter relates to that person's job. When work packages are developed for a person's job, with that person's active participation, standards for evaluating an individual's performance exist. The management functions of planning, motivating, directing, and controlling within the context of that person's job is more meaningful and effective. That person knows—as does his supervisor— what is expected by way of contribution to the organization's mission, objectives, and goals. Communication is facilitated simply because the members of the organization understand their roles and how these roles relate, *in specific terms,* to other organizational roles. The nature of the work packages depend on the mission of the organization. Table 2 portrays an excerpt from an LRC for employee relations in a matrix organization.

3. The heart of the LRC is the interface points at the intersections of the organizational positions and the work packages. Both vertical and horizontal, these interface points are where the action is carried out that makes the organization function effectively. The vertical interface points portray the hierarchical levels in a larger work package. (For example, in Figure 1, a summation of the vertical interface points gives a view of the work packages involved in an organizational position—a work breakdown structure of that position.) The horizontal interface points show a work package related to supporting organizational positions. The specificity of these interface points is described through the use of a legend.

4. The legend simply describes *who does what with respect to the work package* at the interface point. There are several alternative ways of describing what goes on at the interface point. A typical summary legend with accompanying definitions is described at the bottom of Table 2.

The legend and the definitions portray a complex of people (and work package) relationships centering on the nature of the work to be accomplished; the legend and accompanying definitions must be agreed to by all persons who are participating in the development of the chart. A discussion of the nature of the legends is presented below.

    a. *Primary Responsibility (P)*—Has prime authority and responsibility for accomplishment of the work package. Someone must assume leadership for the work package to see that the work is accomplished on time, is within budget, and meets performance standards. The person who has primary responsibility is "it" for doing what needs to be done. Primary responsibility (P) normally includes work is done (W), and approval (A).

Table 2. Linear Responsibility Chart.

Work Packages	Operations Center	Contract Management	Finance & Admin.	PL Division	PL Division	Marketing & Strat. Plan.	Management Council
Sales Prospecting				P		I	
Prosposal Preparation	I	O, W	P, I		I		
Present Bid to Customer				P			

Legend:

(P) Primary Responsibility – The prime authority and responsibility for accomplishment of work package.

(R) Review – Reviews key output of work package.

(N) Notification – Is notified of key output of work package.

(A) Approval – Approves work package.

(O) Output – Receives key output of work package.

(I) Input – Provides key input to work package.

(W) Work is Done – Accomplishes actual labor of work package.

P includes W
P includes A
A includes R
unless otherwise specified

b. *Review (R)*—Reviews key output of the work package. This individual reviews the quality and quantity of the work package to determine if predetermined standards have been met, e.g., a quality control specialist reviews certain output of a production line. A financial executive reviews the financial credibility of a bid price on a proposal submitted to a customer. The review is carried out to obtain certain input to enable the reviewer to accomplish his job in some part of the organization.

c. *Notification (N)*—Receives notice of key output of the work package. This legend is used to indicate that an organizational position is to be notified of something involving the work package. The individual occupying that position judges whether or not any action should be taken as a result of this notification. For example, the sales department might notify the contract management of an intent to bid on a proposed request for a proposal.

d. *Approval (A)*—Approves work package. When an authentication of a work package is required, this legend is used. For example, the approval of a capital project by the chief executive officer for a corporation. Approval (A) always includes review (R) unless otherwise stipulated.

e. *Output (O)*—Receives key output of the work package. The recipient of the output of the work package takes the output and integrates it into the work being accomplished in the recipient's organizational position. For example, the contract administration officer receives an advance copy of an engineering change, so that the effect of that change on the terms and conditions of a project contract could be determined by the contract administrator.

f. *Input (I)*—Provides key input to the work package. To complete a work package, input is required from different positions in the organization. For example, for a merit salary increase, the results of an employee performance review would have to be provided to the employee relations office. The manager of employee relations would then forward appropriate documentation to the finance office for notation on the employee's pay records.

g. *Work is Done (W)*—Accomplishes the actual labor of the work package. This legend is used when it is desired to accomplish the work in an organizational position other than where primary responsibility resides. For example, responsibility for the preparation of a project proposal would normally reside in the sales manager with the physical preparation of the proposal accomplished by central publications of the organization.

When roles are defined through the use of an LRC little is left to change. The professional has a better chance of understanding his individual role and the relationships with:

- The supervisor
- The subordinates
- The peer group

Figure 2 illustrates these relationships in the context of authority, responsibility, and accountability tied together by the work package.

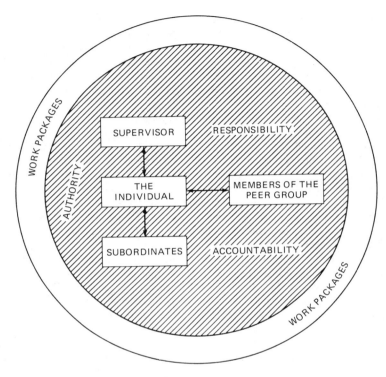

Figure 2.

The Importance of Role Definition

The use of an LRC process helps the individual to understand better the specific responsibility that is expected in the performance of his role in the organization. Each work package has an individual designated who has primary responsibility for planning and executing the work package. Other individuals who have some collateral responsibility involving the work package are also identified. When these collective roles have been identified there remains "no place to hide in the organization." If the work package is not being completed on time or does not meet the performance standard that has been established for the work, someone can be identified who is responsible. Responsibility, authority, and accountability—the triad of personal performance in organized life—is not left to doubt when the LRC process is used in organizations.

Many problems in matrix organizations can be traced to an important oversight: someone failed to clarify roles of the team. Who does what? Who works for whom? As a result of this failure, much psychological and social energy is tied up trying to determine or avoid responsibility and authority or trying to seize more power in the organization. When roles are not adequately defined, the inevitable power struggles and conflicts that develop tie up a lot of the time and energy of people. Conflicts that are not confronted in the organization may be played out in indirect and destructive ways.

Professionals tend to relate to each other as members of a community having similar interests. When a matrix organization has a staff of professionals who can work together in supporting a common purpose, shared accountability results. Professional roles are blurred as they work together as a team in formulating plans and strategies to support project objectives. Being a project team member helps each individual to perform duties more astutely, because there is more of an opportunity to work with interdisciplinary peers, rather than just through the discipline of the functional entity. The resulting teamwork is tied together in a sharing context of decision making, results, and accountability. Within such a context the individual has more visibility to be heard and to influence the course of events in the organization. As the professional grapples with decisions as a member of the project team, that individual begins to think and act somewhat as a general manager, as well as a functional specialist. The individual who is not a contributor is soon found out and will not be around for long. Peer pressure will sort out the nonperformers; those who survive find that the increased contacts with peers in different disciplines, managers, and other contributing personnel enhance career opportunities. The demands on the individual to improve interpersonal skills and communication abilities are many—but worth the effort for those professionals whose roles have been defined.

Summary

The introduction of matrix management changes the prevailing culture of the organization. One of the first changes perceived by the discerning professional is the multiple authority-responsibility-accountability patterns that evolve in the matrix organization. The fluidity of the matrix organization is often a puzzlement to the professional. Conflicting directives, uncoordinated activities, territorial battles, professional jealousies, interpersonal strife, role ambiguities, and many other dysfunctional influences may be perceived by the professional in first experiences in the matrix organization. Such perceptions may be factual or imaginative, but can create substantive human problems depending on the reality of the situation.

Adequate definition of individual and collective roles is critical to personal satisfaction and mission accomplishment in the matrix organization. When the professional participates in the development of these roles, improved organizational effectiveness will result.

Questions

1. What are some other terms that might be used to depict the interface points in a linear responsibility chart?
2. How might a traditional organizational chart be used with LRC?
3. Many traditional organization charts have dotted lines to describe an organizational relationship. What do these dotted lines mean?

4. What are the advantages of the LRC over the traditional organization chart?
5. Work breakdown structuring precedes the development of an LRC. Do you agree with this statement? Why or why not?
6. The process of developing the LRC may be more important than the completed LRC. Do you agree with this statement? Why or why not?
7. Participative management and LRCs have something in common. What is it?
8. Assume that the organization from which Table 2 is taken is an aerospace firm. What are some additional work packages that would be appropriate to project management in such an enterprise?
9. Some managers resist the development of an LRC for their organization. What are some of the possible reasons for such resistance?
10. In the final analysis organizational roles must be identified, negotiated, and resolved for both individuals and organizational teams. Do you agree with this statement? Why or why not?

SITUATION 10:   PROJECT MANAGER CANDIDATE SPECIFICATIONS[1]

Develop a profile of a project manager's ideal *characteristics* and *modus operandi.*

The Situation

As a result of "the need for enhanced effectiveness and productivity," project management is being introduced in your organization, and you have just been appointed a project manager.

Your chief executive has informed his entire organization that each manager should make any or all of his people available to staff the new management system. The chief executive also stated that as a project manager, each of you will determine and communicate *specifically* what you are looking for (background, experience, personal style, potential, energy level, human resources capabilities, etc.) in your new position. You agree with your employee relations manager's suggestion that a position candidate specification should be documented and must be easily communicated and "defendable, meaning obviously related to the work which must be done."

In developing the list of specifications, it has occurred to you that because the work of project management is to complement the contribution of other functions, then specifications for these functions might also need to be reconsidered.

Your Small Work Group Task

As a group, after considering work content, define a set of candidate specifications for an assumed project manager position, to be used in staffing your project management system.

---

[1] Source: *Systems Analysis and Project Management,* 3rd edition, by David I. Cleland and William R. King, McGraw-Hill Book Co., New York, 1983. Used by permission.

Have a representative for your small work group present your findings.

SITUATION 11: PROJECT MANAGEMENT ROLES[1]

The Situation

Table 3 lists a series of roles with supporting definitions that can be used to describe what a project manager does in a project management situation. One way of classifying these roles is

1. Primary (P)
2. Supportive (S)

Place a P or S in each column segment to appropriately describe the role or roles each of the managers carries out. If you think a manager does not carry out a particular role, leave that column blank.

Be prepared to defend your team's choice of roles.

Have the team leader present your findings.

Table 3.   Role of the Key Managers in Project Management.

Role & Definition	Project Manager	General Manager	Work Package Mgr	Chief Executive	Resource Facilitations Manager
TECHNOLOGIST—Provides leadership to establish technical (engineering, production, finance, etc.) objectives, goals and strategies					
AGENT—Represents and acts for another in a transaction					
NEGOTIATOR—Arranges an agreement on an issue					
LOGISTICIAN—Produces, distributes, maintains, and replaces human and nonhuman resources for the organization					
STRATEGIST—Uses science and art in the development of a sense of future direction for an organization					

[1] David I. Cleland and William R. King, *Systems Analysis and Project Management,* 3rd edition, McGraw-Hill Book Co., New York, 1983. Used by permission.

Table 3.   Role of the Key Managers in Project Management.

Role & Definition	Project Manager	General Manager	Work Package Mgr	Chief Executive	Resource Facili-tations Manager
COUNSELLOR—Participates in an exchange of opinions and ideas and provides advice and guidance					
DISCIPLINARIAN—Enforces organizational policies and procedures and keeps the organization on the most promising path toward objectives					
MOTIVATOR—Provides an environment whereby people attain social, psychological, and economic satisfaction in their work					
ORGANIZER—Organizes human and nonhuman resources					
DECISION MAKER—Chooses the alternative that the organization will follow					
FIGUREHEAD—Represents the organization in all matters of formality					
LEADER—Leads people along a way					
LIAISON OFFICER—Interacts with peers and "systems" community to gain favors for the organization					
MONITOR—Receives and collects information that permits an understanding of the organization					
DISSEMINATOR—Distributes information					
SPOKESMAN—Disseminates organization information in the environment					
ENTREPRENEUR/INNOVATOR—Initiates change in the organization					
DISTURBANCE HANDLER—Takes charge when the organization is threatened					
SUBORDINATE—Receives direction from a superior in the organization					

Table 3.   Role of the Key Managers in Project Management.

Role & Definition	Project Manager	General Manager	Work Package Mgr	Chief Executive	Resource Facili- tations Manager
CONTROLLER—Establishes standards and judges results					
COORDINATOR—Synchronizes activities with respect to time and place					
TEACHER—One whose purpose is to instruct					
OTHER?					

SITUATION 12: PROJECT MANAGEMENT "MAGNA CARTA"

Purpose

To develop a Magna Carta for Project Management within a profit center division.

Situation

For project management to operate successfully within a profit center division, a basic overall document establishing the legitimate role of project management should be developed. This document—a Magna Carta—should deal with a basic enumeration of authority and responsibility of the people who must work together in the matrix organization.

Your Task

Develop a document for a division. Some items you might wish to consider in developing this document include:

authority of managers in one function vis-à-vis other functional managers
role of top management (profit center manager)
the profit center's cultural ambience
the project-functional interface
resolution of project-functional conflicts
responsibilities of general manager, functional managers, manager of projects, and project manager

Section IV
The Execution of Projects[1]

The act or process of executing action in managing projects is largely where ultimate success or failure of the project is determined. The design, development, and execution of a matrix management system require a philosophy that conceptualizes the totality of its elements. In the project-driven matrix the project objective becomes the leading element for the entire system to support the organizational mission. But necessary to the effectiveness of the system and intrinsic to its philosophy is the ability to synergize all the system's elements. This section examines the several synergistic elements of project-driven matrix management and their importance in the successful execution of projects.

The conceptual model of Figure 1 shows these elements. The figure represents an operationally useful way of describing the totality of the matrix system. An understanding of its elements and their interrelationships is essential in developing a philosophy for the execution of projects.

There are hierarchical relationships among these elements that naturally occur when an organizational mission is designated. But interaction and interdependency link the elements together in such complex ways that actions taking place in any element can produce far-reaching reverberations within the matrix management system. Once the project-oriented company assumes a mission, each of the projects supporting that mission will have specific financial, schedule, and technical performance objectives. And the degree to which the organizational mission is accomplished depends on the synergistic effectiveness of all the elements that follow: project objectives, goals, strategies, organizational structure and roles, style, and resources.

In this section we will discuss the organizational mission, project objectives, goals, and project team roles.

---

[1] Material in this section paraphrased from David I. Cleland, "Pyramiding Project Management Productivity," paper presented at Project Management Institute Seminar/Symposium, Houston, Texas, October 1983.

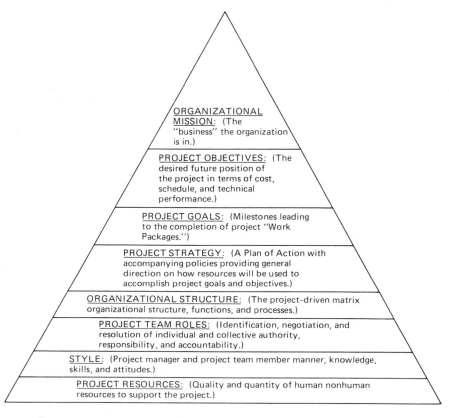

Figure 1.   Elements in the Project–Driven Matrix Management System.

Organizational Mission

At the apex of our triangular model is the organization's mission, the culminating strategic point of all organizational activity. An organization's mission is the most general strategic choice that must be made by its managers. An organization's mission tells what it is, why it exists, and the unique contribution it can make. The organization's mission answers the basic question: "What business are we in?" One project-oriented firm defined its mission as: "We are in the business of designing, developing, and installing energy management systems and services for a domestic, nonresidential market."

Organizations that consciously consider, choose, and continually review their mission, or basic "business," have a better chance to survive and prosper.

Such a mission becomes a symbol on which all effort in the organization is focused. The mission of an organization should provide the driving force to design suitable implementation strategies. Unfortuantely many project organizations do have a concept of their mission, but fail to develop a comprehensive strategy for the consumption of resources to accomplish that mission. They fail to "work" the organization down through the successive levels of the model depicted in Figure 1. Herein lies one of the difficulties of managing in matrix—the failure to recognize and deal with the "systems effects" of matrix management.

Project Objectives

While the mission of an organization is the common thread that binds together the resources and activities of an organization, a *project objective* designates the future positions or destinations that it wishes to reach in its "projects" business. Project objectives are the end result of managing the financial, schedule, and technical performance work packages of the project in consonance with the project plan. The accomplishment of project objectives contributes directly to the mission of the organization. This contribution can be measured. The proper selection and management of project objectives are essential steps in the strategic management of the organization. Such objectives are the building blocks of the project management organization's mission. Project objectives are supported by project goals.

Project Goals

The distinctive features of project goals are their specificity and measurements on time-based points that the project team intends to meet in pursuit of its project objectives. For instance, in the management of a project, the completion of a work package in the project work breakdown structure means that progress has been made toward the objective of delivering the project on time, within budget, and in satisfaction of its operational objectives.

Mission, objectives, and goals are the triad of organizational direction. But this triad is not enough. The execution of organizational resources in support of this triad is contained in the project strategies.

Within a matrix organization, the performance of both individual and collective roles plays an important part in maintaining the organizational balance. All too often when roles are inadequately defined, they jeopardize an effective system and style in an organization. In the next few paragraphs we briefly present a technique for defining and negotiating roles in organizations.

Project Team Roles

The structure of an organization defines the major territories that are assigned to each manager. Within each territory—production, finance, marketing, and so forth, specific roles require identification and negotiation, particularly in terms of the interaction of individuals with peers, subordinates, and supervisors. Figure 2 illustrates the interdependencies that exist among the individuals. To be effective, each one must understand how to work with the others. These role-interrelationships come to focus through work packages and are held together by accepted authority, responsibility, and accountability of the project management team. Work packages are major work elements at the hierarchical levels of the work breakdown structure within the organization or within a project. They are used to identify and control work flows in the organization and have the following characteristics:

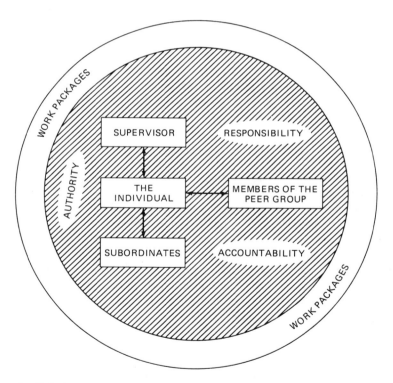

Figure 2.   Role Interdependencies. (Dundar F. Kocaoglu and David I. Cleland, "RIM Process in Participative Management," *Management Review*, October 1983. Used by Permission.)

1. A work package represents a discrete unit of work at the appropriate level of the work breakdown structure (WBS) where work is assigned.
2. Each work package is clearly distinguished from all other work packages.
3. The primary responsibility of completing the work package on schedule and within budget can always be assigned to a member of the project team and never to more than one organizational unit.
4. A work package can be integrated with other work packages at the same level of the WBS to support the work packages at a higher level of the WBS.

Work packages are level-dependent, becoming increasingly more general at each higher level of the WBS and increasingly more specific at each lower level. A general manager would be expected to have primary responsibility to set project objectives where a contract manager would be expected to take the lead in corporate maintenance agreements for a profit center manager to use in supporting equipment that has been delivered to a customer. An individual is designated as having primary responsibility for each work package. Others who have collateral responsibility involving the work package are also designated. When these collective roles have been designated there remains no place to hide in the organization. If the work package is not completed on time or does not meet the performance standards, someone can readily be identified and held responsible and accountable for that work. Responsibility, authority, and accountability—the triad of personal performance in organized life—is not left to doubt when individual and collective roles have been adequately defined. This definition can be carried out through the process of Linear Responsibility Charting (LRC).[2]

LRC is a valuable tool as a succinct description of organizational interfaces. It conveys more information than several pages of job descriptions and policy documents by delineating the authority/responsibility relationships and specifying the accountability of each organizational position. However, by far the most important aspect of LRC is the process through which the people on the project team prepare it. If LRC is developed in an autocratic fashion by the project manager, it simply becomes a document portraying the organizational relationships. On the other hand, if it is prepared through a participative process with the project team members, the final output becomes secondary to the impacts of the process itself. The open communications, broad discussions, resolution of conflicts, and the achievement of consensus through

---

[2] The concept of the LRC process has been defined elsewhere in the literature. For instance, see Chapter 11 in Cleland and King, *Systems Analysis and Project Management,* 3rd edition, McGraw-Hill Book Co., New York, 1983.

participation provide a solid basis for project team development and team harmony.

By the time LRC is developed this way, the team goes through such an education that the chart becomes secondary. Because their vested interests are amplified by the participative process in understanding their role, team members subscribe to the ideas behind LRC and protect its integrity. And the understanding of roles in the project-driven matrix organization is of prime importance. For instance, at the innovation-oriented culture at Intel Corporation, control of the sprawling organization is accomplished with a matrix management system that gives managers multiple bosses, each with specialized functions. Apparently this kind of system can be overextended. *Business Week* posits that although the matrix system worked well when the company was smaller, it has been strained by Intel's growth. And former employees say that uncertainty was caused by people *not understanding the (role) relationships* in this large and complex organization.[3]

The following cases and situations portray the forces and factors involved in the execution of projects and other forms of matrix.

RELEVANT BIBLIOGRAPHY

Archibald, Russell D. *Managing High-Technology Programs and Projects.* John Wiley & Sons, New York, 1976.

Butler, Arthur G., Jr. "Project Management—Its Functions and Dysfunctions." In *Project Mangement Handbook,* edited by D.I. Cleland and W.R. King. Van Nostrand Reinhold Co., New York, 1983, p. 59.

Cascino, Anthony E. "How One Company Adapted Matrix Management in a Crisis." *Management Review,* November 1979, pp. 57–61.

Cathey, Paul. "Matrix Method Builds New Management Muscle at ESB." *Iron Age,* June 20, 1977.

Cleland, David I. "Pyramiding Project Management Productivity," paper presented at Project Management Institute Seminar/Symposium, Houston, Texas, October 1983.

Colvin, Geoffrey. "The Astonishing Growth of DEC." *Fortune,* May 3, 1982, pp. 93–96.

Devore, Tim, James K. McCollum, and William N. Ledbetter. "Project Engineering in a Plant Environment." *Project Management Quarterly,* September 1982, pp. 25–30.

Drucker, Peter F. "New Templates for Today's Organizations." *Harvard Business Review,* January–February 1974.

George, William W. "Task Teams for Rapid Growth." *Harvard Business Review,* March–April 1977.

Gray, J.L. "Matrix Organizational Design as a Vehicle for Effective Delivery of Public Health Care and Social Services." *Management International Review,* 1974/6.

Harrison, F.L. *Advanced Project Management.* Gower Publishing Co. Ltd., Hants, England, 1983.

Herbert, T.T., and R.W. Estes. "Improving Executive Decisions by Formalizing Dissent: The Corporate Devil's Advocate." *Academy of Management Review,* October 1977.

"How to Stop the Buck Short of the Top." *Business Week,* January 17, 1978, pp. 82–83.

"Kaiser Aluminum Flattens Its Layers of Brass." *Business Week,* February 24, 1973.

---

[3] "Why They're Jumping Ship at Intel," *Business Week,* February 14, 1983, pp. 107–108.

Kerzner, Harold. "The R&D Project Manager." *Project Management Quarterly,* June 1981, pp. 20–24.

Kotter, John P. "Power, Dependence and Effective Management." *Harvard Business Review,* July–August 1977.

Ladner, Hayward P. "Who's Really Running the Show?" *Program Manager,* March–April 1983, pp. 33–35.

McConkey, Dale D. "Participative Management: What it Really Means in Practice." *Business Horizons,* October 1980.

McIntyre, Shelby H. "Obstacles to Corporate Innovation." *Business Horizons,* January–February 1982, pp. 23–28.

Mashburn, James I., and Bobby C. Vaught. "Two Heads are Better Than One." *Management Review,* December 1980.

Morris, Peter W.G. "Managing Project Interfaces—Key Points for Project Success." In *Project Management Handbook,* edited by D.I. Cleland and W.R. King. Van Nostrand Reinhold Co., New York, 1983, p. 3.

Rogers, Lloyd A. "Guidelines for Project Management Teams." *Industrial Engineering,* December 1974.

Smith, William H. "The Role of the Technical Manager in the Program Office." *Program Manager,* January–February 1983, pp. 25–28.

Spirer, Herbert F. "The Basic Principles of Project Management." *Operations Management Review,* Fall, 1982, p. 8.

———. "Phasing Out the Project." In *Project Management Handbook,* edited by D.I. Cleland and W.R. King. Van Nostrand Reinhold Co. 1983. p. 245.

Stuckenbruck, Linn C. "Project Manager—The Systems Integrator." *Project Management Quarterly,* vol. IX, no. 3, September 1978.

"Texas Instruments Shows U.S. Business How to Survive in the 1980s." *Business Week,* September 18, 1978.

Thamhain, Hans J., and David L. Wilemon. "Conflict Management in Project Life Cycles." *Sloan Management Review,* vol. 16, no. 3, Spring, 1975.

The Initiation and Implementation of Industrial Projects in Developing Countries: A Systematic Approach. United Nations Industrial Development Organization, United Nations, New York, 1975.

Ullman, P.E. "Project Management Teams—What's The Score?" *Process Engineering,* September 1978.

Von Bergen, C.W., Jr., and R.J. Kirk, "Groupthink: When too Many Heads Spoil the Decision." *Management Review,* March 1978.

Wolff, Michael F. "The Joy (and Woe) of Matrix." *Research Management,* March 1980.

CASE STUDY 20:   FEDERAL RADAR CORPORATION[1]

On the morning of November 14, 1964, John Taylor, Space Warning Network (SPAWN) Program Manager, was getting ready for a private meeting with Paul Shaifer, President of the Federal Radar Corporation (FedRad). Mr. Shaifer had sched-

---

[1] The issues presented in this case are based on actual experience; however, the circumstances, program, customer, and personnel involved have been disguised. Prepared by L. Wallace Clausen and Alfred G. Zappala under the direction of Dr. J. Sterling Livingston, the case is intended to provide a basis for seminar discussion, rather than to illustrate either effective or ineffective handling of an administrative situation. Copyright © by Peat, Marwick, Mitchell & Co; used by permission.

uled the meeting to discuss the problems that had plagued the company's important SPAWN program during its first year-and-a-half. These problems, which included unauthorized design changes and Taylor's inability to control the program's cost, schedule, and technical performance, had contributed to a cost overrun and schedule delay, estimated at 30 percent and four months respectively, and a general loss of customer confidence.

The November 14th meeting was specifically precipitated by a series of delays in the scheduled date of the first prototype acceptance tests and by strong evidence of customer concern and loss of confidence in FedRad's management. By November, Taylor was still unable to set a firm date for the tests that had been originally scheduled for August. The test slippage, supplemented by cost overruns and technical problems, had caused Colonel Grace, the Air Force's System Program Office (SPO) Director for SPAWN, to write a highly critical letter to a FedRad manager.

The Federal Radar Corporation

Since its founding in 1940, FedRad had been preeminent in the radar field. FedRad's scientists and engineers were prominent figures in the development of radar and, over the years, the name FedRad was synonymous with technical excellence in building radar equipment. Financial success had rewarded the company's technical skills in the production of surface, navigational, and fire control radar equipment for the military services and large prime contractors. In recent years, however, sales, employment, and profits had declined appreciably as heavy competition reduced FedRad's contract capture rate.

During the years, FedRad's largest customer by a substantial margin was the Navy. Air Force business was growing rapidly, however, and FedRad thought it might eventually equal the Navy's volume. The SPAWN program accounted for most of the company's Air Force business and was the largest single program in-house during 1964.

The Space Warning Network (SPAWN)

FedRad won the SPAWN prime contract in mid-1963. SPAWN was an advanced warning system to detect, track, and report weapons fired from space. It was to consist of four major subsystems: (1) radar installations to detect the threat; (2) computers to translate and analyze the signals from the radar in order to identify the objects, determine their position and velocity, and calculate their course and probable target; (3) communication equipment to relay the information to NORAD headquarters and the various command and control sites; and (4) display equipment to be used by the operators.

SPAWN was the logical follow-on to the aircraft warning system and the ballistic missile early warning system. It was designed to extend USAF's detection and response capability to the growing threat of armed satellites and spacecraft.

The SPAWN radar subsystem required several advances over earlier radar systems because of unique scanning and tracking problems. The other major subsystems were similar to those of existing manned aircraft and missile warning systems, but the performance and reliability requirements for the system as a whole were considerably more stringent because successful reaction to a space attack required an extremely fast and accurate response.

FedRad's Program Management History

Although FedRad had always made significant contributions to radar's state of the art, most of the radar equipment it had developed prior to the SPAWN program was based on the same fundamental principles. In addition, the major portion of its contracts had required only the redesign and improvement of existing components to meet new specifications. Consequently, the company was able to follow a management approach characterized by functional groups performing traditional tasks. Although program coordination existed, there was very little centralized control over a total program.

FedRad first departed from its traditional approach to organization in 1963, when the company won the SPAWN contract. To win the competition, FedRad had established and described in its management proposal both a SPAWN program office and a programs department. There were two reasons for this departure from tradition: first, the recent loss of a key Navy contract, primarily because of an unsatisfactory management proposal, and second, the Air Force's current attitude toward contractors' management organizations and procedures.

The SPAWN competition took place shortly after FedRad's loss, in 1962, of the Navy's Shish Kebab interceptor fire control contract. Shish Kebab, an advanced system, would have placed FedRad in a favorable position to win during the next decade, several hundred million dollars in direct follow-on and related development. The loss was a severe blow, and FedRad's management was determined to make any changes necessary to assure winning other key contracts.

The first step taken was an effort to identify and correct any management deficiencies that might have contributed to the Shish Kebab loss. At the Navy's debriefing, Paul Shaifer had learned that his company placed second in the competition. The company had lost the award primarily because its management proposal failed to demonstrate FedRad's ability to manage and control an advanced development program.

The October 3, 1962 Management Meeting

At an October 3, 1962 meeting held at the company's California headquarters, Shaifer conveyed the debriefing information to FedRad's top management (see Figure 3).

"From Navy's comments," Shaifer added, "I inferred that FedRad's management structure is considered obsolete and probably would not win any significant future Navy contracts unless it shaped up."

Mr. Hereford, Vice-President, Marketing, agreed. "All the services seem to be taking a stronger and more specific look at the relative merits of contractor management approaches. The Air Force is strongly oriented toward program management and is currently our main potential source of business."

"Important programs of the type we need to maintain our operations are scarce,"

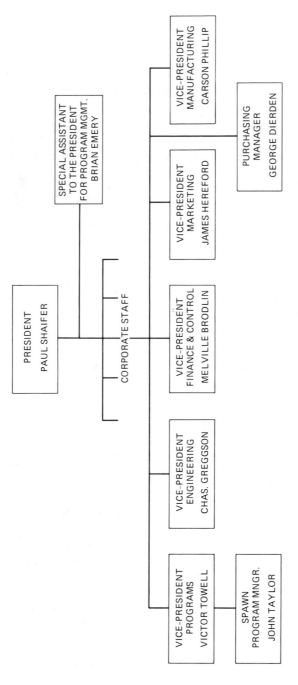

Figure 3. Federal Radar Corporation Organization Chart.

Hereford continued. "We have only one in the fire now, the Air Force SPAWN proposal, which we've been working on for several months. We expect the RFP in late 1962 and the award in mid-1963."

Mr. Hereford next amplified his comment on current attitudes toward contractor management. "An Air Force SPO is a powerful organization headed by a single officer. Air Force officials increasingly want contractors to provide an equally authoritative single point of contact for each program. My staff is preparing the SPAWN management proposal now, and it looks like a loser at this point. The closest we come to centralized responsibility is the program coordinator in the engineering department. This person, however, has no broad program responsibility and authority. Unless we can develop and present a modern, centralized type of organization, I don't think we'll win the SPAWN award or any other major contract."

James Hereford's comments touched off a lengthy discussion. Charles Greggson, Vice-President, Engineering, favored FedRad's present organization, noting the company's reputation for excellent technical work, the close relationship between the engineering and manufacturing departments, and the long and close association between his staff and many customer technical personnel. He concluded, "I'm inclined to discount all this supposed customer pressure for a new kind of organization. I think the men who talked to Paul and James were probably administrative types attempting to persuade us to adopt some 'ideal' organization structure. I'll bet a customer technical man wouldn't want us to change. These new organizational ideas would remove control from our integrated engineering team and hand it to administration types who don't have adequate insight into our technical problems. A move in that direction would interfere with our methods, which, after all, have made us number one in the radar business. I'm convinced that political considerations lost us the Shish Kebab contract—nothing more."

Carson Phillips, Vice-President, Manufacturing, agreed with Greggson, adding, "I'd be the first to go along with a change if I felt it were necessary. I do resist any changes that would risk our present very successful setup unless somebody can show me how they will improve our management capability."

After further similar discussion, Paul Shaifer declared, "Gentlemen, I've not been completely open with you. I made some decisions on this matter before the meeting, but I wanted to hear you express your own opinions before I announced them."

"I believe we must meet the new emphasis on program-oriented management if we are to be successful in the future. We need to establish and present to our prospective customers some coordinating organization that can monitor our programs as they pass through the marketing, engineering, and manufacturing phases. We all agree that our present management organization and techniques are sound, but I think we'll also agree that superimposing a coordinating group can't do any harm, might help us manage large programs, and most certainly will appeal to our friends in the military.

"With this introduction, I'd like to announce the formation of a programs department and the promotion of Victor Towell to the office of Vice-President, Programs. Vic's performance as financial manager has been exceptional, and I believe his demonstrated grasp of the intricacies and interdependencies of our financial structure proves his ability to watch over our program efforts. He'll direct the overall program effort by guiding the activities of program offices, each consisting of a program manager and a small staff. In the future, a program office will be established for each major program. Within the next week, Vic and I will choose, with your concurrence, a program manager for the SPAWN proposal.

"I also plan to create and fill another new position in the near future—that of Special Assistant to the President for Management. This man will act as a proposal consultant, troubleshooter, and management specialist, keeping an eye on the effectiveness of our organization and management of defense programs. He'll be an outsider and, hopefully, will be familiar with government and military management techniques."

Establishing Program Management for the SPAWN Proposal

On October 18, in a memorandum to all FedRad personnel, Paul Shaifer announced the appointment of Col. Brian Emery (USAF, Retired), formerly Assistant Deputy Commander for Systems and Logistics, Air Force Systems Command, to the newly created position of Special Assistant to the President for Management. His appointment was to be effective November 15.

At the same time, John Taylor, formerly Ordnance Fabrication Shop Supervisor, was appointed to assist in the preparation of the SPAWN management proposal and to take over as program manager if FedRad won the award.

Victor Towell, the new Vice-President, Programs, was 55 and had been with Fed-Rad for 25 years. After 10 years, in engineering and manufacturing positions, he was appointed chief financial officer. In that position, he reported to the vice-president, finance and control and was responsible for the corporation's financial management. He also assisted the marketing department in its efforts to identify and capture new business.

Brian Emery, 48, was a veteran Air Force procurement officer. He had participated in procurements ranging from nuts-and-bolts items to billion-dollar weapon systems and had a unique insight into the key elements of military management. Emery had directed two substantial Air Force development programs and, during the preceding two years, had helped formulate the latest USAF systems management techniques. Shaifer had selected Emery because of his demonstrated competence and forceful personal impression.

Shaifer and Towell chose John Taylor to head the SPAWN program because they considered him well-qualified, with wide experience in military and contractor organizations. After receiving his electrical engineering degree in 1942, Taylor had served four years in the Army Corps of Engineers. From 1946 to 1953, he was employed by the World-wide Electronics Corporation; from 1953 to 1957, by Uniradar Systems, Inc. He had served in positions that included contracting officer, administrative manager, and shop supervisor. In 1958, Taylor joined FedRad. During his years with the company he had served in various supervisory and administrative positions in both the engineering and manufacturing departments.

After his appointment, the marketing department gave Taylor the task of completing the management proposal. Work had progressed further on the technical and cost sections of the proposal, and Taylor did not work on those sections.

By mid-November, 1962, Taylor had consulted his associates in other departments and had set up a proposed program management organization. It was strictly an information-collecting and liaison organization and included, in addition to Taylor, a manager for the administrative systems required by the RFP and engineering, manufacturing and quality control liaison representatives. In the meantime, Colonel Emery had joined FedRad. Because his first assignment was to assume responsibility for preparing the SPAWN management proposal, it was to Emery that Taylor submitted his proposed organization.

When Emery inspected Taylor's five-man program office he was shocked. "Why, the 'staff-coordinator' approach to managing a large development program was abandoned two or three years ago! A weak program orientation," he told Taylor, "caused several programs to go completely out of control technically, financially, schedulewise, or all three. In each case, the Air Force SPO manager had to ride it out at great expense to his budget and reputation or, through drastic application of SPO personnel and techniques, actually had to take over the management of the contractor's effort. Most Air Force procurement officers are aware of this and consequently view this approach with dismay. This type of organization will never work with an advanced, complex program like SPAWN."

Bolstered by the Colonel's knowledge and persuasion, Taylor joined Emery in another attempt to structure a strong program management organization. Emery suggested that they approach the job from the standpoint of an Air Force evaluator's preference. According to the colonel, this would be a program office that had the capability, responsibility, and authority to plan and direct the essential elements of the SPAWN program. Furthermore, it should be the only Air Force contact at FedRad for information and action.

Noting that nearly half the SPAWN program would be subcontracted, Emery added subcontract management to the program office's list of responsibilities. He asserted, moreover, that the organization and management techniques described in the proposal should correspond to the Air Force's SPO management system. Each member of the SPO should be able to perceive who would be responsible for his particular area and to be confident that both the defined position and the man filling it would meet his requirements.

By late December 1962, Emery and Taylor had a long and complete description of the SPAWN program office (see Figure 4 for the organizational structure).

Selling the SPAWN Program Office

Emery and Taylor presented the new organization to key engineering, manufacturing, purchasing, and marketing personnel. Their attempt to solicit support for the new SPAWN program office was a complete failure. Most engineering managers vigorously resisted the concept that a centralized program organization should have overall responsibility for a program's technical, cost, and schedule elements.

"Technical integration has always been performed by the engineering department," declared Charles Greggson, "and, as far as I am concerned, always will. I plan to appoint a program engineer, the staff administrator we traditionally use to monitor program activities. He'll handle the program office's contacts with engineering, and

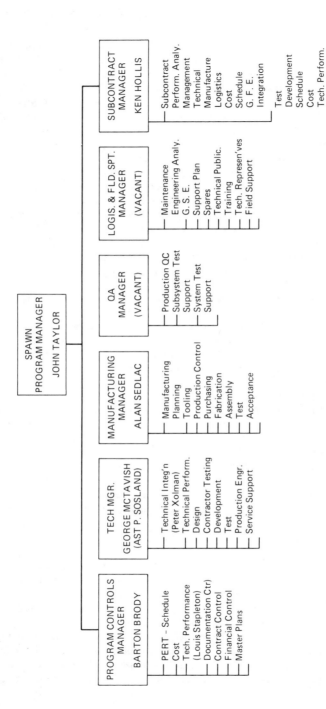

Figure 4. Spawn Program Office.

I'll conduct my own engineering budgeting and scheduling. I think your proposed provision that all customer contact be conducted through the program office is unnecessary and unworkable."

The purchasing department resented the appointment of a subcontracts manager and felt that anything he would do directly with the subcontractors was a violation of its prerogatives. The marketing department opposed the idea that Taylor should play a major role in the marketing effort and should become acquainted with both the Air Force SPO director and higher level military and DOD officials. Otherwise, they favored a strong program office because they felt the Air Force desired it.

Emery and Taylor presented and discussed the new organization on many occasions during the next three weeks. Each presentation led to lengthy arguments and terminated in disagreement. By the third week in January, it was apparent to both men that there was no time for additional persuasion. The proposal's deadline was February 1, 1963, and a prompt decision had to be made regarding the SPAWN management proposal. After due consideration, Emery, Taylor, and marketing department personnel agreed that FedRad would not win the award if the proposal lacked a strong program office. The only realistic approach was to propose a "paper organization" that had not been approved.

In a memorandum dated January 18, Emery requested Shaifer's permission to propose a SPAWN management organization that did not exist. Emery stated that he was convinced that this organization was needed not only to win the contract, but also to manage the program and recommended that it be included in the proposal. He also recommended that strong steps be taken to implement this description if FedRad won the contract, informing Shaifer that he and Taylor had been unable to convince others in the company of its desirability.

Shaifer replied two days later that, although he had not gone over the proposed description in detail, he would go along with Emery's opinion that it was required to win. The management proposal was written accordingly, and the SPAWN proposal was submitted to the Air Force on February 1, 1963.

The SPAWN Award

On May 13, 1963, the Air Force announced that FedRad had won the SPAWN contract award. FedRad's management breathed a sigh of relief as the anxiety generated by steadily decreasing work was lifted. After the initial ebullience had subsided, however, a few FedRad managers felt mixed emotions. Emery and Taylor knew that their real work was just beginning. They again attempted to convince engineering and other FedRad management personnel that the proposed organization had contributed significantly to winning the award. The other managers, however, claimed that the award could be attributed to the company's superior technical design and sound engineering reputation.

At this point, Emery was assigned to another task. Consequently, establishing an operational SPAWN program office was left entirely to Taylor. By June 1, when the actual engineering work was to begin, Taylor had been able to secure, for his office, only five men from the engineering department. These men were responsible for technical management and program control. Greggson refused to give Taylor additional engineers. Taylor was able to obtain from other departments one man to perform manufacturing liaison work and another to act as subcontracts manager.

Taylor felt insecure about his organizational support, as SPAWN moved into high gear in June 1963. His feeling was borne out during the next six months. By January 1964, the SPAWN program was two months behind schedule, and a cost overrun of from 10–25 percent was projected. The problems leading to the January situation are described below.

Technical Management Problems

The program office's technical management team consisted of George McTavish, technical manager, Philip Sosland, assistant technical manager, and Peter Kolman, system integration coordinator. All three men remained on the engineering department payroll. McTavish was assigned 80 percent to the program office. Sosland was assigned 100 percent to the program office as necessary, but continued to report to his engineering department superior. McTavish and Sosland had backgrounds in manufacturing, engineering, and project engineering. Kolman was the only one with recent experience in systems design work. As stated in the management proposal, these three men were to define the system, subsystem, and end-item design objectives; to prepare data for the work breakdown structure; to design performance tests; to control the technical interfaces between the various FedRad, Air Force, and subcontractor design groups; and to evaluate the effect of technical deficiencies and proposed changes on system objectives.

By July 1963, it was apparent that the program office was technical manager in name only. The engineering department's technical integration section continued to perform the same functions it traditionally had performed for programs managed within the department. Engineering personnel contacted Air Force representatives without going through the program office, explaining, when questioned by Taylor, that channelling technical communications through a third organization only confused matters. In two instances, Taylor learned about unauthorized design changes after the redesign work was almost completed. Though both changes would result in improved technical performance, Taylor doubted that the improvements would justify the schedule delay and cost increase. He learned that FedRad engineers had obtained informal approval for the changes from lower level Air Force engineers, but he was not certain that the SPO director would approve funding for the changes.

Program Control Problems

Taylor's program control team consisted of Barton Brody, program control manager, and Louis Stapleton, PERT supervisor. Both were assigned full time to the program office. Although they had experience in program planning and cost analysis, neither had prior experience with PERT networking. The description of the work breakdown structure and the PERT network, both of which were included in the SPAWN proposal, had been prepared by Antole Kalmis, a project administrator in the engineering department. Kalmis had worked with Taylor and the marketing department during proposal preparation, but was recalled to handle detailed networking and changes full time for the engineering department after the program began.

As defined in the SPAWN management proposal, Brody and Stapleton were responsible for PERT, which included maintaining the work breakdown structure and master plans; revising and updating the PERT networks; preparing system output reports, such as management summary reports; and recommending corrective action for problems revealed by the reports.

During the first months of the program, however, their roles were reduced to monitoring the actual planning and control work conducted within the engineering department and trying to integrate this information into the total program plan. These plans encompassed the other FedRad departments, contractors of major subsystems, and Government Furnished Equipment (GFE).

Several incidents occurring between June and January had created problems for the program office. In one case, Stapleton was not informed of a network revision made by the engineering department to reflect a schedule slippage caused by a shortage of engineers. This revision was discovered only shortly before a set of drawings was scheduled to go to the computer subcontractor. As a result, the subcontractor's schedule also was delayed, and several engineers were placed on idle time.

On another occasion, FedRad engineers had provided Air Force representatives with work breakdown charts detailed below the level furnished the program office. The SPO engineering deputy had a question regarding the charts and called Taylor to inquire about it. He ascertained in short order that Taylor was both unaware of the charts in question and uninformed about the overall status of the engineering effort. Following this incident, the SPO officer developed the habit of contacting FedRad engineers directly to obtain information.

Subcontractor Management Problems

FedRad had three SPAWN subcontractors for the major computer and communications subsystems and the smaller display subsystem. The subcontracted portion represented about 45 percent of total contract dollars. All three subsystems were closely interdependent and were expected to meet stringent quality and reliability requirements. Of the three, FedRad previously had worked with only the computer subcontractor.

Ken Hollis, assigned 50 percent as program office subsystems manager, was responsible for monitoring and analyzing subcontractor performance. The purchasing department was responsible for all contractual, price, and delivery matters. George Dierden, purchasing department manager, had made it clear during the proposal effort that his organization was fully competent to negotiate with vendors and had promised to object if any unnecessary duplication or interference by the program office came to his attention. In fact, Towell and Greggson had to intervene while the proposal was being prepared to settle a conflict between the program office and the purchasing department regarding Taylor's right to monitor and approve work statements the engineering department prepared for subcontractors.

Taylor had several problems involving subcontractor management during the June–

January period. The most significant of these was a series of revised proposals submitted by the communications subcontractor during negotiations with Purchasing. As of January 1964, requirements changes had escalated contract costs by 15 percent and the contract still had not been finalized. An additional group of 25 engineering change proposals was awaiting approval by the FedRad engineering department, following which they would be negotiated by Purchasing.

Another difficulty involved the display subcontractor. The terms of that subcontract had not defined a specific set of management and control procedures, and the subcontractor's procedures were very difficult to translate accurately into categories useful to FedRad. As a result, Ken Hollis was unable to monitor the display program's status or even to identify the single person in the subcontractor's organization who could talk knowledgeably with him. George Dierden refused to help Hollis, stating that since the contracts people had affirmed to him the subcontractor's intention and ability to meet requirements, he saw no need for additional information.

The Program Office Staff Increase

By January 1964, John Taylor felt that he had lost control of the SPAWN program. Because of his limited authority and staff, he was able to determine program status only after a one- to-two-month lag. His inability to provide prompt answers to the customer had caused SPO personnel to contact FedRad and subcontractor personnel directly. Many decisions that Taylor believed he should make were presented to him as accomplished facts. Also, he felt that technical decisions were being made without due consideration of their cost and schedule impact. Consequently, he described his problem to Paul Shaifer and asked Shaifer to take some action to increase his effectiveness as program manager.

Shaifer responded by securing the release of several additional men to the program office. Two of these men were appointed to the previously vacant positions of logistics and field support manager and quality assurance manager. Others provided additional support to the program control and technical managers. With his staff increased to 13 men, Taylor felt better prepared to face his responsibilities, which were now focused on the Air Force acceptance testing of the first prototype unit, scheduled for August 1964.

By early March, Taylor was able to report that his expanded staff had given him substantially greater control over the program. This improved control, however, was largely brought about by better liaison and information-gathering capability. The actual role of the program office remained the same, since the functional managers still were reluctant to yield those responsibilities that, through years of experience, they were confident they could discharge effectively.

The Translator Module Design Change

Taylor's new feeling of control soon vanished. Early in April, he saw a FedRad memorandum referring to a significant design change in the sensing unit with the computer subsystem. The change surprised him because he had thought the Translator design was finalized at the beginning of the program. Any change in the Translator concerned him because it constituted the interface between the radar and computer subsystems. In addition to the expense of the change itself, any change might have significant impact on those subsystems.

Taylor began investigating to determine why the change was deemed necessary, what it could cost, and what effect it would have on the program requirements. It took him two weeks to gather the full story. He learned that a senior systems engineer who had joined the SPAWN program two months earlier had developed a new approach to the Translator design. After obtaining the chief engineer's permission, he conducted a parallel design study, which demonstrated that his design would substantially improve translation speed. The chief engineer then tabled the original Translator design and instructed his engineers to work out the new design and to make any necessary changes in the radar unit. He ordered the computer interface to be redefined and communicated to the computer subcontractor after several technical problems had been solved. When questioned, the chief engineer apologized to Taylor for not first checking with him, but explained that Taylor had been out of town when the new approach originally came up.

Further checking revealed that, as a result of forced delays in other parts of the computer design, the computer subcontractor had accelerated the design of certain components that were highly interdependent with the Translator. Consequently, a redefinition of the translator-computer interface would generate considerable added costs and schedule delays. Some radar redesign would also be required.

When Taylor reviewed the data he had collected, he determined that the new design meant a clear improvement in Translator speed, increasing it 20 percent. A reliability problem was still unsolved, however, as well as possible problems in the redesign necessary to take advantage of the increased speed. Taylor estimated that $70,000 had been spent on the change so far and predicted an additional $100,000 and one-month schedule slippage to complete the change. On the other hand, it would entail a $25,000 expense and a one-week schedule slippage to go back to the old Translator design. At this point, Taylor called Colonel Grace to report the situation and to get a decision on whether or not to proceed with the design change.

Colonel Grace was displeased by Taylor's news. "You know as well as I do that we're already exceeding our cost and time schedules," he told Taylor. "The old design met requirements and we bought it. Let's go back to it. You can charge your little experiment to company-funded research. Furthermore, I advise you to find out how many more unreported changes you've piled up. At this point, I really wonder who runs the show at FedRad."

The Test Date Slippage and Colonel Grace's Concern

By spring 1964, it was apparent that FedRad would be unable to meet the deadline for the Air Force acceptance tests of the first prototype unit, originally scheduled for August. During the summer, the anticipated test date was projected successively to September, November, and December. Taylor declared that the inaccurate projections were due to delays in end-item completion, reported to him at the last minute. The slippage was accompanied by a projected cost overrun of 30 percent, which, Taylor assured the customer, could be reduced to about 5 percent by anticipated shortcuts in the development of the second prototype unit. Colonel Grace was pessimistic about this, however, and it was clear that he had lost confidence in FedRad's management capability.

In October 1964, Colonel Grace wrote to Colonel Emery, an old Air Force friend. Among other things, Grace wrote, "I'm worried by the persistent slippage in the test date and I'm under pressure from my superiors. My position is very sensitive because it's more and more apparent that I should have stepped in and put tighter controls on FedRad several months ago. I'd appreciate anything you can do to explain good program management to FedRad's executives."

After receiving Grace's letter, Emery obtained permission from Paul Shaifer to make a study of the SPAWN program's problems. Emery was appalled by what he found, and wrote a confidential memorandum to Shaifer, which included the following comments.

"John Taylor's efforts to direct and control the SPAWN program are being frustrated by the functional managers. With such a limited program office, successful direction depends on the managers' support and cooperation. Without their help, we risk fumbling the program. There are two major problems, as I see it.

"First, the acceptance test date has already slipped four months, and we are unable even now to set a definite date for these tests. A survey of the considerable correspondence between the program office, the engineering and purchasing departments, and subcontractors during the past several months reveals two difficulties. Number one, no single department is coordinating the effort of all the organizations involved in the tests. Engineering's radar design and systems design test sections have a general plan on paper. This plan is being monitored by the program office. The detailed test plan, however, is known only to engineering's test personnel and has not been communicated adequately to the other parties involved. The second point that emerges is that the tests are vitally important to the customer. They are the SPO's first chance to demonstrate the success of the program. Unless we improve our organization and that of our major subcontractors, it is doubtful that the acceptance tests will be performed satisfactorily.

"Second, a serious threat to our reputation currently exists. Colonel Grace is thoroughly disgusted with our disorganization and mismanagement. In addition, continued poor performance may bring visits from higher level Air Force officials. I can assure you that, whatever the technical merits of FedRad's management approach, our program management concept as it has been implemented on the SPAWN program will be sharply criticized.

"In conclusion, I believe we will be in serious trouble as long as we retain our present approach to program management. I urge you to expand Taylor's group and to strengthen and clarify his relationship to the functional managers."

Shaifer's Meeting with Taylor

Colonel Emery succeeded in arousing Shaifer's concern. Shaifer contacted Taylor and arranged a meeting for the morning of November 14. He suggested that Taylor prepare a list of the changes he wanted in staff, organization, procedures, and any other areas he believed necessary to making SPAWN's program management a success.

Shaifer said he would do the same and ended the conversation with the comment, "Maybe between the two of us we can come up with a plan of action that will really work!"

CASE STUDY 21: PROJECT MANAGEMENT IN THE AUTOMOTIVE INDUSTRY[1]

Francis M. Webster
School of Management
University of Michigan-Flint
Flint, Michigan

Introduction

When the Project Management Institute meets, much of the conversation is focused on megabuck projects, such as nuclear reactors, power dams, and Alaskan pipelines. These are certainly interesting if not awesome projects. With far less visibility and fanfare, equally interesting and perhaps, if the facts were really known, also awesome projects are undertaken in the automotive industry year after year.

Consider the following facts drawn from newspapers during the last several months.

- General Motors will spend $40 billion on new product development and associated new and rehabilitated facilities over the five-year period from 1980–1984.
- Ford plans to spend an average of $4 billion per year over the period from 1979 through 1985.
- Chrysler is spending some $700 million for plant modernization to produce the K car. This includes:
    $100 million to refurbish the Jefferson Avenue Assembly Plant in Detroit.
    $50 million to refurbish the Newark, Delaware, Assembly Plant.
    $300 million to retool the Trenton, Michigan, Engine Plant to produce 2.2 liter, 4-cylinder engines.
- American Motors Corporation spent $54.6 million in 1979 and plans to spend $85 million in 1980.
- Mr. Murphy, Chairman of General Motors, in summarizing all this said that the U.S. automotive industry will spend $80 billion in the five year period 1980–1984 to develop new fuel-efficient cars and trucks and construct or rehabilitate the plants necessary to produce them.

Compare this to the $9 billion cost of the Alaskan Pipeline. Indeed that is a propitious comparison, for the manufacture of automobiles can be likened to a giant

---

[1] Francis M. Webster, School of Management, University of Michigan, Flint, Michigan *Project Management Institute 1980 Proceedings,* "Communications" Seminar/Symposium, Phoenix, Arizona, October 1980, The Project Management Institute, Drexel Hill, Pennsylvania. Used by permission.

pipeline system in which one inoperable component can shut down the entire system.

While the Alaskan Pipeline was dramatic in its total size, it was actually done as many subprojects, not unlike the many subprojects of the auto companies. General Motors is building at least three completely new assembly plants and substantially rehabilitating others. The new assembly plants are estimated to cost at least $350 million each. They include complete new overhead conveyor lines instead of the in-the-floor conveyors that have been used by GM. They also include almost completely automated welding and painting lines that use as many as 100 robots per plant. All the car companies are building new plants and rehabilitating others to produce the new engines, transmissions, and other drive train components as well as the variety of other parts for these all new vehicles. One such plant, Ford's Essex Engine Plant in Windsor, Ontario, is a 1.3-million square foot building (equivalent to 24 football fields) and contains complex automatic transfer lines for machining parts and computerized engine test facilities.

What is not readily apparent is that all these subprojects are scheduled for completion to support the introduction of completely new car lines. Be assured, all subprojects will be completed on time because job number 1, the first car off the assembly line, cannot be sold if it is missing even a single component.

The auto companies are noted primarily for the efficient management of stable, mass production typified by the assembly line. It is precisely this mass production feature that which complicates many of these subprojects. Chrysler's Jefferson Avenue Plant was converted from the large car to the K car production in 15 weeks. The Newark, Delaware, plant was allowed 10 weeks. That's 10 weeks from production of the last 1980 model car until the first 1981 car! Of course, a lot of preparatory work was done before and, no doubt, some cleanup will be done afterward. Nevertheless, job number 1 will go down the line on schedule.

What is required to accomplish this? What are the communications and coordination problems?

A Functional Organization

In one major manufacturing complex, there may be several different plants, each with its own workforce, management, and problems. Each of these may be divided into several manufacturing plants and departments. The primary responsibility of these manufacturing plants and departments is to produce the parts necessary for all the current year's vehicle production and to assemble those vehicles. In addition, the complex may have a complete management structure with appropriate support groups. These support groups include:

- Product engineering responsible for:
  detail design of products to be produced
  solving problems on current production
- Production engineering responsible for:
  developing manufacturing processes
  tooling design

machine design

coordinating large machinery purchases

compiling, coordinating, and disseminating information on large projects in their conceptual phases and monitoring physical progress during the implementation phases (the Project Control Group)

solving problems on current production

- Industrial engineering responsible for:

    work methods

    floor space utilization

    layout

    packaging

    product costing

    coordinating with manufacturing departments to maintain efficient production on current products

    solving problems on current production

- Plant engineering responsible for:

    building capacities (utilities and structure)

    maintain all existing facilities

    install new equipment

    design materials handling systems

    maintain a construction gang

    solving problems on current production

- Purchasing responsible for:

    purchase equipment, materials, and supplies required in project work

    purchase parts for current production

- Appropriations analysis (accounting) responsible for:

    review of project requests for economic justification

    review of in-process projects for past and future spending and savings

    publish quarterly status reports on all projects

    formally close projects

- Work order control (accounting) responsible for:

    issuing work order numbers

    collecting costs against work orders

    closing the work orders upon their completion

- Production scheduling responsible for:

    establishing banking (in process inventory) requirements for current production

    establishing production schedules and ensuring their feasibility on current production

    expediting delivery of production parts

    scheduling machines and lines for shutdown for changeover

These line manufacturing plants and functional support groups may at any one time be working on one or more of the following project types:

- new car (model change), e.g., GM's X and J cars, Chrysler's K car, and Ford's Escort
- new truck (model change), e.g., GM's new small pickup truck
- component parts, e.g., a new transmission plant
- capacity related, e.g., expand an existing engine plant
- plant modernization, e.g., replace the cupolas in a foundry with electric melt furnaces
- replacement, e.g., replace obsolete or worn-out facilities or equipment
- cost savings and new methods, e.g., installing computer control of the melt process in a foundry
- EPA/OSHA, e.g., installing pollution control equipment or changing the switches on all machines to meet requirements
- all others

All these are processed through rather well-defined procedures requiring agreement and approval of the various manufacturing plants and support groups and then careful coordination of their implementation. To aid in understanding this process, consider a typical complex involving eight manufacturing plants and eight functional support groups.

Model Change Project

A typical project, one that occurs cyclically and with a definite completion date, is a model change. It is typically one project for the entire division and varies in cost and complexity from year to year.

Usually, general plans are formulated five years in advance, with periodic updates and reevaluation. In the beginning, general concepts are outlined from a projection of product demands over the coming five years. These product concepts are translated into facilities concepts and, as the needs become more concrete and defined, are evaluated for divisional importance and economic implications. This overall divisional perspective is broken down into the requirements of each of the manufacturing plants. A series of evaluation and approval meetings solidify the products to be produced and the facilities to manufacture them.

At a point in time far enough ahead to ensure completion of the model change, an overall project request is formulated. Manufacturing, along with its support groups, breaks down the facility's requirements far enough to get an accurate price tag on the total model change project.

General Project Path

Figure 5 shows a general project path the project takes from conception to completion. While the project may simultaneously be the concern of several different groups, each with its own needs, each review point listed is a point the entire project experiences at once. Thus, all the needs have to be defined and compiled before a request can be formulated.

On the top line are activities that occur at the uppermost managerial levels of the division, in coordination with and with the approval of the corporation as the

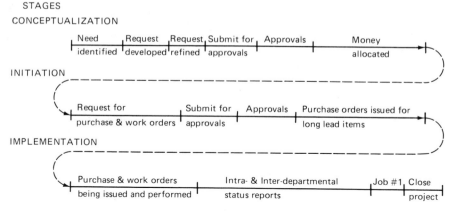

STAGES

CONCEPTUALIZATION

Figure 5.   General Project Path.

project develops in the conceptual stage. Not shown in detail are the specific steps involved in corporate approval. For example, similar requests are prepared by other divisions, which must be considered simultaneously at corporate level, as they pertain to the same new model car introduction.

The middle line shows activities at the middle-management levels of the division after general corporate approval. The manufacturing and support groups subdivide the total allocation into smaller, easier to manage segments called *work orders* and *purchase orders.* Here the long lead items are purchased, contracts let, and the support groups start detailing their portions of the responsibilities. It is here that the project is transformed from the conceptual stage to the initiation stage.

The bottom line concerns that time in the project when monies and plans are converted into actual facilities, i.e., the implementation stage. In this stage the largest number of people are involved, time becomes an important factor, and contingency plans are most likely to be effectuated. From here to the conclusion of the project, manufacturing, which is of course primarily structured to maintain mass-production operations, shares its responsibilities for model change with three of its support groups, i.e., production engineering, industrial engineering, and plant engineering.

At every point along this path there is an accounting-related function, with the intensity of the accounting function involvement increasing as the project progresses from conceptualization through implementation.

A Synopsis

With the variety of projects that may be in process simultaneously, work groups organized along functional lines, and with an absence of a specific project organization, a relatively specific set of rules and procedures is needed to guide a project to completion. These rules and procedures tie together the progress of the project even though responsibilities for the various points along the path may seem ill-defined, and the responsibilities for these points fall to different groups at different times. Physical

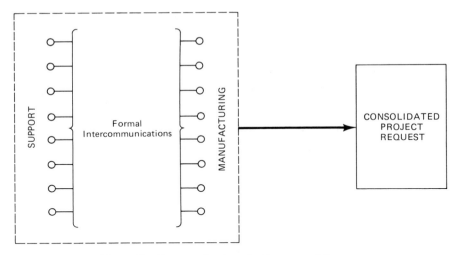

Figure 6. Communications in Conceptual Stage.

progress along the path is the responsibility of the originating group (usually manufacturing), and the financial control of the project ultimately rests with accounting.

Because of the entwining of functions, responsibilities, record keeping, and coordination, it is helpful to look at the projects from one more point of view. This view will define some of the communications channels necessary to complete a model change project.

Communications

Figure 6 presents a generalized concept of the communications necessary to accomplish the conceptualization stage of a project. The formal lines of communication exist from each one of the eight manufacturing groups to each one of the eight support groups. After a period of interaction, the manufacturing groups submit a consolidated statement to the corporation for approvals. The far-reaching decisions and directions are arrived at during this stage.

During this process the communications channels remain open, although the amount of traffic diminishes while the project is at corporate. Formally, a support group receives information about another support group's activities only through the concerned manufacturing group. Of course there are any number of informal communications channels in the system.

The formal communication channels necessary to accomplish the initiation stage of Figure 5 are shown in Figure 7. The monies are apportioned at this middle-management level, the support groups communicating with the manufacturing groups along much the same lines as in Figure 6, with some notable exceptions:

- There are typically more people involved within each group.
- Accounting becomes more dominant in gathering information formally from all sources.

- The production engineering group, as primary coordinator for the manufacturing groups, gathers information from many sources.

With more people becoming formally involved in most groups, the communications structure becomes more involved. In the first communications structure (Figure 6), assuming one person in each group communicates for the entire group, there would be 64 (8 × 8) formal channels of communication. In the structure applicable to the initiation stage (Figure 7), if there are only two people in each group, there would be as many as 256 (16 × 16) different formal channels. Some of these channels are never used, but in many instances there are more than two persons representing any single group. Furthermore, this does not take into consideration the large number of persons within each group that may be involved in the project in some way.

Even though a portion of production engineering becomes directly involved in compiling, coordinating, and dispersing information on the project, another part of this support group is still in the more structured support mode, as are various parts of accounting, so they cannot be removed from the support group column.

As the production engineering work progresses, the thrust of the model change moves to industrial engineering, where information, primarily from manufacturing, production engineering, and plant engineering is combined to form the first detailed rendering of the final physical facilities, the layout. Industrial engineering has at least two people for each manufacturing plant responsible for layouts as part of their work. The more involved manufacturing plants usually designate one of their number as "Model Change Coordinator" representing manufacturing's interests in the layout. The rest of the support groups monitor layout progress for a need for their involvement. The layout represents an important point in the communication chain because it is at this point that communications again subdivide. (See Figure 8.) Because of the importance of layouts, approvals may be required by the division general manager.

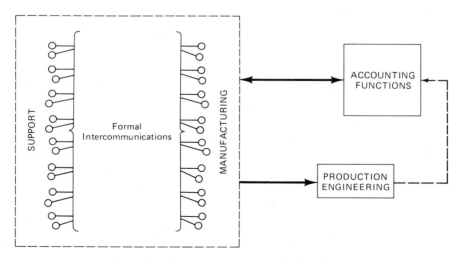

Figure 7.   Communications in Initiation Stage.

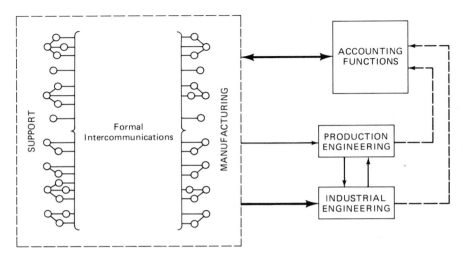

Figure 8.   Communications in Initiation Implementation Stage.

The layouts and associated information are forwarded to plant engineering for translation into the final facilities. They take the lead in the construction of the facilities, coordinating with industrial engineering and maintaining direct communication channels with manufacturing (through the model change coordinator if there is one), accounting, and production engineering. Indirect channels are maintained with the other manufacturing and support groups as a whole. (See Figure 9.)

Because the progression from the initiation stage to the implementation stage is not instantaneous, but rather is transferred piecemeal over a considerable period of time, production engineering and industrial engineering continue to be shown on Figure 9. Eventually the roles of these two departments in the project diminish until the project is formally closed by accounting. By this time concern of these departments turns to the continuing operations of the new equipment and facilities and, probably, to the next round of projects already coming through the system.

Conclusion

The communications section was intended to show the complexity of the communication system for a model change project. Admittedly this is by far the most involved project of the nine types, and all channels are not used all the time. Nevertheless, it is complex. It shows that the cohesive factor holding the model change project together is not a well-defined project organization nor an efficient communications system. Rather, the cohesive factor seems to be the procedures for approvals as the project is conceptualized and the transfer of responsibility as it moves through initiation and implementation.

While this system has worked well, it has some major potential deficiencies. First, there are extreme pressures placed on the managerial staff. These pressures come

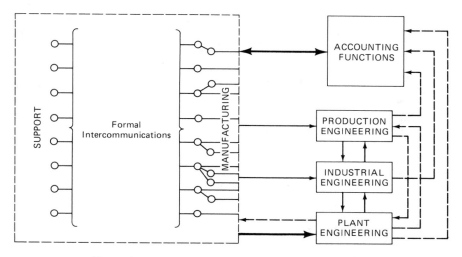

Figure 9.   Communications in Implementation Stage.

from the emphasis that the project *will* be completed on time in order that job number 1 *will* come off the line as scheduled and as a complete vehicle. Pressure also comes from a very strong and effective financial management system that constantly reviews actual and planned expenditures to prevent over expenditure.

These pressures create a stress on the individuals and encourage a certain amount of what might be called *gamesmanship*. Those who rise in the organization learn early to conduct themselves in such a manner as to stay out of the spotlight of failure, to share decision making, to ensure they have met the letter, if not the spirit, of the requirements on them. Those who get caught in the spotlight of failure to perform to schedule may quickly fall off the ladder.

On the other hand, a situation is created that encourages a dual bookkeeping practice. Accounting keeps the official books, but first-line supervision maintains the accurate books. Foremen keep track of their expenditures of labor and materials against each work order. Seldom do they report a work order completed until it is completely expended. To some extent at least, this is sanctioned by plant managers. If a work order is underspent, the money often goes back to corporate with no benefit to the plant. By turning the other way on this matter, the plant manager often finds those little jobs taken care of for which he has been unable to obtain funds through normal corporate procedures.

In many instances, even with the strong financial control system and control of physical progress, these two vital systems are not directly related. A work order may span several months for one trade, sometimes for activities on unrelated physical features of the plant. As a result, it is often impractical, if not impossible, to accurately relate physical progress and money spent.

In short, the projects accomplished by the automotive industry on a regular basis are truly amazing when more fully understood. *And* these projects are accomplished in a functional organization where the principal pressure is to achieve daily production goals in a mass production system while the projects are being planned and implemented. It works almost every time. Occasionally, some component is late, and every vacant field in town is filled with almost-complete cars. They are later completed at a substantial penalty cost.

Improvements could be made in the communications networks, using some of the concepts of modern project management. Efforts are under way to learn how to do this. They will be incorporated very carefully, because the cost of a mistake in the automotive industry is very high.

CASE STUDY 22:   PROJECT MANAGEMENT AT FLUOR UTAH, INC.[1]

Project management is more an art than a science, and, therefore, it is not practical to attempt to define it in precise terms. There are, however, certain basic truths or concepts used by Fluor Utah project managers in directing the execution of engineering, procurement, and construction contracts that meet the project objectives imposed or agreed upon with the client. As has been stated by a past president of Fluor Corporation, the first of these basics might be "Don't refer to an owner as a client until he comes to you with repeat business." In this paper, we confidently use the word *client* rather than *owner* to refer to the contracting party.

To some degree, Fluor Corporation has always operated under a strong task force organization headed by a project manager. When Si Fluor, Sr., acted as project manager over the small engineering and construction projects performed at the company's beginning, he recognized long before the term *task force* was conceived, that advantage accrued to the owner and the project by having total responsibility under a single individual and a single organization. Then, as technology grew and projects became larger and more sophisticated—and Fluor began performing a number of these larger projects simultaneously—it became necessary to develop a different type of organization and method of managing the company and its projects. From this need was developed what we refer to as the task force/department *matrix-type* organization at Flour.

During the early 1960s, after hundreds of projects had been completed, it became apparent that many projects successfully achieved their basic project objectives, but some failed to achieve budget, schedule, and performance objectives originally established.

The history of many of these projects was carefully reviewed to identify conditions and events common to successful projects, vis-à-vis those conditions and events that occurred frequently on less successful projects.

A common identifiable element on most successful projects was the quality and

[1] Robert K. Duke, *Vice President Project Management,* H. Frederick Wohlsen, *Manager of Projects,* and Douglas R. Mitchell, *Project Manager,* Fluor Utah, Inc. *Realities in Project Management,* Proceedings of the 1977 Project Management Institute, International Seminar/Symposium, Chicago, Illinois, October 1977, The Project Management Institute, Drexel Hill, Pennsylvania. Used by permission.

depth of early planning by the project management group. Execution of the plan, bolstered by strong project management control over identifiable phases of the project, was another major reason why the project was successful.

This review provided the first recognition of the phased concept and subsequent project execution of phase control. Since that beginning, the task force method of executing projects by phase control has been developed to the point where Fluor is fully dedicated to the task force/project management concept of performing projects.

Fluor Utah executes projects by the task force approach on small- and medium-size projects up through the very largest, including the $750 million turnkey Cuajone copper complex in Peru, which was completed on schedule in late 1976.

As it is not practical to cover all facets of project management in a single paper, we have selected several subjects to illustrate project management as it is practiced at Fluor Utah. These are: task force organization; task force and departmental responsibilities; corporate management and the task force; prime project management considerations; communications with the client; project execution by phase control; variables in the practice of project management; Fluor Utah's project manager development program; and a summary. Because we believe phase control plays a major role in successful project execution, it is discussed in greater detail than other concepts.

Task Force Organization

We structure the task force under the direction of a project manager who is primarily responsible for the company's performance of the contract. The task force comprises engineering, procurement, construction, project controls, and administrative personnel functioning under the direction of the project manager. These persons are assigned to each task force by the various section or department heads, who retain certain authority and responsibility for the quality of the work in accordance with established company procedures. Now, let us take a moment to examine a typical task force organization chart (Figure 10).

This organization was used for a medium-size domestic project. It indicates the key personnel reporting to the project manager and the functional responsibilities of each of the key members of the task force. Shown on this organization chart are the dotted lines between each of the key personnel and his respective department or section manager. The latter has responsibility for furnishing personnel to the task force and giving necessary technical direction to assure the quality of work.

Task Force and Department Responsibilities

The definition of the respective authorities and the responsibilities of the project manager and his key task force personnel, with respect to the department and section managers, are the keys to the orderly functioning of a matrix organization such as ours. To achieve an accepted definition of these responsibilities, we prepared division-of-responsibility matrices.

Figure 11 shows a representative division of responsibility matrix chart. It partially delineates the responsibilities of various task force and engineering department person-

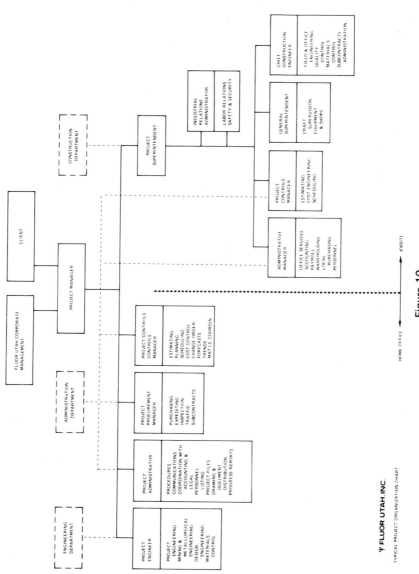

Ψ FLUOR UTAH, INC.

TYPICAL PROJECT ORGANIZATION CHART

Figure 10.

FLUOR UTAH, INC.	DIVISION OF RESPONSIBILITY ENGINEERING				
Legend R – RESPONSIBLE FOR COLLECTION AND COORDINATION OF DATA A – APPROVE I – INPUT OF DETAILED DATA C – CHECK – REVIEW FOR COMMENT	Task Force			Department	
ACTIVITY	PROJECT MANAGER	PROJECT ENGINEER	DISCIPLINE CHIEF ENGINEERS	SECTION MANAGERS	
CONCEPTUAL ADEQUACY	A	R		A	
TECHNICAL ADEQUACY		R	A		
PROCESS CRITERIA	A	R		A	
DESIGN CRITERIA	A	R	A		
PROJECT CRITERIA	A	R			
PREPARE MANHOUR BUDGET	A	R	I	A	
MANPOWER PLANNING		R	I	A	
ENGINEERING SCHEDULE	A	R	I	I	
TECHNICAL SPECIFICATIONS		R	A		
DESIGN CALCS & DRAWINGS		R	A		
BID EVALUATION	A	R			
ASSIGNMENT OF KEY PERSONNEL	A			R	
ASSIGNMENT OF OTHER PERSONNEL		A	R		

Figure 11.

nel. Figure 12 shows a similar chart showing a portion of the construction department's division of responsibilities.

Corporate Management and the Task Force

Corporate management and project managers recognize that even though we are fully dedicated to the task force concept, corporate management cannot abdicate its responsibilities when delegating authority to a project manager. We instill in our project managers the ability to determine when they should meet management or seek management's advice. Also, the project manager must make the dotted-line relationships work. If a specialist on the task force is not receiving dotted-line, technical direction from his department, then the project manager and his key task force personnel are at fault for not fulfilling one of their prime responsibilities.

Section and department managers also have responsibility to see that assigned task force personnel receive proper technical direction. These managers fulfill their responsibility by being involved in the conceptual design, in some of the project planning and in participating in and approving project procedures relating to their area of expertise. They also make periodic visits to the task force, are present at certain task force meetings, and approve appropriate project documents in accordance with company and project procedures.

⚈ FLUOR UTAH, INC.	DIVISION OF RESPONSIBILITY CONSTRUCTION								
Legend	**Task Force**					**Department**			
R – RESPONSIBLE FOR COLLECTION AND COORDINATION OF DATA A – APPROVE I – INPUT OF DETAILED DATA C – CHECK – REVIEW AND COMMENT	PROJECT MANAGER	PROJECT SUPERINTENDENT	CHIEF CONSTRUCTION ENGR	GENERAL SUPERINTENDENT	V P CONSTRUCTION	MGR CONSTRUCTION ENGR	MGR CONSTRUCTION ADMIN		
ACTIVITY									
ESTABLISH CONSTRUCTION PLAN	A	R	I	I	C	I			
SCOPE – SUBCONTRACTS	A	R	I	I	C				
PREPARE CONSTRUCTION SCHEDULE	A	R	I	I	C	I			
ESTABLISH FIELD ORGANIZATION	A	R	I	I	C	I			
ASSIGNMENT OF KEY PERSONNEL	A	I			R		I		
ASSIGNMENT OF OTHER PERSONNEL		A			R		I		
DEVELOP CONSTRUCTION EQUIPMENT LIST	A	R	I	I	C	I			
DEFINE TEMPORARY FACILITIES	A	R	I	I		I			
MANPOWER PLANNING	A	R	I	I	C				
H.O. MANHOUR BUDGET	A	I	I	I	A	R			

Figure 12.

While Fluor Utah corporate management is informed of the project's status on an informal basis, it is at the quarterly project reviews that a complete, formal review of the project is made. These quarterly reviews are held in two sessions chaired by the project manager. The first, involving key task force and section management personnel, is an in-depth working review of the project's status. Attending this meeting are the project manager, senior task force personnel, and appropriate section and department managers.

Agenda for this meeting is:

- Project plan
- Cost forecast/estimate
- Schedule
- Organization
- Manpower plan
- Productivity
- Specific problem areas
- Section managers' comments

The purpose of the second meeting is to inform corporate management of the project's status, seek management's guidance and advice on policy matters, and obtain any required approvals.

Attending this meeting are the project manager; president; senior vice-presidents of operations, administration, and marketing; and the vice-presidents of project management, construction, and engineering.

Agenda for this meeting is:

- Project plan-revisions
- Cost forecast/estimate
- Schedule
- Organization
- Performance of key individuals
- Contract status
- Financial status (client payment)
- Nonreimbursable costs
- Manpower plan
- Productivity
- Client relations
- Task force/department relations
- Specific problem areas
- Department V.P. comments

An important function of this meeting is to review the performance of key task force individuals. Outstanding work as well as personnel problems are discussed and acted upon.

Prime Project Management Considerations

On every project there are four prime project management considerations, namely:

- Task force performance
- Project cost and schedule
- Client relations
- Fluor Utah business interests

One facet of the art of project management stressed at Fluor Utah is for the project manager to keep these four major considerations in balance. When concentration of effort is on one, two, or even three of the above, without full consideration of the others, the result is always a less successful project. Neither the interests of the client, nor the engineering construction company, nor the project cost and schedule should have an overriding influence on the project manager's execution of the project. It is the project manager's responsibility—because of his position, as well as his experience, training, and knowledge—to see that the four factors are kept in balance.

Communications with Client

Proper communication with the client's organization is another important part of project management, particularly on reimbursable-type work. To facilitate this, we aim for the following:

- Obtain owner input and approval of the project plan and procedures; make these "live" documents by their review and revision.
- Establish a team approach with the client.
- Schedule and hold periodic summit meetings with top-level client and Fluor Utah management personnel to assure that both are kept fully informed, and that the client understands and supports instructions being given by his resident engineers.
- Assure understanding by the client of the estimates and cost forecasts presented to him.
- Strive for owner representation at home office for duration of activities to make decisions and give timely approvals. Similar representation in the field is highly desirable.

Project Execution by Phase Control

Project execution by phase control is a management system used by Fluor Utah to control projects. This system, which divides a project into identifiable phases, enables Fluor Utah to complete projects on schedule and within budget. Each phase contains a defined work function with a specific input and goal. Phase control eliminates unexpected difficulties by identifying adverse trends in their early stages, from which positive corrective action is taken to reverse these trends. Thus, by monitoring and controlling the progress of each phase, it is possible to control an entire project.

As stated earlier, total responsibility is placed in our project manager. He is totally responsible for the execution of a project from its earliest stages right through to completion. We recognize the need to keep Fluor Utah Management totally informed, so that it may apply its expertise to any problems that may arise.

Last, and most important, we recognize the need to keep the client fully informed so he is totally involved. Only in this way can we work together as a team in the successful execution of a project.

A typical project is divided into seven phases:

Phase I   —planning, data gathering and procedures

Phase II   —studies and basic engineering

Phase III —major review

Phase IV   —detail engineering

Phase V   —detail engineering/construction overlap

Phase VI   —construction

Phase VII—testing and commissioning

Phases are divided into periods as percentages of total project time. Each phase contains a defined work function with a definitive input and a recognizable result.

As the project moves from phase to phase, the number of persons and the talents are changed. Changes in staffing are continuous in order to respond to changing job conditions. Control features allow continuous job progress while providing for necessary reviews. As you see on the bar chart (Figure 13), various phases may overlap in time. Every project will vary from this example.

In addition to calendar reviews, specific reviews are required at phase change points. These identify positive control points, typical of which is the status of schedule and cost.

Project execution phase charts indicate how an engineering and construction project is controlled in each phase. The same phases shown on the flow chart (Figure 14) were previously shown on the bar chart.

The flow chart and each individual phase chart show Fluor Utah's organization on the lower line and the client organization on the upper line. They run concurrently through the life of the project. For example, Phase V—detail engineering/construction overlap (Figure 15) shows the peak of functional activities and persons involved. Various symbols are used to depict different functions, locations, or length of assignment, as shown in the legend.

Note that an individual or a group maintains the same code throughout each phase chart and that both the client's and Fluor Utah's organizations are assigned specific tasks during each phase of the project.

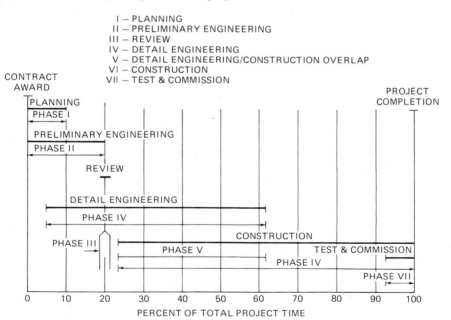

Figure 13.

TYPICAL PHASE EXECUTION FLOW CHART

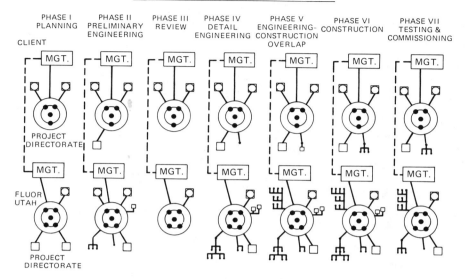

Figure 14.

We will now explain the phases in detail and enumerate the salient responsibilities of each organization during each phase.

Phase I—Planning, Data Gathering, and Procedures

Phase I begins upon contract award, or letter of intent. Its purpose is to establish the work plan for the entire project.

In the planning phase, we have a typical planning organization consisting of a project engineering manager, project controls manager (who is responsible for estimating, scheduling and cost engineering), and project procurement manager.

This key group, augmented by other personnel for a specific project as required, forms a project directorate, which stays with a project throughout its life, relocating as necessary. It is the project directorate that performs the vital planning and control functions.

The phase chart also indicates the client's parallel organization and project directorate. In this case, we have simply shown a project manager, process engineer, general representative, and site representative.

We have indicated a communications link between Fluor Utah management and client management.

The various phase charts indicate the principal activities of Fluor Utah and the Client. During Phase I, Fluor Utah establishes the task force, develops the project execution plan and procedures, gathers data from site and client, prepares project execution flow chart, and recommends a program of studies.

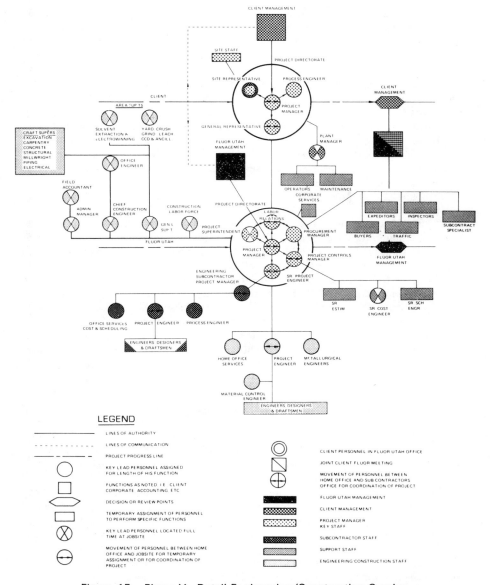

Figure 15.   Phase V—Detail Engineering/Construction Overlap.

Concurrently during Phase I, the client will establish his project team, define scope of work, provide site and available process data, provide information on work to be performed directly by client or others, approve project execution plan and procedures, review and agree to program of studies. A project manager and his key task force members make a more detailed review of the proposed project plan, as well as the available technical and general data, to determine what additional data should be obtained and what revisions to the proposed project plan may be required. Alternative conceptual design studies may be required by the contract or may be suggested by task force members in the interest of improved performance, cost and schedules.

The financing for the project is reviewed to determine what restrictions may be imposed by the loaning agencies. The alternatives to construction versus construction management will be reviewed.

Standard project procedures will be reviewed and modified for applicability to the project and for later discussions with the client.

Shortly after the initial task force meeting, arrangements and an agenda for the very important initial client meeting will be made. Major agenda items for this meeting will be transmittal of data, establish communication procedures, agree upon document distribution, review and confirm scope of project, arrange for detail site visit, and review Fluor Utah's plan of execution and project procedures.

One of the tasks Fluor Utah performs during this initial planning phase is to prepare charts, such as Figure 15, to identify each phase and to indicate what must be accomplished by Fluor Utah and the client during each phase.

Prior to moving to the next phase, there is a joint review of progress with the client's and Fluor Utah's management. This and similar joint review meetings provide assurance to the client that he has total control over the execution of the project or as much control as he wishes to maintain.

Phase II—Studies and Basic Engineering

In the preliminary engineering phase, a larger engineering organization is at work in either Fluor Utah's home office or in the office of the engineering subcontractor than existed in Phase I. The client's organization may likewise change during this preliminary engineering phase.

Objective of Phase II is to provide a complete engineering package for the project or portions thereof, to the point where the work has been fully defined and its completion becomes routine. This will permit production man-hour and cost budgets, staffing, scheduling, and work plan to be accurately and realistically produced and reported.

During Phase II, the following basic engineering will be accomplished: process flowsheets, preliminary piping and instrument diagrams, electrical one-line diagrams, initial general arrangement drawings and plot plans. Specifications for long-lead items will be prepared, quotations received and analyzed, and recommendations made to client for purchase. Final engineering and procurement schedules will be developed during this period.

The construction and material plan will be developed during this phase, and construction methods will be investigated to suit site conditions and the availability of construction equipment. A review of capabilities of local subcontractors will be made to amplify the construction plan.

The project control estimate of engineering and construction costs, as well as the overall project schedule, will be developed during this phase. Project procedures will be finalized during Phase II.

The project manager has the responsibility for preparing project procedures as soon as possible after contract award and for preparing them in general accordance with Fluor Utah's standard procedures. He is also responsible for explaining procedures to the client and other parties, and obtaining all necessary approvals. Preparation of the project procedures early in the job will force all the task force supervisors and the client to think through and understand how they will execute all phases of the project. Many problems can be minimized or avoided by preparation of comprehensive procedures covering all facets of the client's participation. These include who the client's representatives will be, where they are to be located, who is to receive what information, and which client representative has approval and decision making authority in each area of project operations.

Near the completion of Phase II activities, a major review meeting is arranged with the client. This is called Phase III.

Phase III—Major Review

Before proceeding to the detail engineering Phase IV, it is necessary to ensure before the build-up of a large staff that the design is basically frozen. It is important to determine that the client is satisfied with process flowsheets, piping and instrument diagrams, electrical one-lines, plot plans, general arrangements, etc. This makes possible a one-pass engineering effort. For this reason, a major or summit review phase is scheduled prior to proceeding with detail engineering.

Most important, we make sure all parties understand that this package (scope, design criteria, flowsheets and piping and instrument drawings, one-line electrical drawings, equipment lists, specifications, general arrangement drawings, estimate, and schedule) becomes the basis for controlling project costs and schedule. Any changes from the data base will result in project trend reports or change orders covering either costs or schedules, or both!

Upon completion of the Phase III Review, we are ready to begin production of detail engineering.

We—at times—perform only this portion of the engineering and other tasks in the home office. For these projects, we transfer a preliminary engineering package to another office overseas along with key task force engineers and managers to complete the work. This is another reason for adopting the phased concept of project execution.

Phase IV—Detail Engineering

In the first three phases, the project has been described by flowsheets, equipment specifications, and general arrangement drawings. Its construction cost has been estimated, and execution has been scheduled and planned. All these activities have been discussed with and approved by the client. Orders have been given to proceed with the project.

With all this preparation, we should be able to sit back and watch the project develop. Unfortunately, as we all know, things just don't work out that way. Our project planning must continue to the project's end because many forces are constantly at work that could cause changes to the best of plans.

Some typical changing conditions that must be dealt with are:

- Product specification variations
- Site conditions
- Weather
- Labor relations
- Material and equipment shortages
- Political stability
- Project financing requirements

In addition to project plan revisions caused by these factors, supplementary plans must be developed in detail for the successful completion of the project:

- Detail engineering
- Procurement
- Construction
- Testing and commissioning

During the detail engineering (Phase IV) Fluor Utah will prepare construction drawings and specifications, material take-off, subcontract documents and continue procurement activities as developed in earlier phases. Costs of engineering and purchased items will be monitored. Their effect on schedules and control estimate will be evaluated.

Fluor Utah's activities during this phase include material take-off and bulk orders of piping and electrical materials. Bulk materials are combined with the equipment list on a computer inventory program. Purchasing information, expediting reports, and scheduling requirements are constantly added to the program, so that the status of all major equipment and materials is monitored to project completion.

Detail engineering and procurement schedules are prepared during this phase and are integrated into the construction schedule. The time for receipt of data from the client and client approval is an important part of such schedules.

It should be noted that approval to start detail engineering and construction is often specifically delineated in the prime contract between the client and Fluor Utah. The procedure for approvals of other items is agreed upon during preparation of project procedures in Phase II, as mentioned earlier. In day-to-day meetings in our home office, the authorized client representative will approve the items developed during the design engineering phase.

Phase V—Detail Engineering and Construction Overlap

The phase during which the most diverse activities proceed concurrently is known as Phase V, detail engineering and construction overlap. Coordination between all parties—engineering, procurement, construction, and the client—uring this phase forms the basis for the ultimate success of the project. At this time, all planning to date gets its first major test and is revised as required.

In Phase V, the field staff is mobilized by Fluor Utah, and initial construction is started. Subcontractors are selected and their work supervised. Material and equipment are received. A detail construction schedule is developed. Design is completed and construction drawings and specifications issued.

Client representation at both the field and home office by persons with authority to act is vital in this phase, so that timely approvals can be obtained.

Phase VI—Construction

Detail construction schedules of the subcontractors and Fluor Utah construction superintendents are coordinated and implemented during this phase.

The organizational arrangement in Figure 15 shows the start of the build-up of personnel engaged in construction activities. This build-up reaches its peak in Phase VI. Lead design engineers are held available for advice, design interpretation, and support during the construction phase.

Although members of the client's operating organization may be available during earlier design phases, it is necessary that managers of operations and maintenance be on hand during this phase to familiarize themselves with various systems and maintenance procedures.

During this phase, the construction planning of earlier phases meets its greatest test as material shortages, late equipment deliveries, labor relations problems, subcontractor difficulties, and weather uncertainties necessitate constant monitoring of schedules and costs with timely reevaluations.

Even though we are in the early stages of construction, planning of the final project stages is an important activity. The preoperational checkout procedures are completed. These procedures will be used to check out all piping, electrical, material handling, and control systems with their attendant instrumentation.

Toward the end of this phase, the project completion schedule is developed, showing detail times of construction completion of the project units. Preoperational checkout and testing and the transfer of care, custody, and control of such units to the client are shown in detail.

Phase VII—Testing and Commissioning

Final phase of the project (Phase VII) is where organizational arrangements change slightly to show the addition of checkout or startup engineers. The testing, commissioning, startup, and Fluor Utah's closeout activities occur in this phase.

Whereas the client has been a part of the team during the life of the project, Fluor Utah's project manager is the leader of the team until preoperational testing and checkout have been completed. At this point, the client's operations management accepts care and custody of the plant and becomes the leader.

With the assistance of Fluor Utah process, checkout, and startup engineers and construction supervisors, the client's staff starts up and operates the plant. Equipment vendor warranties are enforced and equipment functions checked out under operating conditions.

Although the project facilities are basically completed at the plant's commissioning, closeout activities continue for some time after that to button up the punch lists and paper work.

Fluor Utah has a program of periodic followup visits to the project by project management and process engineers to review plant operations and performance after startup and project closeout have been completed.

Variables in the Practice of Project Management

It would be less than candid to conclude without acknowledging that the approach to, and the practice of, project management at our company vary considerably depending upon a number of factors that influence the manner in which we execute projects.

Several examples of these variables are:

- The prime contract
- Financial restraints
- International project considerations
- Client attitude or philosophy
- Geographical location of project
- Services provided by client or third parties
- The project manager himself

Because of these considerations, no contract is performed precisely like any other. We have found it of value to accommodate these variables by preparing a comprehensive project plan with detailed project procedures at the beginning of each job. The insistence upon early planning for each project assures that the project team thinks through, in advance, how it will perform each aspect of the job. This gives us the necessary flexibility required and assures the proper communication among the key members of the task force, the client, and responsible third parties.

Project Manager Development Program

We would like to make reference to something that is much more important to successful project management than the most highly developed state of the art. That something is our project managers. We recognize that no system, procedures or state of the art as practiced by any organization can perform the most routine project management function. Only people manage or perform anything. Because of this conviction, we have established a project manager development program, participated in by all project managers and by some personnel from other departments. In this comprehensive program, we strive not only to improve the skills of the participants, in order to better manage our projects, but also to improve the state of the art of project management as practiced at Fluor Utah.

We recognize the value of developing our own project managers rather than relying on recruiting such highly skilled individuals from outside the organization. With this emphasis on internal development, our project managers over a period of time become thoroughly familiar with our systems and procedures, our organization and its key personnel, and the corporate philosophy and approach to executing projects, and thus gain the confidence of corporate management. With this confidence, management becomes more comfortable in delegating maximum responsibility. This is essential when projects are being executed under a strong project management/task force concept.

Summary

In summary, the state of the art of project management at Fluor Utah is a commitment to the task force approach to project execution.

Strong project management, with clearly defined authority to direct all project activities within a matrix organization, is basic to our approach. The roles of functional departments in supporting project execution are clearly defined to provide the checks and balances necessary to keep the project manager and corporate management advised of project progress.

Strong emphasis is given to client communications and early project planning, facilitated by project execution by phase control.

Finally, we have built into our approach the flexibility to respond to the many restraints and special client requirements that influence each project in a different way.

CASE STUDY 23:   CLIENT REACTION TO INEFFECTIVE PROJECT MANAGEMENT[1]

Introduction

In the *Project Management Institute Quarterly,* ASCE *Journal of the Construction Division, Engineering News-Record, The Constructor, Construction Methods and Equipment,* and many other construction-related publications, there are stories of successful projects employing innovative methods to solve difficult construction management problems. However, publications rarely discuss projects plagued with problems of varying degrees and various natures that cause delays and cost overruns on almost every activity. Therefore, the following case study of what can and often does go wrong on a project may be equally important as published success stories, if not more so, to owners, design engineers, constructors, and educators.

Background Information

The rapidly changing technology of multimillion dollar industrial projects has resulted in new processes with innovative and sophisticated approaches, but, in turn, it has

---

[1] John Borcherding, "Client Reaction to Ineffective Project Management—A Case Study," paper presented at the Project Management Institute Seminar/Symposium, Anaheim, California, October 1978. Used by permission.

generated more complex engineering design and construction management problems. In addition, for the past several years, the government has become increasingly dictatorial in its attempt to lessen the adverse effects on the environment by large product producing industries through enforcement of proliferating regulations, restrictions, and specifications. Similarly, greater attention is being directed toward the safety and well-being of individuals with occupations that make them susceptible to serious injury, by requiring engineers and constructors to follow published safety procedures.

Achieving successful construction projects that satisfy all these demands requires new approaches to previously standard construction practices. However, changing design procedures, as well as new methods of construction, inevitably increase the chance of errors. By pointing out some of these errors in the following case study, plus other problems that occur during the construction of a new process plant, future design and construction may prove more profitable.

Case Analysis

This study of a large project troubled with problems may be contrasted with productive industrial sites to point out what is going wrong versus what is going right. Though there may be a tendency to consider the many problems as a contrived horror story, this is a true description of an actual project.

During the analysis of the organizational structure, site layout, and design approach, the reader may recognize the following underlying, yet general, factors creating an unfavorable work atmosphere on this project:

1. Poor communication throughout levels of the hierarchy
2. Duplication of effort
3. Numerous modifications to plans
4. A state of very low morale by the work force
5. Schedules consistently slipping

It is even more important, however, for readers to note specific solutions and refrain from offering generalizations, such as more intelligent field operations with better cooperation and communication between engineering and construction will minimize mistakes and solve problems.

Organizational Structure

Basically, the organization and communication between construction field representatives and office engineering personnel was established as shown in Figure 16.

The field consisted of the senior process engineer, process engineer, project engineer, field superintendent, and several engineering inspectors, all employed by the same engineering company.

Included in construction activities was the general contractor handling major equipment installation and structural steel erection. Subcontractors consisted of electricians, pipefitters, excavators, vessel fabricators, and various other building and industrial

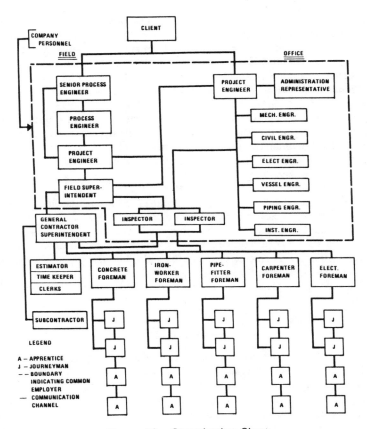

Figure 16.   Organization Chart.

craftsmen. This large number of supervisory personnel added to confusion over authoritative responsibilities, for the functions of all personnel were not clearly identified.

Awarding the Contract

The process engineers interpret and develop the client's ideas into a workable engineering package. The process package is then fully developed and assembled into a workable
contract by design engineers and then released for competitive bidding. During the
bid period, a conference is arranged between the interested contractors and the design
engineers to clarify any discrepancies in the contract that might exist. This meeting
should have solved many future potential conflicts. However, many contractors arrived
for the primary purpose of examining the physical site without having detailed knowledge of overall contract presentation and intent.

After the contract is awarded and construction begins, the only line of communication between the contractor and the engineers is through the project engineer or the engineering inspector. This organizational structure inherently caused significant delays in communications. First, the problem was passed through several parties before reaching the individual who could give the answer. Second, questions became subject to misinterpretation. Third, often questions or answers were not immediately communicated to the concerned parties.

The company field supervisor worked closely with the general contractor superintendent, the engineering inspectors, and the project engineer. But the general contractor had no direct communication with the engineering office. So before the construction of the project ever became active, basic problems were present. At this point, potential conflicts could have been reduced by:

1. Defining responsibilities and status of all personnel in the field acting in an administrative or authoritative capacity. This includes engineering representatives, financiers, process representatives, and construction personnel.
2. Defining the exact purpose and extent of prebid meetings between engineering and contractors. Segregate the site visit and other activities from this meeting and allow ample time for contractor preparation.
3. Establishing a single link between the field and design office for direct communication.

Site Layout

Relatively easy access and open working areas were provided at the plant site as shown by Figure 17. However, most activities were concentrated in and around the process area, consisting of a four-level steel structure.

Due to the various phases of engineering, and a concern for material deliveries, three main steel fabricators became confused over tie points, resulting in duplicating or omiting steel members. In many cases, the contractor had to field-cut and fit previously fabricated pieces to complete the structure, which added to the cost and delayed schedules.

The control building was originally designed by a local architectural firm, but had to be modified to accommodate changes in design. Again, the burden was put on the contractor to incorporate these changes in his schedule.

North of the process area was the tank farm. Storage tanks of many different sizes and structural requirements were grouped and placed within the confines of a 4-foot-high concrete dike wall. Installation of tanks that were to be field-erected was subcontracted, while the general contractor provided the foundations. Proper construction sequencing was vital in this area, and the problems encountered due to design and construction changes will be examined below, in a section entitled "Addenda."

To the north of the tank farm were the tank car loading and unloading facilities. At this point, two different fabricators were involved in providing the structural steel to be erected by the general contractors. A separate vendor was to supply hose supports, and another supplied adjustable gangways that were to be supported on

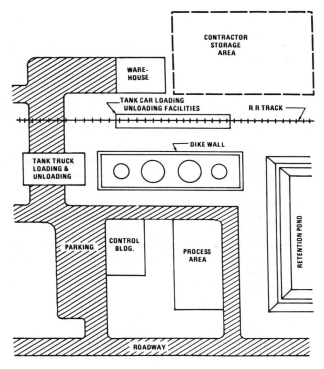

Figure 17.   Site Plan.

the structural steel, all installed by the general contractor. Although a simple structure, construction became complicated, and lack of coordination among the crafts appeared to be a major problem. Alterations in design requirements caused additional field modifications and contributed to further construction difficulties.

The tank truck loading and unloading station was also supplied by a separate building fabricator, and all foundation and erection work was to be done by the main contractor. Special adjustments to this building were later required by law before it could be used. Furthermore, safety devices and other equipment that provided easier and safer access to the tank trucks during loading or unloading were installed.

The warehouse building provided the contractor with a shelter to store fragile items and other small pieces of equipment. The area east of the warehouse was used as storage for structural steel, long runs of prefabricated pipe, and large equipment.

Performance Factors

Job performance on this project hinged on several important factors.

1. The contract was awarded to a nonunion contractor who was relatively unfamiliar with process plants. This may have contributed to the lack of industrial

construction experience by many craftsmen and other personnel. Additional inexperienced personnel were given responsible positions in important activities.

2. The contract was awarded to the lowest bidder. Undoubtedly, any oversights in the original bid could be compensated for by extras, of which there were many. Since reliable cost checks were not accurately maintained, friction developed among the many groups represented in the field.

3. The bid package contained many areas that were marked "Hold for Construction" with the understanding that these areas would be negotiated at a later date. Adequate design information was not available to complete construction details when the contract was bid on these items. When the construction details were finally issued, usually changes to already finished items were required. Work completed had to be redone, adding to the frustration of crew members.

4. Three main structural steel fabricators were involved in complicated and closely related areas. Since a very early steel contract was released to fabricators due to a concern about delivery, a magnitude of negotiations and changes resulted in defining existing and modified items.

5. Many different manufacturers from areas throughout the country were involved in production and delivery of various standard and custom-made items used on the job. Late deliveries resulted in delayed construction schedules, and inadequate vendor design required some items to be either returned or modified in the field.

6. The actual process involved in producing the marketable end product was continuously being revised, even during the construction phase. This led to a constant flow of field change orders and construction addenda.

Problems

Interpretation of engineering drawings. Consistent complaints were registered by the superintendents of the three major construction crafts (electrical, ironworker, pipefitter) because of the difficulty in interpreting the exact intent of a major portion of the engineering drawings. Understanding the overall job was difficult, so supervisors hesitated to take the initiative to complete specific tasks that were unfamiliar to them.

Many of the specifications governing the installation of important items were detached from the detailed construction drawings. Therefore, the supervisor needed to spend time researching through volumes of written specifications before performing each step in the construction sequence to verify that his approach was correct and that he was not violating or omitting necessary requirements. He complained that the references from the details to the specifications and vice versa were unclear and confusing. The contractor was not accustomed to operating under such a system of strict guidelines required by the close tolerances and technology involved.

The contractor soon found that, due to his mistakes and omissions, he was not able to maintain his construction schedule. A more diligent review of the details and specifications by the superintendent before the construction work for that particular activity began would have eliminated many of the difficulties. In addition, a general review of all information, including the indexing and reference system, could have been conducted by field managers with their foremen and general foremen.

Material procurement. During the time this construction project was active, manufactured materials were difficult to obtain, mostly due to the existing national economic conditions. Major vendors were requiring that specified delivery dates be extended on some materials. A few of the manufacturers listed on engineering drawings were no longer in business or they had discontinued that particular product line. The contractor, therefore, inherited the responsibility of substituting some construction materials with what was available. In cases where several engineering firms were involved in joint design of a certain system, the contractor found incongruencies in the details and construction sequences. Again, these conflicts were not detected until construction work on that activity was actually being performed. The contractor had to stop until the conflict could be resolved. This sometimes took days before a satisfactory solution was found, which further delayed his construction schedule.

Verification of vendor documents. In cases where supports were required for stabilizing equipment, contractor verrification of support details with certified vendor documents was required. This check was not performed until the actual construction began. The differences in support details between the construction drawings and vendor drawings were numerous. In a majority of the cases, most of the vendors altered dimensions from their preliminary data, which were used as a basis for setting dimensions on engineering drawings. The contractor again was forced to halt construction to make the necessary alterations in support details, further delaying the construction schedule.

One illustration of such discrepancy occurred during the construction of a compressor deck. The system involved two large compressor units mounted on a composite, sloping concrete slab 10 feet above the ground, supported on a rigid steel frame. The contractor worked overtime one weekend on this structure in an attempt to get back on schedule. He erected the steel and formed up the deck to be ready to pour concrete at the beginning of the following week. However, after the forming was complete, he noticed that there were no block-outs specified in the drawings for pipe penetrations through the floor slab. He, therefore, had to delay pouring until he received this information. While plotting the pipe location, the latest vendor documents on the compressor showed a 3-inch offset on the compressor supports. Therefore, the contractor had to take down all the form work, shift the four supporting compressor beams by 3 inches, and then reform the deck. At this point, he realized that meeting a schedule under such circumstances was impossible.

Another major setback occurred when the contractor had to alter a ringwall foundation for a large storage tank located in the tank farm area. To alter the foundation, the contractor had to demolish a section of the dike wall, remove the slab, rework the foundation, then replace the slab and the section of wall. Although the contractor adjusted his bid to perform the alteration, he lost valuable production time.

Equipment deliveries. To prevent congesting storage space, the contractor attempted to have the supports and foundations in place so he could immediately position equipment upon its arrival. When inspecting the process equipment as it arrived, parts were found to be damaged and missing. Some items were not properly secured during transportation, which caused damage; inspection of welds showed some to have faulty seams, and on others, connections and fittings were incorrectly fabricated. These items were, therefore, returned to the manufacturer for repair, further delaying progress. The situation became so bad that at one point it became necessary to stop construction for two days until all changes could be interpreted and their effects analyzed.

Addenda.   One of the major points of contention that contributed to many of the problems listed above and added to the contractor's inability to accomplish work on schedule was the continuous flow of revisions throughout the construction phase. Some of the causes for this confusion were due to changes in engineering design, types of supports required for certain items, structural systems, location of equipment, electrical schedules, quantities of materials, type of materials, size and type of piping, pump sizes, motor sizes, etc. Many of the superintendents became confused as to exactly what was their work. One ironworker superintendent said, "Due to the series of revisions, we are not sure where we stand. Steel that is already erected shows up later as deleted. Foundations already installed at one location show up later as needed in a different location."

Attitude of Workforce

In light of the difficulties encountered in almost every phase of the project, one can easily imagine the disillusionment and frustrations encountered by skilled craftsmen. When effort is exerted to complete a task properly and within schedule, there is much disappointment when time and time again that effort ends up fruitless. This disappointment is reflected by the displays of sarcastic, derogatory leaflets hung up about the change shacks and directed toward the skill and planning of construction managers and supervisors, engineers, architects, vendors, and the client. Displayed throughout the job are copies of "Murphy's Laws," which state the continuous unavoidable confrontations with errors.

These attitudes definitely do not produce success. The only satisfaction realized from this type of job is eight hours' pay for eight hours work, for there is little present to create incentive, excite the imagination, or increase performance.

Basically, most of the qualities of work regularly causing dissatisfaction were present on this site.[3,4] In particular, mistakes and field change orders that required craftsmen to redo work were most dissatisfying to previously productive workers.

Major dissatisfiers for foremen were related to poor engineering plans and specifications, unorganized planning and activity schedules, and slow progress. As mentioned, supervisors, and especially foremen, complained about the difficulty in cross-referenc-

---

[3] John D. Borcherding, "An Exploratory Study of Attitude Affects on Human Resources in Building and Industrial Construction," Dept. of Civil Engineering, Stanford University, Stanford, California, 1972.

[4] John D. Borcherding and Clarkson H. Oglesby, "Job Dissatisfaction in Construction Work," ASCE *Journal of Construction,* vol. 101, CO2, June 1975, pp. 415–434.

ing between the plans and specifications. They hesitated to exercise their full responsibility for fear of overlooking pertinent information, which would then result in mistakes and having to tear work out.

Likewise, maintaining job schedules proved to be a difficult task, due to equipment and material delays, along with the changes to engineering and process designs. Ultimately, these problems produced very slow progress, which magnified the foremen's frustrations.

Suggestions for Improvement

Initial confrontation with such a volatile work situation should have been a warning to construction management personnel to review its organizational approaches in planning and scheduling. Fundamental steps that could have been employed to minimize the adverse effects from lack of clarity and from changes inherent in this project were:

1. Require frequent (biweekly) meetings with foremen, general foremen, and super-intendents to discuss schedules and anticipated problems likely to occur.
2. Conduct a close review of specifications and construction details for each activity before commencing work.
3. Employ an individual whose prime responsibility is to check the latest issues of vendor documents against construction details. If a conflict exists, notify the project manager and immediately correct the construction detail.
4. Require foremen or general foremen to list the project activities to be accomplished each day, with an alternative schedule to follow in case of delays.
5. Keep a close account of all extras encountered during each day. Inform the client as these extras occur.
6. Explain the client's philosophy and how construction management is organized to accommodate this philosophy to all levels of the field hierarchy.

Conclusion

The circumstances encountered in this case study are by no means unique. Problems that impede progress, create low worker moral, and cause inefficient work environments have always been and will continue to be common to the construction industry. In each case, management's responsibility is to understand his client's attitude, which is reflected in the presentation of the contract package. Additionally, he needs to know the character of the site, the vendors, and the general economic trends to properly prepare and organize the construction approach.

The objective of presenting a case study of what can go wrong on a project was to assist, not criticize, owners, design engineers, construction managers, and field supervisors. Although projects can be turned around after they are classified "sick" and appear to be out of control, this is not an easy task to accomplish. Therefore, many of the suggested solutions for the project's problems were of a preventive type— this is what you should do to prevent a problem from occurring. The frequent techniques of outlasting problems at considerable cost and time are often all that is left when a project seeks a cure to its sickness.

When the entire contractor's organization makes an early commitment to stay on top of a job, there is a high likelihood for success. That is a major reason contracts with a large margin between the low and second bidder often turn out very successful.

Likewise, the client and engineer must make every effort to provide the necessary information in a timely manner if they want contractors to bid process plant work. If problems arise early in the job, similar to those examined in the case study, the contract should be altered to time and materials rather than a fixed price with many extras.

CASE STUDY 24:   THE CASE OF THE PRECARIOUS PROGRAM[1]

Foreword

The following case, though hypothetical, reflects the kinds of real problems faced by the growing number of companies, especially in advanced-technology industries, that have experimented with program management. Joseph J. Hansen, who has had firsthand experience with his subject, is a Senior Management Analyst with Raytheon Company. He is the author of two "Problems in Review" cases in past issues.

The scene is the office of George Miller, general manager of the Aircraft Products Division of Admor Company, a manufacturing company located on the perimeter of a major city. With him is Paul Ostroff, manager of the company's program management office. Miller and Ostroff have just returned from a meeting in another part of the plant. Sitting at his desk, Miller keeps glancing distractedly at different papers and memoranda that he must attend to later. Ostroff looks glumly at a note he made during the meeting.

Miller: Well, that session was a fiasco. I thought we were going to have a program review meeting—not a confrontation of enemy camps!

Ostroff: If we could only agree on some basic principles . . .

Miller: I just don't understand it, Paul. You've headed up the program management office for a year-and-a-half now, and the friction between your group and the line managers hasn't diminished a bit. This hydraulic control business—why can't you fellows get together and figure out how to do it? Why do *I* have to be dragged into the middle every time? Frankly, I'm beginning to question the whole program management concept.

Ostroff: But what's the alternative, George? We can't turn the clock back. After all, we didn't just decide one day on a whim to use program management. We were forced into it; our contracts were changing. Remember, we used to do mostly military

---

[1] By Joseph J. Hansen. *Reprinted by permission of the Harvard Business Review.* Copyright © 1968 by the president and fellows of Harvard College; all rights reserved.

jobs that started as cost-plus-fixed-fee development programs and then became fixed-price production contracts. But a couple of years ago, when we did begin getting contracts involving both engineering and production, the schedules didn't let us finish the design phase before we had to start production planning. You remember what *that* was like! There were commitments for personnel and for facilities and orders for materials and parts to subcontract with long lead times—we had to start doing all that long before the design got frozen. And we couldn't do it under the old system. We had coordination problems we'd never dreamed of before.

Miller: And PERT, bless it! Remember when we had to start using PERT in our reports? What a time that was. . . .

Ostroff: And the other status reports we had to make for a contract in progress, and all the figures and dates customers were asking us for, even before we started manufacturing. That's what I mean, George. There had to be somebody to coordinate, and you know we didn't have it under the old system. It doesn't matter whether you call it *program management* or something else, but you've got to have it. Not all the time, of course—but for jobs like this, yes. (Table 1 shows the charter for the program management office.)

Miller: We're a month behind schedule on this job.

Ostroff: We can make it up and deliver on schedule. I told them that at the meeting.

Miller: We're overspent by $110,000.

Ostroff: We can trim it to $60,000. I said that, too.

Table 1. Charter of the Program Management Office[a]

The program management office is responsible for (a) planning for and meeting contractual requirements on programs assigned to it, and (b) meeting profit objectives on these programs as established by division management.

In the planning stage the program management office will:

☐ Prepare schedules, in cooperation with operating departments, for the execution of all tasks in accordance with program requirements.

☐ Prepare budgets and negotiate them with operating departments, consistent with contractual funds available and division profit.

During the execution of a contract the Program Management Office will:

☐ Monitor technical and contractual progress with a frequency sufficient to ensure the timely detection of problem areas.

☐ Work with operating department managers to provide corrective action on any problem areas and bring serious or unresolved problems to the attention of the Division General Manager.

☐ Be the main contact point for the customer, handling his requests for information, processing requests for cost estimates of progressive changes, furnishing status reports, and so forth.

☐ Coordinate, in cooperation with the sales department, all bids and proposal activity of a follow-on nature stemming from a current contract.

[a] From a directive issued by George Miller, general manager of the Aircraft Products Division.

Miller: Engineering doesn't agree. It predicts $150,000—and a month late with delivery on top of that.

Ostroff: Engineering always exaggerates. Last September, remember, on that instrumentation for . . .

Miller: I know, I know. The point is, why can't you people *get together* on these figures? Why do I always have to arbitrate? There must be something wrong with the system, and we've just got to get at it, Paul. We can't go on like this; *I* can't, anyway.

Ostroff: One thing is that my program coordinators and I have no line authority. I'm not complaining, but you've got to remember that. We're more like a general contractor than anything else. We negotiate work statements, budgets, and schedules with line departments, and then we follow up on them to make sure they are living up to their agreements. If they fall down on the job, there isn't much we can do except exert pressure by threatening to take the job away from them and subcontract it outside. And that threat is more theory than practice, as you know, because we've never carried it out.

You say you're in the middle. *We're* the ones who have to talk with the customer, answer his questions, and generally keep him out of the hair of the operating groups. Talk about being in the middle!

Miller: How about your staff? Do you have the right men and enough of them to do the job?

Ostroff: I'd say so. We're able to handle the planning, budgeting, and monitoring of programs well enough. What we *can't* do is the program tasks themselves—there we have to depend on the line people.

Miller: Let's see. How many men have you got? Five?

Ostroff: Three are program coordinators. This hydraulic control contract takes all the time of one of them. The other contracts are divided up. Then I've got a man for scheduling and status review; he helps the program coordinators, and he knows all about PERT and LOB and the rest. And I've also got a cost control expert; he helps us with the division controller, he helps the program coordinators with budgets, and sometimes he helps us in pricing negotiations with customers.

Miller: I've asked Larry and Vic to meet me in a few minutes to try to work out these differences on the hydraulic control job. Maybe you should join us.

Ostroff: Okay, but I've got a one o'clock lunch.

Miller: We should be through by then.

Larry Rivera and Victor Stekler come into the office. Rivera is engineering department manager; Stekler is a section head for engineering department services. (See Table 2 for a partial organization chart of the Aircraft Products Division.) The two men draw up chairs near Paul Ostroff.

Table 2. Partial Organization Chart of the Aircraft Products Division of Admor Company.

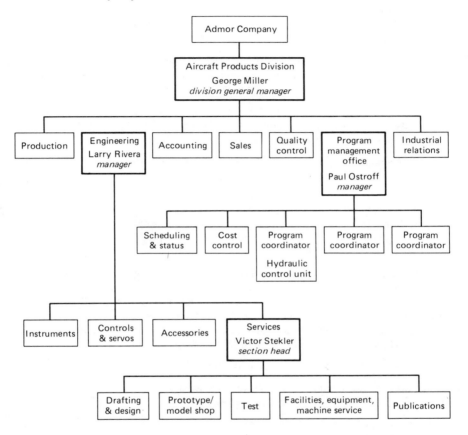

Miller: I've just told Paul, and I don't mind telling you fellows as well, that I thought this morning's meeting was a fiasco. Here we are halfway down the pike on the program, and we still can't agree on when we should be able to finish or what the final cost will turn out to be.

Rivera: I've reviewed all the engineering department estimates with my section heads again, and it just wouldn't be realistic to change them at this point. It still looks as though we'll deliver a month late with an overrun of $150,000.

Ostroff: I don't see why!

Rivera: I'll tell you why. When a job is under the control of your program management office, we don't get authorization to proceed—we can't move—without your okay. Your men have to give us work statements, budget breakdowns, and schedules that we all agree on. In this case, we didn't get the green light until three full weeks after the program was supposed to have started! So, you see, only one week of the month delay can be charged against engineering. Your office will have to take the blame for the other three weeks.

Ostroff: Now wait a minute. Those three weeks were spent waiting for *you* to make up your mind whether or not you were going to accept the budgets and schedules we'd prepared. We had them in your hands on time; you held them up!

Riveria: I didn't accept them because I knew right from the start we couldn't meet your budget. You took our estimates and pared them to suit your own ideas. That's also why we have a cost overrun today.

Ostroff (holding up a budget with Riveria's approval signature on it): But you *did* accept it.

Rivera: Yes, finally—but only because my back was against the wall. I've a limited amount of overhead funding for holding people who don't have contract work to support them. It was either give in or else lay off the people I needed most to do the job. I figured they might as well be doing something productive as waiting around while we argued about budgets.

Stekler: That's doubly true for the service departments, Paul. In engineering department services there's an irreducible minimum we have to keep, say, in the model shop to maintain our versatility. When you give me a budget that's 20 percent low in my opinion, and then say "take it or leave it," I may as well take it and face up to the overrun later. The only alternatives are to put everyone on waiting time—an overhead charge, as you know—or close up the shop.

Ostroff: I know that. I recognize your problem.

Miller (pulling out a printed schedule for the hydraulic control program and staring at it): Now, let's take this, for instance. How does that apply to this?

Stekler: My people have been expecting to build the model of the control unit in April. Everything's been programmed with that in mind. So when I get the preliminary release a whole month late, how can you expect me to stay within the original budget? I have the same overhead budget problem that Larry just described. I'm going to have to charge those people to the hydraulic job whether they're working on it or not, unless I let them go; and if I do that, we won't be able to do the work when we *do* get it!

And, by the way, what happens to the other work we have lined up for May? I expect to have the whole crew tied up on the channel selectors for the entire month.

Ostroff: The channel selector job isn't under the control of my office.

Stekler: Which means I've got to fight with somebody else about the May schedule.

Rivera: Vic's right about the charges. If you change the schedule, it's going to cost you money and maybe time, too. Engineering agreed to the budgets, I'll admit, but only as a package: budgets, work statements, *and* schedule. Change any element, and the whole package is subject to review.

Ostroff: Nobody changes anything for the sake of change. We've got a customer to worry about.

Rivera: That reminds me of another thing that's bothering me. After we had barely started, your program coordinator came in with a whole list of questions from the customer: Could we operate on a minimum of 75 pounds per square inch instead of the 100 in the original spec? Could we get the overall weight down under 17 pounds? What viscosity range could we stand? And so on. At least a week of the schedule delay is attributable to these questions. It took time and money to get the answers, and I don't see anything in my original work statement that says I have to spend two or three days a week getting information for the program management office to pass along to the customer. I thought your program office staff was supposed to keep those people *off* our necks! Why don't they answer the questions themselves?

Ostroff: If we could, we would. We'd do the engineering as well.

Rivera: That's not the issue. We don't mind giving you technical opinions, but it takes time and money. What about the contract? Does it stipulate that we have to supply all this extra information at no additional cost?

Ostroff: No. But if you don't, you'll never see a follow-on contract!

Rivera: Well, if all you do is take the questions in, pass them on to us, and then send our answers back out, whey do we need the program management office? I don't have these problems on the jobs I run myself.

Ostroff: Maybe that's because all the tough programs are assigned to my office. You'd be surprised how many nontechnical questions we handle ourselves without bothering you and how many data and report requests we turn down, because we believe they're outside the contract scope and can safely be refused. Without the program management office, how would you furnish monthly PERT reports? Who would write the status reports? Who would bear the responsibility for profit? Who'd watch performance? These coordination problems aren't trivial, and that's why we have a program management office. We're a professional group, and my men are specialists.

We try to set up schedules and budgets that are a reasonable compromise between what the departments want and what we would like to give them. If we let everyone set his own targets, you'd have overruns on every job.

Rivera: I'm not arguing against the need for coordination.

Ostroff: There's another point. Not every program is run through this office. I'm not blaming you, Larry, or your people, but the top priorities for manpower always seem to go to the programs where the entire responsibility is yours. for example, last week when the drafting effort on the channel selector was in trouble, what did you do? You took draftsmen off the hydraulic control unit.

Miller sighs audibly, pushes his chair back, and walks to the window. The others wait silently. Finally, Miller turns to face them.

Miller: Do you think you'd be more effective, Paul, if you had control of all programs rather than just those that seem to require extensive coordination? Then you could establish priorities.

Rivera: Wait a minute! Even if the program management office *coordinates* all jobs, it's my job to *run* engineering. *I* have to decide where best to use my people and resources, not Paul. I'll accept responsibility for meeting my budgets and schedules as far as possible; but I'm the one who has to worry about how to support my people, how to maintain capability, what areas need strengthening.

Ostroff: Isn't that really the heart of the problem? I have responsibility for the job, but every other department has authority to run things any damned way it wants.

Miller: Suppose we do it another way. Suppose that whenever we have a major program starting up, we assemble all the talent needed to do the job—borrowing them from various departments—and assign them directly to you, Paul, on a line basis for the duration of the program. I've read that many companies operate that way.

Rivera: And what happens to the people when the job is over? Then I get them back, I suppose. What if my budget can't stand it at that point?

Ostroff: I have to agree with Larry because I've been in that spot myself. The line manager is perpetually running a juggling act with his program budgets, overhead, manpower forecasts, and all the other problems. When someone is sick, it's his problem. When there's not enough work, he worries about covering his people, because next month he'll be swamped.

Miller: Think it over. We won't decide anything right now, but we've got to do something soon. One thing I know: we'd better make some changes.

Ostroff, Rivera, and Stekler leave the office as Miller walks back to his desk.

Query to Readers

Many companies have used and are using the program management concept to help solve difficult problems of coordination and control. Some have been successful; others—like Admor—have found that the change to program management has increased tensions within the organization and caused more problems than it solved.

To get a variety of points of view on why this conflict-laden situation arose and how it should be resolved, HBR sought opinions from several commentators, each with a different background. Why not take a moment now to collect your own thoughts on this case. What would you do if you were George Miller? How can other companies avoid the mistakes made by Admor? Then compare your own views with those of the panel, which follow.

Adequate Accountability

Our commentators have identified many seeming faults in Admor's modus operandi. They are in agreement, however, that when a technique such as program management is introduced, it must be accompanied by a rational and careful assignment of responsibility and authority.

Jay S. Mendell, Assistant Project Engineer at Pratt & Whitney Aircraft, sees a lack of continuity at Admor in the chain of responsibility from the corporate to the individual level:

> Admor must build the hydraulic control system according to prearranged conditions: in a certain period, at a definite price, according to customer specifications. Meanwhile the corporation must carry on equally important projects of research, development, and production. As things stand, no one person is accountable for all aspects of building the required control system on time and a profit.

Melvin Silverman, author of *The Technical Program Manager's Guide to Survival*[2] and formerly Manager of Program Management at the Kearfott Division of General Precision, Inc., underscores the role of the program manager as a manager first and a coordinator second, but reserves the responsibility for specific performance and authority decisions to line managers supervising specific sections of the program. He states:

> The program manager cannot 'second guess' the line managers in their areas of specialization, since they—not he—are doing the work. He has enough to do just as a 'generalist' and a manager. He can suggest alternatives and ask for reevaluations; but when the line managers finally say 'that's it,' he either accepts their conclusion or changes the line managers.

Broadening this point to a diagnosis of Admor's cost problem, Mr. Silverman argues for a realistic approach from the beginning:

> If the total of all cost estimates submitted by line managers for the functional work statements is equal to or less than that of the original contract, Ostroff's major task becomes that of coordinating, since the quotation of the original contract was managed well. If the total is greater than that of the contract, a default or loss is coming up, and Miller had better know about it in the beginning. Then his alternatives are less restricted because no company funds have, as yet, been spent. A follow-on contract might be well worth a loss or added division efforts. Or, Miller might want to cancel this contract and take a small penalty to avoid the potentially larger loss pointed up by Ostroff's total budget. In any event, Ostroff will have presented an objective picture; and any changes

---

[2] John Wiley & Sons, Inc., New York, 1967.

later on cannot be attributed to poor planning, squeeze plays, or other devious ploys.

Other commentators suggest assigning full responsibility to the program manager, with authority commensurate to the task. Looking at the case from his vantage point as Assistant Program Officer, Occupational Health Program, U.S. Department of Health, Education, and Welfare, Bill B. Benton, Jr., considers the possibility that the program manager's office be inserted directly into the chain of command:

> Elevating Ostroff's office to a line position between the general manager and the operating departments appears to be the only means of fulfilling the terms of the program management office's charter. Ostroff would have the authority to take the actions necessary to ensure the fulfillment of the project plans, subject to the review of the general manager. Project plans, once formulated, would serve as an organizational control mechanism similar to a contract within the organization.

Managerial Maturity?

To several of our commentators, the crux of Admor's problem is not so much the formal organization as it is the way in which the individuals have performed. Herbert A. Freimark, a Project Manager with the Professional Development Division of the American Institute of Certified Public Accountants and also a CPA, looks at the specific requirements of program and line organizations and questions the capabilities of Admor's staff to meet them:

> Project management is always subject to priority pressures and tends to create a shifting of personnel from project to project. Successful project management also depends heavily on the acumen of the project manager. Unfortunately, Admor Company doesn't appear to have the caliber of men, on the line, required to make project management a viable method. An intensive analysis of Admor's human resources is definitely required to ascertain that qualified men are being deployed in all departments. The current confrontations seem to indicate that some personnel changes may be required.

H.M. Hendry, Project Superintendent, Hendry Corporation, concurs. Wondering whether Admor's line managers had a hand in the choice of jobs to be subject to program management, he comments:

> Ostroff should be well aware of the hostile attitude of engineering toward program management, should soothe rather than aggravate, assist and persuade rather than dictate. Even if the program manager had final line authority, he would need the complete and *active* support of engineering to obtain desired results.
> The hydraulic control program management assignment was determined on whose recommendation? Certainly engineering had no part in this assign-

ment—or so it seems. Were all aspects of the assignment fully explored? Just who does determine that certain projects be earmarked as special?

Did Miller Do Enough?

Most of HBR's commentators feel that to bring some reasonable measure of schedule and budget control to a project like Admor's hydraulic control contract, the general manager must become directly and personally involved. One of the men who feels strongly about this point is Otto Klima, Jr., Manager, Systems and Technologies, Re-Entry Systems Department, at the Missile and Space Division of General Electric Company. He says:

> The general manager's personal involvement at this point is critical. Here is where he vividly demonstrates that he will provide the necessary leadership until he feels the program is back on its feet.
>
> It's important to emphasize that in this case Miller must provide both *action* and *communication*. He cannot afford to wait; in this business, delay itself is a decision—and a costly one. The program manager approach is a proven success—but like most meaningful efforts, it takes strong, decision making leadership and excellence in communication. The general manager can afford no less, if he seeks an immediate solution and a lasting future for his business.

Mr. Benton concurs, but wonders whether the conflict might now have gone too far to be resolved by Miller:

> The Admor Company's traumatic experience in program management could have been alleviated with more direct leadership by the general manager in defining objectives and criteria. On the surface, anticipation of conflict areas by Miller could, in effect, have resolved the friction between Ostroff and Rivera, as well as other operative department managers. It is my feeling, however, that the opportunity for success through this approach has passed.

Mr. Hendry would counsel the general manager to hear all sides of the story before acting:

> Miller should critically examine his reasoning and methods in the marshaling of available capacities for program success. He should counsel further with *all* individuals (How about the program coordinator?), singly and in groups, to ensure that he is equipped to manage his division with less chaos and greater profitableness.
>
> There now exists an acute problem, and the division manager will have to use his broad experience and astute management instincts to subdue or control the existing conflicts and chaos and to guide the individual program tasks to desired ends.

What Organizational Changes?

As a corollary requirement to strong leadership, several members of our panel see the need for some kind of organizational change. This could be a minor change, serving primarily to clarify present responsibilities, or a fairly broad change, involving wide shifts in individual roles. Interestingly, none of HBR's commentators think that program management should be scrapped by Admor; all believe it can be made workable in some form. This consensus, which will surprise many readers, may reflect the growing renown of program managers in U.S. industry and increasing confidence in a concept that which not many years ago was a black sheep in the management family.

Donald K. Jellow, whose experience includes both program management and line management at Hazeltine Corp., would strengthen and restructure the program management group on a product line basis:

> The original charter for program management must be strengthened to provide authority commensurate with the currently defined responsibilities. A revision of the charter should provide for complete product responsibility and for a separate program management group for each product line. Each group would be headed by a product line manager. All contracts in a product line would be under the control of one man who would be solely responsible for their success or failure. Small or miscellaneous contracts would be best served if they were collectively assigned to a program management group as one entity.
>
> Organizationally there must be informal lines of communication between the program management representatives and their counterparts in the line organization. This provides for a better means of problem solving and a free flow of technical information acquired from various programs.
>
> Personnel assignment to the various programs must be the responsibility of the line manager. He knows the special talents, as well as the strong and weak points, of each of his employees and is more qualified to place them in programs for which they are best suited.

Dr. Mendell would continue to use the program management office for its staff activities, but would place more responsibility on key individuals in the line organization. He argues:

> A project engineer, reporting to either Rivera or the production manager, should have the authority, responsibility, and accountability. Miller should give this project a priority according to its importance and turn the project engineer loose to do his job. Design, test, and procurement will act as service groups— as will the project management office. The latter should not be allowed to interfere once it has completed its assistance in planning. Ostroff's group should furnish advice and services on request.
>
> As for the program management office, it should furnish certain tools that "build" the solution to difficult problems. These tools (PERT, LOB, budgeting techniques) can be requested by the project engineer and "operated" by the

expert program coordinator. The project management office should educate the line managers and project engineers. It should teach them that planning and budgeting are nothing less than attempts to foresee a partly unpredictable and uncontrollable future. The resulting forecasts are probabilistic guesses intended to maximize the chances of success. When planning is viewed in this light, some friction may disappear.

Mr. Benton dissents from this view because its implementation would place the responsibility for coordination of various programs with the general manager. He states:

> With little difficulty the responsibility for the preparation of the products of the present program management system could be assigned to the operative departments. If the company's conception of the value of program management lies solely in the preparation of PERT charts and status reports, technicians could be assigned to the operative departments accomplishing the resolution of conflict. On the basis of a coordination criterion, however, this responsibility would have to be assumed by the general manager. Such an assumption would appear to demand more time of Miller, preempting all but a superficial review of competing demands. Additionally, this alternative would reduce program management to meaningless paper work or, at best, a necessary evil.

Mr. Freimark, in his recommendations, assigns full authority for all operations to the program manager:

> A centralized management setup (project life cycle management) should be instituted at once. Under the centralized system Ostroff would assume complete responsibility for all jobs. Of course, placing overall responsibility on the shoulders of one man is no panacea. Production planning and the attendant time and cost estimating that go with it can only be perfected with experience.
>
> Although line authority would be vested in Ostroff under the proposed system, Rivera would still be able to reassign personnel, because the manpower forecasts would originally be coordinated with the program management office. Thus Rivera's budget should not reflect an adverse variance due to excessive idle time.
>
> Moreover, a centralized system would change the organization chart. The new chart would place the program management office directly under the division general manager and above the engineering department, which would remain in its present position. This organization should take Miller out of the middle of the arguments Ostroff is currently having with the line managers, for the line managers would be reporting to Ostroff not to Miller.

Striking a middle ground, Mr. Hendry would have Miller retain the authority for assigning priorities, but would make extensive use of the program manager and his staff to help implement this authority. He says:

Program management was originally chartered to assist, influence, and guide—with the best studied opinion available—the all-inclusive effort of assigned programs. The program manager should assist, negotiate, and guide the formulation of budgets and schedules and act as adviser to the division general manager, while concurrently acting as principal customer contact and participating in followup effort with the sales department. I believe it would be advisable for Miller to remove all doubt and firmly establish that Ostroff is not charged with line authority.

Program management is a sound idea and can be very helpful; Ostroff and his department can coordinate and assist with excellent results. One program coordinator can be assigned to one or several more complicated programs. In doing this, management, with staff assistance, would beef up programs that need additional coordination and better and more thorough reporting techniques. Ostroff should coordinate and assist, persuade, and promote rational justification of alteration and adjustment, rather than try to dictate and insist that his budgets and schedules be accepted by the engineering department.

The Next Step?

Mr. Klima outlines a positive action program for the general manager:

Miller's dilemma is that he has allowed himself to be maneuvered into the position of being a referee between the program management office and engineering. He needs promptly to demonstrate a "take-charge" attitude, and he needs an immediate and effective education program to explain the program management concept, so that both his program people and his line operating people know what he expects from them. The general manager is going to have to make a personal commitment to get deeply involved.

What's lacking is a total understanding of the mutual responsibilities of the program manager and engineering. This particular program manager obviously hasn't learned to balance pressure with persuasion. He's shown little vision of those factors from upstream that have an impact on matters of cost and schedule.

Meanwhile Rivera, the engineering department manager, has avoided managing. He has assumed that the various programs must share his workload and overhead burdens. He is looking around for this supporting crutch, instead of generating study contracts and doing other similar activities that help to level out the business picture.

Right now Miller should assign the two adversaries in the case to spend the night formulating an agreed-on, positive plan to take care of schedule, cost, and manpower problems and to assure sound technical performance on this hydraulic control contract. By morning these two, joined by the manager of marketing, should be ready to present their story at a meeting chaired by the general manager. His marketing manager should be present to assess possible customer sensitivity to the decisions that are being made.

Conclusion

That program management is no panacea for the problems of engineering-product coordination and customer liaison has become apparent to all companies that have used it. Equally apparent is that it can be a workable form of organization that can handle numerous communication and coordination activities that are simply beyond the scope of the line organization.

Unquestionably, program management in any form creates lines of authority and responsibility that differ from traditional patterns. Is this bad? Mr. Silverman comments:

> A split responsibility, such as that which occurs in program management, is by itself neither helpful nor harmful to the company. It depends on how it's handled. There are many split responsibilities in life—for instance, the differing responsibilities of the student toward his teacher, classmates, parents, and minister or the varying responsibilities of a manager toward his comanagers and bosses.
>
> It is the company management itself that determines if the split responsibility is helpful or harmful. In this case Miller's less than enthusiastic support of program management causes confusion and harm to his division. Ostroff does not accomplish his job when he forces tight budgets and schedules through, because any later chance to miss the mark will certainly be grabbed by the managers whom he has coerced. But then it is possible that this forcing of managers was Ostroff's adjusting to his company's management philosophy. Without condoning this action, I think it is possible that Ostroff felt he could accomplish his task in no other manner, because he did not have the direct authority he needed.

In Admor's case, introduction of program management without sufficient forethought regarding possible conflicts has certainly diminished its effectiveness. Little wonder that a power struggle between the program manager and the line managers resulted; this struggle was the only mechanism provided for them to test and resolve their new assignments of authority.

As our commentators have observed, a clearer statement of the specific responsibilities of the program management office, with a firm commitment on Miller's part to back the statement up, would almost certainly have avoided the worst features of this conflict. At the very least, the issues would have been brought out into the open earlier, a confrontation would not have been delayed until the company faced a possible large loss and missed schedules on its most important contract.

Change of any kind almost always brings problems. The ability to foresee these problems and to take steps in advance to mitigate their adverse effects is a distinguishing characteristic of mature and successful management.

CASE STUDY 25:   THERMODYNE, INC., AND THE *PEGASUS* PROGRAM[1]

On February 13, 1979, Charles Lanzell, Manager of *Pegasus* Program of Thermodyne, Inc., was worried and deeply discouraged as he reviewed the January budget report (Table 3) for his Pegasus project. Lanzell had conceived Thermodyne's role in this program, had prepared the proposal, and had managed the project since receiving the contract the previous February. Now that the originally scheduled completion date was approaching, it was apparent that the program could not be satisfactorily completed for at least another four to five months. Contract costs were overrun, and a request for additional funding, submitted the previous November, had not yet been approved. Even this would not be adequate to see the project through to completion. Interim spending authority, granted by the board of directors pending action on the funding request, would be exhausted in another month at the present rate of expenditure. An even more serious problem was the possibility of losing essential prospective follow-on business because of late delivery.

History of Thermodyne, Inc.

Thermodyne, Inc., was founded in 1974 by several scientists and engineers from the Propulsion Division of Cascade Industries, Inc. After first operating as a consulting group on thermodynamics problems, the company undertook several development projects. Although not highly profitable, these projects had been technically successful and had helped to establish Thermodyne's reputation for competent development work in the thermodynamics field.

One especially successful project was a lightweight, highly efficient, portable power unit. Called the *Sirocco,* it was developed for use in the Phobos space program. It was believed that Thermodyne's success in this project, and its general capability in aerodynamics and thermodynamics, was instrumental in obtaining a contract for the boundary layer control system on the *Aurora,* an experimental transport aircraft under development for the Air Force. This was, by Thermodyne's standard, a large contract and one that showed good future volume and profit potential for the production phase.

The *Aurora* contract was received in July 1979, 19 months ago. It necessitated a heavy recruiting program for technical personnel and a considerable refinement of the organization. From June to October of 1977, employment rose from 350 to 600. In the same period, manufacturing was established as a separate organizational function, and technical operations were reorganized. Figure 18 shows the general organization of the company at that time.

Charles Lanzell had joined Thermodyne three years ago. He had been employed by Cascade Industries, and, although not one of the original founders of Thermodyne,

[1] This case is a revision of an earlier case prepared by David C. Howard under the direction of Dr. J. Sterling Livingston as a basis for class discussion, rather than to illustrate either effective or ineffective handling of an administrative situation. The current revision was prepared by J. Ronald Fox, Lecturer, Harvard Business School, June 1980.

Table 3.   Thermodyne, Inc., and the Pegasus Program: *Monthly Budget Report—Pegasus Project for the month ending January 31, 1979* **($1000)**

	This month (Jan. 1979)			Cumulative for Project		
	Budget	Actual	Variance	Budget	Actual	Variance
Direct Labor	*			*		
Laboratory	—	—	—	20	16	(4)
Eng. & Design	$ 30.8	$ 37.0	$ 6.2	310	364	54
Manufacturing	12.0	11.6	(.4)	80	60	(20)
Test	14.8	11.4	(3.4)	120	80	(40)
Total	$ 57.6	$ 60.0	$ 2.4	530	520	(10)
Overhead	57.6	59.6	2.0	472	464	(8)
Material and						
Direct Charges	4.0	12.2	8.2	84	52	(32)
General and						
Administrative	20.4	22.4	2.0	170	162	(8)
Total	$139.6	$154.2	$14.6	1,256	1,198	(58)

* Original Contract Budget	$1,002,000
Budget Authorized Pending Approval of Funding Request	400,000
Total Budget	$1,402,000

he was well known and respected as an unusually able and promising physicist. Lanzell became senior engineer of the thermodynamics group on the Sirocco project, and it was believed that his work had contributed appreciably to the success of the Sirocco unit.

Pegasus

Lanzell came across the *Pegasus* job almost accidentally. While making a presentation to an Army evaluation group on the Sirocco unit in January of last year, Lanzell learned of the Army's interest in an alternative system of emergency and auxiliary power for the *Pegasus,* a new high-capacity, troop- and cargo-carrying helicopter.

The prime systems contractor for the *Pegasus* program was the Vertech Corporation, but Western Kinetics, Inc., was responsible for the propulsion and power subsystems. Under the approach taken by Western Kinetics, primary lift and propulsion power was furnished by gas turbine engines, with emergency lifting power supplied by rotor tip ramjet units. After discussing the system with Army engineers, Lanzell concluded that the tactical applications of the *Pegasus* offered a good potential for high-efficiency rocket type thrust units. Although these would involve more complicated fuel handling, tankage, and hardware and more difficult integration, these disadvantages would be offset by substantially higher performance for short intervals.

Lanzell discussed his thoughts with Army engineers, who expressed enthusiastic

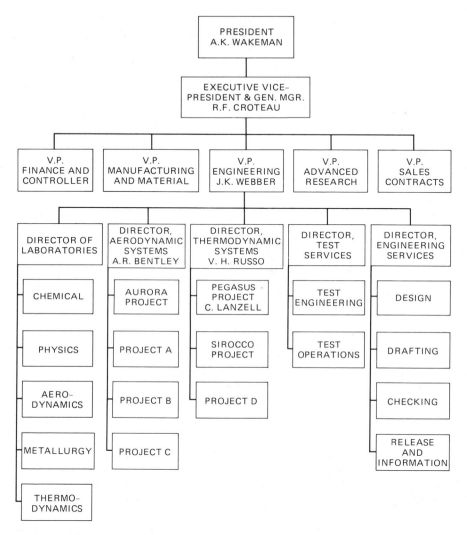

Figure 18.   Thermodyne, Inc., and the Pegasus Program. Organization Chart.

interest and urged him to submit a proposal for developing the system. Since very little time was available for proposal preparation, Lanzell immediately started work on it. The following day, a Saturday, Lanzell telephoned J.K. Webber, Vice-President of Engineering, to discuss the *Pegasus* proposal. His immediate senior, Victor Russo, Director of Thermodynamic Systems, was vacationing in Florida. Webber, who was about to depart on a business trip, expressed enthusiasm and instructed Lanzell to "drop whatever else you're doing. Take charge of this thing and get out a proposal."

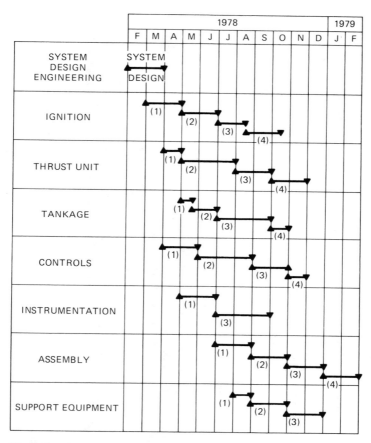

(1): Engineering
(2): Design and Drafting
(3): Procurement and Manufacturing
(4): Test

Figure 19.   Thermodyne, Inc., and the Pegasus Program. Time Projection–Pegasus Project.

Lanzell accordingly worked around the clock Saturday and Sunday. The technical approach offered no problem. To obtain estimates, he relied heavily on his Sirocco experience and on rate projection material that he found in J.K. Webber's office. The time estimates had to be compatible with the overall program schedule, which called for auxiliary power unit testing and evaluation in March 1979. Figure 19 shows the worksheet used by Lanzell in developing these time estimates. Table 4 shows the development of direct labor costs, based on hourly estimates priced at the rates shown in J.K. Webber's rate projection data. For current pricing use, this

Table 4. Thermodyne, Inc., and the *Pegasus* Program. *Direct Labor Estimate Pegasus Proposal.*

		Feb	Mar	Apr	May	June	July	Aug	Sept	Oct	Nov	Dec	Jan	Feb	Total Hours	Total Dollars
Chem.	Hours @	100	200												500	
	$12.00	1,200	2,400													6,000
Metal-lurgy	Hours @		120	120	120										360	
	$12.00		1,440	1,440	1,440											4,320
Thermo-dynamic	Hours @		200	200	200	200									800	
	$12.00		2,400	2,400	2,400	2,400										9,600
Engi-neering	Hours @	450	1,200	1,200	1,200	1,200	1,200	1,200	900	900	600	600	500	500	11,540	
	$12.00	5,400	14,400	14,400	14,400	14,400	14,400	14,400	10,800	10,800	7,200	7,200	6,000	6,000		139,800
Design	Hours @				2,000	2,000	2,000	2,000	2,000	2,000					12,000	
	$10.00				20,000	20,000	20,000	20,000	20,000	20,000						120,000
Shop	Hours @						1,000	1,500	1,500	1,500	1,000	1,000			7,500	
	$8.00						8,000	12,000	12,000	12,000	8,000	8,000				60,000
Test	Hours @						1,000	1,000	1,200	1,500	1,500	1,000	1,200	1,600	10,000	
	$10.00						10,000	10,000	12,000	15,000	15,000	10,000	12,000	16,000		100,000
Total	Hours	550	1,720	1,720	3,520	3,400	5,200	5,700	5,600	5,900	3,100	2,600	1,700	2,000	42,810	
	Dollar	6,600	20,640	20,640	38,240	36,800	52,400	56,400	52,800	57,800	30,200	25,200	18,000	22,000		439,720
Cumu-lative	Dollar	6,600	27,240	47,880	86,120	122,920	175,320	131,720	286,520	344,320	374,520	399,720	417,720	439,720		

also showed an overhead rate of 80 percent of direct labor and a general and administrative expense rate of 15 percent.

In summary, Lanzell's estimate was as follows:

Direct Labor	$440,000
Overhead at 80%	352,000
Material and Direct Charges	80,000
	$872,000
General and Administrative Expense at 15% (G & A)	130,000
Total Cost	$1,002,000
Fee	60,000
Total Price	$1,062,000

Although proposals normally were reviewed by the vice-president of finance and the vice-president of sales and contracts, neither could be reached by telephone when the proposal was finished late Sunday evening. Consequently, Lanzell mailed his finished proposal, satisfied that the proposed program offered an excellent new business opportunity for the company.

A week after the proposal was submitted, Victor Russo returned from vacation, and Lanzell briefed him on the proposed *Pegasus* work. Russo was impressed with the new business potential presented by the proposed system, but was slightly dubious about the time and cost estimates.

Early in February 1978, Thermodyne received a letter of intent authorizing work to proceed on the *Pegasus* project as proposed. Lanzell immediately assumed responsibility for the job, and Russo appointed him project manager. Russo would have preferred to select Stanley Fram, an experienced propulsion engineer, for Lanzell was relatively inexperienced and had never before held overall project responsibilities. Russo felt that Lanzell's appointment was necessary, however, because he had personally conceived and "sold" the idea, and because J.K. Webber had authorized Lanzell to take charge. Furthermore, Russo was not sure that it would be fair, either to the project or to the personnel involved, to ask someone else to assume responsibility for carrying out the work proposed within the time and cost limits Lanzell had established.

The first serious problem was finding technical personnel to assign to the job. Russo's organization, Thermodynamics Systems, had been drained of qualified technical personnel to man the *Aurora* project, under Alvin Bentley, Director of Aerodynamics Systems. Russo now requested Bentley's cooperation in returning several experienced engineers. Unfortunately, the specific men requested by Russo were deeply involved in critical tasks and could not be removed without creating serious technical problems. Bentley was able to make available two engineers, one of whom, Bernard Hausmann, had an exceptional amount of aerodynamic experience. Hausmann had joined Thermodyne a year-and-a-half ago, too recently to have become critically involved in the *Aurora* project and therefore could be made available to the *Pegasus* job. Hausmann being the most experienced engineer available, Lanzell decided to appoint him project engineer, and Russo agreed.

Monitoring Progress

Russo and Lanzell also discussed arrangements for surveillance of progress in the *Pegasus* project, as follows:

Russo: Chuck, I haven't been very close to this job, and I think it's just going to spread me too thin if I try to get into it very deeply.

Lanzell: I agree, Vic. With all the planning I've done so far, it would be kind of tough for anyone to really get on board. I think I've got it pretty well under control.

Russo: I'm sure you have, and so is Webber. Said so to me the last time he was in town. Now, of course, I am going to need a monthly progress report.

Lanzell: Vic, we just don't have time for a lot of paper. These reports take a lot of work to prepare. Why don't we just have a chat every few weeks, and you can put down whatever you think is important.

Russo: Chuck, I have to have something in writing. Give me a memo—short, nothing elaborate. At a minimum I have to have percent expended, percent completed, and a brief paragraph or two on technical progress and problems. I don't want to make a lot of work, but I have to answer for quite a few projects and can't keep them all at my fingertips without some kind of notes. Also, I have to have something to give J.K. [Webber] for monthly project review meetings.

Lanzell: Why don't I just carbon copy him on the memos to you?

Russo: O.K. with me. Incidentally, we'll probably be on the agenda for a presentation at several project review meetings, so keep it in mind. Now, you've got the ball, so you're going to take care of the government reports and all that, right?

Lanzell: Right.

Following these arrangements, Lanzell used his original estimate to prepare a project budget, which projected monthly expenditures of engineering and laboratory labor, design labor, shop labor, test labor, and materials and other direct charges. He distributed this budget to affected managers. Within a few days, several reactions occurred:

The assistant to the controller telephoned to say that the direct labor rates were inadequate; they failed to include a general increase in professional, technical, and scientific salaries and fringe benefits schedules for April of last year.

J.K. Webber forwarded a memorandum he had received from the vice-president of manufacturing questioning the adequacy of shop labor and material dollars and pointing out that he could not accept the budget without knowing exactly what was required. He also pointed out the immediate need for requisitioning long-lead-time materials.

Russo received a memo from the test director, who pointed out that his organization simply could not provide the hours required for *Pegasus* on a straight-time basis and that half the work, if done at all, would have to be at premium rates.

From these comments and from discussion with Hausmann, Lanzell concluded that contract funds might prove inadequate by approximately $100,000. He was confident, however, that overrun funds would be provided if necessary and felt that a request should be deferred until there had been considerable technical achievement and the adequacy of funding could be determined more precisely.

Because of staffing problems, Lanzell omitted the February progress report. The March report showed $42,000 expended. This was less than projected, but, in Lanzell's opinion, was roughly equivalent to technical accomplishment. Progress was generally satisfactory, although metallurgical problems had proved more difficult than anticipated.

During May, $74,000 was expended, bringing total expenditures to about $150,000, or 15 percent of estimated costs. Technical performance was only 12 percent because of continuing metallurgical problems and release of designs in inefficient lots. Although the May schedule called for 2,000 design hours, the preliminary design work had not progressed as rapidly as hoped, and very little work was ready for design. At the insistence of the design manager, who had arranged for the necessary staff to be available, some work was released to design in a dubious state of readiness. This provided some work for the designers earmarked for *Pegasus,* although it was, in Lanzell's opinion, of questionable value.

At a project review meeting in mid-June, J.K. Webber was questioned on the status of *Pegasus* by the executive vice-president and general manager, and by the vice-president of manufacturing. Webber asked Lanzell to join him at the meeting and to present a brief report. Lanzell discussed the metallurgical and design problems, but stated that he believed they had been overcome. At this meeting, Daniel McAlester, Vice-President of Manufacturing, questioned Lanzell:

McAlester: Lanzell, your schedule calls for shop work to start July 1—1,000 shop-hours next month. OK, I've hired the men and I'll be waiting. What worries me is, are you going to be ready? What you've said so far hasn't eased my mind any.

Lanzell: I'd let you know if there were any problems.

McAlester: OK. Now you understand, I hope, what we need—good prints in time to do our shop planning and get our tools and material toegether and load the jobs. Incidentally, what with your metallurgy problems, I hope you have all your materials lined up in stores. No exotic stuff, now?

Lanzell: I can't tell you exactly, but we'll be using mostly stainless and nickel alloys.

McAlester: That's six-month stuff; we don't carry it in stores and I know you haven't given Purchasing one blessed requisition. Might as well have a layoff right now. We'll save everybody money in the long run.

Lanzell: Listen Dan, we won't need very much, and I'm almost sure I know where you can pick up whatever you need.

McAlester: I hope so. Now what about paper. I need good prints with two-week lead time. That means right now, today; I need pictures if I'm going to get my own shop paper together.

Lanzell: It's going to be pretty tight, because we had to schedule this job close to meet the customer's needs. We're all going to have to give a little. With a little luck, we'll have usable prints ready the first of July. If that isn't enough time, we'll send our engineers right down to the machinists to make sure they understand what we need.

McAlester: I'll tell you one thing, you're not sending any wildeyed junior achievement engineers into *my* shop.

Webber: Well now, look fellows, this isn't getting us anywhere. Dan, we'll see what we can do to help out—what more can we do?

After the meeting, Webber called Lanzell and stressed the importance of having some work ready for the shop by July 1. Lanzell assured him that some orders would be ready, although perhaps not worked out completely. Accordingly, design work was pushed, and releases were readied on tankage and on two alternative ignition configurations. After considerable delay and difficulty in locating materials, the buyer was finally able to borrow some material from a nearby plant. Manufacturing was started in mid-July, although considerable difficulty was caused by the lack of tooling and shop operation sheets. Serious welding problems also developed due to faulty tankage dimensions, and extensive redesign work became necessary.

At the end of August, expenditures were $452,000, or 45 percent of estimated costs. Lanzell and Hausmann estimated technical completion at 35 percent, but believed that the worst technical problems were past and that performance would quickly overtake expenditures.

Early in October, Russo and Lanzell reported on the status of the *Pegasus* project at the project review meeting. Lanzell said that as of the end of September, funds were 57 percent expended, and accomplishment perhaps 45 to 50 percent. One minor setback had occurred in September when both ignition configurations failed to meet their design specifications in preliminary tests. Some redesign would be necessary, and had already been started. It was now apparent that the overrun might be $100,000 to $140,000.

At this meeting, Lanzell also reported on his visits to the Army evaluation center and to other contractors involved in the *Pegasus* program. Army technical and contracting personnel had been very much impressed with his description of the design approach and progress and had been sympathetic with the design problems and the schedule pressure imposed on Thermodyne. It was Lanzell's impression that the contracting officer would be receptive to a request for overrun funds, if necessary. Lanzell had outlined some advanced approaches and hoped that these might be incorporated into the contract as scope of work changes, thus justifying additional fee for increased funding. In fact, considerable engineering time had already been applied to exploring these approaches.

Lanzell had also visited Vertech and Western Kinetics. Although Western Kinetics had received him cordially, Lanzell felt there had been some underlying reserve, if not hostility. He believed this meant that Western Kinetics was concerned that the Thermodyne approach indeed might prove superior to its own auxiliary lift system.

Following Lanzell's report, the problems of proposing overrun were discussed, and it was agreed to defer the discussion until October results were known.

At this same meeting, the controller reported that funding on the major *Aurora* effort was virtually exhausted. Unless some favorable action were taken on the pending proposals for *Aurora* continuation work, the company faced the immediate possibility of personnel reassignment or layoff and an increase in overhead. The vice-president of sales and contracts reported that he was confident the Air Force would accept the continuation work as proposed.

Additional problems were encountered during the remainder of October. The two test unit thrust chambers exploded during static firings, and it became clear that the entire system needed very extensive redesign.

On October 27, the Air Force awarded a continuation contract on *Aurora* at approximately one-quarter of the level proposed. Its immediate effect was to raise overhead and G & A rates appreciably. It made available, however, several of the more experienced engineers for assignment to *Pegasus.*

At the end of October, Webber told Russo of his concern for the *Pegasus* project, "Vic, you'd better get close to that job. It's your responsibility, you know, and I'm afraid that Lanzell has been flying pretty high, wide, and handsome."

That same day, Russo met Lanzell and, after a thorough technical review, asked Lanzell for a complete status report and an estimate of completion time and cost. Lanzell pointed out that meeting the schedule was mandatory, since the overall program schedule still called for delivery and evaluation of emergency lift subsystems in March, only five months away. They, therefore, would have to increase the effort in the remaining months through multiple-shift operations in the shop and in test and extensive overtime in engineering and design.

Lanzell's estimate of costs to complete was as follows:

Direct Labor	$240,000
Overhead at 100%	240,000
Material	58,000
	$538,000
G & A at 17%	91,460
Required to Complete	$629,460
Unexpended	274,182
Additional Funding Required	$355,278

Russo felt that Lanzell's estimate might be unduly optimistic. Accordingly, he increased it to $400,000, prorating the increase among the various cost elements.

Russo then advised Lanzell that he was assigning three additional *Aurora* senior engineers to *Pegasus* and that he expected them to be given broad responsibilities, commensurate with their experience. Lanzell objected to this, but Russo insisted.

At the November review meeting, Russo reported on the *Pegasus* project. Expenditures were running from $150,000 to $160,000 per month. Total expenditures were now $728,000, or 73 percent of contract funds. Due to setbacks arising from the test failures, technical completion was only 40 percent. Russo stressed the importance of completing the project on time and presented the revised estimate of the new funds required. He recommended, with the endorsement of J.K. Webber, that a funding request be submitted to the Army for increased work scope to cover costs and negotiated with some profit if possible, but without profit if necessary. The executive vice-president and general manager concurred and instructed the vice-president of sales and contracts to handle the matter. The vice-president of sales and contracts, however, was virtually certain that no scope increase could be obtained, because he had heard that the Army Materiel Development and Readiness Command (DARCOM) was extremely rigorous on granting overrun coverage. He was certainly not confident of rapid approval and warned the group that Thermodyne might have to provide its own financing to complete the work.

Russo replied that Lanzell has received more optimistic reports from the contracting officer, but that in any case the work should continue as rapidly as possible.

The funding request was submitted to the army early in November 1978.

November expenditures remained at about $154,000 for the month. (This figure was to remain constant during the following three months.) Overtime was heavy in all the supporting departments. Overhead and G & A remained high because of the overall drop in volume caused by the reduced *Aurora* effort. Premium prices had to be paid for materials procurement and subcontracting because of short lead times. Operations in design, manufacturing, and test continued to be inefficient as a result of the piecemeal release of specifications, drawings, and hardware. Frequently, for example, design checkers assigned to check urgently needed design packages would wait most of the day without work, and then work long overtime hours to complete the check-in time for reproduction and release to the shop on the following shift.

The vice-president of sales and contracts made frequent personal checks at a high level in DARCOM to expedite the additional funding. He was repeatedly advised that no definite answer could be given, but that cost reduction pressures from the Department of Defense were extremely heavy, and therefore the present time was not the most propitious for raising overrun questions.

Russo became more active in the project and was kept current on design and schedule problems. He contributed greatly to coordinating interface problems with manufacturing, purchasing, and test—areas that had been especially troublesome for Lanzell and Hausmann.

By the end of December, the original funding was exhausted. The contracting officer assured Lanzell that approval of new funding was almost certain, although DARCOM headquarters did not reflect this optimism. At its December 23 meeting, the board of directors approved a recommendation made by the president and the executive vice-president and general manager to expend a maximum of $400,000 in corporate funds to cover additional work on the *Pegasus* project.

Substantial progress was made in December and January. The worst design problems were solved or at least alleviated. Test units of most major components were successful in meeting minimum test objectives. Nevertheless, it became clear that it would be impossible to complete a fully integrated, tested, and instrumented system by the end of February. Russo estimated that this would require another $400,000 to $500,000 and four additional months.

Russo and Lanzell met on February 12, 1979, to explore the situation at length, discussing several alternative courses of action. Lanzell suggested setting up a rough system assembly not completed to specification, but capable of indicating the system's potential. He felt this could be accomplished by March 1, within the funding limitation established by the board of directors. On a recent trip to the Evaluation Center, he had heard a rumor that Western Kinetics was also having schedule and cost difficulties on its emergency lift system. A preliminary systems evaluation might be advantageous to Thermodyne and lay the groundwork for more funding.

Another course was to request additional funding from the Thermodyne board. Russo was pessimistic about receiving executive endorsement for such a request, but felt that in the long run it might be advisable. Lanzell also suggested initiating an aggressive sales campaign among other propulsion and helicopter contractors, seeking additional markets, and perhaps financing, for the project.

After their discussion, Russo asked Lanzell to give him a full report of the situation with a recommended course of action. In the meantime, Russo would formulate his own thoughts. After receiving Lanzell's report, Russo would submit his formal recommendations to J.K. Webber for consideration by company executives and officers.

CASE STUDY 26:   THE BLUE SPIDER PROJECT[1]

"This is impossible! Just totally impossible! Ten months ago I was sitting on top of the world. Upper-level management considered me one of the best, if not the best, engineer in the plant. Now look at me! I have bags under my eyes, I haven't slept soundly in the last six months, and here I am, cleaning out my desk. I'm sure glad they gave me back my old job in engineering. I guess I could have saved myself a lot of grief and aggravation had I not accepted the promotion to project manager."

History

Gary Anderson had accepted a position with Parks Corporation right out of college. With a Ph.D. in mechanical engineering, Gary was ready to solve the world's most traumatic problems. Parks Corporation, at first, offered Gary little opportunity to do the pure research he eagerly wanted. However, things soon changed. Parks grew into a major electronics and structural design corporation during the big boom of the late 1950s and early 1960s when the Department of Defense (DOD) contracts were plentiful.

---

[1] Copyright © 1978 by Harold Kerzner.

Parks Corporation grew from a handful of engineers to a major DOD contractor, employing some 6,500 people. During the recession of the late 1960s, money became scarce, and major layoffs resulted in lowering the employment level to 2,200 employees. At that time, Parks decided to get out of the R&D business and compete as a low-cost-production facility, while maintaining an engineering organization solely to support production requirements.

After attempts at virtually every project management organizational structure, Parks Corporation selected the matrix form. Each project had a program manager who reported to the director of program management. Each project also maintained an assistant project manager, normally a project engineer, who reported directly to the project manager and indirectly to the director of engineering. The program manager spent most of his time worrying about cost and time, whereas the assistant program manager worried more about technical performance.

With the poor job market for engineers, Gary and his colleagues began taking coursework toward an M.B.A. degree should the job market deteriorate further.

In 1975, with the upturn in DOD spending, Parks had to change its corporate strategy. Parks had spent the last seven years bidding on the production phase of large programs. But now, with the new evaluation criteria set forth for contract awards, those companies winning the R&D and qualification phases had a definite edge on being awarded the production contract. The production contract was where the big profits could be found. In keeping with this new strategy, Parks began to beef up its R&D engineering staff. By 1978, Parks had increased in size to 2,700 employees. The increase was mostly in engineering. Experienced R&D personnel were difficult to find for the salaries that Parks was offering. Parks was, however, able to lure some employees away from the competitors, but relied mostly upon the younger, inexperienced engineers fresh out of college.

With the adoption of this corporate strategy, Parks Corporation administered a new wage and salary program, which included job upgrading. Gary was promoted to senior scientist, responsible for all R&D activities performed in the mechanical engineering department. Gary had distinguished himself as an outstanding production engineer during the past several years, and management felt that his contribution could be extended to R&D as well.

In January 1978, Parks Corporation decided to compete for phase I of the Blue Spider project, an R&D effort that, if successful, could lead into a $500-million program spread out over 20 years. The Blue Spider project was an attempt to improve the structural capabilities of the Spartan missile, a short-range tactical missile used by the Army. The Spartan missile was exhibiting fatigue failure after six years in the field. This was three years fewer than the original design specified. The Army wanted new materials that could result in a longer life for the Spartan missile.

Lord Industries was the prime contractor for the Army's Spartan program. Parks Corporation would be a subcontractor to Lord if it could successfully bid and win the project. The criteria for subcontractor selection were based not only on low bid, but also on technical expertise and management performance on other projects. Parks' management felt it had a distinct advantage over most of the other competitors because, it had successfully worked on other projects for Lord Industries.

The Blue Spider Project Kickoff

On November 3, 1977, Henry Gable, Director of Engineering, called Gary Anderson into his office.

Henry Gable: "Gary, I've just been notified through the grapevine that Lord will be issuing the RFP for the Blue Spider project by the end of this month, with a 30-day response period. I've been waiting a long time for a project like this to come along, so that I can experiment with some new ideas that I have. This project is going to be my baby all the way! I want you to head up the proposal team. I think it must be an engineer. I'll make sure that you get a good proposal manager to help you. If we start working now, we can get close to two months of research in before proposal submittal. That will give us a one-month's edge on our competitors."

Gary was pleased to be involved in such an effort. He had absolutely no trouble in getting functional support for the R&D effort necessary to put together a technical proposal. All the functional managers continuously remarked to Gary that, "This must be a biggy. The director of engineering has thrown all his support behind you."

On December 2, the RFP was received. The only trouble area that Gary could see was that the technical specifications stated that all components must be able to operate normally and successfully through a temperature range of −65°F to 145°F. Current testing indicated that Parks Corporation's design would not function above 130°F. An intensive R&D effort was conducted over the next three weeks. Everywhere Gary looked, it appeared that the entire organization was working on his technical proposal.

A week before the final proposal was to be submitted, Gary and Henry Gable met to develop a company position concerning the inability of the preliminary design material to be operated above 130°F.

Gary Anderson: "Henry, I don't think it is going to be possible to meet specification requirements unless we change our design material or incorporate new materials. Everything I've tried indicates we're in trouble."

Henry Gable: "We're in trouble only if the customer knows about it. Let the proposal state that we expect our design to be operative up to 155°F. That'll please the customer."

Gary Anderson: "That seems unethical to me. Why don't we just tell the truth?"

Henry Gable: "The truth doesn't always win proposals. I picked you to head up this effort because I thought you'd understand. I could have just as easily selected one of our many moral project managers. I'm considering you for program manager after we win the program. If you're going to pull this conscientious crap on me like the other project managers do, I'll find someone else. Look at it this way; later we can convince the customer to change the specifications. After all, we'll be so far downstream that he'll have no choice."

After two solid months of 16-hour days, the proposal was submitted. On February 10, 1978 Lord Industries announced that Parks Corporation would be awarded the Blue Spider project. The contract called for a 10-month effort, negotiated at $2.2 million at a firm-fixed price.

Selecting the Project Manager

Following the contract award, Henry Gable called Gary in for a conference.

Henry Gable: "Congratulations, Gary! You did a fine job. The Blue Spider project has great potential for ongoing business over the next 10 years, provided we perform well during the R&D phase. Obviously you're the most qualified person in the plant to head up the project. How would you feel about a transfer to program management?

Gary: "I think it would be a real challenge. I could make maximum use of the M.B.A. degree I earned last year. I've always wanted to be in program management."

Henry Gable: "Having several master degrees, or even doctorates for that matter, does not guarantee that you'll be a successful project manager. There are three requirements for effective program management; you must be able to communicate both in writing and orally; you must know how to motivate people; and you must be willing to give up your car pool. The last one is extremely important in that program managers must be totally committed and dedicated to the program, regardless of how much time is involved.

"But this is not the reason I asked you to come here. Going from project engineering to program management is a big step. There are only two places you can go from program management: up in the organization or out the door. I know of very, very few engineers who failed in program management and were permitted to return."

Gary: "Why is that? If I'm considered the best engineer in the plant, why can't I return to engineering?"

Henry Gable: "Porgram management is a world of its own. It has its own formal and informal organizational ties. Program managers are outsiders. You'll find out. You might not be able to keep the strong personal ties you now have with your fellow employees. You'll have to force even your best friends to comply with your standards. Program managers can go from program to program, but functional departments remain intact.

"I'm telling you all this for a reason. We've worked well together the past several years. But if I sign the release so that you can work for Grey in program management, you'll be on your own, like hiring into a new company. I've already signed the release. You still have some time to think about it."

Gary: "One thing I don't understand. With all the good program managers we have here, why am I given this opportunity?"

Henry Gable: "Almost all our program managers are over 45 years old. This resulted from our massive layoffs several years ago when we were forced to lay off the younger, inexperienced program managers. You were selected because of your age and because all our other program managers have worked on only production-type programs. We need someone at the reins who knows R&D. Your counterpart at Lord Industries will be an R&D type. You have to fight fire with fire.

"I have an ulterior reason for wanting you to accept this position. Because of the division of authority between program management and project engineering, I need someone in program management I can communicate with concerning R&D work. The program managers we have now are interested only in time and cost. We need a manager who will bend over backward to get performance also. I think you're that man. You know the commitment we made to Lord when we submitted that proposal. You have to try to achieve that. Remember, this program is my baby. You'll get all the support you need. I'm tied up on another project now. But when it's over, I'll be following your work like a hawk. We'll have to get together occasionally and discuss new techniques.

"Take a day or two to think it over, If you want the position, make an appointment to see Elliot Grey, Director of Program Management. He'll give you the same speech I did. I'll assign Paul Evans to you as chief project engineer. He's a seasoned veteran, and you should have no trouble working with him. He'll give you good advice. He's a good man."

The Work Begins

Gary accepted the new challenge. His first major hurdle occurred in staffing the project. The top priority given to him to bid the program did not follow through for staffing. The survival of Parks Corporation depended upon the profits received from the production programs. In keeping with this philosophy, Gary found that engineering managers (even his former boss) were reluctant to give up their key people to the Blue Spider program. However, with a little support from Henry Gable, Gary formed an adequate staff for the program.

Right from the start Gary was worried that the test matrix called out in the technical volume of the proposal would not produce results that could satisfy specifications. Gary had a milestone, 90 days after go-ahead, to identify the raw materials that could satisfy specification requirements. Gary and Paul Evans held a meeting to map out their strategy for the first few months.

Gary Anderson: "Well, Paul, we're starting out with our backs against the wall on this one. Any recommendations?"

Paul Evans: "I also have my doubts in the validity of this test matrix. Fortunately, I've been through this path before. Gable thinks this is his project, and he'll sure as hell try to manipulate us. I have to report to him every morning at 7:30 with the raw data results of the previous day's testing. He wants to see them before you do. He also stated that he wants to meet me alone.

Lord will be the big problem. If the test matrix proves to be a failure, we're going to have to change the scope of effort. Remember, this is an FFP contract. If we change the scope of work and do additional work in the earlier phases of the program, then we should prepare a tradeoff analysis to see what we can delete downstream so as to not overrun the budget."

Gary Anderson: "I'm going to let the other project office personnel handle the administrative work. You and I are going to live in the research labs until we get some results. We'll let the other project office personnel run the weekly team meetings."

For the next three weeks Gary and Paul spent virtually 12 hours per day, seven days a week, in the research and development lab. None of the results showed any promise. Gary continuously tried to set up a meeting with Henry Gable, but always found him unavailable.

During the fourth week, Gary, Paul, and the key functional department managers met to develop an alternate test matrix. The new test matrix looked good. Gary and his team worked frantically to develop a new workable schedule that would not impact the second milestone, which was to occur at the end of 180 days. The second milestone was the final acceptance of the raw materials and preparation of production runs of the raw materials to verify that there would be no scale-up differences between lab development and full-scale production.

Gary personally prepared all the technical handouts for the interchange meeting. After all, he would be the one presenting all the data. The technical interchange meeting was scheduled for two days. On the first day, Gary presented the data, including test results, and the new test matrix. The customer appeared displeased with the progress to date and decided to have its own in-house caucus that evening to go over the material presented. The following morning the customer stated his position:

"First of all, Gary, we're quite pleased to have a project manager who has such a command of technology. That's good. But every time we've tried to contact you last month, you were unavailable or had to be paged in the research laboratories. You did an acceptable job presenting the technical data, but the administrative data were presented by your project office personnel. We at Lord do not think that you're maintaining the proper balance between your technical and administrative responsibilities. We prefer that you personally give the administrative data and your chief project engineer present the technical data.

We did not receive an agenda. Our people like to know what will be discussed and when. We also want a copy of all handouts to be presented at least three days in advance. We need time to scrutinize the data. You can't expect us to walk in here blind and make decisions after seeing the data for 10 minutes.

To be frank, we feel that the data to date are totally unacceptable. If the data do not improve, we will have no choice but to issue a stop workage order and look for a new contractor. The new test matrix looks good, especially since this is a firm-fixed-price contract. Your company will burden all costs for the additional work. A tradeoff with later work may be possible, but this will depend upon the results presented at the second design review meeting, 90 days from now.

We have decided to establish a customer office at Parks to follow your work more closely. Our people feel that monthly meetings are insufficient during R&D activities. We would like our customer representative to have daily verbal meetings with you or your staff. He will then keep us posted. Obviously, we had expected to review much more experimental data than you have given us.

Many of our top-quality engineers would like to talk directly to your engineering community, without having to continuously waste time by having to go through the project office. We must insist upon this last point. Remember, your effort may be only $2.2 million, but our total package is $100 million. We have a lot more at stake than you people do. Our engineers do not like to get information that has been filtered by the project office. They want to help you.

And last, don't forget that you people have a contractual requirement to prepare complete minutes for all interchange meetings. Send us the original for signature before going to publication.

Although Gary was unhappy with the first team meeting, especially with the requests made by Lord Industries, he felt that Lord had sufficient justification for its comments. Following the team meeting, Gary personally prepared the complete minutes. "This is absurd," thought Gary. "I've wasted almost one entire week doing nothing more than administrative paperwork. Why do we need such detailed minutes? Can't a rough summary just as well suffice? Why is it that customers want everything documented? That's like an indication of fear. We've been completely cooperative. There has been no hostility between us. If we've gotten this much paperwork to do now, I hate to imagine what it will be like if we get into trouble."

A New Role

Gary completed and distributed the minutes to the customer, as well as to all key team members.

For the next five weeks testing went according to plan, or at least Gary thought that it had. The results were still poor. Gary was so caught up in administrative paperwork that he hadn't found time to visit the research labs in over a month. On a Wednesday morning, Gary entered the lab to observe the morning testing. Upon arriving in the lab, Gary found Paul Evans, Henry Gable, and two technicians testing a new material, JXB-3.

Henry Gable: "Gary, your problems will soon be over. This new material, JXB-3, will permit you to satisfy specification requirements. Paul and I have been testing it for two weeks. We wanted to let you know, but were afraid that if the word leaked out to the customer that we were spending his money for testing materials that were not called out in the program plan, then he would probably go crazy and might cancel the contract. Look at these results. They're super!"

Gary Anderson: "Am I supposed to be the one to tell the customer now? This could cause a big wave."

Henry Gable: "There won't be any wave. Just tell them that we did it with our own IR&D funds. That'll please them because they'll think we're spending our own money to support their program."

Before presenting the information to Lord, Gary called a team meeting to present the new data to the project pesonnel. At the team meeting, one functional manger spoke out:

> This is a hell of a way to run a program. I like to be kept informed about everything that's happening here at Parks. How can the project office expect to get support out of the functional departments if we're kept in the dark until the very last minute? My people have been working with the existing materials for the last two months and you're telling us that it was all for nothing. Now you're giving us a material that's so new that we have no information on it whatsoever. We're now going to have to play catch-up, and that's going to cost you plenty.

One week before the 180-day-milestone meeting, Gary submitted the handout package to Lord Industries for preliminary review. An hour later the phone rang.

Customer: "We've just read your handout. Where did this new material come from? How come we were not informed that this work was going on? You know, of course, that our customer, the Army, will be at this meeting. How can we explain this to the Army? We're postponing the review meeting until all our people have analyzed the data and are prepared to make a decision.

"The purpose of a review or interchange meeting is to exchange information when both parties have familiarity with the topic. Normally, we (Lord Industries) require almost weekly interchange meetings with our other customers, because we don't trust them. We disregarded this policy with Parks Corporation based upon past working relationships. But with the new state of developments, you have forced us to revert to our previous position, for we now question Parks Corporation's integrity in communicating with us. At first we believed this was due to an inexperienced program manager. Now, we're not sure."

Gary Anderson: "I wonder if the real reason we have these interchange meetings isn't to show our people that Lord Industries doesn't trust us. You're creating a hell of a lot of work for us, you know."

Customer: "You people put yourself in this position. Now you have to live with it."

Two weeks later Lord reluctantly agreed that the new material offered the greatest promise. Three weeks later the design review meeting was held. The Army was definitely not pleased with the prime contractor's recommendation to put a new untested material into a multimillion dollar effort.

The Communications Breakdown

During the week after the design review meeting, Gary planned to make the first verification mix to establish final specifications for selection of the raw materials. Unfortunately, the manufacturing plans were a week behind schedule, primarily due to Gary, because he had decided to reduce costs by accepting the responsibility for developing the bill of materials himself.

Gary called a meeting to consider rescheduling the mix.

Gary Anderson: "As you know we're about a week to 10 days behind schedule. We'll have to reschedule the verification mix for late next week."

Production Manager: "Our resources are committed until a month from now. You can't expect to simply call a meeting and have everything reshuffled for the Blue Spider program. We should have been notified earlier. Engineering has the responsibility for preparing the bill of materials. Why isn't it ready?"

Engineering Integration: "We were never asked to prepare the bill of materials. But I'm sure that we could get it out if we work our people overtime for the next two days."

Gary: "When can we remake the mix?"

Production Manager: "We have to redo at least 500 sheets of paper every time we reschedule mixes. Not only that, we have to reschedule people on all three shifts. If we were to reschedule your mix, it will have to be performed on overtime. That's going to increase your costs. If that's agreeable with you, we'll try it. But this will be the first and last time that production will bail you out. There are procedures that have to be followed."

Testing Engineer: "I've been coming to these meetings since we kicked off this program. I think I speak for the entire engineering division when I say that the role that the director of engineering is playing in this program is suppressing individuality among our highly competent personnel. In new projects, especially those involving R&D, our people are not apt to stick their necks out. Now our people are becoming ostriches. If they're impeded from contributing, even in their own slight way, then you'll probably lose them before the project gets completed. Right now I feel that I'm wasting my time here. All I need are minutes of the team meetings and I'll be happy. Then I won't have to come to these pretend meetings any more."

The purpose of the verification mix was to make a full-scale production run of the material to verify that there would be no material property changes in scale-up from the small mixes made in the R&D laboratories. After testing, it became obvious that the wrong lots of raw materials were used in the production verification mix.

A meeting was called by Lord Industries for an explanation of why the mistake had occurred and what the alternatives were.

Lord: "Why did the problem occur?"

Gary: "Well, we had a problem with the bill of materials. The result was that the mix had to be made on overtime. And when you work people on overtime, you have to be willing to accept mistakes as being a way of life. The energy cycles of our people are slow during the overtime hours."

Lord: "The ultimate responsibility has to be with you, the program manager. We at Lords think that you're spending too much time doing and not enough time managing. As the prime contractor, we have a hell of a lot more at stake than you do. From now on we want documented weekly technical interchange meetings and closer interaction by our quality control section with yours."

Gary: "These additional team meetings are going to tie up our key people. I can't spare people to prepare handouts for weekly meetings with your people."

Lord: "Team meetings are a management responsibility. If Parks does not want the Blue Spider program, I'm sure we can find another subcontractor. All you (Gary) have to do is give up taking the material vendors to lunch, and you'll have plenty of time for handout preparation."

Gary left the meeting feeling as though he had just gotten raked over the coals. For the next two months, Gary worked 16 hours a day, almost every day. Gary did not want to burden his staff with the responsibility of the handouts, so he began preparing them himself. He could have hired additional staff, but with such a tight budget, and having to remake the verification mix, cost overruns appeared inevitable.

As the end of the seventh month approached, Gary was feeling pressure from within Parks Corporation. The decision making process appeared to be slowing down, and Gary found it more and more difficult to motivate his people. In fact, the grapevine was referring to the Blue Spider project as a loser, and some of his key people acted as though they were on a sinking ship.

By the time the eighth month rolled around, the budget had nearly been expended. Gary was tired of doing everything himself. "Perhaps I should have stayed an engineer," thought Gary. Elliot Grey and Gary Anderson had a meeting to see what could be salvaged. Grey agreed to get Gary additional corporate funding to complete the project. "But performance must be met since there is a lot riding on the Blue Spider project," asserted Grey.

Gary called a team meeting to identify the program status.

Gary: "It's time to map out our strategy for the remainder of the program. Can engineering and production adhere to the schedule that I have laid out before you?"

Team Member, Engineering: "This is the first time that I've seen this schedule. You can't expect me to make a decision in the next 10 minutes and commit the resources of my department. We're getting a little unhappy being kept in the dark until the last minute. What happened to effective planning?"

Gary: "We still have effective planning. We must adhere to the original schedule or at least try to adhere to it. This revised schedule will do that."

Team Member, Engineering: "Look, Gary! When a project gets in trouble it is usually the functional departments that come to the rescue. But if we're kept in the dark, then how can you expect us to come to your rescue? My boss wants to know, well in advance, every decision that you're contemplating with regard to our departmental resources. Right now, we . . ."

Gary: "Granted, we may have had a communications problem. But now we're in trouble and have to unite forces. What is your impression as to whether your department can meet the new schedule?"

Team Member, Engineering: "When the Blue Spider program first got in trouble, my boss exercised his authority to make all departmental decisions regarding the program himself. I'm just a puppet. I have to check with him on everything."

Team Member, Production: "I'm in the same boat, Gary. You know we're not happy having to reschedule our facilities and people. We went through this once before. I also have to check with my boss before giving you an answer about the new schedule."

The following week the verification mix was made. Testing proceeded according to the revised schedule, and it looked as though the total schedule milestones could be met, provided that specifications could be adhered to.

Because of the revised schedule, some of the testing had to be performed on holidays. Gary wasn't pleased with asking people to work on Sundays and holidays, but had no choice, for the test matrix called for testing to be accomplished at specific times after end-of-mix.

A team meeting was called on Wednesday to resolve the problem of who would work on the holiday that would occur on Friday, as well as staffing Saturday and Sunday. During the team meeting Gary became quite disappointed. Phil Rodgers, who had been Gary's test engineer since the project started, was assigned to a new project, which the grapevine called Gable's new adventure. His replacement was a relatively new man, only eight months with the company. For an hour-and-a-half, the team members argued about the little problems and continuously avoided the major question, stating that they would have to first coordinate commitments with their boss. It was obvious to Gary that his team members were afraid to make major decisions and therefore "ate up" a lot of time on trivial problems.

On the following day, Thursday, Gary went to see the department manager responsible for testing, in hopes that he could use Phil Rodgers this weekend.

Department Manager: "I have specific instructions from the boss (director of engineering) to use Phil Rodgers on the new project. You'll have to see the boss if you want him back."

Gary Anderson: "But we have testing that must be accomplished this weekend. Where's the new man you assigned yesterday?"

Department Manager: "Nobody told me you had testing scheduled for this weekend. Half my department is already on an extended weekend vacation, including Phil Rodgers and the new man. How come I'm always the last to know when we have a problem?"

Gary Anderson: "The customer is flying down his best people to observe this weekend's tests. It's too late to change anything. You and I can do the testing."

Department Manager: "Not on your life. I'm staying as far away as possible from the Blue Spider project. I'll get you someone, but it won't be me. That's for sure!"

The weekend's testing went according to schedule. The raw data were made available to the customer, under the stipulation that the final company position would be announced at the end of next month, after the functional departments had a chance to analyze it.

Final testing was completed during the second week of the ninth month. The initial results looked excellent. The materials were within contract specifications, and, although they were new, both Gary and Lord's management felt that there would be little difficulty in convincing the Army that this was the way to go. Henry Gable visited Gary and congratulated him on a job well-done.

All that now remained was the making of four additional full-scale verification mixes in order to determine how much deviation there would be in material properties between full-sized production-run mixes. Gary tried to get the customer to concur (as part of the original tradeoff analysis) that two of the four production runs could be deleted. Lord's management refused, insisting that contractual requirements must be met at the expense of the contractor.

The following week, Elliot Grey called Gary in for an emergency meeting concerning expenditures to date.

Elliot Grey: "Gary, I just received a copy of the financial planning report for last quarter, in which you stated that both the cost and performance of the Blue Spider project were 75% complete. I don't think you realize what you've done. The target profit on the program was $200,000. Your memo authorized the vice-president and general manager to book 75 percent of that, or $150,000, for corporate profit spending for stockholders. I was planning on using all $200,000, together with the additional $300,000 I personally requested from corporate headquarters, to bail you out. Now I have to go back to the vice-president and general manager and tell him that we've made a mistake and that we'll need an additional $150,000."

Gary Anderson: "Perhaps I should go with you and explain my error. Obviously, I take all responsibility."

Elliot Grey: "No, Gary. It's our error, not yours. I really don't think you want to be around the general manager when he sees red at the bottom of the page. It takes an act of God to get money back once corporate books it as profit. Perhaps you should reconsider project engineering as a career instead of program management. Your performance hasn't exactly been sparkling, you know."

Gary returned to his office quite disappointed. No matter how hard he worked, the bureaucratic red tape of project management seemed to always do him in. But late that afternoon, Gary's disposition improved. Lord Industries called to say that, after consultation with the Army, Parks Corporation would be awarded a sole-source contract for qualification and production of Spartan missile components using the new longer life raw materials. Both Lord and the Army felt that the sole-source contract was justified, because Parks Corporation had all the technical experience with the new materials, provided that continued testing showed the same results.

Gary received a letter of congratulations from corporate headquarters, but no additional pay increase. The grapevine said that a substantial bonus was given to the director of engineering.

During the 10th month, results were coming back from the accelerated aging tests performed on the new materials. The results indicated that although the new materials would meet specifications, their life would probably be shorter than five years. These numbers came as shock to Gary. Gary and Paul Evans had a conference to determine the best strategy to follow.

Gary Anderson: "Well, I guess we're now in the fire instead of the frying pan. Obviously, we can't tell Lord Industries about these tests. We ran them on our own. Could the results be wrong?"

Paul Evans: "Sure, but I doubt it. There's always margin for error when you perform accelerated aging tests on new materials. There can be reactions taking place that we know nothing about. Furthermore, the accelerated aging tests may not even correlate well with actual aging. We must form a company position on this as soon as possible."

Gary Anderson: "I'm not going to tell anyone about this, especially Henry Gable. You and I will handle this. It will be my throat if word of this leaks out. Let's wait until we have the production contract in hand."

Paul Evans: "That's dangerous. This has to be a company position, not a project office position. We had better let them know upstairs."

Gary Anderson: "I can't do that. I'll take all responsibility. Are you with me on this?"

Paul Evans: "I'll go along. I'm sure I can find employment elsewhere when we open Pandora's box. You had better tell the department managers to be quiet also."

Two weeks later, as the program was winding down into the testing for the final verification mix and final report development, Gary received an urgent phone call asking him to report immediately to Henry Gable's office.

Henry Gable: "When this project is over, you're through. You'll never hack it as a program manager or possibly a good project engineer. We can't run projects around here without honesty and open communications. How the hell do you expect top management to support you when you start censoring bad news to the top? I don't like surprises. I like to get the bad news from the program managers and project engineers, not second-hand from the customer. And of course, we cannot forget the cost overrun. Why didn't you take some precautionary measures?"

Gary Anderson: "How could I when you were asking our people to do work such as accelerated aging tests that would be charged to my project and were not part of the program plan? I don't think that I'm totally to blame for what's happened."

Henry Gable: "Gary, I don't think its necessary to argue the point any further. I'm willing to give you back your old job in engineering. I hope you didn't lose too many friends while working in program management. Finish up final testing and the program report. Then I'll reassign you."

Gary returned to his office and put his feet up on the desk. "Well," thought Gary, "perhaps I'm better off in engineering. At least I can see my wife and kids once in awhile." As Gary began writing the final report, the phone rang:

Functional Manager: "Hello, Gary. I just thought I'd call to find out what charge number you want us to use for experimenting with this new procedure to determine accelerated age life."

Gary Anderson: "Don't call me! Call Gable. After all, the Blue Spider project is his baby."

CASE STUDY 27:   CORWIN CORPORATION

By June 1982, Corwin Corporation had grown into a $150-million-per-year corporation with an international reputation for manufacturing low-cost, high-quality rubber components. Corwin maintained more than a dozen different product lines, all of which were sold as off-the-shelf items in department stores, hardware stores, and automotive parts distributors. The name *Corwin* was now synonymous with *quality*. This provided management with the luxury of having products that maintained extremely long life cycles.

Organizationally, Corwin maintained the same structure for more than 15 years (see Figure 20). The top management of Corwin Corporation was highly conservative and believed in a marketing approach to find new markets for existing product lines rather than to explore for new products. Under this philosophy, Corwin maintained a small R&D group whose mission was simply to evaluate state-of-the-art technology and its application to existing product lines.

Corwin's reputation was so highly regarded that it continually received inquiries about the manufacturing of specialty products. Unfortunately, the conservative nature of Corwin's management created a do-not-rock-the-boat atmosphere, which opposed taking any type of risks. A management policy was established to evaluate all specialty product requests. The policy required that the following questions be answered:

- Will the specialty product provide the same profit margin as existing product lines, i.e., 20 percent?
- What is the total projected profitability to the company in terms of follow-on contracts?
- Can the specialty product be developed into a product line?
- Can the specialty product be produced with minimum disruption to existing product lines and manufacturing operations?

These stringent requirements forced Corwin to no-bid more than 90 percent of all specialty product inquiries.

Corwin Corporation was a marketing-driven organization, although manufacturing often had different ideas. Almost all decisions were made by marketing with the exception of product pricing and estimating, which was a joint undertaking between manufacturing and marketing. Engineering was considered merely a support group to marketing and manufacturing.

For specialty products, the project managers would always come out of marketing, even during the R&D phase. The company's approach was that if the specialty product should mature into a full product line, then there should be a product line manager assigned right at the onset.

The Peters Company Project

In 1980, Corwin accepted a specialty product assignment from Peters Company because of the potential for follow-on work. In 1981, and again in 1982, profitable

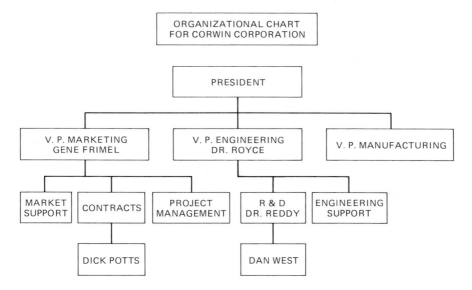

Figure 20.

follow-on contracts were received, and a good working relationship developed, despite Peters' reputation as difficult to work with.

On December 7, 1982, Gene Frimel, Vice-President of Marketing at Corwin, received a rather unusual phone call from Dr. Frank Delia, Marketing Vice-President at Peters Company:

Delia: Gene, I have a rather strange problem on my hands. Our R&D group has $250,000 committed for research toward development of a new rubber product material, and we simply do not have the available personnel or talent to undertake the project. We have to go outside. We'd like your company to do the work. Our testing and R&D facilities are already overburdened.

Frimel: Well, as you know, Frank, we are not a research group, even though we've done this once before for you. And furthermore, I would never be able to sell our management on such an undertaking. Let some other company do the R&D work and then we'll take over on the production end.

Delia: Let me explain our position on this. We've been "burned" several times in the past. Projects like this generate several patents, and the R&D company almost always requires that our contracts give them royalties or first refusal for manufacturing rights.

Frimel: I understand your problem, but it's not within our capabilities. This project, if undertaken, could disrupt parts of our organization. We're already operating lean in engineering.

Delia: Look Gene! The bottom line is this: we have complete confidence in your manufacturing ability to such a point that we're willing to commit to a five-year production contract if the product can be developed. That makes it extremely profitable for you.

Frimel: You've just gotten me interested. What additional details can you give me?

Delia: All I can give you is a rough set of performance specifications that we'd like to meet. Obviously, some tradeoffs are possible.

Frimel: When can you get the specification sheet to me?

Delia: You'll have it tomorrow morning. I'll ship it overnight express.

Frimel: Good! I'll have my people look at it, but we won't be able to get you an answer until after the first of the year. As you know, our plant is closed down for the last two weeks in December, and most of our people have already left for extended vacations.

Delia: That's not acceptable! My management wants a signed, sealed, and delivered contract by the end of this month. If this is not done, corporate will reduce our budget for 1983 by $250,000, thinking that we've bitten off more than we can chew. Actually, I need your answer within 48 hours so that I'll have some time to find another source.

Frimel: You know, Frank, today is December 7th, Pearl Harbor Day. Why do I feel as though the sky is about to fall in?

Delia: Don't worry, Gene! I'm not going to drop any bombs on you. Just remember, all that we have available is $250,000, and the contract must be a firm-fixed-price effort. We anticipate a six-month project with $125,000 paid upon contract signing and the balance at project termination.

Frimel: I still have that ominous feeling, but I'll talk to my people. You'll hear from us with a go or no-go decision within 48 hours. I'm scheduled to go on a cruise in the Carribean, and my wife and I are leaving this evening. One of my people will get back to you on this matter.

Gene Frimel had a problem. All bid and no-bid decisions were made by a four-man committee composed of the president and the three vice-presidents. The president and the vice-president for manufacturing were on vacation. Frimel met Dr. Royce, Vice-President of Engineering, and explained the situation.

Royce: You know, Gene, I totally support projects like this, because it would help our technical people grow intellectually. Unfortunately, my vote never appears to carry any weight.

Frimel: The profitability potential, as well as the development of good customer relations, makes this attractive, but I'm not sure we want to accept such a risk. A failure could easily destroy our good working relationship with Peters Company.

Royce: I'd have to look at the specification sheets before assessing the risks, but I would like to give it a shot.

Frimel: I'll try to reach our president by phone.

By late afternoon, Frimel was fortunate enough to be able to contact the president and received a reluctant authorization to proceed. The problem now was how to prepare a proposal within the next two to three days and be prepared to make an oral presentation to Peters Company.

Frimel: The boss gave his blessing Royce, and the ball is in your hands. I'm leaving for vacation and you'll have total responsibility for the proposal and presentation. Delia wants the presentation this weekend. You should have his specification sheets tomorrow morning.

Royce: Our R&D Director, Dr. Reddy, left for vacation this morning. I wish he were here to help me price out the work and select the project manager. I assume that, in this case, the project manager will come out of engineering rather than marketing.

Frimel: Yes, I agree. Marketing should not have any role in this effort. It's your baby all the way. And as for the pricing effort, you know our bid will be for $250,000. Just work backward to justify the numbers. I'll assign one of our contracting people

Table 5. Proposal Cost Summaries.

Direct Labor and Support	$ 30,000
Testing (30 tests at $2,000 each)	60,000
Overhead at 100%	90,000
Materials	30,000
G&A (General & Administrative, 10%)	21,000
Total	$231,000
Profit	19,000
Total	$250,000

to assist you in the pricing. I hope I can find someone who has experience in this type of effort. I'll call Delia and tell him we'll bid it with an unsolicited proposal.

Royce selected Dan West, one of the R&D scientists, to act as the project leader. Royce has severe reservations about doing this without the R&D director, Dr. Reddy, being actively involved. With Reddy on vacation, Royce had to make an immediate decision.

On the following morning, the specification sheets arrived, and Royce, West, and Dick Potts, a contracts man, began preparing the proposal. West prepared the direct labor man-hours, and Royce provided the costing data and pricing rates. Potts, being completely unfamiliar with this type of effort, simply acted as an observer and provided legal advice when necessary. Potts allowed Royce to make all decisions, even though the contracts man was considered the official representative of the president.

The proposal was finally completed two days later. The proposal was actually a 10-page letter that simply contained the cost summaries (see Table 5) and the engineering intent. West estimated that *30 tests* would be required. The text matrix described only the test conditions for the first five tests. The remaining 25 test conditions would be determined at a later date, jointly by Peters and Corwin personnel.

On Sunday morning, in a meeting at Peters Company, the proposal was accepted. Delia gave Royce a letter of intent, which authorized Corwin Corporation to begin working on the project immediately. The final contract would not be available for signing until late January, and the letter of intent simply stated that Peters Company would assume all costs until such time as the contract was signed or the effort was terminated.

West was truly excited about being selected as the project manager and being able to interface with the customer, a luxury that was usually given only to the marketing personnel. Although Corwin Corporation was closed for two weeks over Christmas, West still went into the office to prepare the project schedules and to identify the support he would need in the other areas. West felt that if he presented these to management on the first day back to work, management would be convinced that West had everything under control.

The Work Begins

On the first working day in January, 1983, a meeting was held with the three vice-presidents and Dr. Reddy to discuss the support needed for the project. (West was not in attendance at this meeting, although all participants had a copy of his memo.)

Reddy: I think we're heading for trouble in accepting this project. I've worked with Peters Company previously on R&D efforts, and they're tough to get along with. West is a good man, but I would never have assigned him as the project leader. His expertise is in managing internal rather than external projects. But, no matter what happens, I'll support West the best I can.

Royce: You're too pessimistic. You have good people in your group, and I'm sure you'll be able to give him the support he needs. I'll try to look in on the project every so often. West will still be reporting to you for this project. Try not to burden him too much with other work. This project is important to the company.

West spent the first few days after vacation soliciting the support he needed from the other line groups. Many of the other groups were upset that they had not been informed earlier and were unsure about what support they could provide. West met Reddy to discuss the final schedules.

Reddy: Your schedules look pretty good, Dan. I think you have a good grasp of the problem. You won't need very much help from me. I have a lot of work to do on other activities, so I'm just going to be in the background on this project. Just drop me a note every once in a while telling me what's going on. I don't need anything formal. Just a paragraph or two will suffice.

By the end of the third week, all the raw materials had been purchased, and initial formulation and testing was ready to begin. In addition, the contract was ready for signature. The contract contained a clause specifying that Peters Company had the right to send an in-house representative into Corwin Corporation for the duration of the project. Peters Company informed Corwin that Patrick Ray would be the in-house representative, reporting to Delia, and would assume his responsibilities on or about February 15.

By the time that Pat Ray appeared at Corwin Corporation, West had completed the first three tests. The results were not what was expected, but gave promise that Corwin was heading in the right direction. Pat Ray's interpretation of the tests was completely opposite to that of West. Ray felt that Corwin was way off base and redirection was needed.

Ray: Look Dan! We have only six months to do this effort and we shouldn't waste our time on marginally acceptable data. These are the next five tests I'd like to see performed.

West: Let me look over your request and review it with my people. That will take a couple of days and, in the meanwhile, I'm going to run the other two tests as planned.

Ray's arrogant attitude bothered West. However, West decided that the project was too important to "knock heads" with Ray and simply decided to cater to Ray as well as he could. This was not exactly the working relationship that West expected to have with the in-house representative.

West reviewed the test data and the new test matrix with engineering. Corwin personnel felt that the test data were inconclusive yet and preferred to withhold their opinion until the results of the fourth and fifth tests were made available. Although this displeased Ray, he agreed to wait a few more days if it meant getting Corwin Corporation on the right track.

The fourth and fifth tests appeared to be marginally acceptable, just as the first three had been. Corwin's engineering people analyzed the data and made their recommendations.

West: Pat, my people feel that we're going in the right direction and that our path has greater promise than your test matrix.

Ray: As long as we're paying the bills, we're going to have a say in what tests are conducted. Your proposal stated that we would work together in developing the other test conditions. Let's go with my test matrix. I've already reported back to my boss that the first five tests were failures and that we're changing the direction of the project.

West: I've already purchased $30,000 worth of raw materials. Your matrix uses other materials and will require additional expenditures of $12,000.

Ray: That's your problem. Perhaps you shouldn't have purchased all the raw materials until we agreed on the complete test matrix.

During February, West conducted 15 tests, all under Ray's direction. The tests were scattered over such a wide range that no valid conclusions could be drawn. Ray continued sending reports back to Delia confirming that Corwin was not producing beneficial results and that there was no indication that the situation would reverse itself. Delia ordered Ray to take whatever steps necessary to ensure a successful completion of the project.

Ray and West met again, as they had for each of the previous 45 days, to discuss the status and direction of the project.

Ray: Dan, my boss is putting tremendous pressure on me for results, and thus far I've given him nothing. I'm up for promotion in a couple of months, and I can't let this project stand in my way. It's time to completely redirect the project.

West: Your redirection of the activities is playing havoc with my scheduling. I have people in other departments who just cannot commit to this continuous rescheduling. They blame me for not communicating with them when, in fact, I'm embarrassed to.

Ray: Everybody has his own problems. We'll get this problem solved. I spent this morning working with some of your lab people in designing the next 15 tests. Here are the test conditions.

West: I certainly would have liked to have been involved with this. After all, I thought I was the project manager. Shouldn't I have been at the meeting?

Ray: Look, Dan! I really like you, but I'm not sure that you can handle this project. We need some good results immediately, or my neck will be stuck out for the next four months. I don't want that. Just have your lab personnel start on these tests, and we'll get along fine. Also, I'm planning on spending a great deal of time in your lab area. I want to observe the testing personally and talk to your lab personnel.

West: We've already conducted 20 tests and you're scheduling another 15 tests. I priced out only 30 tests in the proposal. We're heading for a cost overrun.

Ray: Our contract is a firm-fixed-price effort. Therefore, the cost overrun is your problem.

West met Dr. Reddy to discuss the new direction of the project and potential cost overruns. West brought along a memo projecting the costs through the end of the third month of the project (see Table 6).

Dr. Reddy: I'm already overburdened on other projects and won't be able to help you out. Royce picked you to be the project manager, because he felt that you could do the job. Now, don't let him down. Send me a brief memo next month explaining the situation, and I'll see what I can do. Perhaps the situation will correct itself.

During the month of March, the third month of the project, West received almost daily phone calls from the people in the lab stating that Pat Ray was interfering with their job. In fact, one phone call stated that Ray had changed the test conditions from what was agreed upon in the latest text matrix. When West confronted Ray on his meddling, Ray asserted that Corwin personnel were very unprofessional in their attitude and felt that this was being carried down to the testing as well. Furthermore, Ray demanded that one of the functional employees be removed immediately from the project because of incompetence. West stated that he would talk to the employee's department manager. Ray, however, felt that this would be useless and said, "Remove him or else!" The functional employee was removed from the project.

Table 6. Projected Cost Summary at the End of the Third Month.

	Original Proposal Cost Summary for the Six-Month Project	Costs Projected at the End of the Third Month
Direct Labor/Support	$ 30,000	$ 15,000
Testing	60,000 (30 tests)	70,000 (35 tests)
Overhead	90,000 (100%)	92,000 (120%)[a]
Materials	30,000	50,000
G&A	21,000 (10%)	22,700 (10%)
	$231,000	$249,700

[a] Total engineering overhead was estimated at 100%, whereas the R&D overhead was 120%.

By the end of the third month, most Corwin employees were becoming disenchanted with the project and were looking for other assignments. West attributed this to Ray's harassment of the employees. To aggravate the situation even further, Ray met with Royce and Reddy and demanded that West be removed and a new project manager be assigned.

Royce refused to remove West as project manager and ordered Reddy to take charge and help West get the project back on track.

Reddy: You've kept me in the dark concerning this project, West. If you want me to help you, as Royce requested, I'll need all the information tomorrow, especially the cost data. I'll expect you in my office tomorrow morning at 8:00. I'll bail you out of this mess.

West prepared the projected cost data for the remainder of the work and presented the results to Dr. Reddy (see Table 7). Both West and Reddy agreed that the project was now out of control, and severe measures would be required to correct the situation, in addition to more than $250,000 in corporate funding.

Reddy: Dan, I've called a meeting for 10:00 A.M. with several of our R&D people to completely construct a new test matrix. This is what we should have done right from the start.

West: Shouldn't we invite Ray to attend this meeting? I'm sure he'd want to be involved in designing the new test matrix.

Reddy: I'm running this show now, not Ray! Tell Ray that I'm instituting new policies and procedures for in-house representatives. He's no longer authorized to visit the labs at his own discretion. He must be accompanied by either you or me. If he doesn't like these rules, he can get out. I'm not going to allow that guy to disrupt our organization. We're spending our money now, not his.

West informed Ray of the new test matrix, as well as the policies and procedures that would be placed upon in-house representatives. Ray was furious over the new

Table 7.   Estimate of Total Project Completion Costs.

Direct Labor/Support	$ 47,000[a]
Testing (60 tests)	120,000
Overhead (120%)	200,000
Materials	70,000
G&A	47,000
	$517,000
Peters Contract	250,000
	$267,000
Overrun	$267,000

[a] Includes Dr. Reddy.

turn of events and stated that he was returning to Peters Company for a meeting with Delia.

On the following Monday, Frimel received a letter from Delia stating that Peters Company was officially cancelling the contract. The reasons given by Delia were as follows:

1. Corwin had produced absolutely no data that looked promising.
2. Corwin continuously changed the direction of the project and did not appear to have a systematic plan of attack.
3. Corwin did not provide a project manager capable of handling such a project.
4. Corwin did not provide sufficient support for the in-house representative.
5. Corwin's top management did not appear to be sincerely interested in the project and did not provide sufficient executive-level support.

Royce and Frimel met to decide upon a course of action in order to sustain good working relations with Peters Company. Frimel wrote a strong letter refuting all the accusations in the Peters letter, but to no avail. Even the fact that Corwin was willing to spend $250,000 of its own funds had no bearing upon Delia's decision. The damage was done. Frimel was now thoroughly convinced that Pearl Harbor Day is the wrong time to accept a contract.

CASE STUDY 28:   TRW SYSTEMS GROUP (D)[1]

TRW Systems Group of Redondo Beach, California, was a successful supplier of systems and hardware in the aerospace industry. A major operating group of TRW, Inc., which was headquartered in Cleveland, Ohio, TRW Systems Group employed nearly 17,000 people, many of whom were technical professionals.

This case will describe the history and organization of TRW Systems Group as it existed in the late summer of 1967, to provide background for the E and F cases of the series.

History of TRW, Inc., and TRW Systems Group

TRW, Inc., was a highly diversified company formed by the merger of two distinctly different companies—Thompson Products, a leading maker of auto and aircraft parts in Cleveland, Ohio, and Ramo-Wooldridge, an aerospace company founded by Caltech scientists Simon Ramo and Dean Wooldridge. In 1953 these two men left Hughes Aircraft Company and established their business with the Thompson Company's financial backing. Winning a contract for the systems engineering and technical direction of the Air Force's ICBM program, Ramo-Wooldridge quickly became one of the most respected "think factories" in the United States. This contract established

---

[1] Copyright © 1968 by the president and fellows of Harvard College. This case was prepared by John J. Gabarro under the supervision of Jay W. Lorsch as a basis for class discussion, rather than to illustrate either effective or ineffective handling of an administrative situation. Reprinted by permission of the Harvard Business School.

a special relationship that made Ramo-Wooldridge (R-W) the technical supervisor for all ICBM contracts.

During this period, a nucleus of highly competent people was attacted to R-W. In the words of one senior manager:

> The leverage of our activities in the old systems engineering and technical direction business was great. With a few decisions, we had great influence in the aerospace industry. Because of this, we were able to attract the best people. Some of these people were put on assignments that were not really up to their capability, because we put the very best man possible on every job. We had an extremely competent group, and this is reflected in the character of the organization. If you put a fellow with a terrific background in a fairly moderate job, he's not about to be pushed around. So this strength of individuality showed up in the organizational structure. We started out with that core of individuals, and they're still here.

R-W's merger with Thompson into TRW, Inc., occurred in 1958. The two firms' amicable relations and complementary capabilities made the merger a natural evolution of their earlier relationship. TRW Systems Group was the successor to the Ramo-Wooldridge arm of the merger.

In 1959 TRW Systems decided to give up its privileged relationship with the Air Force's ICBM program, because its role as technical director precluded it from competing for Air Force contracts. The transition from a sheltered captive of the Air Force to an independent, competitive company was successfully completed by 1963. By 1967, TRW Systems was in some way engaged in 90 percent of the government's missile and space projects, including such diverse contracts as the Comsat communications satellites, NASA's Orbiting Geophysical Observatory, and engines for the Apollo Lunar Excursion Module. TRW Systems' strategy was to have as many small, diverse contracts relating to the same technology as possible to avoid dependence on one large contract, thus providing internal stability for the long run.

The "Matrix" Relationship

TRW's projects ranged from major space vehicle contracts and large subcontracts requiring integration of many capabilities, to small projects within a single discipline. Its functional capabilities included expertise in such varied specialties as guidance and control systems, digital systems, telecommunications, electronic detection, rocket propulsion systems, electrical power systems, and solar array batteries. In addition, TRW provided systems analysis in thermodynamics, space vehicle structures, and orbital and trajectory mathematics. A large hardware contract for a space vehicle would require the integration of all these capabilities to produce the systems engineering and detailed vehicle design, called *software,* and the actual fabrication and testing of the vehicle, called *hardware.* Even small contracts required the coordination of different disciplines. Interdependency was inherent in virtually every project regardless of size.[2]

---

[2] The terms *project* and *program* were used interchangeably at TRW.

To handle these projects, TRW Systems had developed an organization that it described as a "matrix." On one side of the matrix were the project offices that directed and coordinated the projects, and on the other side of the matrix were the functional departments that provided the manpower and technical resources needed by the project offices.

Typically, a project office had a small group of 30 to 40 people assigned to it. These people were concerned with the planning, coordinating, and systems engineering of the project. The project office called on the functional departments in its division and other divisions to perform the actual design and other technical work. As a result, the engineers working on a project were not members of the project office, but rather of functionally specialized departments, even though they might work on a project for several months or longer. The reasons for this organization were described in the report of a working committee formed to study the TRW Systems organization:

> TRW Systems is in the business of applying advanced technology. The hardware work that we do is awarded by our customers in bid packages that usually require the integration of hardware from several technical fields into a single end item. We have hundreds of these projects in operation at a time. The number of people assigned to them ranges from three or four to several hundred. Most of the projects are small—only a few fall in the "large hardware project" category we are mainly concerned with in this document.
>
> From the standpoint of personnel and physical resources, it is most efficient to organize by specialized groups of technologies. To stay competitive, these groups must be large enough to obtain and fully utilize expensive special equipment and highly specialized personnel. If each project had its own staff and equipment, duplication would result, resource utilization would be low, and the cost high; it might also be difficult to retain the highest caliber of technical specialists. Our customers get lowest cost and top performance in organization by specialty.
>
> For these reasons, the company has been organized into units of technical and staff specialties. As the company grows, these units grow in size, but a specialty is normally not duplicated in another organization. Each customer's needs call for a different combination of these capabilities. [Hence] a way of matching these customer needs to the appropriate TRW organizational capabilities is necessary. The use of the project office and matrix organization allows TRW Systems Group to make this fit.

Project Management

The project manager was responsible for the technical effort through all phases of development. He was also responsible for the control of project schedules and costs and in a total sense the profit of the project. As project manager, he controlled the funds and was ultimately responsible for their expenditure.

The work of the project office was carried out with the aid of a staff and several assistant project managers (APMs), whose responsibilities varied with the needs of the specific contract. Certain of these APMs had line responsibility over one or more subprojects. These APMs were responsible for preparing the subsystem specifications and coordinating their design. Other APMs provided services for all of the subprojects. For example, the APM for planning and control was responsible for cost and schedule control and PERT costing. In a sense he performed the functions of a local comptroller and master scheduler. The APM for systems engineering was responsible for formulating the project's systems requirements and making sure that everything was designed to fit together in the end. And the APM for product integrity was responsible for developing and implementing a reliability program for the entire project, including all its subprojects.

Subproject Management

The total project effort was divided into subprojects by the project office. A typical hardware subproject was in the $2 million to $4 million range, with an average manpower level of 50 people and a peak of over 100. The effort consisted of the analysis, design, development, and fabrication of perhaps four different assemblies comprising a subsystem. Typically, these assemblies were new designs, and five to eight of each were produced over a two-year period.

Each hardware subproject was assigned to a specific functional organization. The manager of that functional organization appointed a subprogram manager (SPM) with the concurrence of the project manager. The SPM was responsible for the total subproject and was delegated management authority by both the functional management and the APM to whom he reported operationally for the project. Normally he reported administratively to a laboratory or department manager in the functional organization.

The SPM worked full-time directing his subproject, but was not a member of the project office; he remained a member of his functional organization. He represented both the program office and functional management in his authority over the divisional people working on his subproject. He spoke for the project in such matters as scheduling personnel and facility assignments, expenditure of funds, customer requirements, and design interfaces. He also, however, represented the laboratory or division in such issues as technical approach, cost-effective scheduling, and the impact of design changes. The project manager provided his evaluation of the SPM's performance to the SPM's functional manager for the SPM's salary review.

Work Packages

The SPM was responsible for proposing a "work breakdown structure" of his subproject for the project manager's approval. In this work breakdown structure the subproject effort was successively subdivided into work packages, work units, and tasks for schedule, cost, and performance control. Job numbers were assigned at each level.

The functional engineer or supervisor receiving project direction from the SPM was called the work package manager (WPM). Below the level of the WPM, the work was managed within the functional structure but the project manager maintained project control through the APM-SPM-WPM chain. The work package was generally performed entirely within one functional department.

Functional Organization

TRW Systems was organized into five operating divisions; specifically, the space vehicles, electronic systems, systems laboratory, power systems, and systems engineering and integration divisions. Each of the divisions served as a technology center that focused on the disciplines and resources necessary to practice its technology. Although each division was organized differently, they shared a similar pattern, or organization.

Reporting to the division general manager were several operations managers. These operations managers were each in charge of a group of laboratories that were engaged in similar technologies. Each laboratory included a number of functional departments organized around technical specialties. Most divisions had a fabrication or manufacturing operations group headed by an operations manager.

Though a project could be conducted entirely within one or two divisions, work for projects that were too complex or large for one laboratory to handle were organized into project offices reporting to the division manager or an operations manager for projects.

Functional Operations Managers

Functional operations managers were responsible for directing the activities of two or three laboratories dealing in "adjacent" technologies. The operations manager level of management was a relatively new development, and the job was not yet defined in detail. His major concern was matching TRW's technical competence to developments in the changing aerospace environment. He also spent considerable time monitoring the administrative aspects of his organization's operations with respect to cost and schedule. His review of subprojects conducted within his operations area was limited to general proposals and plans. His influence and attention, however, were strongly felt when a subproject was in technical or cost-schedule problems.

The operations manager also played a strong role in determining the allocation of TRW's IR&D (Independent Research and Development) funds within his and other operational areas. IR&D funds were appropriated for use in research and development not directly associated with contract work, their purpose being to maintain TRW's technical capability by developing the state of the art.

Laboratories

The typical laboratory contained from 100 to 300 personnel and was engaged in anywhere from 2 to 10 subprojects. The laboratory manager spent about half of his time reviewing the progress of these subprojects and reviewing new proposals. His main concerns also included the assignment of personnel and facilities to meet new demands on the laboratory or in anticipating impending problems. Many laboratory managers had an assistant who was in charge of the subprogram managers and responsible for monitoring the subproject work being performed in the lab. In other cases the subproject managers were responsible to department managers.

Departments

The number of departments in a laboratory might vary from two to six. A typical department could have from 25 to 100 people assigned to it, and most departments were divided into at least two sections. Few had more than five. Normally the departments were organized so that their activities were confined to a single technical specialty. The department manager was responsible for developing and maintaining the technical capabilities of his particular specialty.

Unlike the laboratory manager, the department manager might be involved in giving technical supervision of a detailed nature. He was responsible for the professional growth and personnel management of his people, as well as capital planning and other resource administration. The department manager had a small budget for the operation of his department, but had to rely mainly on project work and IR&D (to a much smaller degree) for funding the department's operation.

Section

A typical section contained between 5 and 15 engineers or scientists and an equal number of support personnel. Sections differed widely in the number and type of project tasks they handled. The section head provided the day-to-day direction of his personnel, although larger sections were sometimes divided into groups with group leaders for this purpose. The number of project tasks in a single section might vary from 1 to 10. Sometimes the entire section was committed to a single unit or subsystem on an important project.

A Typical Large Hardware Project

An organizational chart of a typical large hardware project is shown in Figure 21. To the left of the dotted line is the project organization described in the early portion of this case, showing the link between the PM and APM. To the right of the line is the functional organization with the operations manager, laboratory manager, and department managers, described in the latter part of this case.

The SPM, although formally in the functional side of the matrix was, in reality, in the middle.

Because most projects went through a life cycle of several phases from their conception to their completion, both the size and the individual membership of the project team constantly shifted. For instance, the organizational structure changed significantly as task emphasis shifted from conceptual design to detailed design and production. Figure 22 shows four shifts in emphasis and the accompanying shifts in organization that took place during the life cycle of one such project.

The case writer talked to members of two project offices considered typical of medium to large hardware programs and to the functional people supporting these projects. One of the projects was the Vela Space Vehicle Program, which was sponsored by the space vehicles division, although much of its work was being conducted in other divisions, especially the electronic systems division. The second was the LMDE project (Lunar Module Descent Engine), which, unlike the Vela program, was almost entirely conducted within the power systems division—its sponsoring division.

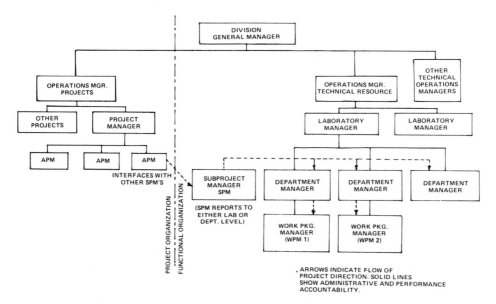

Figure 21.   TRW Systems Group (D). Organization of a Typical Large Hardware Project Showing the APM-WPM Chain.

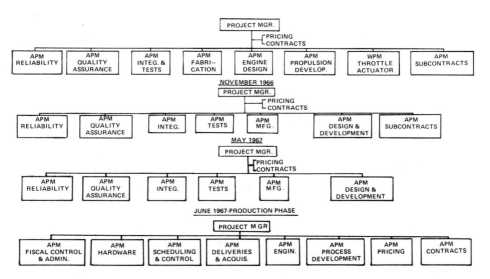

Figure 22.   TRW Systems Group (D). LMDE Project Office Organizations June 1966 to June 1967. June 1966–Development Phase.

Building a Project Team

Mr. Gene Noneman, project manager of the Vela project, described how he put together a project team:

> First I look at the project office's workload as a function of time, so that no one person's workload peaks while the rest of the people in the organization have little to do. We want everyone busy with small peaks if possible.
>
> Then I take various cuts of how we could organize the project office. If a guy is overloaded on the first cut, I adjust and so forth. It is a "real-time" thing that you assess day by day even after you have made your basic organization.
>
> The next step I take is to look at how I am going to split up the total work along the functional side of the matrix. What departments will be needed? What will have to be subcontracted?
>
> In doing this there are overlaps. It's then a question of defining where one subproject begins and where one ends. Another question is how big should each subproject be? Do I need two subprojects to accomplish something or do I need one? This requires a lot of thought on our part and collaboration with the functional departments. We've tried to develop some criteria over the years for defining subprojects.
>
> One criterion is the dollars that a subproject manager is going to have to look after. Second is the number of people within the company that his man is going to direct and monitor. The third criterion is the number of technical interfaces he has. How many technical people and how many discrete technical problems does he have to work with? The fourth factor is the management interfaces involved. How many functional departments is he going to have to interface with from a management point of view? A fifth key factor is the number of subcontracts and the nature of the procurement. Is it easy to do or is it protracted, technically detailed, demanding subcontract work? And the sixth one is the nature of the total effort. Here's where risk comes in. Does the job border on basic research, where you're dealing with factors that are not yet known, or is it more applied?
>
> Generally, we go to the divisions with our requirements and our initial breakdown of the work within the program office, and probably some subsystems in mind, and say, "Look, this is how I think it should be worked out—how does it look to you?" We have to compromise. I take the original cut because I know the requirements and interfaces, but then we sit down and work out the details with them.
>
> When I go to the functional departments, I have specific people in mind who I'd like to have work for me—people I know can do the job.
>
> In the end we put together a team for every contract. A lot of times it's a question of their not having people available to help us. One of the department manager's concerns is who can he give me that I'll be happy with. I never ask for a hotshot to do a small project, because I know they can't afford to give him to me and it wouldn't be a proper utilization of his time. If the

company were shrinking instead of expanding, all this might be different. But now they aren't worried about keeping their men busy. Rather they are worried about who they can give to whom and when. Now their concern is, "When can I have this guy back to put him on something else," rather than "I've got to keep this guy going."

Internal Control System

TRW Systems management was concerned about the effectiveness of project cost control because of changes in the contracting environment from cost-plus-fixed-fee contracts to contracts with a fixed cost plus incentive fee based on performance, target cost, and schedule.

There was no single control system that applied to all projects in early 1967, although control personnel were working on developing a cost-reporting system flexible enough to apply in all situations. Many major project offices had developed their own cost control systems based on the perceived needs of the project.

The reporting systems used by the project offices were intended for use at the project office level. These systems were not intended, nor detailed enough, for use by the SPMs for their subprograms or by work package managers. SPMs and WPMs made their own control systems. The assistant project manager for project planning and control of the Vela project described subprogram control in the following way:

> The reports we generate in this office are not intended for use by the SPMs in controlling their subprograms. They have to develop their own system to do this. We don't dictate formats—only the information that we need out of their reports. We try to leave it as flexible as possible, so they can do the managing. All we want is the correct information, so we know that they are not in trouble. We sit down with each SPM once a month or so, and if he is in trouble, at least once every two weeks. We've been putting pressure on the SPM to make sure he is using the tools that he has available to control his costs and schedule, and also that he is working at least one level greater in detail than we are here in the project office.

The assistant project manager for fiscal control on the LMDE project described how the cost control system used in that project was constructed and how it was related to the development of a management organization.

> When the job is first estimated in a proposal, we establish a control matrix and a work breakdown structure. Across the top is the work breakdown structure, which has all the work packages and work units and the major significant tasks. On the vertical axis we have the customer requirements. In this particular case our customer requires that we report to him the progress we were making by hardware line item, the throttle actuator, the injector, the nozzle extension, and so on. Essentially the customer imposes this kind of an axis on the matrix. Ultimately all this information goes into a data bank for estimating costs on new jobs.

CASE STUDY 29: TRW SYSTEMS GROUP (E)[1]

The extent to which relationships in the matrix should be defined and procedures standardized was a major organizational issue facing TRW Systems Group managers in the early summer of 1967. There were three principal reasons for that concern. Customers who did not understand the matrix relationships became uneasy with the project office's seeming lack of control over laboratory and shop resources. Second, TRW Systems meteoric growth from 2,000 to 14,000 employees in less than 10 years caused some managers to worry that operating without rigidly defined organizational relationships would become difficult, especially since many new employees were accustomed to more traditional structured organizations. Their inability to understand the organizational ambiguity led them to interpret it as confusion. The most significant factor, however, was the increasing number of large hardware projects being won by TRW. These projects required the control of tens of millions of dollars annually and brought extremely complex interdependencies into the organization.

An APM's comment was typical of one point of view on this issue:

> There is no question that for utilizing talent, the matrix organization is superior to a strict project organization. However, in the matrix you end up with a large overlay of management—too much management structure. I see this as a problem every time we negotiate with the customer. We have to sell the program office, the SPMs, the SPM staff, the functional organization, and then all the staff functions.
>
> We need more control because we're getting too big. You can't run a large hardware project with expenditures of millions of dollars a year in the same informal way that we have operated in in the past. There is a strong need for more consistent definition of tasks and organizational units.

Other managers were less concerned about a need for clear definition and control, as was the manager who made this comment:

> I think you find more frustration with the matrix in the manufacturing and scheduling operations where people tend to be oriented to more traditional organizations. For example, I can think of an SPM who is a real "heavy" in manufacturing, and he is very unhappy here because he's been used to calling the shots and having people jump, or if there is a problem going up the ladder to get a definite answer.
>
> We have procedures, but procedures are guides. Procedures show people how things are done. But you can never write down on a piece of paper everything that makes a highly development-oriented organization like this go. Maybe you can do it at the post office department, but this isn't the post office.

[1] Copyright © 1968 by the president and fellows of Harvard College. This case was prepared by John J. Gabarro under the supervision of Jay W. Lorsch as a basis for class discussion, rather than to illustrate either effective or ineffective handling of an administrative situation. Reprinted by permission of the Harvard Business School.

Feeling About the Matrix

Although differences of opinion existed over the need for procedures, most TRW managers and engineers felt that the matrix was on balance a very satisfactory way of organizing, given TRW's resources and business. One department manager in the power systems division described its advantages:

> "The matrix organization is of value when you reach the point where you don't need the specialist full time for a long period on any one given project. We have encouraged the matrix system because most of our projects are small, and we need the flexibility."

Mr. Robert DiBono, a former APM in the Vela Project recently promoted to manager of another project, said he believed the matrix organization was fundamentally good. It allowed a man to do whatever he was best at all the time, whether he was oriented toward systems work, management, or technical jobs:

> "There is a complete spectrum of work available and you can't help but find a good fit. And the company can't help but get a good fit."

Mr. DiBono also felt that the matrix organization made poor unilateral decisions almost impossible, because so many people interfaced with the program manager. However,

> Some of the bad aspects are that it's really difficult to pinpoint responsibility, and it's also hard to identify yourself with a specific accomplishment, because there are so many other people involved in that accomplishment. Personal identity is sometimes hard for people in the program office to feel, so I would imagine that it is even harder for someone in a functional lab. . . .
>
> Stress is concentrated on those people who feel responsible. I can't say where most of the stress is in the organization. It's an individual thing. I think this goes along with the difficulty in pinpointing responsibility. You either feel responsible or you don't. The very nature of the matrix distributes stress over a number of people.

Richard Gress, liaison engineer from LMDE's customer, National Aircraft Company, saw the TRW matrix system this way:

> It's quite an unusual atmosphere here. I don't know what your impression is, but my first impression coming from an aircraft company four years ago was that nothing was being done here. But I found as I stayed here, that it's not that way at all. People accomplish a lot more. The key to their success is their ability to recognize a problem and to put all their effort toward solving it. If any of their jobs have problems, the first thing they do is find out what they can do to correct it. Not, what to do to *hide it.*
>
> We find in our exposure to other companies that lots of times the first

thing they do is hide a problem so they can quietly solve it and then tell us. They don't do that here. They'll tell you most things as soon as they know them.

Differences in the Orientations of the Functional and Project Organizations

Many managers felt that one inevitable characteristic of the matrix organization was the difference that existed between the orientation and objectives of the functional and project organizations.

The manager of a PSD design and development laboratory summed up the basic differences by explaining that the program office controlled the program by allocation of resources, by interpreting the often obscure customer requirements, and by the probing and testing of progress. The engineering organization, however, believed itself to be the "doer" organization and resented program office restraints on development activities.

A manager of another development department engaged in the LMDE Project explained that another difference in orientation was the tendency of engineers to produce a good technical product (sometimes at the cost of lengthening the schedule and exceeding the budget), while the project office "pulled too hard the other way." He commented: "The engineers don't really understand the project implications nor are they interested in controlling the project. The project people don't really understand the technical implications of what they are doing, and often don't present technical things well enough to the customer or screen the customer's unreasonable demands from getting into the work. So natural conflict begins to arise."

Mr. Lionel Hammet, whose laboratory was involved in the Vela Project, elaborated on these different concerns:

Noneman (Vela Program manager) looks at the problem with the 2792 system a little differently than I do.[2]

I'm close to the numbers. I've talked to the experts in the area and I feel I have a much stronger feeling for what will happen than he has. He comes to me and he asks me, "Well, have you talked to the experts?" and I say, "Yes, I have talked to this fellow and that fellow, etc." He says, "Have you checked them, have you doublechecked what they said?"

We are just as concerned as he is but in a more detailed way. We are concerned with a given location of the relay. I see the detailed analyses that are conducted, and I know pretty much what the engineers are thinking. He's concerned because another program has had trouble with a component similar to the one we are using, and we've had some problems with it too. He's not concerned with the numbers we have to show him; he wants to see the box itself working. He wants to be able to shake the box up and see what happens to the relays. He wants to get maximum attention from the department managers, which you can't blame him for.

---

[2] The 2792 was a subsystem that had been having difficulties. A difference of opinion existed between the laboratory and the Vela Project office as to the source and extent of the problem.

The comments of two managers who had served in both sides of the matrix summed up the differences between the project and functional organizations and particularly emphasized the difference in personal satisfactions. Mr. John Wyman, a line manufacturing manager and a former APM, described his feelings

> I have spent most of my life in line organizations, and I feel I have more control over my destiny there than I do in the project. Maybe it is a personal thing for me. For example, in the project office I had difficulty in getting the attention of people working on the project in the functional area. You're assigned men of various capabilities from the functional areas to work for you. But whatever he's like you've got to depend on him to get the job done. If he's not performing, you can go to his boss. But your project is just one of many to his boss. And he's in a different organization than you, so you have little direct control there. If you keep hammering on his boss's door every day, the man himself will resent it and is not going to be effective.

A recently assigned APM described his point of view another way:

> I was in development engineering until the middle of March of this year, so I have been on the other side of the fence doing the design and development of the engine and always complaining about those "dirty guys over in the project office." Now I'm in the project office. When you're sitting over in development engineering, you're trying to do a good technical job—an engineer likes to get a thing perfect. The guys in development and design engineering are not looking at it from a business standpoint. That is why you have a project office. Somebody has to make a profit for the company.

He went on to express his feeling that perhaps there was more satisfaction to be found in the functional organization, since the engineers found solutions to detailed technical problems themselves, while the project managers dealt with problems that had to be solved by others; the project manager's satisfaction seemed to be in getting the total job done within the schedule and the budget.

Project Office Involvement in Integrating Activities

The project office focused on directing and coordinating the project's work in the various departments. Thus, the working relationships between people in the project office and in the line and the handling of differences between them were of special interest to project office managers. Mr. DiBono, former Vela APM, described these concerns:

> How do you maintain a relationship with the guy in the functional department so that he gives you maximum creativity and his best efforts while also getting what is required for the project? It's an influence sort of thing. You never have direct control over your resources. You have to know how the other people operate, and in many cases it is a completely individual relationship

with each one of the men who work on your part of the project. You work it out by having some good healthy discussion with the SPMs and the key people in the functional departments. The people over whom you have control in the project office also have to interface outside and be influencers in the functional departments.

The matrix organization is really an interlacing of personal relationships. For example, everyone who had worked with us on the last launch at the test site wanted to do a good job, and people really put out. As a result you make a lot of personal arrangements with the people who work for you in the functional area. For example, company policy says that unless a man is sent to a test location for more than 45 days he can't go on per diem or take his family. Well, when you have technicians who have been working fantastic overtime for you, much more than you can humanly expect, you do everything you can to let them take their families to Florida even though it's not strictly in accordance with company policy.

But people have a devotion here to their work that you can't find anywhere else. For example, it's common on the test site for technicians, at the end of a 14-hour day, to leave the number of the bar or restaurant that they're going to after work in case a problem comes up and they're needed. And they are hourly people; they aren't salaried.

But people have to feel that they're important to do this. They have to know you and trust you. Another part of establishing a good relationship is making sure that the line people in your project are recognized by their bosses for a good job. You help them look good in front of their bosses.

Mr. Robert Wilder, a younger APM in the Vela Program, described his job as "making sure that the right thing is being done at the right time." Unable to work on technical problems in any great detail, Mr. Wilder explained that he had to rely on strong working relationships. He had initiated off-site meetings at the beginning of the design phase for his SPMs and some of the other APMs, and he felt that these sessions were important in helping people get to know each other. According to Wilder, at one such session Professor James Clarke of UCLA had explained the "arc of dissonance" concept: "He explained that every person projects an arc of dissonance, which is a measure of the inconsistency or incongruence that people see in him, mainly referring to his openness and honesty. His studies have shown that the most successful leaders have small arcs of dissonance. That made a lot of sense to me, and since then I've tried to be as open as possible."

Mr. Wilder felt that team building was extremely important in an organization where so many people were dependent on each other. In his opinion coordination was essential to a successful project and, in addition, he noted, "You have to have trust and understanding to make this kind of organization work . . . if you don't have it you're dead."

Mr. Morris Adler, an SPM on the Vela Project in Wilder's area, also discussed the effect of team building on his subprogram's success:

I attribute a lot of the success our subsystem has had to our relationship with the project office and my relationship with the people who worked on it. The project office started by having off-site meetings. Wilder actually initiated it with his SPMs and some of the APMs who were involved with us, and he chaired these meetings. We started by going to a restaurant where we had dinner and a couple of drinks and just talked to each other. But we did it under a different atmosphere. We weren't under the pressures of daily problems. The first session was more friendly than anything else—getting to know each other. In later sessions, however, we really grappled with some meaty problems. We dealt with relationships and problems directly, bringing a lot of things into the open. For example, we found out that there were a lot of problems within one of the functional areas, and it helped me prevent similar things from occurring in my own area. It also helped the guys in that area clear up their own.

Adler was impressed enough by this experience to obtain funding for similar meetings with his own unit engineers:

When we sat down, we got a lot of things squared away. It was an opportunity for everyone to talk about problems they were having by themselves and problems that others were causing. For example, when a design engineer wants to make a change, the production engineer screams at him because the change screws up his operation. Now, the production guy has a good feeling for what problems the design engineer has and vice versa, and they can talk to each other. This was all a very important part of making my people project-oriented, and I think was behind our success.

The thing I have to remember to appreciate team building is that no one works for me on a solid-line basis but my secretary.

Many other TRW personnel, both functional and program office, also stressed the importance of communication and trust in the reconciliation of differences in outlook between them. Mr. DiBono expressed his belief that no unresolvable differences in outlook existed between the specialists and the program office people; the specialists were extremely anxious to do a good job, and the key was simply to get both parties looking at the same problem. He had encountered difficulty only when the program office had failed to define the nature of problems to people in the functional area.

DiBono explained that many misunderstandings developed over documentation. As an example he explained that equipment specifications for orbital operations equipment had to be user-oriented, but design people would give design-oriented equipment specifications unless the exact need was communicated to them. Sometimes it was necessary to take a man out of the lab and up to the test site to achieve this understanding. He gave a further example:

I had a case where I couldn't communicate to a group of design people what it was that I needed for equipment specs. I tried, but it was obvious that I wasn't getting across. So I took the design information that was available and tried to translate it into operating specs myself. With this in hand, I went back to them and showed it to them. They said, "Boy, that's pretty bad."

And they were right, it was pretty bad because it wasn't really detailed enough. But this gave them an opportunity to see what I wanted.

Some program office personnel, however, found the relationship with the functional areas frustrating. Mr. Wyman, for example, a former APM on the LMDE Program, described his feelings in the following way:

> The real problem we have in many of the divisions is that the work is left to the man down at machine, and his boss is in an office somewhere and doesn't know what is really going on. You are more or less at the mercy of that particular man. If you get one that you don't have rapport with, then you have to go work on his boss to get him moving, and frequently it is difficult to get a number of things done except under extreme pressure. This is because of the buddy system. A guy down there has a friend and he will put other people's work aside to help his buddy out.

Mr. Wyman stated that there were times in the course of a program when he was dependent on a whole department for assistance. He described a situation when electronic hardware operations didn't have enough of a special wire in stock:

> This was critical to us, so we actually had people go over there and work with them to find out how much wire they really had and how we could steal a little bit here and there.
>
> When we first started into this, we had a very negative reaction. Then Anderson and I had the manager in charge of that department over for supper. We laid out our problem to him and told him why we needed his help and what it meant to the company and what we were risking. There was a little lag in getting their cooperation while the desires of the lab supervisor filtered down to the lower levels. In other words they had to get interested in the things their boss was interested in, but we ended up getting a lot of cooperation, and everything turned out OK. That's the important thing in this business— how it ties together. It really is not so important what people think of you in the middle of all these things as it is what they think of you when you come to the end of it.

Subprogram Manager's Role

The SPM was a key person in the accomplishment of project work since he was responsible for managing the efforts of a major business subsystem of the project. Although he was in actuality a member of a functional area and reported administratively to a laboratory or department manager, his full-time effort was directed toward his subprogram. Mr. Joe Kranz, an APM on the Vela Project who was formerly an SPM, described the SPM as "the one person in the functional area who can ensure that costs and schedules are maintained for a part of the project." This job was difficult because an SPM represented both the project office and the functional organization, and their aims were often dissimilar. An SPM made many decisions affecting the project and its profitability, and it was essential that he balance the objectives of both organizations. The SPM's job is probably one of the most uncomfortable yet rewarding positions a man can have. I think it needs strengthening the most, with more support staffed to him. Let's face it, that's where the interfacing takes place between the line and the project office and in large programs that's where most of the technical direction takes place."

Mr. Kranz stated that although the project office and lab could put pressure on an SPM, both organizations "know that if you put too much pressure on that point, it will break down . . . especially because it has so much stress on it already." He categorized SPMs as two types: "the kind of guy who is strong technically and the kind of guy who isn't." Technically capable SPMs were received with respect and cooperation by the engineers, while the not-so-competent SPM was perceived as an outsider from the program office. Mr. Kranz felt that an SPM had to be competent technically in order to communicate with people about detailed technical problems. He talked about his own experiences:

I think I had this respect as an SPM because when I decided to transfer to the project side of the house, the people in the laboratory didn't want me to go and tried to talk me into staying. It's hard to explain, but I felt that when I was an SPM my own position as a member of the laboratory was unchallenged because people accepted me and they realized that I was a capable guy and a pretty good engineer. I guess it was easier for me to look after the best interests of the program office because I didn't have to worry about my standing as a member of the laboratory.

An SPM for a fabrication subproject of the Vela Program attempted to describe the role he played as the intermediary between the project office and the functional area:

I have asked our people to treat the project office like a customer, that is, honest and so forth, but discrete. I've encouraged contact between our working guys and the project office for information purposes. All other things and the technical direction come through me.

One of the dangers of being in this job is that you identify too much with the project office. You can't become so identified with a project that you lose sight that the guy who is in trouble is in your department. It's possible to be so program-oriented that you're throwing stones at your own guys. You're the frontline representative of the program office, but you're still getting paid by the lab manager . . . there is no question in my mind that he's my boss.

I also have conflicts with other SPMs. It's easy for problems to develop when two projects are coming down the same assembly line. We're all TRW, so it's a question of figuring out who has the worst problem and helping each other. Sometimes I have problems working in another lab, and I have to make sure that we're getting the internal management there that we need without my being there eight hours a day.

Mr. Adler, the SPM for an electronic subprogram, whose comments were introduced earlier, felt differently about the SPM's conflicting loyalties:

> The question of divided loyalties doesn't really come up very often. I feel responsibility for both the program office and the functional area. I won't carry people for the functional department for free on a project, for example. But, on the other hand, I won't push people for an early completion just to feel safe—especially when it means these people are going to be sitting around after it's done. I've found that if I'm objective with both sides and focus on the subprogram's needs I'm not squeezed. A good part of this is because my lab manager says, "Your charter is to look out for your subprogram, period."
>
> I'm sure there are several labs that have their SPMs more functionally oriented than we are, and it's not because the SPM wants to be. It's because the lab manager wants him to be. If the lab manager wants an SPM to be functionally oriented first and foremost, you can say anything you want and write all the reports you want, they will be functionally oriented.

The frustrations and satisfactions of being an SPM were also described by Ray La Flamme, another SPM on the Vela Project. He said his satisfaction came from seeing his ideas develop into tangible accomplishment, from living with a minimum of information, and from combining technical work and management responsibility within a broad program picture. Further, he noted:

> I get my greatest satisfaction when we're able to carry off the plan with a minimum of changes. My frustrations, they're legion: organization, personal relationships, misinformation on overruns, adapting to changes constantly in design plans, schedule, etc. But it has to be that way, because that's the nature of the job. I enjoy this kind of excitement and going into meetings. It's part of the romance of the job.
>
> There are a lot of binds that an SPM can find himself in. The most typical one is when there is a difference of technical opinion between the project office and the functional department manager. I think my own position is harder because I'm on the department manager's staff, and not the lab manager's. I'm at a level where I can't quite get out of the detail stuff. It also makes it hard for me to interface with other department managers.

Another frustration described by SPMs was getting someone with management status to look at the work going on in the departments between crises, and occasionally during problem periods.

Many SPMs transferred into the project offices as assistant project managers after one or two assignments as an SPM. Joe Kranz had left the SPM's job primarily because he felt there was no recognition to be gained from doing project management-type work in a functional division, and the program office was the place to do this type of work. He felt that a tour as an SPM might be a good learning experience for a man who wanted to stay in the functional side of the house, but after more than one or two stints as an SPM a man would lose touch with the state of the art. Thus he became less effective both in the lab and as an SPM. Kranz concluded that there was little to be gained from remaining very long in the SPM's job.

Other TRW managers, however, did not all feel that the SPM's future career path was a problem. An APM stated that SPMs were an important source of program office people, since they were close to the program office as well as to their discipline, and their work was visible to many people.

Temporary Membership in the Project Offices

As the comments above suggest, one characteristic of a project office was that it had a finite life as an organization, ending when the project was completed. Managers other than SPMs also spoke about how this affected their outlook. One APM listed three alternative courses that could be followed after the closing of a project: (1) get followup work on the old project, (2) find a new customer for a new application of your old project, or (3) hunt for a new job. He stated that the company did not necessarily have a new job waiting at the end of a program, but finding something had not been a problem. If a man had done a good job, finding the next job was easy, because new program offices always looked for a man whose judgment and competence could be trusted. He commented:

> If we were starting a new program office, we'd look for people who we knew had the capability to do the job. If you can't find them directly, then you go to people whose judgment you can trust and ask them whom they would recommend.
>
> The company still works on the basis that a man's competence and personal reputation are very important. Competence and knowledge are a way in which a man can provide for the future and reduce the uncertainty of a career in the project side of the house.

This particular APM's predecessor had lost an opportunity outside his project because he had been "indispensable"; the current APM intended to replace himself before the project ended in order to avoid this. He added, "Noneman (Vela Program manager) now requires that people brought into the project office have the capacity to grow into the APM job, but sometimes this requirement is overlooked because of the need for people."

APM Bob Wilder of the Vela Program commented that the issue of temporary membership was no problem because of TRW's continuing growth; no one felt threatened about job security. If the company were in a declining stage, however, he thought he might be worried and the program office would no longer be as attractive a place to work. He continued:

> I'd imagine that if I were not too sure about my present performance, I might be pretty worried. But I say to myself, I'm a pretty good guy and I'm valuable to TRW; things would have to be pretty bad for me to go, and a lot of other people would go before me. My personal competence as a manager is very

important to me, and I gain my sense of security by knowing that there is a fairly wide recognition of my competence.

I will admit though that occasionally I think about TRW not yet having faced the aerospace cycle—big boom and bust—that most other outfits have. We're counting on our diversity and large number of small projects to prevent our ever facing one.

A third APM described the procedure of looking for another assignment after a project drew to a close:

Around this place you look for a job; they don't look for you. Like everything else here it is unstructured. I don't really like the way it's done. You find another assignment by nosing around the company, seeing who has what. If I were looking for another assignment, I would tell all my friends I was available and Gene Noneman, the project manager, would also. I remember a guy who was about to phase out of a project. He started looking about a month before and just couldn't find anything, so he stayed on two months or so. This is really unusual. More often than not, a guy is needed on another project before he can leave the project he's working on.

This APM thought that people should not be kept in a program office too long because of the pressure: "You can't ever really relax." He suggested rotating people, perhaps to a functional area.

The Functional Manager's Views of the Functional-Program Relationship

The functional managers, like their program office counterparts, felt that most of the conflicts caused by different orientations were resolved. Dr. Drake, manager of a development department engaged in the LMDE program, explained that different orientations sometimes crystallized around situations where his organization felt more work should be done and the program office wanted them to stop. Such problems were only occasionally resolved by going up to the lab manager—program manager level. Dr. Drake thought that people higher in the organization tended to be more mature and broad-minded.

Drake explained that similar conflicts arose within the technical organization; for example, design engineers felt subjugated to development engineers in the same way that development engineers felt subjugated to program office people. In a period of significant technical problems, however, Drake felt that the project organization was at the mercy of the technical organization, and there had to be a feeling of trust and mutual purpose.

There have been times when nobody has known clearly what to do, and where the pressures have been intense, budgets were exceeded, schedules slipped, problems became almost unbearable, personal workloads were high, tempers short, and clumsiness made everyone irritable. You literally get to the point where you may have some nervous breakdowns. The force of a few personalities becomes very important at that point. The same people are not quite so important when things are running smoothly.

The matrix requires you to be aware of the individual you are dealing with in judging the way he presents his case. . . . We have had problems when personalities are not well-balanced. It's a bad situation when one personality is much stronger than the other. The stronger begins to dictate, and the balance between line and project office is lost. We had a very strong development engineer in one area, and his counterpart on the project side was weak. The development engineer was in control. No doubt about it. The project office in that situation was providing service, keeping the budget and documents straight, and everybody worked for this development engineer. At exactly the same time there was another area where the project engineer was a very strong personality, and the development engineer was not. The project was in absolute control there because it controls the funds to begin with.

In referring to the functional-project office relationship, another department manager, whose area was involved in the Vela Project, described the value he saw in the looseness of this relationship:

Everything can't always be put on paper. We can't play the same game that a vendor plays with a customer. That's our strength. We don't live to the letter of the law. We meet the spirit and the intent. We're not subcontractors. We maintain a pretty flexible and loose relationship with the project office, but, at the same time, if I don't stay involved, this relationship can cause some problems.

One of the problems is that the department manager and section heads are not pulled into project work early enough when problems come up. The SPMs have interfaced pretty closely with the development engineer causing him to feel he's taking direction from the SPM. This has led to cases where the department manager or the section heads aren't involved until it gets really bad. In essence, the department managers are left out of the information loop until costs or problems are too big. This also results in under- or overdesign.

In speaking about their jobs, laboratory managers pointed out that they were generally involved in nontechnical problems (such as capital and manpower planning), rather than detailed technical problems. The exception was very major technical problems, in which they became deeply involved.

Mr. Hammet stated that there were a lot of frustrations involved in being a lab manager due to personalities and the nebulous nature of problems. But the satisfaction came from solving these same problems and from being able to see people who were involved grow. He also felt that it was not true that functional personnel were dissatisfied because they could not work on a project from beginning to end:

Everyone in the lab who's worked on a project gets satisfaction out of seeing a good launch. The manager of the integration and test lab and I have worked out a pretty fluid relationship between our areas, which enables us to transfer people so that they can follow the project through right to the launch. The surprising thing is that few of the designers ever want to do that. They would rather design. In many respects having a designer follow his project through to the launch would be good, because the launch experience would have a good effect on his future design work. But, we've had few takers.

All the department managers and most of the SPMs reported to Mr. Hammet. He said that his SPMs were theoretically equal in organizational status to the department managers, but the department managers felt more important because they had the people needed by the SPMs. However, an SPM was in a very visible position and was therefore able to make or break himself, while the department manager's performance averaged out.

A development engineer working on the LMDE program discussed the functional project relationship in a manner typical of development and design engineers:

One of the ways in which being an engineer here is different from other places is that you have technical responsibility and in effect no authority. We've had problems on the shut-off valve. They were technical problems that I, as a development engineer, felt needed correction. But the project office thought that it was satisfactory the way it was and that no changes were required. It's not so much the dollar that the project office is concerned with as schedules. . . .

It's very difficult when you feel you have the responsibility, knowledge, and experience, but not the funds to authorize more work. You have to convince other people who are not familiar or experienced that it's necessary. Unfortunately, with valves, it's hard to justify them until you've had a series of failures and have actually stopped delivery of an engine. When this happens they sometimes look at you and ask why you didn't push harder. It's happened here, but they've always been man enough to accept the responsibility.

Assessing Priorities between Programs

An important part of the functional manager's role was to assess the priorities between projects competing for resources. A manager of a design department in the Power System Division said that it never had enough people to do everything at once, and some jobs had to slide at the decision of the department manager. He said priorities were allocated by discussing jobs with the responsible people in the various programs, trying to establish which was most urgent; if no agreement could be reached, then someone up the line, a lab manager or operations manager, might be approached.

Another department manager put it this way: "When you really come down to it, the real job is to keep all your projects with passing grades. If one of them looks like it's heading for a D or an F, you put more effort into it, regardless of whether you like one better than you do another. If things are equal, I'll admit that I find all sorts of justifications to work on the things I like to work on, rather than on those I don't."

An APM on the LMDE project felt that the procedure used was satisfactory to the project office:

> Everyone in the project office thinks his is the highest-priority job, and that's, of course, what he should think. But you have to look at it from a company standpoint. Recently there was a case where we had a guy over in development engineering and we needed him to do some work on our program. However, they had him assigned to another spacecraft project because of a very difficult problem they were having. If he did not work on this one, it meant a large sum of money to the company. They were in some kind of a contractual situation, where if they did not start a certain test at a certain day, they would lose a lot of the fee. So the LMDE Program suffered a little bit.
>
> If there is a conflict, as in this case, it gets up to the project manager. He goes over and has a chat with the laboratory manager and they have a meeting of the minds about it. What means more to the company? We know that you want this man for your project, but we need him over here. So an agreement is generally worked out.

Control

As one indication of the concern for better control and better definition of jobs, TRW had in the planning stages a control system that was being designed specifically for controlling project-type work. As it had not been fully developed by August of 1967, a control system called a *work breakdown structure* was being used to control projects.

The APM for planning and control for the LMDE Project said that in the matrix system the difficulty of trying to collect costs accurately, promptly, and in enough detail to manage effectively arose because most department heads, section heads, and engineers were working a number of projects simultaneously; they therefore had a lot of job numbers against which to charge their time and materials. For example:

> In the early days of LM, we had 250 charge numbers, for example, and about 650 "equivalent people" working on the program. We had as many as 2,000 individual people charging the program—some as little as half an hour a month. The part-time chargers, particularly, due to unfamiliarity with the program, tend to mischarge inadvertently.
>
> People don't realize that you're trying to segregate recurring and nonrecurring costs or development activity from production activity. We have a control matrix that gives you all kinds of sophisticated information if it's properly used. But this sophistication has to be conveyed well to all the people charging the program.
>
> You find a subtle conflict of interest because the engineer has a natural desire to polish and improve the product to the ultimate degree. Maybe he's in the middle of a redesign, or maybe he isn't quite finished, so he'll work an extra hour or day or the rest of the week to do what he thinks is necessary

from an engineering standpoint. You never know this because he continues to work on the program while charging another number. So you have an inherent inaccuracy in the data itself for that reason.

The APM explained that as the program progressed, the work breakdown structures and matrix were revised, certain development numbers were closed, and production numbers opened. People tended, however, to keep using an old number because they remembered it. Inaccuracy was minimized by a high response system for collecting and reporting charges: each individual had a number and where he worked had a cost center code identifying his division, laboratory, and department. It was possible to tell by the actual charge where and who the individual was; it was difficult, however, to know what was *not* being charged to a project although, presumably, charges made to another project would be detected by that project's APM.

A development engineer provided the viewpoint of some professionals at his level about the matters of controls:

I'm somewhat of a maverick. I'm of the firm opinion that once you've got a contract you should throw the budget out the door, in effect, and do the job. Of course keep accounting records of how much it costs you. And the hell with what you estimated it was going to cost. That's water under the bridge. Your job, once you have a contract, is to do it as efficiently as possible and at a minimum of cost. And do it properly. If you're keeping the name for the company you have to do a good job.

The project office will very often come up and say we can't fix it because we don't have the money. This is a ridiculous statement. You have to fix it. Where they get the money is their problem. You ought to keep budget records, because you have to know how much it costs and use that information to improve your estimate on the next contract.

What sometimes happens when we run out of funds is that other phases of the program are charged, because this other phase might be overbudgeted and yours is underbudgeted. You end up with data that are not entirely accurate. We continue to underestimate, because we really don't know what it costs. The other facet of this is that most good development engineers work a lot of overtime for which they're not paid and never shows up in accounting records. They work twice as much as actually shows up, including nights and Saturdays.

Moonlighting is standard practice for a conscientious engineer to solve a problem now so that when the problem hits he has a solution for it. You don't want to spend nights, Saturdays, and Sundays when it does hit because it affects your personal life and you don't do a good job solving problems that you didn't have the time to think about. When the problem comes up and you say, "I happen to have the answer right here," they're overjoyed. They don't say, "How come you were working on that?" I think the answer would be somewhat embarrassing to them and very seldom do they go into that. They just take it, and usually give the engineer very little credit for it.

The APM for control in the Vela Project explained that a big problem in controlling costs was knowing when people were merely tracking costs. TRW's reputation for technical excellence at any cost affected cost control, in that individuals in the functional organization were not evaluated on management skills, but on technical skills, that is, how good were the boxes they built: "I think customers realize that we are expensive. I think they know, though, that if they come here, it will be expensive but good—better than it could be done anywhere else."

He explained that this was a question of management philosophy, and basic change in orientation had to come from the top on down. The president of TRW Systems was beginning to put more emphasis on cost management because of customer concern, however, and he felt that costs would become an item of greater importance to the organization.

Mr. Gene Noneman, the Vela Project manager, said that the subprogram plan was a very important tool in defining the tasks that had to be completed in establishing a cost and time schedule for control. The plan had to be made up by the SPM early in the program and in such a way that it could be understood by everyone. The finished plan was sent to the APM, and Noneman said that this was how he knew that the SPM understood the requirements of the job and that the people in his department and all the departments he interfaced with would understand the job.

As described in TRW Systems Group (D), the SPMs designed their own control systems and were required to give key inputs only to the program office. Mr. Ray La Flamme, an SPM in the Vela Program, felt that this and the work breakdown structure had a number of limitations:

> The program office is often naive in realizing how much it costs to do work in a shop. My own recognition and documentation, of these added costs has not been adequate, and for this reason we're "overrun" on manpower and money. I find it very hard to keep up with the documentation.
>
> There's nothing that's set up in our cost control system with which you can document a change rapidly and efficiently. If I had it to do all over again, I'd attempt to develop a system whereby everyone realizes the impact of what he's doing to us.
>
> The other influence on controlling costs lies with the departments doing the work. If someone there doesn't feel responsible for meeting and beating cost where possible and preventing costly overdesign, you've had it.

Formalizing the Matrix Relationships

Many TRW managers stressed that formalizing and standardizing the matrix relationships and control system had to be considered in the context of the TRW Systems organization and its distinct characteristics. Robert Anderson, operations manager for projects in the Power Systems Division, was one of the most articulate in making this point:

> I'd like to talk just a little bit about the character of the company, because I think it influences the capability of this kind of system to work in a good way: This outfit is always *working the problem*. I have never seen anything

like it. It just seems that this whole company is infused with the idea of working hard and making itself better.

It is the most self-critical place you have ever seen, and as a result it is not stagnant. Everything is sort of continuously changing, and there is always a little degree of fuzziness around. But they are all working, and not just on their own problems. A guy is just as likely to work on somebody else's problems. It is none of his business, but he's doing it anyway, presumably from pure motives. He is trying to help the other guy to do better. Organizational definitions are not really rigid.

Every year they get a little more so. And many of us look at that with fear and trepidation and beat them down every now and then just for fun.

But in this organization there is enough diversity and enough talent so that the organization sort of evolves as needs change. The good parts of the organization grow and prosper, and the bad parts of the organization sort of don't.

You could argue that it makes for empire building, but if the strong and needed parts survive it's a valid empire.

CASE STUDY 30:   ROBERT L. FRANK & COMPANY[1]

It was Friday afternoon, a late November day in 1978, and Ron Katz, a project purchasing agent for Robert L. Frank, pored over the latest, man-hour figures. The results kept pointing out the same face—the Lewis project was seriously over budget. Man-hours expended to date were running 30 percent over the projection, and, despite this fact, the project was not progressing sufficiently to satisfy the customer. Material deliveries had experienced several slippages, and the unofficial indication from the project scheduler was that, due to delivery delays on several of the project's key items, the completion date of the coal liquefaction pilot plant was no longer possible.

Katz was completely baffled. Each day for the past few months, as he reviewed the daily printout of project time charges, he would note that almost the entire purchasing and expediting departments were working on the Lewis project, which was not an unusually large project, dollarwise, for Frank. Two years before, Frank was working on a $300 million contract, a $100 million contract, and a $50 million contract concurrently with the Frank Chicago purchasing department responsible for all the purchasing, inspection, and expediting on all three contracts. The Lewis project was the largest project in house and was valued at only $90 million. What made this project so different from previous contracts and cause such problems? There was little Katz could do to correct the situation. All that could be done was to understand what had occurred in an effort to prevent a recurrence. He began to write his man-hour report for submission to the project manager the next day.

---

[1] This case is partially fictitious and was prepared by Robert J. Hamill under the direction of Harold Kerzner as a basis for discussion, rather than to illustrate either the effective or ineffective handling of an administrative situation.

Company Background

Robert L. Frank and Company is an engineering and construction firm serving the petroleum, petrochemical, chemical, iron and steel, mining, pharmaceutical, and food processing industries from its corporate headquarters in Chicago, Illinois, and its worldwide offices. Its services include engineering, purchasing, inspection, expediting, construction, and consultation.

Frank's history began in 1947, when Robert L. Frank opened his office. In 1955, a corporation was formed, and by 1960 the company had completed contracts for the majority of the American producers of iron and steel. In 1962, an event that was to have a large impact on Frank's future occurred. This was the merger of Wilson Engineering Company, a successful refinery concern, with Robert L. Frank, now a highly successful iron and steel concern. This merger greatly expanded Frank's scope of operations and brought with it a strong period of growth. Several offices were opened in the United States in an effort to better handle the increase in business. Future expansions and mergers enlarged the Frank organization to the point where today it has 15 offices or subsidiaries located in the United States and 20 offices worldwide. Through its first 20 years of operations, Frank had over 2,500 contracts for projects having an erected value of over $1 billion.

Frank's organizational structure has been well suited to the type of work undertaken. The projects Frank contracted for typically had a time constraint, a budget constraint, and a performance constraint. They all involved an outside customer, such as a major petroleum company or a steel manufacturer. Upon acceptance of a project, a project manager is chosen (usually contained in the proposal). The project manager heads the project office, typically consisting of the project manager, one to three project engineers, the project control manager, and the project secretaries. The project team then includes the necessary functional personnel from the engineering, purchasing, estimating, cost control, and scheduling areas. Figure 23 is a simplified graphical depiction. Of the functional areas, one is nearly unique in its organization.

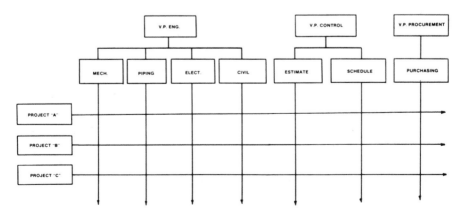

Figure 23.   Frank Organization.

The purchasing department is organized on a project management basis, much as the project as a whole is organized. Within the purchasing department, each project has a project office, which includes a project purchasing agent, one or more project expeditors, and a project purchasing secretary. Within the purchasing department, the project purchasing agent has line authority over only the project expeditor(s) and project secretary. However, for the project purchasing agent to accomplish his goals, the various functions within the purchasing department have to commit sufficient resources to that end. Figure 24 illustrates the organization within the purchasing department.

History of the Lewis Project

Since 1976, the work backlog at Frank has been steadily declining. The Rovery project, valued at $300 million, had increased company employment sharply since its inception in 1973. In fact, the engineering on the Rovery project was such a large undertaking that, in addition to the Chicago office's participation, two other U.S. offices, the Canadian office, and the Italian subsidiary were heavily involved. However, since the Rovery project completion in 1976, not enough new work was received to support the work force, thus necessitating recent layoffs of engineers and even a few project engineers.

Company officials were very disturbed with the situation. Point 1 of Frank's com-

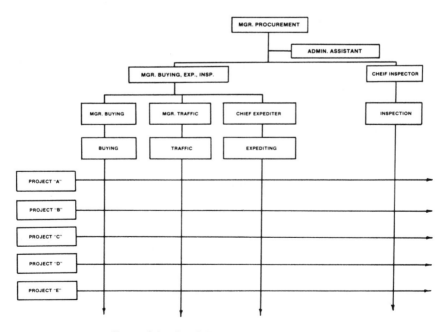

Figure 24.   Frank Purchasing Organization.

pany policy was to "maintain an efficient organization of sufficient size and resources, and staffed by people with the necessary qualifications, to execute projects in any location for the industries served by Frank." However, the recent downturn in business meant that there was not enough work, even with the reduction in employees. Further cutbacks would jeopardize Frank's prospects of obtaining future projects, as prospective clients look to contractors with a sufficient staff of qualified people to accomplish their work. On the other hand, supporting employees out of overhead was not the way to do business either. It became increasingly important to "cut the fat out" of the proposals being submitted for possible projects. Despite this, new projects were few and far between, and the projects that were received were small in scope and dollar value and therefore did not provide work for very many employees.

When rumors of a possible facility for a new coal liquefaction pilot plant started circulating, Frank officials were extremely interested in bidding for the work. It was an excellent prospect for two reasons. Besides Frank's desperate need for work, the Lewis process being used for the pilot plant would benefit Frank in the long run. If the pilot plant project could be successfully executed, when it came time to construct the full-scale facility, Frank would have the inside track, because it had already worked with the technology. The full-scale facility offered prospects exceeding the Rovery project, Frank's largest project to date. Top priority was therefore put on obtaining the Lewis project. It was felt that Frank had a slight edge due to successful completion of a Lewis project six years ago. The proposal submitted to Lewis contained estimates for material costs, man-hours, and the fee. Any changes in scope after contract award would be handled by change order to the contract. The functional department affected would submit an estimate of extra man-hours involved to the project manager who would review the request and submit it to the client for approval. Frank's preference is for cost-plus-fixed-fee contracts.

One of the unique aspects about the Lewis proposal was the requirement for participation by both Frank Chicago's operating divisions. Previous Frank contracts were well suited to either Frank's Petroleum and Chemical Division (P & C) or the Iron and Steel Division (I & S). However, due to the unusual process, one that starts with coal and ends up with a liquid energy form, one of the plant's three units was well suited to the P & C Division and one was well suited to the I & S Division. The third unit was an off-site unit and was not of particular engineering significance.

The acceptance of the proposal six weeks later led to expectations by most Frank personnel that the company's future was back on track again.

The Lewis Project

The project began inauspiciously. The project manager was a well-liked, easy-going sort who had been manager of several Frank projects. The project office included three of Frank's most qualified project engineers.

In the Purchasing Department, the project purchasing agent (PPA) assigned to the project was Frank's most experienced PPA. Bill Hall had just completed his assignment on the Rovery project and had done well, considering the magnitude of the job. The project had its problems, but they were small in comparison with the achievements. He had alienated some of the departments slightly, but that was to be expected. Purchasing upper management was somewhat dissatisfied with him, in that, due to the size of the project, he didn't always use the normal Frank purchasing methods; rather, he used whatever method he felt was in the best interest of the project. Also, after the Rovery project, a purchasing upper management reshuffling left him in the same position but with less power, rather than receiving a promotion he felt he had earned. As a result, he began to subtly criticize the purchasing management. This action caused upper management to hold him in less than high regard, but, at the time of the Lewis project, Hall was the best man available.

Due to the lack of float in the schedule and the early field start date, it was necessary to "fast start" the Lewis project. All major equipment was to be purchased within the first three months. This, except for a few exceptions, was accomplished. The usual problems occurred, such as late receipt of requisition from engineering and late receipt of bids.

One of the unique aspects of the Lewis project was the requirement for purchase order award meetings with vendors. Typically, Frank would hold award meetings with vendors of major equipment, such as reactors, compressors, large process towers, and large pumps. However, almost each time Lewis approved purchase of a mechanical item or vessel, it requested that the vendor come in for a meeting. Even if the order was for a fairly stock pump or small drum or tank, a meeting was held. Initially, the purchasing department attendees included the project purchasing agent, the buyer, the manager of the traffic department, the chief expeditor, and the chief inspector. Engineering representatives included the responsible engineer and one or two of the project engineers. Other Frank attendees were the project control manager and the scheduler. Quite often these meetings would accomplish nothing except the reiteration of what had been included in the proposal, or what could have been resolved with a phone call. The project purchasing agent was responsible for issuing meeting notes after each meeting.

One day at the end of the first three-month period the top-ranking Lewis representative and Larry Broyles, the Frank project manager, met.

Lewis Rep: Larry, the project is progressing, but I'm a little concerned. We don't feel we have our finger on the pulse of the project. The information we are getting is sketchy and untimely. What we would like to do is meet with Frank every Wednesday to review progress and resolve problems.

Larry: I'd be more than happy to meet with any of the Lewis people, because I think your request has a lot of merit.

Lewis Rep: Well, Larry, what I had in mind was a meeting among all the Lewis people, you, your project office, the project purchasing agent, his assistant, and your scheduling and cost control people.

Larry: This sounds like a pretty involved meeting. We're going to tie up a lot of our people for one full day a week. I'd like to scale this thing down. Our proposal considered meetings, but not to the magnitude we're talking about.

Lewis Rep: Larry, I'm sorry, but we're footing the bill on this project and we've got to know what's going on.

Larry: I'll set it up for this coming Wednesday.

Lewis Rep: Good.

The required personnel were informed by the project manager that, effective immediately, meetings with the client would be held weekly. The meetings were held and, due to Lewis's dissatisfaction with the results of the meetings, the Frank project manager informed his people that a premeeting would be held each Tuesday to prepare the Frank portion of the Wednesday meeting. All the Wednesday participants attended the Tuesday premeetings.

Lewis requests for additional special reports from the Purchasing Department were given into without comment. The project purchasing agent and his assistants (project started with one and expanded to four) were devoting the great majority of their time to special reports and "putting out fires," instead of being able to track progress and prevent problems.

For example, recommended spare parts lists are normally required from vendors on all Frank projects. Lewis was no exception. However, after the project began, Lewis decided it wanted the spare parts recommendations early in the job. Usually spare parts lists are left for the end of an order. For example, on a pump with 15-week delivery, normally Frank would pursue the recommended spare parts list 3 to 4 weeks prior to shipment, as it will tend to be more accurate. This improved accuracy is because at this point in the order all changes probably have been made. In the case of the Lewis project, spare parts recommendations had to be expedited from the day the material was released for fabrication. Changes could still be made that could dramatically affect the design of the pump. Thus, a change in the pump after receipt of the spare parts list would necessitate a new spare parts list. The time involved in this method of expediting the spare parts list was much greater than the time involved in the normal Frank method. Added to this situation was Lewis's request for a fairly involved biweekly report on the status of spare parts lists on all the orders. In addition, a full-time spare parts coordinator was assigned to the project.

The initial lines of communication between Frank and Lewis were initially well defined. The seven in-house Lewis representatives occupied the area adjacent to the Frank project office (see Figure 25). Initially all communications from Lewis were channeled through the Frank project office to the applicable functional employee. In the case of the Purchasing Department, the Frank project office would channel Lewis requests through the purchasing project office. Responses or return communications followed the reverse route. Soon the volume of communications increased to the point where response time was becoming unacceptable. In several special cases, in an effort to cut this response time, Larry Broyles told the Lewis people to call or go see the functional person (i.e., buyer or engineer) for the answer. However, this practice soon became the rule rather than the exception. Initially, the project office was kept informed of these conversations, but this soon stopped. The Lewis personnel had integrated themselves into the Frank organization to the point where they became part of the organization.

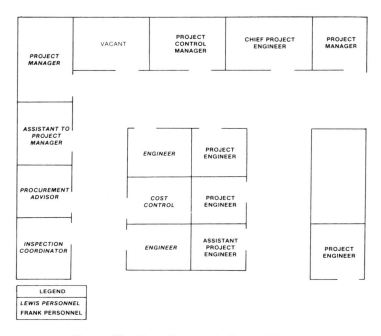

Figure 25.   Floor Plan—Lewis Project Teams.

The project went on, and numerous problems cropped up. Vendor's material delays occurred, companies with Frank purchase orders went bankrupt, and progress was not to Lewis's satisfaction. Upper management became aware of the problems on this project due to its sensitive nature, and soon the Lewis project was receiving much more intense an effort than it had been previously. Upper management sat in on the weekly meetings in an attempt to pacify Lewis. Further problems plagued the project. Purchasing management, in an attempt to placate Lewis, replaced the project purchasing agent. Ron Katz, a promising young M.B.A. graduate, had five years experience as an assistant to several of the project purchasing agents. He was most recently a project purchasing agent on a fairly small project that had been very successful. It was thought by purchasing upper management that this move was a good one for two reasons. First, it would remove Bill Hall from the project as PPA. Second, by appointing Ron Katz, Lewis would be pacified, as Katz was a promising talent with a successful project under his belt.

However, the project under the direction of Katz still experienced problems in the purchasing area. Revisions by engineering to material already on order caused serious delivery delays. Recently requisitioned material could not be located with an acceptable delivery promise. Katz and purchasing upper management, in an attempt to improve the situation, assigned more personnel to the project, personnel that were more qualified than the positions dictated. Buyers and upper-level purchasing officials were sent on trips to vendors' facilities that were normally handled by traveling expediters.

In the last week the Lewis representative met with the project manager, Broyles:

Lewis Rep: Larry, I've been reviewing these man-hour expenditures, and I'm disturbed by them.

Larry: Why's that?

Lewis Rep: The man-hour expenditures are far outrunning project progress. Three months ago, you reported that the project completion percentage was 30 percent, but according to my calculations, we've used 47 percent of the man-hours. Last month you reported 40 percent project completion, and I show a 60 percent expenditure of man-hours.

Larry: Well, as you know, due to problems with vendors' deliveries, we've really had to expedite intensively to try to bring them back in line.

Lewis Rep: Larry, I'm being closely watched by my people on this project, and a cost or schedule overrun not only makes Frank look bad, it makes me look bad.

Larry: Where do we go from here?

Lewis Rep: What I want is an estimate from your people on what is left, man-hour wise. Then I can sit down with my people and see where we are.

Larry: I'll have something for you the day after tomorrow.

Lewis Rep: Good.

The functional areas were requested to provide this information, which was reviewed and combined by the project manager and submitted to Lewis for approval. Lewis's reaction was unpleasant to say the least. The estimated man-hours in the proposal were now insufficient. The revised estimate was for almost 40 percent over the proposal. The Lewis representative immediately demanded an extensive report on the requested increase. In response to this, the project manager requested man-hour breakdowns from the functional areas. Purchasing was told to do a purchase-order-by-purchase-order breakdown of expediting and inspection man-hours. The buying section had to break down the estimate of the man-hours needed to purchase each requisition, many of which were not even issued.

CASE STUDY 31:   THE LYLE PROJECT[1]

At 6:00 P.M. on Thursday in late November of 1978, Don Jung, an Atlay company project manager assigned to the Lyle contract, sat in his office thinking about the

---

[1] This case is partially fictitious and was prepared by R. A. Popelmayer under the direction of Harold Kerzner as a basis for discussion, rather than to illustrate either the effective or ineffective handling of an administrative situation.

comments brought up during a meeting with his immediate superior earlier that afternoon. During that meeting Fred Franks, the supervisor of project managers, criticized Don for not promoting a cooperative attitude between himself and the functional managers. It seems that Fred Franks had a high-level meeting with the vice-presidents in charge of the various functional departments (i.e., engineering, construction, cost control, scheduling, and purchasing) earlier that day. One of these vice-presidents, John Mabby, head of the purchasing department, had indicated that his department, according to his latest projections, would overrun its man-hour allocation by 6,000 hours. This fact had been relayed to Don by Bob Stewart, the project purchasing agent assigned to the Lyle project, twice in the past, but Don had not seriously considered the request, for some of the purchasing was now going to be done by the subcontractor at the job site, who had enough man-hours to cover this additional work. John Mabby, during this meeting, complained that, even though the subcontractor was doing some of the purchasing in the field, his department still will overrun its man-hour allocation. He also indicated to Fred Franks that Don Jung had better do something about this man-hour problem now. At this point in the meeting, the vice-president of engineering, Harold Mont, stated that he was experiencing the same problem, in that Don Jung seemed to ignore requests for additional man-hours.

Also at this meeting the various vice-presidents indicated that Don Jung had not been operating within the established standard company procedures. In an effort to make up for time lost due to initial delays that occurred in the process-development stage of this project, Don and his project team had been getting the various functional people working on the contract to "cut corners" and in many cases to "buck" the standard operating procedures of their respective functional departments in an effort to save time. His actions and the actions of his project team were alienating the vice-presidents in charge of the functional departments. During this meeting, Fred Franks received a good deal of criticism due to this fact. He was also told that Don Jung had better shape up, because it was the joint opinion of these vice-presidents that his method of operating might seriously hamper the project's ability to finish on time and within budget. It was very important that this job be completed in accordance with the Lyle requirements, because it will be building two more similar plants within the next 10 years. A good effort on this job could further enhance Atlay's chances for being awarded the next two jobs as well.

Fred Franks related these comments and a few of his own to Don Jung. Fred seriously questioned Don's ability to manage the project effectively and told him so. However, Fred was willing to allow Don to remain on the job if he would begin to operate in accordance with the various functional departments' standard operating procedures and if he would "listen" and be more attentive to the comments from the various functional departments and do his best to cooperate with them in the best interests of the company and the project itself.

Inception of the Lyle Project

In April of 1978, Bob Briggs, Atlay's vice-president of sales was notified by Lyle's vice-president of operations (Fred Wilson) that Atlay had been awarded the $60 million contract to design, engineer, and construct a polypropylene plant in Louisiana. Bob Briggs immediately notified Atlay's president and other high-level officials in the organization (see Figure 26). He then contacted Fred Franks to finalize the members of the project team. Briggs wanted George Fitz, who was involved in developing the initial proposal, to be the project manager. However, Fitz was in the hospital and would be essentially out of action for another three months. Atlay then had to scramble to choose a project manager, for Lyle wanted to conduct a "kickoff meeting" with all the principals present in a week. One of the persons most available for the position of project manager was Don Jung. Don had been with the company for about 15 years. He had started with the company as a project engineer and then was promoted to the position of manager of computer services. He was in charge of computer services for six months until he had a confrontation with Atlay's upper management regarding the policies under which the computer department was operating. He had served the company in two other functions since—the most recent position, that of being a senior project engineer on a small project that was handled out of the Chicago office. One big plus was the fact that Don knew Lyle's Fred Wilson personally, because they belonged to the same community organization. It was decided that Don Jung would be the project manager and John Neber, an experienced project engineer, would be assigned as the senior project engineer. The next week was spent advising Don Jung regarding the contents of the proposal and determining the rest of the members of the project team.

A week later, Lyle's contingent arrived at Atlay's headquarters (see Figure 27). Atlay was informed that Steve Zorn would be the assistant project manager on this job for Lyle. The position of project manager would be left vacant for the time being. The contingent then introduced the rest of Lyle's project team. Lyle's project team consisted of individuals from various Lyle sections around the country—Texas, West Virginia, and Philadelphia. Many of the Lyle project team members had met each other for the first time only two weeks ago.

During this initial meeting, Fred Wilson emphasized that it was essential that this plant be completed on time because its competitor was also in the process of preparing to build a similar facility in the same general location. The first plant finished would most likely be the one that would establish control over the southwestern United States market for polypropylene material. Mr. Wilson felt that Lyle had a six-week head start over its competitor at the moment and would like to increase that difference if at all possible. He then introduced Lyle's assistant project manager who completed the rest of the presentation.

At this initial meeting the design package was handed over to Atlay's Don Jung, so that the process engineering stage of this project could begin. This package was, according to the inquiry letter, so complete that all material requirements for this job could be placed within three months after project award (because very little additional design work was required by Atlay on this project). Two weeks later, Don contacted the lead process engineer on the project—Raphael Begen. He wanted to get Raphael's opinion regarding the condition of the design package.

Begen: Don, I think you have been sold a bill of goods. This package is in bad shape.

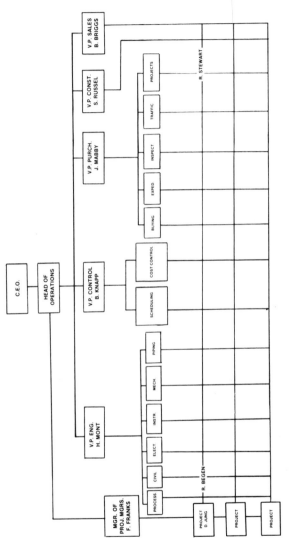

Figure 26. Atley and Company Organizational Chart.

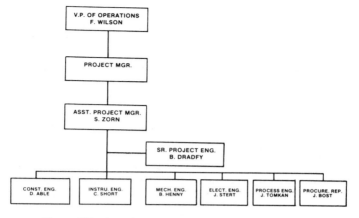

Figure 27.   Lyle Project Team Organizational Chart.

Jung: What do you mean this package is in bad shape? We were told by Lyle that we would be able to have all the material on order within three months because this package was in such good shape.

Begen: Well in my opinion, it will take at least six weeks to straighten out the design package. Then within three months from that point you will be able to have all the material on order.

Jung: What you are telling me then is that I am faced with a six-week delay right off the bat due to the condition of the package.

Begen: Exactly.

Don Jung went back to his office after his conversation with the lead process engineer. He thought about the status of his project. He felt that Begen was being overly pessimistic and that the package wasn't really all that bad. Besides, a month shouldn't be too hard to make up if the engineering section would do its work quicker than normal and if purchasing would cut down on the amount of time it takes to purchase materials and equipment needed for this plant.

Conduct of the Project

Thus, the project began. Two months after contract award, Lyle sent in a contingent of representatives. These representatives would be located at Atlay's headquarters for the next 8 to 10 months. Don Jung had arranged to have the Lyle offices set up on the other side of the building from his project team. At first there were complaints from Lyle's assistant project manager regarding the physical distance that separated Lyle's project team and Atlay's project team. However, Don Jung assured him that there just wasn't any available space that was closer to the Atlay project team than the one it was now occupying.

The Atlay project team, operating within a matrix organizational structure, plunged right into the project (see Figure 28). It was made aware of the delay incurred at the onset of the job (due to the poor design package) by Don Jung. His instructions were to cut corners whenever doing so might result in a time savings. The team was also to suggest to members of the functional departments that were working on this project methods that could possibly result in quicker turnaround of the work required of them. The project team coerced the various engineering departments into operating outside their normal procedures, due to the special circumstances surrounding this job. For example, the civil engineering section prepared a special preliminary structural steel package, and the piping engineering section prepared preliminary piping packages, so that the purchasing department could go out on inquiry immediately. Normally, the purchasing department would have to wait for formal take-offs from both these departments before it could send out inquiries to potential vendors. Operating in this manner could result in some problems, however. For example, the purchasing department might arrange for discounts from the vendors based on the quantity of structural steel estimated during the preliminary take-off. However, after the formal take-off has been done by the civil engineering section, which would take about a month, it might find out that it underestimated the quantity of structural steel required on the project by 50 tons. Knowing that there was an additional 50 tons of structural steel might have aided the purchasing department in securing an additional discount of $.20 per pound, or $160,000 discount for 400 tons of steel.

Also, in an effort to make up for lost time, the project team convinced the functional engineering departments to use catalogue drawings or quotation information whenever they lacked engineering data on a particular piece of equipment. The engineering section leaders pointed out that this procedure could be very dangerous and could

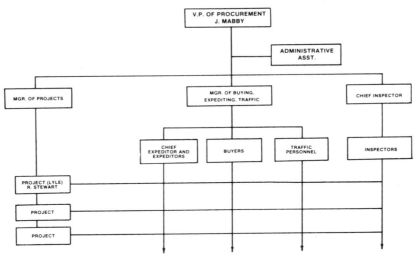

Figure 28. Atlay Company Procurement Department Organizational Chart.

result in additional work and further delays to the project. If, for example, you base the dimensions for the scale model being built on this project on preliminary information without the benefit of having certified vendor drawings in house, you run the risk of building an inaccurate scale for that section of the model. When the certified data prints are later received, and it is apparent that the dimensions are incorrect, you may have to disassemble that portion of the model and rebuild it correctly. This would further delay the project. However, if the information does not change substantially, you could save approximately a month in engineering time. Lyle was advised in regard to the risks and potential benefits involved when Atlay operates outside of its normal operating procedure. Steve Zorn informed Don Jung that Lyle was willing to take these risks in an effort to make up for lost time. The Atlay project team then proceeded accordingly.

The method that the project team was utilizing appeared to be working. It seemed as if the work was being accomplished at a much quicker rate than what was initially anticipated. The only snag in this operation occurred when Lyle had to review/approve something. Drawings, engineering requisitions, and purchase orders would sit in the Lyle area for about two weeks before they would be reviewed by Lyle personnel. Half the time these documents were returned two weeks later with a request for additional information or with changes noted by some of Lyle's engineers. Then the Atlay project team would have to review the comments/changes, incorporate them into the documents and resubmit them to Lyle for review/approval. They would then sit for another week in that area before finally being reviewed and eventually returned to Atlay with their final approval. It should be pointed out that the contract procedures stated that Lyle would have only five days to review/approve the various documents being submitted. Don Jung felt that part of the reason for this delay had to do with the fact that all the Lyle team members went back to their homes for the weekends. Their routine was to leave around 10:00 A.M. on Friday and return around 3:00 P.M. on the following Monday. Therefore, essentially two days of work by the Lyle project team out of the week were lost. Don reminded Steve Zorn that, according to the contract, Lyle was to return documents that needed approval within five days after receiving them. He also suggested that if the Lyle project team would work a full day on Monday and Friday it would probably increase the speed at which documents were being returned. However, neither corrective action was undertaken by Lyle's assistant project manager, and the situation failed to improve. All the time the project team had saved by cutting corners was now being wasted, and further project delays seemed inevitable.

In addition to the above, there were other problems that were being encountered during the interface process between the Lyle and Atlay project team members. It seems that the Lyle project team members, who were on temporary loan to Steve Zorn from various functional departments within the Lyle organization, were concerned with producing a perfect end product. They did not seem to realize that their actions, as well as the actions of the Atlay project team, had a significant impact on this particular project. They did not seem to be aware of the fact that they were also constrained by time and cost, as well as performance. Instead, they had a very relaxed and informal operating procedure. Many of the changes made by Lyle were given to Atlay verbally. They explained to the Atlay project team members that written confirmation of the changes was unnecessary because we are all working "on the same team." Many significant changes in the project were made when a Lyle engineer was talking directly to an Atlay engineer. The Atlay engineer would then incorporate the changes into the drawings he was working on and sometimes failed to advise his project engineer about the changes. Because of this informal way of operating, there were instances in which Lyle was dissatisfied with Atlay because changes were not being incorporated or were not made in strict accordance with its requests. Steve Zorn called Don Jung into his office to discuss this problem:

Steve: Don, I've received complaints from my personnel regarding your team's inability to follow through and incorporate Lyle's comments/changes accurately into the P & ID drawings.

Don: Steve, I think my staff has been doing a fairly good job of incorporating your team's comments/changes. You know the whole process would work a lot better, however, if you would send us a letter detailing each change. Sometimes my engineers are given two different instructions regarding the scope of the change by your people. For example, one of your people will tell our process engineer to add a check valve to a specific process line, and another will tell him that check valves are not required in that service.

Steve: Don, you know that if we documented everything that was discussed between our two project teams we would be buried in paperwork. Nothing would ever get accomplished. Now, if you get two different instructions from my project team you should advise me accordingly, so that I can resolve the discrepancy. I've decided that since we seem to have a communication problem regarding engineering changes, I want to set up a weekly engineering meeting for every Thursday. These meetings should help to cut down on the misunderstandings as well as to keep us advised of your progress in the engineering area of this contract without the need of a formal status report. I would like all members of your project staff present at these meetings.

Don: Will this meeting be in addition to our overall progress meetings that are held on Wednesdays?

Steve: Yes. We will now have two joint Atlay/Lyle meetings a week—one discussing overall progress on the job and one specifically aimed at engineering.

On the way back to his office Don thought about the request for an additional meeting. That meeting will be a waste of time, he thought, just as the Wednesday meeting is. It will just take away another day from the Lyle project team's available time for approving drawings, engineering, requisitions, and purchase orders. Now there are three days during the week where at least a good part of the day is taken up by meetings, in addition to a meeting with his own project team on Mondays in order to freely discuss the progress and problems of the job without intervention by Lyle personnel. A good part of his project team's time, therefore, was now being spent preparing for and attending meetings during the course of the week. Well, Don rationalized, Zorn represents the client and if he desires a meeting then I have no alternative but to accommodate him.

Jung's Confrontation

When Don returned to his desk he saw a message stating that John Mabby (vice-president of procurement) had called. Don returned his call and found out that John requested a meeting. A meeting was set up for the following day. At 9:00 A.M. the next day Don was in Mabby's office. Mabby was concerned about the unusual procedures that were being utilized on this project. It seems as though he had a rather lengthy discussion with Bob Stewart, the project purchasing agent assigned to the Lyle project. During the course of that conversation it became very apparent that this particular project was not operating within the normal procedures established for the purchasing department. This deviation from normal procedures was the result of instructions given by Don Jung to Bob Stewart. This upset John Mabby, for he felt Don Jung should have discussed these deviations with him prior to his instructing Bob Stewart to proceed in this manner:

Mabby: Don, I understand that you advised my project purchasing agent to work around the procedures that I established for this department, so that you could possibly save time on your project.

Jung: That's right John. We ran into a little trouble early in the project and started running behind schedule, but by cutting corners here and there we've been able to make up some of the time.

Mabby: Well I wish you would have contacted me first regarding this situation. I have to tell you, however, that if I had known about some of these actions I would never have allowed Bob Stewart to proceed. I've instructed Stewart that from now on he is to check with me prior to going against our standard operating procedure.

Jung: But John, Stewart has been assigned to me for this project. Therefore, I feel that he should operate in accordance with my requests, whether they are within your procedures or not.

Mabby: That's not true. Stewart is in my department and works for *me.* I am the one who reviews him, approves the size of his raise, and decides if and when he gets a promotion. I have made that fact very clear to Stewart, and I hope I've made it very clear to you also. In addition, I hear that Stewart has been predicting a 6,000 man-hour overrun for the purchasing department on your project. Why haven't you submitted an extra to the client?

Jung: Well, if what Stewart tells me is true, the main reason your department is short man-hours is because the project manager who was handling the initial proposal (George Fitz) underestimated your requirements by 7,000 man-hours. Therefore, from the very beginning you were short man-hours. Why should I be the one to go to the client and tell him that we blew our estimate when I wasn't even involved in the proposal stage of this contract? Besides we are taking away some of your duties on this job and I personally feel that you won't even need those additional 6,000 man-hours.

Mabby: Well, I have to attend a meeting with your boss Fred Franks tomorrow and I think I'll talk to him about these matters.

Jung: Go right ahead. I'm sure you'll find out that Fred stands behind me 100 percent.

SITUATION 13:   "ADVANTAGES/DISADVANTAGES PROFILE" OF MATRIX MANAGEMENT[1]

Matrix management is not a panacea—it's not for every organization. Even where it is used, it has advantages and disadvantages. An appreciation of both aspects is important for the manager/professional who is responsible for producing results within a cultural context of matrix management systems.

The Situation

The continued design and development of some form of matrix management continues in the XYZ Company. Some of the cultural changes accompanying this management system appear to emerge as advantages/disadvantages, as perceived by the people involved. Your general manager would like to have a workshop to discuss these advantages/disadvantages in the near future. He is hopeful that such a discussion will lead to a better appreciation by all concerned of what matrix management can do and cannot do for his organization.

Your Small Work Group Task

Take the attached profile of the Advantages/Disadvantages of Matrix Management in the context of a general manager's environment. Develop the "remedial strategy" or "capitalization strategy" appropriate to the advantages/disadvantages. Some factors you might wish to consider in developing this profile include the impact of matrix management on:

- Strategic decision making
- Operational decision making
- Resource control
- Interpersonal relationships
- Authority and responsibility patterns
- Organizational effectiveness

Make whatever assumptions you feel are necessary to carry out this assignment.

Prepare a summary briefing, and select a representative to share your ideas with the other small work groups.

---

[1] This case is adopted in part from David I. Cleland and William R. King, *Systems Analysis and Project Management,* 3rd edition, McGraw-Hill Book Co., New York, 1983. Used by permission.

Matrix Management Cultural Factors.

Advantages	Capitalization Strategy

–Higher profit generation
–Increased competitive ability
–More open channels of communication
–More participative working environment
–Better balance of authority
–Accountability is closer to authority-responsibility
–More visible results
–Top management has more time for strategic planning
–Greater organizational flexibility
–Develops people
–Develops more people with general manager knowledge, attitudes, and skills
–Provides for both specialization and integration of organizational activities
–Unleashes creative talent
–Productivity increases
–Reduces profit center parochialism
–People gain more insight into organizational objectives, goals, and strategies
–Provides a single "organization" oriented to a single goal
–Facilitates a peer-to-peer "checks and balances"
–More responsive reaction to the marketplace
–Facilitates new disciplines/capabilities in the organization
–People who make decisions have best information and knowledge
–Provides an additional career path—promotions, opportunities
–More efficient utilization of professional/skilled manpower
–Promotes technology transfer
–Critical self-appraisal of organization's ability to produce results
–Frees top management from day-to-day responsibilities

Advantages	*Capitalization Strategy*

Advantages

–Contributes to a "new company" atmosphere
–Improves morale
–Facilitates quick feedback
–Impossible to hide anything
–High performance (and failure) is quickly visible
–More visibility for the manager-to-be
–Fosters innovation
–Provides scale economies
–Provides adaptability of "small team" culture
–People have more responsibility and freedom
–Provides a peer group to which a commitment can be made
–Technology can be nurtured— functionally and by project
–Permits better sharing of scarce resources
–People are more aware of the other fellow's problem
–People are forced to listen to each other
–Provides for the coexistence of decentralization and centralization
–More compatible with the value systems of the younger professional/ management generation
–Facilitates phasing in and out of new business opportunities
–Resource allocations are more proportionate to expected results
–Other

Matrix Management Cultural Factors.

Disadvantages	*Remedial Strategy*

Disadvantages

–Major issues take longer to resolve
–Decision process deteriorates into a political compromise
–More meetings
–Gamesmanship and political jockeying become widespread
–More detailed analysis required

Disadvantages	*Remedial Strategy*

-"Buck passing"

-Fragmented accountability

-Extra bookkeeping

-Promotes unhealthy internal conflict/
tension

-Increases overhead costs (double/triple
up on management)

-Dual/multiple authority and
responsibility never work

-Duplication of effort

-Interpersonal skills required don't exist
in many people

-Lack of employment continuity (e.g.,
projects come and go)

-Functional (engineering, finance, R&D,
marketing, production) state of the art
deteriorates

-Creates tendency to argue more

-Group decision making reduces
individual decision initiative

-Power struggles develop

-Takes too long to implement

-Too much top management dedication
required

-Adjustment of people is difficult and
takes time

-Too much time spent keeping people
informed

-Personnel are assigned to several
projects/issues, consequently lose
control of them

-It's necessary to share limited resources
too often

-No single person is really responsible for
results

-There are always unresolved questions
about how much authority a matrix
manager has

-Tries to make managers out of
professionals too quickly

-Top management has to make all the
decisions

-More formal planning and control
required

Advantages   *Capitalization Strategy*

−No sense of security for the individual
 (no reference base for the individual)
−Authority and responsibility are not
 equal
−Profit-and-loss responsibility is
 splintered
−Endless time building personal
 relationships
−Organization is too complex
−Information systems are too complex
−Impossible to react quickly
−Priorities become a problem
−Conflicting project and functional goals
−Role conflict produces stress, anxiety,
 reduced job satisfaction
−People resist the change to a matrix form
−Top management dedication is
 necessary; many executives don't have
 the strategic patience required
−Too much time spent on negotiation
−More training and education are
 required
−Other?

SITUATION 14: PERCEPTIONS OF MATRIX MANAGEMENT

The Situation

The profit center division of a large corporation had the mission of supplying semiconductor components and services to a worldwide industrial market. The division manager was concerned about the ability of the division to keep abreast of semiconductor technology in the field and, at the same time, increase the market share of the division.

Basic and applied research support for the profit center divisions in this corporation came from the centralized laboratory of the corporation. This central research organization was responsive to the business mission of the profit centers. The research laboratory was centralized to facilitate research within the environment of extreme diversification in the kind of products and services offered by the corporation.

Funding for the central R&D laboratory of the corporation came from the profit centers, government or private research agencies, and through direct support from the corporate headquarters. For those projects funded by the profit center, R&D was viewed as the initial phase of the life cycle of the product.

Because the profit center was paying the costs of the R&D work done at the central laboratory, the profit center manager was anxious to design and operate a project management system that would provide for optimum performance by both R&D and profit center managers and professionals. The profit center managers required information on the status of the project they had funded, both within the R&D laboratory, as well as any effort expended on the project within the profit center itself.

Each R&D project had a project manager; each profit center manager also appointed a manager within the profit center. The R&D project manager was committed to the scope and objective of the project, as specified by the P&L center management.

Corporate management sees a pair of important advantages resulting from this arrangement:

1. Corporate R&D resources are focused to support profit center market needs.
2. Technology is introduced into the strategic projects by virtue of having a member of the profit center serve as a member of the R&D laboratory project team.

The profit center manager has elected to introduce project management into the organization and has engaged the services of an organizational development (OD) consultant from the corporate human resources to help. After gaining a brief indoctrination into the organizational and operational strategy of the profit center, the OD consultant interviewed key managerial and professional personnel of the profit center. The purpose of these interviews was to gain an appreciation of how these people viewed matrix management in the profit center to support profit center/R&D laboratory objectives, goals, and strategies. These interviews were conducted in a spirit of diplomatic immunity; thus no identification of the comments of a particular person was feasible. The comments were finally organized into topical classification.

The material that follows takes each classification topic and summarizes the findings gleaned from the interviewees' comments.

Degree of knowledge of matrix management. A few people in the division have some knowledge of matrix management through previous work experience. However, there is a general lack of understanding of what matrix management is and what it will do for the division.

Because of a lack of understanding of matrix management, it is perceived with skepticism by some people; others have adopted a wait-and-see attitude.

Extent of matrix management within the division. Matrix management is recognized as a technique that has been practiced in the division in several different contexts: controller, applications engineering, Polish project, marketing, and in the operations group (plant and equipment maintenance).

Concern about two-boss situation. There is a deep concern on the part of both managers and professionals concerning the "two-boss" situation of matrix management. This concern stems from a lack of definition of what the "two-boss-one professional" relationship should be. This concern will continue until a relationship has been defined and is understood and accepted by the managers and professionals of the division.

Authority and responsibility patterns of matrix management. Practically all people are concerned about the delineation of the specific authority and responsibility of matrix management, in terms of such things as: personal development; budgeting; normal supervisory relationships; merit evaluation; matrix managers-professional relationships; promotions; priority setting; cost charges; resource control; and personnel tasking.

Need for education in matrix management.   There is a very strong agreement on the need for matrix management education for all managers and professions at the division to start. This education should take the form of workshops to explain the theory and practice of matrix management and be followed by more specific instruction with the principal matrix managers/professionals.

Additional resources required at the division.   Additional professionals are required at the division. There is some support for adding additional equipment at the division.

Supporting systems for matrix management.   There is a recognition of the need to develop supporting systems (budget, financial, information, cost accounting) for the projects, to give project managers adequate visibility and control.

General comments about matrix management.   There are some general concerns about matrix management at the division. In addition to those that are expressed elsewhere in this report, the people singled out the following:

- Relationship of MBO and matrix management
- Potential threat of matrix management to excellent people relationships
- Project/functional interfaces
- Functional managers' support
- Advantages/disadvantages
- Authority/responsibility patterns
- Personnel actions
- Personnel utilization

General comments on the division.   On balance, the division is perceived as a success-ful, satisfying, and friendly place to work. The organizational approach being taken by the programs management department is well received. Understanding of the division's competition could be improved. There is some concern about the ability of the managers to accept innovative ways of improving management through personal recognition programs. There is a minority opinion concerning the need for people-oriented education for managers at the division.

Degree of commitment to matrix management.   Most people, although admitting that they don't understand matrix management, are committed to making it work.

Recommendations regarding matrix management within the division.   Monthly review meetings on the major projects are needed. There is some concern that the R&D representative should be tied more closely to matrix management. Several specific actions are noted to improve project management within the division, such as:

- Closer working relationship between program manager and functional managers.
- Be judicious in the application of matrix management.
- Establish profit-loss responsibility for programs management.

Comments on general manager.   The general manager is perceived as a strong leader whose current work to improve the strategic posture of the division should be continued and accelerated.

Matrix-management-related problems at the division.   Certain people feel strongly about and are able to discourse on the project management problems on the hybrid program. Those problems include:

- Management style of project manager
- Lack of functional support
- Previous adverse cultural ambience for matrix management at the division
- Inadequate resources
- In addition, technical documentation is singled out as a troublesome area.

Specific comments on the "X" program.   Program manager is recognized as a logical choice for managing the program. There is confidence in the program, but there is some concern over the marketing of the program and progress in the development of the program.

What not to do in matrix management.   Matrix management should be used in the division only where it is needed. We should not reorganize across the board to accommodate matrix management. We should be candid and forthright in describing matrix management to the people at the division.

Future direction of the division.   On balance, people see the transistor program as the right way to go. The current direction of the division is correct, although there is some concern over the long-term profitability of the division without the tax advantage of Puerto Rico, particularly in the "cash cow" context, in which the division is believed to be viewed by corporate management. The pace at which the division is developing products should be accelerated according to most people. The marketing of the "X" product should be intensified. A key concern is raised as to the willingness of corporate management to make the investments required to enable the division to cope with emerging market opportunities. There is concern over the lead time required to obtain new equipment. Some concern was expressed over the lack of understanding of the strategic objectives of the division. The key role of the programs management department in developing the division's future is clearly recognized.

After reading these comments, the profit center manager wondered how the senior management of the profit center would react to the findings. After it had reacted to the comments, he pondered what action, if any, would it recommend be taken.

Your Assignment

If you were a senior manager in this division, how would you react?

SITUATION 15: INDUSTRIAL SYSTEMS, INCORPORATED (ISI)

D. I. Cleland[1]

Industrial Systems, Inc., a joint venture of a U.S. and a German firm, was chartered in July 1981, to design, develop, and install electrical drive systems and process control in the mining, pulp and paper, heavy materials handling, and primary metals

---

industries. The German parent is one of the world's leading electrical equipment manufacturers with a broad base of products for use in the supply of electric power by utilities and for use in the construction of electrical power by industry. The German parent also manufactures heavy machinery for the mining, primary metals, processing, and transportation industries. The U.S. parent is a world leader in heavy machinery for construction, mining, and other material handling applications. It also manufactures electrical equipment to power its machinery and supplies similar electrical equipment to other manufacturers.

ISI puts together the strengths of both parents: the German parent, with its advanced technology and wide industry acceptance, and the U.S. company, with its reputation for rugged-duty, high-performance drive systems, especially associated with mining machinery and cranes. ISI will produce AC and DC drive systems control and computer-based process control utilizing both parent's designs. The parent companies are principal suppliers of motors, brakes, and associated devices necessary to put together total systems. In addition to the installation of new systems, ISI will have a full range of parts and service support. A complete stock of replacement parts is to be maintained for shipment from strategically located warehouses, with quality guaranteed to equal or exceed the performance of the original parts. Service organizations will be on call 24 hours a day; in-stock parts will be shipped within 48 hours after receipt of order. Parts books and service manuals will be supplied with each system provided. ISI plans to have total systems expertise and responsibility. It is made up of experience-proven marketing, sales, engineering, manufacturing, product line management, contracts, and service personnel ready to explore the U.S. market. Sales forecasts for the end of the second year of operation have been established at $50 million. The parents have capitalized the company at $5 million and have committed a total of $19 million front-end money to make the company a viable, tough competitor in the U.S. marketplace.

In the first eight months of operation, key managerial and professional personnel have been hired, and a comprehensive analysis of the markets, appropriate market segments, and competitive strengths and weaknesses has been accomplished. A $3.5 million contract to install the first system sold by ISI is currently being negotiated with a customer in Lexington, Kentucky. Key corporate staff members have recently completed an analysis of the organizational structure of ISI and have reorganized along the lines indicated in Figure 29. However, these key managers recognize the shortcomings of the traditional organizational chart to portray managerial relationships and are concerned about the effectiveness of the corporate staff to function as an effective team. Consequently, they have elected to better organize themselves through linear responsibility charting (LRC) to improve team effectiveness.

A summary of the key responsibilities, authority, and accountability of the organization of ISI follows:

Contract Management—Responsible for providing legal and contract management services.

Operations Center—Includes manufacturing, assembly, and associated services on a sharing context for the corporation.

Finance & Administration—Provides personnel, finance, accounting and administrative services to the corporation.

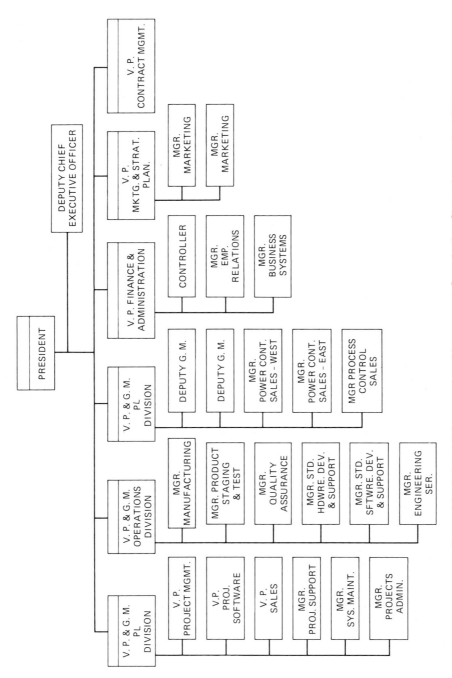

Figure 29. Industrial Systems, Inc., Management Organization Chart, January 1, 1982.

369

PL Division—A profit center responsible for product line and project management for the corporation.

Marketing and Strategic Planning—Manages the marketing and strategic planning process for the company.

Management Council—A plural executive where key operating and strategic decisions are reviewed and made.

Some of the key work packages to be found in this company include, but are not necessarily limited to, the following:

- Management of work package system
- Corporate goals
- Corporate objectives
- Customer OEM agreement document
- Corporate maintenance agreement
- Contract entity
- Contract policy
- Process customer contract and backup data
- Negotiate claim settlement
- Process invoicing information
- Proposal preparation
- Manage warranty
- Booking forecasts
- Selling rental parts and repair service
- Bid-no-bid committee
- Customer interface
- Proposal bid price
- Project schedules
- Technical library
- Configuration management
- Training software/hardware
- Master schedule operation
- Standard product drafting
- Facilities, plant, building
- Purchased materials management
- New product development
- Win/loss analysis
- Customer image assessment
- Prebid selection and prospect
- Product price lists
- Bid strategies
- Competitive analysis
- Prepare marketing brochures
- Product assembly
- Publications/documentation management
- Quality assurance management
- Merit increase salary adjustment

Table 8. Industrial Systems, Inc., Linear Responsibility Chart.

Work Packages	Contract Management	Operations Center	Finance & Admin.	PL Division	PL Division	Marketing & Strat. Plan.	Management Council	Comments

Legend:

(P) Primary Responsibility — The prime authority and responsibility for accomplishment of Work Package.

(R) Review — Reviews output of Work Package.

(N) Notification — Is notified of output of Work Package.

(A) Approval — Approves Work Package.

(S) Support — On line Human Services.

(O) Output — Receives output of Work Package.

(I) Input — Provides input to Work Package.

(W) Work is Done — Accomplishes actual labor of Work Package.

P includes W
P includes A
A includes R
Unless otherwise specified

- Employee recruitment
- Key personnel lists
- Employee communications
- Manpower planning
- Work authorization system
- Management of corporate information systems
- Development of project management information systems
- Insurance and taxes
- Annual budgeting
- Invoicing
- Major appropriation requests
- Limits of authority guidelines
- Establishment of standard costs
- Terms and conditions
- Contract negotiations

Your Task

1. Develop a linear responsibility chart for Industrial Systems, Inc., based on the existing organizational chart and the work packages that are given. Use Table 8 as a model for the linear responsibility chart. In addition to carrying out this responsibility, please accomplish the following additional work as you see appropriate:

  a. Identify some additional key work packages for the company that have not been included in the case writeup.
  b. Identify those work packages among those listed where it appears that territorial conflict will emerge between two or more corporate staff members.
  c. Identify those work packages where limits-of-authority policy should be established for the company.
2. Be prepared to assess the efficacy of interface responsibility charting in contributing to building a managerial team.

Section V
Strategies, Policies,
And Procedures

A strategy is a broad prescription for using resources to accomplish organizational mission, objectives, and goals. A project is reflected in the project plans designating courses of action on how resources will be used to provide *general direction* for the project design, development, and production. Strategies include key policies on product characteristics, market development, production process, financial performance, and research and development. Strategies are the key prescriptions on how it is intended that the project will survive in its competitive and environmental system. The existence of strategies presumes that the environmental and competitive threats and opportunities have been identified, costs and risks have been assessed, and organizational strengths and weaknesses have been evaluated. Strategies provide the parallel pathways that the project must follow to get where it wants to go. Strategies set the pattern for how the enterprises' resources are to be mobilized to accomplish project objectives and goals.

In addition to establishing the general order for committing resources, strategies prescribe matrix structure, key roles, key desired cultural requirements, and organizational systems to support resource utilization. When project strategies are completed, it means that the planning process has been carried out in the organization. What remains is the execution of the project through leadership and cultural strategies expressed in policies and procedures.

Policies

Policies are general statements or principles that the managers of an organization have agreed upon to guide their thinking in making and implementing decisions and reaching goals, objectives, and mission. Managers are expected to exercise judgment in implementing policy. Policies are the corporate code of conduct and should be established on the highest level of business statesmanship. For policies to be most effective, they need to be formulated in collaboration with those managers who will be affected principally by such policies. By participating in policy formulation, people cooperate through understanding. Participating in recommending and formulating policies for an organization is of vital importance to the general morale and espirit de corps with which the policies will be carried out. Participation is a basic part of a modern company's philosophy of management.

Policies should not include detailed rules of procedure. Such rules and details should be incorporated in the procedures, plans, programs, methods, and routines that are formulated to implement action toward objectives, goals, and mission.

Project management policies provide the key basis for the exercise of authority by a member of the project team, through providing the managers and professionals with advice and counsel, specialized assistance, support, and service in accomplishing organizational purposes. Policies are instruments of decentralization.

Procedures

A business procedure prescribes the relationship between functions, physical factors, and people for the purpose of coordinating and facilitating the sequential steps to take in accomplishing a piece of work. Procedures usually do not involve manager and professional discretion.

Matrix management strategies, policies, and procedures are keynoted in the following cases and situations.

RELEVANT BIBLIOGRAPHY

Ackoff, R. L. *Creating the Corporate Future.* John Wiley & Sons, Inc., New York, 1981.

Angrist, Stanley W. "Classless Capitalists." *Forbes,* May 9, 1983, pp. 122–124.

Avots, Ivars. "Why Does Project Management Fail?" *California Management Review,* Fall, 1969.

Clewett, Richard M., and Stanley F. Stasch. "Shifting Role of the Product Manager." *Harvard Business Review,* January–February 1975, pp. 65–73.

Corey, E. R., and S. H. Starr. *Organization Strategy: A Marketing Approach.* Division of Research, Harvard Business School, Boston, 1970.

Hlavacek, J. D. and V. A. Thompson. "Bureaucracy and Venture Failures." *Academy of Management Review,* April, 1978.

Huse, Edgar F., and Michael Beer. "Electric Approach to Organizational Development." *Harvard Business Review,* September–October 1971.

Kolodny, Harvey F. "Matrix Organization Designs and New Product Success." *Research Management,* September 1980.

Kotter, John P. "Power, Dependence, and Effective Management." *Harvard Business Review,* July–August 1977, pp. 125–136.

"Management: GE's Search for Synergy." *The New York Times,* April 16, 1978.

"Management Itself Holds the Key." *Business Week,* September 9, 1972.

Osgood, William R., and William E. Wetzel, Jr. "A Systems Approach to Venture Initiation." *Business Horizons,* October, 1977, p. 42.

Peters, Thomas J. "Beyond the Matrix Organization." *Business Horizons,* October 1979.

————, and Robert H. Waterman, Jr. "Corporate Chariots of Fire." *Across the Board,* May 1983, pp. 40–47.

Sears, Woodrow H. "Conflict Management Strategies for Project Managers." *Project Management Quarterly,* June 1980.

Sherman, Stratford P. "Bausch & Lomb's Lost Opportunity." *Fortune,* January 24, 1983, pp. 104–105.

Slocum, John W., Jr., and Don Hellriegel. "Using Organizational Designs to Cope with Change." *Business Horizons,* December 1979.

Stickney, Frank A., and William R. Johnston. "Delegation and a Sharing of Authority by the Project Manager." *Project Management Quarterly,* pp. 42–53.

Youker, Robert. "Implementing Change In Organizations (A Manager's Guide)." *Project Management Quarterly,* pp. 34–40.

CASE STUDY 32: GREYSON CORPORATION

Greyson Corporation was formed in 1940 by three scientists from the University of California. The major purpose of the company was research and development for advanced military weaponry. Following World War II, Greyson became a leader in research and development. By the mid-1950s, Greyson employed over 200 scientists and engineers.

The fact that Greyson handled only R&D contracts was advantageous. First of all, all the scientists and engineers were dedicated to R&D activities, not having to share their loyalties with production programs. Second, a strong functional organization was established. The project management functions was the responsibility of the functional manager whose department would perform the majority of the work. Working relationships between departments were excellent.

By the late fifties Greyson was under new management. Almost all R&D programs called for establishment of qualification and production planning as well. As a result, Greyson decided to enter the production of military weapons as well and capture some of the windfall profits of the production market. This required a major reorganization from a functional to a matrix structure. Personnel problems occurred, but none that proved to be major catastrophies.

In 1964 Greyson entered the aerospace market with the acquisition of a subcontract for the propulsion unit of the Hercules missile. The contract was projected at $200 million over a five-year period, with excellent possibilities for follow-on work. Between 1964 and 1968, Greyson developed a competent technical staff composed mainly of young, untested college graduates. The majority of the original employees who were still there were in managerial positions. Greyson never had any layoffs. In addition, Greyson had excellent career development programs for almost all employees.

Between 1967 and 1971, the Department of Defense procurement for new weapon systems was on the decline. Greyson relied heavily on its two major production programs, Hercules and Condor II, both of which gave great promise for continued procurement. Greyson also had some 30 smaller R&D contracts, as well as 2 smaller production contracts for hand weapons.

Because R&D money was becoming scarce, Greyson's management decided to phase out much of the R&D activities and replace them with lucrative production contracts. Greyson believed it could compete with anyone in regard to low-cost production. Under this philosophy, the R&D community was reduced to minimum levels necessary to support in-house activities. The director of engineering froze all hiring except for job-shoppers with special talents. All nonessential engineering personnel were transferred to production units.

In 1972, Greyson entered into competition with Cameron Aerospace Corporation for development, qualification, and testing of the Navy's new Neptune missile. The competition was an eight-motor shoot-off during the last 10 months of 1973. Cameron Corporation won the contract due to technical merit. Greyson Corporation, however, had gained valuable technical information in rocket motor development and testing. The loss of the Neptune program made it clear to Greyson's management that aerospace technology was changing too fast for Greyson to maintain a passive position. Even though funding was limited, Greyson increased the technical staff and soon found great success in winning research and development contracts.

By 1975, Greyson had developed a solid aerospace business base. Profits had increased by 30 percent. Greyson Corporation expanded from a company with 200 employees in 1964 to 1,800 employees in 1975. The Hercules program, which began in 1964, was providing yearly follow-on contracts. All indications projected a continuation of the Hercules program through 1982.

Cameron Corporation, on the other hand, had found 1975 a difficult year. The Neptune program was the only major contract that Cameron Corporation maintained. The current production buy for the Neptune missile was scheduled for completion in August 1975, with no follow-on work earlier than January 1976. Cameron Corporation anticipated that overhead rates would increase sharply prior to the next buy. The cost per motor would increase from $55,000 to $75,000 for a January procurement, $85,000 for a March procurement, and $125,000 for an August procurement.

In February 1975, the Air Force asked Greyson Corporation if it would be interested in submitting a sole-source bid for production and qualification of the Neptune missile. The Air Force considered Cameron's position uncertain and wanted to maintain a qualified vendor, should Cameron Corporation decide to get out of the aerospace business.

Greyson submitted a bid of $30 million for qualification and testing of 30 Neptune motors over a 30-month period beginning in January 1976. Current testing of the Neptune missile indicated that the minimum motor age life would extend through January 1979. This meant that production funds over the next 30 months could be diverted toward requalification of a new vendor and still meet production requirements for 1979.

In August of 1975, upon delivery of the last Neptune rocket to the Air Force, Cameron Corporation announced that, without an immediate production contract for Neptune follow-on work, it would close its doors and get out of the aerospace business. Cameron Corporation invited Greyson Corporation to interview all its key employees for possible work on the Neptune requalification program.

Greyson hired 35 of Cameron's key people to begin work in October 1975. The key people would be assigned to ongoing Greyson programs, so as to become familiar with Greyson methods. Greyson's lower-level management was very unhappy about bringing in its 35 employees for fear that they would be placed into slots that could have resulted in promotions for some of Greyson's people. Management then decreed that these 35 people would work solely on the Neptune program, and other vacancies would be filled, as required, from the Hercules and Condor II programs. Greyson estimated that the cost of employing these 35 people was approximately $150,000 per month, almost all of which was being absorbed through overhead. Without these 35 people, Greyson did not believe it would have won the contract as sole-source procurement. Other competitors could have grabbed these key people and forced an open-bidding situation.

Because of the increased overhead, Greyson maintained a minimum staff to prepare for contract negotiations and document preparation. So as to minimize costs, the directors of engineering and program management gave the Neptune program office the authority to make decisions for departments and divisions that were without representation in the program office. Top management had complete confidence in the program office personnel because of their past performance on other programs and years of experience.

In December 1975, the Department of Defense announced that spending was being curtailed sharply and that funding limitations made it impossible to begin the qualification program before July 1976. To make matters worse, consideration was being made for a compression of the requalification program to 25 motors in a 20-month period. However, long-lead funding for raw materials would be available.

After lengthy consideration, Greyson decided to maintain its present position and retain the 35 Cameron employees by assigning them to in-house programs. The Neptune program office was still maintained for preparations to support contract negotiations, rescheduling activities for a shorter program, and long-lead procurement.

In May of 1976, contract negotiations began between the Navy and Greyson. At the beginning of contract negotiations, the Navy stated the three key elements for negotiations:

1. Maximum funding was limited to the 1975 quote for a 30-motor/30-month program.
2. The amount of money available for the last six months of 1976 was limited to $3.7 million.
3. The contract would be cost plus incentive fee (CPIF).

Three weeks of negotiations produced a stalemate. The Navy contended that the production man-hours in the proposal were at the wrong level on the learning curves. It further argued the Greyson should be a lot "smarter" now because of the 35 Cameron employees and because of experience learned during the 1971 shoot-off with Cameron Corporation during the initial stages of the Neptune program.

Because the negotiation teams could not agree, top-level management of the Navy and Greyson Corporation met to iron out the differences. An agreement was finally reached on a figure of $28.5 million. This was $1.5 million below Greyson's original estimate to do the work. Management, however, felt that, by "tightening our belts" the work could be accomplished within budget.

The program began on July 1, 1976, with the distribution of the department budgets by the program office. Almost all of the department managers were furious. Not only were the budgets below their original estimates, but the 35 Cameron employees were earning salaries above the departmental mean salary, thus reducing total man-hours even further. Almost all department managers asserted that cost overruns would be the responsibility of the program office and not the individual departments.

By November 1976 Greyson was in trouble. The Neptune program was on target for cost but 35 percent behind for work completion. Department managers refused to take responsibility for certain tasks that were considered to be usually joint department responsibilities. Poor communication between program office and department managers provided additional discouragement. Department managers refused to have their employees work on Sunday.

Even with all this being considered, program management felt that catchup was still possible. The 35 former Cameron employees were performing commendable work equal to their counterparts on other programs. Management considered that the potential cost overrun was not critical and that more time should be permitted before considering corporate funding.

In December 1976 the Department of Defense announced that there would be no further buys of the Hercules missile. This announcement was a severe blow to Greyson's management. Not only was it in danger of having to lay off 500 employees, but overhead rates would rise considerably. There was an indication last year that there would be no further buys, but management did not consider the indications positive enough to require corporate strategy changes.

Although Greyson was not unionized, there was a possibility of a massive strike if Greyson career employees were not given seniority over the 35 former Cameron employees in case of layoffs.

By February 1977, the cost situation was clear:

1. The higher overhead rates threatened to increase total program costs by $1 million on the Neptune program.
2. Because the activities were behind schedule, the catchup phases would have to be made in a higher salary and overhead rate quarter, thus increasing total costs further.
3. Inventory costs were increasing. Items purchased during long-lead funding were approaching shelf-life limits. Cost impact may be as high as $1 million.

The vice-president and general manager considered the Neptune program critical to the success and survival of Greyson Corporation. The directors and division heads were ordered to take charge of the program. The following options were considered:

1. Perform overtime work to get back on schedule.
2. Delay program activities in hope that the Navy can come up with additional funding.

3. Review current material specifications in order to increase material shelf-life, thus lowering inventory and procurement costs.
4. Begin laying off noncritical employees.
5. Purchase additional tooling and equipment at corporate expense, so that schedule requirements can be met on target.

March 1, 1977, Greyson gave merit salary increases to the key employees on all in-house programs. At the same time, Greyson laid off 700 employees, some of whom · were seasoned veterans. By March 15, Greyson employees formed a union and went out on strike.

SITUATION 16: THE RELUCTANT WORKERS

Tim Aston had changed employers three months ago. His new position was project manager. At first he had stars in his eyes about becoming the best project manager his company had ever seen. Now, he wasn't sure if project management was worth the effort. He made an appointment to see Phil Davies, Director of Project Management.

Tim Aston: "Phil, I'm a little unhappy about the way things are going. I just can't seem to motivate my people. Every day, at 4:30 P.M., all my people clean off their desks and go home. I've had people walk out of late-afternoon team meetings because they were afraid they'd miss their car pool. I have to schedule morning team meetings."

Phil Davies: "Look Tim. You're going to have to realize that in a project environment, people think they come first and that the project is second. This is a way of life in our organizational form."

Tim Aston: "I've continuously asked my people to come to me if they have problems. I find that the people do not think that they need help and, therefore, do not want it. I just can't get my people to communicate more."

Phil Davies: "The average age of our employees is about 46. Most of our people have been here for 20 years. They're set in their ways. You're the first person we've hired in the past three years. Some of our people may just resent seeing a 30-year-old project manager."

Tim Aston: "I found one guy in the accounting department who has an excellent head on his shoulders. He's very interested in project management. I asked his boss if he'd release him for a position in project management, and his boss just laughed at me, saying something to the effect that as long as that guy is doing a good job for him, he'll never be released for an assignment elsewhere in the company. His boss seems more worried about his personal empire than he does in what's best for the company.

   We had a test scheduled for last week. The customer's top management was planning on flying in for first-hand observations. Two of my people said they had programmed vacation days coming and that they would not change under any conditions.

One guy was going fishing, and the other guy was planning to spend a few days working with fatherless children in our community. Surely, these guys could change their plans for the test."

Phil Davies: "Many of our people have social responsibilities and outside interests. We encourage social responsibilities and only hope that the outside interests do not interfere with their jobs.

There's one thing you should understand about our people. With an average age of 46, many of our people are at the top of their pay grades and have no place to go. They must look elsewhere for interests. These are the people you have to work with and motivate. Perhaps you should do some reading on human behavior."

SITUATION 17: REDUCTION IN WORK FORCE

The Situation

An engineering department with an established project management organization determines through resource planning that additional manpower is required to accomplish the goals established by the operating plan. While it is staffing up, a turndown in the economy occurs. Top management's response has caused a reduction in work force within the engineering department without a corresponding reduction in the major projects or goals of the department. The situation has caused the engineering general manager concern, as morale is low and increased productivity is required. As a project manager, you want to help.

Your Task

From the perspective of a project manager, explain what you will do, along with your project management team, to respond to this critical business need. Specifically address the role you and your fellow project managers might play to assure proper resource allocation. Indicate what else you will do to help stimulate the greater overall productivity required. What can you do to help your management team improve overall morale?

How would you handle this situation?

SITUATION 18: PROJECT MANAGEMENT POLICIES

Introduction

Policies are general statements or principles that the managers of an organization have agreed upon to guide their thinking in making and implementing decisions and reaching goals, objectives, and mission. Managers are expected to exercise judgment in implementing policy. Policies are the corporate code of conduct and should be established on the highest level of business statesmanship. For polices to be most effective they need to be formulated in collaboration with those managers who will be affected principally by such policies. By participating in policy formulation, people cooperate through understanding. Participating in recommending and formulating policies for an organization is of vital importance to the general morale and esprit de corps with which the policies will be carried out. Policies provide the key basis for the exercise of staff authority by a member of the corporate staff through providing the line managers with advice and counsel, specialized assistance, support, and service in accomplishing organizational purposes. Policies are instruments of decentralization.

Procedures, on the other hand, prescribe the relationship between functions, physical factors, and people for the purpose of coordinating and facilitating the sequential steps to take in accomplishing a piece of work. Procedures usually do not involve management discretion.

The Situation

A small company is a subcontractor for the design and fabrication of components for an aerospace firm building a missile system for the U.S. Air Force. Recently this small company initiated a project-driven matrix management system. The senior executives of the company decided to initiate a task force to study the need and make appropriate recommendations for the policies and procedures to support the new organizational approach.

Your Task

Assume that you have been appointed chairman of this task force. Develop a list of agenda items you would propose for the first meeting of the task force.

Assume that your first meeting went very well and the other members supported the agenda you proposed. At the next meeting you propose that an initial list of policies and procedures be presented for the members to study. Develop a list of those policies and procedures you feel are necessary to successfully implement project management within the company. Make whatever assumptions are necessary to carry this assignment out.

Section VI
Planning, Scheduling, and Control

Planning in the matrix organization involves thinking about the future in relation to the present in such a way that the future can be affected in ways that benefit the organization. More explicitly, project planning is the process of thinking through and making explicit the strategy, actions, and relationships necessary to accomplish the project objectives on time and within budget. The fundamentals of project planning include:

1. The objective, goals, and strategies of the project
2. The process of reasoning, or thinking through, what resources and what action must be accomplished to reach desired end results
3. Determining the most effective timely allocation of resources and action
4. Establishing methods and approaches for appraising how effectively predetermined strategy and goals are being pursued.

Project planning starts with the development of a work breakdown structure that shows how the total project is broken down into its component parts. Project schedules and budgets are developed, technical performance goals are selected, and organizational authority and responsibility are established for members of the project team. Project planning also involves identifying the material resources needed to support the project during its life cycle. "What are we aiming for and why?" is the key question project planning answers. Project control starts with project planning, because the project plan is the key to the development of adequate control procedures and mechanisms.

Project control provides for the selection of performance standards for the project schedule, budget, and technical performance. It deals with information feedback to compare actual progress with planned progress, and with the initiation of corrective action as required. The rationale for a control subsystem arises out of the need for monitoring the various organizational units that are performing work on the project in order to deliver results on time and within budget. Further, project control is the process of constraining activities and resources to conform to a project plan. Management control is oriented toward achieving objectives by controlling activities and resources. Operational control focuses on the efficient and effective execution of specific tasks.

Feedback system models are commonly used to describe control systems. The feedback loop in such a model represents the flow of information concerning actual performance that is being fed back for comparison with a standard. Project standards are an important aspect of project control. Standards—be they of the financial, schedule, or work package variety—represent the bench marks by which progress is gauged.

In matrix organizations, project control is achieved through both formal and informal channels. Formal controls are usually inadequate in and of themselves. When they are complemented by informal controls, such as those exerted by project team members, a true control system exists. Even though such a system may be difficult to describe or assess, it must itself be kept in control in order to assure the progress of the project.

"Management by exception" is a management philosophy that rests heavily on control concepts. This philosophy directs the project manager to focus his attention on exceptions, rather than on those elements and activities that are progressing normally. In doing so, he directs his attention to those places where control action may be required, and, by omitting other areas from his consideration, he is able to devote to the exceptions the time and energy they may well require.

Thus, planning and control are intrinsically interlinked aspects of the project manager's job. If he does one without the other, he has not fulfilled his duty, and the project-driven organization is unlikely to achieve its objectives.

Planning, scheduling, and control are the primary themes in the cases and situations that follow.

RELEVANT BIBLIOGRAPHY

Alter, S. *Decision Support Systems: Current Practice and Continuing Challenges.* Addison-Wesley Publishing Co., Reading, Massachusetts, 1980.

Anthony, R. M., J. Dearden, and R. F. Vancil. *Management Control Systems.* Richard D. Irwin, Inc., Homewood, Illinois, 1965.

Baker, Bruce N., Dalmar Fisher, and David C. Murphy. *Factors Affecting Success of Project Management.* Paper presented to Annual Meeting of Project Management Institute, Toronto, Canada, October 1973.

Bent, James A. "Project Control: An Introduction." In *Project Management Handbook,* edited by David I. Cleland and William R. King. Van Nostrand Reinhold Co., New York, 1983, p. 421.

Chapman, Chris. "Large Engineering Project Risk Analysis." *IEEE Transactions on Engineering Management,* vol, 1, EM-26, no. 3, August 1979.

Chilstrom, Kenneth O. "Project Management Audits." In *Project Management Handbook,* edited by David I. Cleland and William R. King. Van Nostrand Reinhold Co., New York, 1983, p. 465.

Dane, C. W., C. F. Gray, and B. M. Woodworth. "Factors Affecting the Successful Application of PERT/CPM in a Government Organization." *Interfaces,* November 1979.

Davis, G. B. *Management Information Systems: Conceptual Foundations, Structure, and Development.* McGraw-Hill Book Co. Inc., New York, 1974.

Duke, Robert K. "Project Management at Fluor Utah, Inc." *Project Management Quarterly,* vol. VIII, no. 3, September 1977.

Gildersleeve, Thomas R. *Data Processing Project Management.* Van Nostrand Reinhold Co., New York, 1974.

Gunz, Hugh P., and Alan Pearson. "How to Manage Control Conflicts in Project Based Organizations." *Research Management,* March 1979, pp. 23–29.

Hogarth, R. M., "Cognitive Processes and the Assessment of Subjective Probability Distributions." *Journal of the American Statistical Association,* vol. 70, 1975.

Hollenbach, F. A. "Project Control in Bechtel Power Corporation." In *Project Management Handbook,* edited by David I. Cleland and William R. King. Van Nostrand Reinhold Co., New York, 1983, p. 458.

Howell, Robert A. "Multiproject Control." *Harvard Business Review,* March–April, 1968.

Kahalas, H. "A Look at Major Planning Methods: Development, Implementation, Strengths and Limitations." *Long Range Planning,* August, 1978.

Kerzner, Harold. "Pricing Out the Work." In *Project Management Handbook,* edited by David I. Cleland and William R. King. Van Nostrand Reinhold Co., New York, 1983, p. 383.

King, L. T. *Problem Solving in a Project Environment.* John Wiley & Sons, Inc., New York, 1981.

Kingdon, Donald R. *Matrix Organization: Managing Information Technologies.* Harper & Row Publishers, Inc., New York, 1973.

King, W. R., and D. I. Cleland. "The Design of Management Information Systems: An Information Analysis Approach." *Management Science,* November 1975.

King, William R., and David I. Cleland. "Manager-Analyst Teamwork in MIS Design." *Business Horizons,* vol. 14, April 1971.

Krogstad, J. L., G. Grudnitski, and D. W. Bryant. "PERT and PERT/cost for Audit Planning and Control." *The Internal Auditor,* August, 1979.

Lanford, H. W., and T. M. McCann. "Effective Planning and Control of Large Projects— Using Work Breakdown Structure." *Long Range Planning,* vol. 16, no. 2, pp. 38–50.

Lavold, Garry D. "Developing and Using the Work Breakdown Structure." In *Project Management Handbook,* edited by David I. Cleland and William R. King. Van Nostrand Reinhold Co., New York, 1983, p. 283.

Martin, J. R. "Computer Time-Sharing Applications in Management Accounting." *Management Accounting,* July, 1978.

Martin, Martin Dean, and Kathleen Miller. "Project Planning as the Primary Management Function." *Project Management Quarterly,* March 1982, pp. 31–38.

Miller, Barry M., and Charles D. Williams. *Management Action through Effective Project Controls: A Case Study of a Nuclear Power Plant Project.* 1978 Proceedings of the Project Management Institute, Los Angeles, October 1978.

Moder, Joseph J. "Network Techniques in Project Management." In *Project Mangement Handbook,* edited by David I. Cleland and William R. King. Van Nostrand Reinhold Co., New York, 1983, p. 303.

Morton, Geoffrey H. A. "Human Dynamics in Project Planning." In *Project Management Handbook,* edited by David I. Cleland and William R. King. Van Nostrand Reinhold Co., New York, 1983, p. 265.

Niwa, Kiyoshi, and Koji Sasaki. "A New Project Management Systems Approach: The 'Know-How' Based Project Management System." *Project Management Quarterly,* pp. 65–72.

Shull, F. S., and R. J. Judd. "Matrix Organizations and Control Systems." *Management International Review,* vol. 11, 1971.

Snowdon, Maurice. "Measuring Performance in Capital Project Management." *Long Range Planning,* vol. 13, August 1980, pp. 51–55.

Souder, William E. "Project Evaluation and Selection." In *Project Management Handbook,* edited by David I. Cleland and William R. King. Van Nostrand Reinhold Co., New York, 1983, p. 185.

Thamhain, Hans J., and Wilemon, David L. "Project Performance Measurement: The Keystone to Engineering Project Control." Paper presented at the PMI-Internet Joint Symposium, 1981 Proceedings, Boston.

Van Steelandt, Frank V., and Ludo F. Gelders. "Financial Control in Project Management: A Case Study." *IEEE Transactions on Engineering Management,* vol. 1, EM-26, no. 3, August 1979.

Webster, Francis M. "Tools For Managing Projects." *Project Management Quarterly,* pp. 46–58.

Youker, Robert. *A New Look at WBS (Work Breakdown Structure).* CN-851 Course Note Series, July 1980, International Bank for Reconstruction and Development.

CASE STUDY 33:   CORY ELECTRIC

Frankly speaking, Jeff, I didn't think we would stand a chance in winning this $20 million program. I was really surprised when they said they'd like to accept our bid and begin contract negotiations. As chief contract administrator, you'll head the negotiation team," remarked Gus Bell, Vice-President and General Manager of Cory Electric. You have two weeks to prepare your data and line up your team. I want to see you when you're ready to go.

Jeff Stokes was chief contract negotiator for Cory Electric, a $250 million a year electrical components manufacturer serving virtually every major U.S. industry. Cory Electric had a well-established matrix structure that had withstood 15 years of testing. Job-costing standards were well established, but did include some fat, upon the discretion of the functional manager.

Two weeks later, Jeff discussed the negotiation process with Gus Bell:

Gus Bell: "Have you selected an appropriate team? You had better make sure you're covered on all sides."

Jeff: "There will be four plus me at the negotiating table: the program manager, the chief project engineer who developed the engineering labor package; the chief manufacturing engineer who developed the production labor package; and a pricing specialist who has been on the proposal since the kick-off meeting. We have a strong team and should be able to handle any questions."

Gus Bell: "OK, I'll take your word for it. I have my own checklist for contract negotiations. I want you to come back with a guaranteed fee of $1.6 million for our stockholders. Have you worked out the possible situations based upon the negotiated costs?"

Jeff: "Yes! Our minimum position is $20 million plus an 8 percent profit. Of course, this profit percentage will vary depending upon the negotiated cost. We can bid the program at a $15 million cost—that's $5 million below our target—and still book a $1.6 million profit by overrunning the cost-plus-incentive-fee contract. Here is a list of the possible cases." (See Table 1.)

Gus Bell: "If we negotiate a cost overrun fee, make sure that cost accounting knows about it. I don't want the total fee to be booked as profit if we're going to need it later to cover the overrun. Can we justify our overhead rates, general and administrative costs, and our salary structure?"

Jeff: "That's a problem. You know that 20 percent of our business comes from Mitre Corporation. If it fails to renew our contract for another two-year follow-on effort, then our overhead rates will jump drastically. Which overhead rates should I use?"

Table 1.   Cost Positions.

Minimum Position = $20,000,000
Minimum Fee   =   1,600,000 = 8% of Minimum Position
Sharing Ration   = 90/10%

		Negotiated Fee			
Negotiated Cost	Profit %	Target Fee	Overrun Fee	Total Fee	Total Package
15,000,000	14.00	1,600,000	500,000	2,100,000	17,100,000
16,000,000	12.50	1,600,000	400,000	2,000,000	18,000,000
17,000,000	11.18	1,600,000	300,000	1,900,000	18,900,000
18,000,000	10.00	1,600,000	200,000	1,800,000	19,800,000
19,000,000	8.95	1,600,000	100,000	1,700,000	20,700,000
20,000,000	8.00	1,600,000	0	1,600,000	21,600,000
21,000,000	7.14	1,600,000	−100,000	1,500,000	22,500,000
22,000,000	6.36	1,600,000	−200,000	1,400,000	23,400,000
23,000,000	5.65	1,600,000	−300,000	1,300,000	24,300,000
24,000,000	5.00	1,600,000	−400,000	1,200,000	25,200,000

Assume Total Cost Will be Spent:

Negotiated Cost	% Fee
21,000,000	7.61
22,000,000	7.27
23,000,000	6.96
24,000,000	6.67

Gus Bell: "Let's put in a renegotiation clause to protect us against a drastic change in our business base. Make sure that the customer understands that as part of the terms and conditions. Are there any unusual terms and conditions?"

Jeff: "I've read over all terms and conditions, and so have all of the project office personnel, as well as the key functional managers. The only major item is that the customer wants us to qualify some new vendors as sources for raw material procurement. We have included in the package the cost of qualifying two new raw material suppliers."

Gus Bell: "Where are the weak points in our proposal? I'm sure we have some."

Jeff: "Last month, the customer sent in a fact-finding team to go over all our labor justifications. The impression I get from our people is that we're covered all the way around. The only major problem might be where we'll be performing on our learning curve. We put into the proposal a 45 percent learning curve efficiency. The customer has indicated that we should be up around 50 to 55 percent efficiency, based upon our previous contracts with him. Unfortunately, those contracts the customer referred to, were four years ago. Several of the employees who worked on those programs have left the company. Others are assigned to ongoing projects here. I estimate that we could put together about 10 percent of the people we used previously. That learning curve percentage will be a big point for disagreements. We finished the previous programs with the customer at a 35 percent learning curve position. I don't see how it can expect us to be smarter, given these circumstances."

Gus Bell: "If that's the only weakness, then we're in good shape. It sounds like we have a foolproof audit trail. That's good! What's your negotiation sequence going to be?"

Jeff: "I'd like to negotiate the bottom line only. But that's a dream. We'll probably negotiate the raw materials, the man-hours and the learning curve, the overhead rate, and finally, the profit percentage. I hope we can do it in that order."

Gus Bell: "Do you think we'll be able to negotiate a cost above our minimum position?"

Jeff: "Our proposal was for $22.2 million. I don't foresee any problem that will prevent us from coming out ahead of the minimum position. The 5 percent change in learning curve efficiency amounts to approximately $1 million. We should be well covered.

The first move is up to the other side. I expect an offer of $18 to $19 million. Using the binary chop procedure, that'll give us our guaranteed minimum position."

Gus Bell: "Do you know the guys who you'll be negotiating with?"

Jeff: "Yes. I've dealt with them before. The last time, the negotiations took three days. I think we both got what we wanted. I expect this one to go just as smoothly."

Gus Bell: "OK, Jeff. I'm convinced we're prepared for negotiations. Have a good trip."

The negotiations began at 9:00 on Monday morning. The customer countered the original proposal of $22.2 million with an offer of $15 million. After six solid hours of arguments, Jeff and his teams adjourned. Jeff immediately called Gus Bell at Cory Electric: "The customer's counteroffer to our bid is absurd. He has asked us to make a counteroffer to his offer. We can't do that. The instant we give a counteroffer, we are in fact giving credibility to that absurd bid. Now, he's claiming that if we don't present a counteroffer, we're not bargaining in good faith. I think we're in trouble."

Gus Bell: "Has the customer done his homework to justify that bid?"

Jeff: "Yes. Very well. Tomorrow we're going to discuss every element of the proposal, task by task. Unless something drastically changes in his position within the next day or two, contract negotiations will probably take up to a month."

Gus Bell: "Perhaps this is one program that should be negotiated at the top levels of management. Find out if the person you're negotiating with reports to a vice-president and general manager, as you do. If not, break off contract negotiations until the customer gives us someone at your level. We'll negotiate this at my level, if necessary."

CASE STUDY 34: SPACEAGE, INC. (A)[1]

On Monday, February 4, 1963, a meeting of the strategy board of Spaceage's Aeronics Division was scheduled to review the proposal effort for Project ARIES. On March 1, Spaceage was to submit a proposal to the Air Force for the development of satellites for the ARIES space communications system. In preparing for the ARIES proposal, Spaceage had analyzed and weighted the major technical, management, production, and logistical factors the customer was likely to use in source selection. A competitive evaluation chart (Table 2) was constructed to show the important source selection considerations. Each firm expected to bid on the ARIES contract was rated on this chart; the rating was updated as more information was obtained. The chart became a focal point of discussion at the ARIES strategy board meetings.

Company Background

Prior to 1960, the company name of Spaceage, Inc., was the J. W. Lowry Company. The J. W. Lowry Company was organized just prior to World War II to manufacture aircraft. During the war, the company grew rapidly and achieved a reputation in the airframe industry as a relatively small but high-quality producer. When orders for military aircraft declined after World War II, the Lowry company diversified

---

[1] Copyright © 1963 by the president and fellows of Harvard College. This case was prepared by Louis B. Smith under the direction of J. Sterling Livingston as a basis for class discussion, rather than to illustrate either effective or ineffective handling of an administrative situation. Reprinted by permission of the Harvard Business School.

Table 2. Spaceage, Inc. (A): Competitive Evaluation (February 4, 1963).

Maximum Points	Scientific & Engineering Competence	A. Tech Factors											
		Component Design and Development											
	80	Overall Design	Struct.	Thermal Control	E.P.D.	Telemetry	Re-peater	An-tenna	Ejection & Spin	Fabrication	Test Program	A.G.E.	Reli-ability
	80	150	20	10	10	10	50	10	50	30	50	20	80
Aerospace Corp	70	110	10	7	10	10	40	8	30	10	35	20	40
A.C.E., Inc.	50	60	20	5	5	8	35	7	30	20	30	17	60
American Space Co.	70	100	15	6	8	10	35	9	40	25	35	18	50
Arnold, Inc.	50	80	20	5	5	10	35	7	40	30	50	20	65
Defense Industries, Inc.	70	110	20	7	5	10	35	7	40	30	50	20	65
Diversified Industries, Inc.	70	130	13	10	10	10	45	10	40	20	30	20	20
Dynamics, Inc.	80	130	20	10	10	10	35	10	50	30	50	20	70
Electronic Systems, Inc.	50	80	9	4	5	10	50	9	20	15	25	12	65
F.I.T. Corp.	80	130	20	10	10	10	40	10	40	20	50	15	60
Fulton Corp.	40	60	20	5	5	8	35	7	25	25	30	18	50
General Communications	75	120	10	10	10	10	50	10	30	20	35	15	80
Spaceage	80	130	20	10	10	10	40	8	50	30	50	20	80

Maximum Points	A. Tech. Factors			B. Mgt. Production Logistics							
	Human Engineering	Configuration Mgt.	Safety Engineering	Mgt. Organization and Approach	Master Plan & Sched.	Maintainability	Support & Maint. Plan	Training Plan	Preservation & Packaging	AGE Spares Support to Develop Activities	Tech. Manuals
	5	5	5	100	80	5	5	5	5	5	5
Aerospace Corp.				60	65						
A.C.E., Inc.				70	70						
American Space Co.				75	75						
Arnold, Inc.				60	60						
Defense Industries, Inc.				65	70						
Diversified Industries, Inc.				75	70						
Dynamics, Inc.				100	80						
Electronic Systems, Inc.				60	60						
F.I.T. Corp.				95	80						
Fulton Corp.				60	60						
General Communications				80	75						
Spaceage				70	80						

Table 2. (Cont.)

	Prod. Capability	Subcontractor Program	Facilities	Man-Power	Fin. Capability	B. Mgt. Production Logistics — Cost Reliability: History and Controls	Interference With Other Contractor	Cost and Profit	Quality Control Program
Maximum Points	40	40	100	20	5	200	30	10	60
Aerospace Corp.	30	30	70	18	5	140	30	10	40
A.C.E., Inc.	40	35	65	10	5	160	10	10	40
American Space Co.	40	35	100	20	5	160	20	10	50
Arnold, Inc.	30	30	65	15	5	100	20	10	40
Defense Industries, Inc.	35	30	75	20	5	100	30	10	45
Diversified Industries, Inc.	35	35	90	20	5	160	30	10	45
Dynamics, Inc.	40	40	100	20	5	100	25	10	60
Electronic Systems, Inc.	30	30	70	15	5	120	25	10	45
F.I.T. Corp.	30	35	100	20	5	160	30	10	45
Fulton Corp.	30	30	65	15	5	150	30	10	40
General Communications	40	35	80	20	5	200	25	10	60
Spaceage	40	30	100	20	5	100	30	10	40

B. Mgt. Production Logistics — Totals

Maximum Points 70

	Known Preparation	Labor Surplus Area	A. Total	B. Total	Grand Total
Aerospace Corp.	70		400	568	968
A.C.E., Inc.	40		347	555	902
American Space Co.	60		421	650	1,071
Arnold, Inc.	40		417	475	892
Defense Industries, Inc.	60	+	469	545	1,014
Diversified Industries, Inc.	70	?	458	645	1,103
Dynamics, Inc.	65		525	645	1,170
Electronic Systems, Inc.	65		354	535	889
F.I.T. Corp.	65		495	675	1,170
Fulton Corp.	50		328	545	873
General Communications	30		475	660	1,135
Spaceage	70	+	538	595	1,133

into several industrial products, but retained its interest and market position in the airframe industry. Seeking further diversification, Lowry acquired a small but thriving electronics company in 1954. The Electronics Division proved to be a source of growth to the company through the remainder of the 1950s, in contrast to the stable Industrial Products Division and the declining Military Aircraft Division.

When it became apparent in the mid-1950s that the future of the airplane was questionable and that the missile and space field was to be the big growth area for future defense business, the Lowry company gradually began to make the transition to develop a capability for the missile and space business. Between 1955 and 1960, however, Lowry was not acquiring enough missile and space contracts to compensate for aircraft production, which was phasing out. The result was serious financial strain during this period and several large layoffs. The pace of the transition quickened after 1959, when new management was installed. One of the early decisions of the new management was to change the name of J. W. Lowry Company to Spaceage, Inc. The young and dynamic Spaceage management team aggressively sought to build a solid and diverse capability in missile and space technology and to establish a firm position in the expanding missiles and space market.

The PIONEER Project

Since the late 1950s, the three military services, NASA, and several commercial organizations had been interested in developing a communications system using orbiting satellites. Theoretically, a satellite communications system would provide improved capability compared with existing systems. A satellite communications system would offer increased range, higher reliability, and greater flexibility. The satellite system, however, would augment the overall communications capability, rather than replace current systems.

Spaceage, Inc., had conducted research on communications satellites since 1957. In 1961, the Air Force awarded a major contract to Spaceage to build the spacecraft for a satellite communications system. The responsibility for this highly ambitious program, dubbed Project PIONEER, was divided among the three military services. The Army had responsibility for developing the communications equipment; the Air Force had responsibility for developing the satellites (exclusive of communications equipment), launching the satellites, and maintaining them in orbit; the Navy had responsibility for developing shipborne support stations. The Spaceage contract for the PIONEER satellite development was divided into three phases. Phase I required component development and a breadboard of the system; Phase II required developing a model for system testing; Phase III required development of preproduction prototypes for operational tests.

Because the communications satellite contract was in an entirely new field that appeared to have significant future market potential, Spaceage management decided to form a new division. The Aeronics Division was organized and given the responsibility for the PIONEER contract and for obtaining additional space business. Mr. John Bowles was recruited from Dynamics, Inc., for the position of Aeronics Division general manager.

Mr. Bowles' initial concern was to get additional business for the newly organized division. Within eight months after the Aeronics Division was formed, a second major and several smaller contracts were obtained. In December 1961, at the annual Spaceage planning conference, Mr. Bowles reported that the Aeronics Division was experiencing rapid growth and that the prospect for future space business appeared very bright indeed. In his final speech at the planning conference, the executive vice-president of Spaceage commended the Aeronics Division for a fine job and stated that Spaceage was counting on the Aeronics Division to provide much of the future growth for the company.

During the 18 months after work began on the PIONEER program the various contracts managed by the three military services experienced numerous problems. There were substantial overruns in the costs and serious schedule slippages. The launch vehicle, which was to have launched the PIONEER satellites, fell behind schedule by about two years. More important, the launch vehicle development program encountered serious technical difficulties that caused the vehicle's performance capabilities to fall significantly below expectations. Meanwhile, the PIONEER spacecraft being developed by Spaceage increased 300 pounds in weight, which meant that no substitute booster was available to launch the satellites.

On April 1, 1962, Spaceage was directed to postpone Phases II and III of the PIONEER program and to submit estimated costs and schedule for the remainder of Phase I. On April 28, 1962, Spaceage was advised not to proceed with the full Phase I level of effort, as previously instructed, because of funding limitations. On August 15, 1962, Spaceage received notice of termination of the PIONEER contract, with the exception of a small portion to be completed in six months. On September 5, 1962, the Defense Department announced a major reorientation of the PIONEER project "to bring it into consonance with existing rocket boosters."

The technical redirection of the PIONEER project was of such a fundamental character as to amount to cancellation of the existing program. The Department of Defense instituted studies to ascertain the feasibility of establishing one or more new programs or cancel the defense communication satellite program entirely. Defense Department officials disapproved of noncompetitive reorientation of the PIONEER program because of poor performance by Spaceage and the other major contractors.

Marketing Strategy

On September 1, 1962, Mr. Bowles was transferred to head the marketing department of Spaceage's Military Aircraft Division. Mr. Frank Jackson, a Spaceage employee for 12 years, was promoted to vice-president to head the Aeronics Division. Mr. Jackson and Mr. Joseph Garrett, the Aeronics Division marketing department head, quickly sought to evaluate the competitive position of Spaceage relative to the new communications satellite program expected to be established. A series of meetings were held the first two weeks of September to analyze the situation and to develop a marketing strategy.

At the first meeting, Mr. Garrett observed that, at this time, both the type of program to be undertaken and the selection of contractor were highly uncertain. The problems experienced with PIONEER, the questions of technical feasibility and technical approach, and the high potential cost of the program, indicated that the space communications program was being seriously questioned at high Department of Defense (DOD) levels. Furthermore, Defense Department officials might consider the entire undertaking an unnecessary duplication of effort by DOD because of related programs under NASA auspices and the well-publicized commercial communications satellite developed by the General Communications Company. Mr. Garrett reported that the decisions on the new program in all likelihood would be influenced by the military services, the Office of Defense Research and Engineering (ODR&E), the Secretary of Defense, and possibly White House Executive Offices, as well as legislative Space Committees.

The cancellation of PIONEER had severely disrupted Spaceage's plans for the future. Mr. Jackson found it necessary to reduce the work force of the Aeronics Division by several hundred. More layoffs were scheduled for October and November. These layoffs added to the already relatively high unemployment in the local area.

The Spaceage facility that housed the Aeronics Division was currently operating at approximately one-half capacity. The building was constructed with space satellite development in mind and had the latest test chambers for simulating space environmental conditions. The size and quality of these chambers could not be matched at the present time by another firm in the country.

Mr. Jackson and Mr. Garrett agreed that the companies selected to participate in the reoriented space communications program would enjoy a decided competitive advantage for future space business if the program were successfully completed. They also believed that the space efforts by NASA and the defense establishment offered the best growth potential for future business in sight. As a result, they expected aggressive competition for the contract from well-qualified, strong firms. With these considerations in mind, Mr. Jackson decided to actively and enthusiastically seek the new communications satellite contract for the Aeronics Division of Spaceage.

The analysis of the marketing strengths and weaknesses of Spaceage indicated a position of strength, because of the PIONEER work, in the areas of technical experience, technical understanding of the problem, and reliability. And, of course, the ready availability of facilities, equipment, and qualified personnel needed for the work was a strength. It was felt, however, that in the viewpoint of the customer, Spaceage's most serious weakness was its inability to keep within costs and schedule, as reflected by its work on PIONEER and other current government R&D programs.

Mr. Jackson and Mr. Garrett developed a marketing strategy for the space communications business designed to exploit and enhance Spaceage's strengths and overcome its weaknesses. The major elements of the strategy were:

1. Continuing in-house studies of the satellite communications system and discussion of these studies with appropriate individuals throughout the government, so that the customer would be aware of the continued interest of Spaceage in the program and of Spaceage's technical knowledge and understanding of the problems involved.

2. An extensive campaign in the pre-Request for Proposal (RFP) period by Spaceage's marketing and engineering personnel to establish and maintain contact with the customer at all levels, to determine the technical and management approach, program schedule, and program funding desired by the customer, and to ascertain the customer's opinion and image of Spaceage.

3. Reassessment and improvement of Spaceage's management control and cost techniques and emphasis in the proposal to demonstrate an awareness of the significance of this aspect.

4. Creation of an improved company image in the defense market by high-level contact between Spaceage and defense officials.

5. A weekly strategy board meeting was to be held each Monday to review and evaluate significant aspects of the marketing effort and to plan specific actions to take as necessary. The strategy board was to be composed of key marketing and technical management personnel and Mr. Jackson.

Pre-RFP Effort

On the recommendation of Mr. Garrett, Mr. Jackson selected Mr. Max Post to lead the Spaceage marketing team that would be responsible for preparing the proposal and cultivating the customer. Mr. Post was selected on the basis of his previous experience as the project director on PIONEER. Post had been with Spaceage for five years and was highly respected for his creative design capabilities. Mr. Garrett felt Post's technical understanding of the problems involved in developing communications satellites would prove invaluable in demonstrating to the customer Spaceage's continued interest and capability in the space communications program. Mr. Jackson did not plan for Mr. Post to assume the responsibility for the project in the event Spaceage was awarded the contract. Rather, he felt Mr. Post's capabilities could be more effectively used on another related proposal effort expected to materialize in about six months.

Mr. Post collected a group of engineering and support personnel to assist with the proposal preparation, customer presentations, and other marketing activities. The group grew from 40 people at the beginning of the marketing effort to 100 by the time the proposal was submitted. Some of the technical personnel came from the terminated PIONEER project, while others came from Spaceage projects that were currently phasing out. Although the team worked closely with the Marketing Department and the effort was supported by marketing funds, Mr. Post reported directly to Mr. Jackson.

At its weekly Monday meetings, the strategy board carefully reviewed the marketing activities of the previous week, thoroughly analyzed the situation, established specific plans for future actions, and assigned responsibility for these actions. Mr. Jackson, Mr. Garrett, Mr. Post, and other key technical and marketing personnel regularly participated in the strategy board meetings. The meetings provided a focal point for evaluating marketing intelligence information collected and organized by Mr. Garrett's Marketing Department.

The marketing efforts of Spaceage resulted in close coverage of the day-to-day developments leading toward establishment of the reoriented program. Before the RFP was dispatched, the Spaceage team made more than 500 presentations to interested customer personnel on various facets of the satellite program. Technical personnel on the Spaceage team established close personal working relationships with their customer counterparts. Spaceage management, at the same time, systematically planned and made high-level customer contacts.

Through its intensive marketing efforts, Spaceage influenced the specifications that were later included in the Air Force Request for Proposal (RFP). Indeed, Mr. Garrett was delighted to learn that Spaceage personnel, in effect, wrote 400 pages of the final 900-page RFP. Mr. Garrett estimated that the Spaceage team knew 90 percent of the contents of the RFP before the document was officially received. Mr. Garrett also was aware that several strong competitors for the business influenced the RFP, were equally determined to get the business, and were as thorough as Spaceage in their marketing efforts.

A formal management review of the pre-RFP effort was held in December 1962. In addition to the Spaceage management team, several outside consultants participated in the review. The following points were made at the review and were to be taken into account in preparing the proposal.

1. The communications satellite procurement will probably call for a separate management book, so strive for management novelty. Meet all requirements *plus*. Show how the customer will be able to evaluate performance on the project. Play up reliability in both books (technical and management).

The proposal should contain not only PERT and PERT/cost, but an integrated schedule, cost, *performance* measurement and control scheme *for this job,* which also is compatible with and meets all PERT and PERT/cost requirements. The proposal should clearly indicate what management control reports are to be available.

2. The current climate in the DOD tends to place a balanced emphasis on technical, cost, and schedule performance. This is a shift from the earlier practices of stressing technical and schedule performance, often at the expense of cost overruns. Cost effectiveness analyses are being conducted more frequently in the Department of Defense. These studies analyze the expected value to be derived from initiating and continuing a program in terms of the costs involved and the alternative spending opportunities available. Thus, cost increases, schedule slippages, and performance degradation, when compared with the assumptions upon which the decisions on the initial plans were made, could well mean that the marginal value of the end product might slide below the threshold for justifying continuing the effort.

3. The proposal evaluation (source selection and board evaluation) will, as always, use a point-scoring system. It is assumed that the following will be used:

Engineering Approach (40 percent or less)
   Understanding of problem
   Soundness of approach
   Compliance with requirements
   Special factors (unique ideas)

Performance History (30 percent or more)
   Related experience on programs satisfactorily completed
   Quality of related products
   Overrun history
   Ability to meet schedule

Qualifications Based on Nontechnical Considerations (30 percent)
   Specific experience (directly related, management and technical)

Organization (people and structure)
Equipment and facilities
Management measurement and control

Project ARIES

The RFP for the new communications satellite program, entitled Project ARIES, was received by Spaceage on January 2, 1963. The Air Force, which was again responsible for the satellite portion, invited 35 firms to bid on the ARIES satellites. To select the ARIES contractor, the Air Force would use the contract definition (CD) procedure.[2]

In Phase A, the Air Force screened firms responding to the RFP on the basis of overall performance capability criteria, including technical understanding of the problems, management capability, and costs. The Phase A management and technical proposal was due March 1, 1963. Two or three firms were to be selected from the Phase A competition to continue into Phase B. The Phase B awards were to be announced on May 1, 1963.

In Phase B of contract definition, the two or three contractors selected were to work closely on final systems design specifications with the Air Force and DTS Corp., an Air-Force-associated nonprofit organization. Phase B was to be concerned with such things as defining the number of satellites to be orbited, orbit altitudes, weight, operating characteristics, and specification of the total system configuration. Because of the very close working relationships necessary in Phase B among the contractors, the Air Force, and the DTS Corporation, Mr. Garrett assumed all information from one contractor would inevitably become known to the others. The winner of the development contract award resulting from Phase B competition would be announced on October 1, 1963. Actual development was to commence immediately thereafter.

Mr. Garrett's market intelligence indicated that the winners of the Phase A competition could expect to receive $300,000 to $500,000 to participate in Phase B, while the losers would receive nothing. He noted that the Spaceage effort was expected to cost $600,000 by March 1, and that it would cost an additional $800,000 to participate in Phase B of the final program definition. The excess marketing costs could not be charged directly to the contract in the event it was awarded, and would have to be recovered from profits.

The Aeronics Division Organization

The organization of the Aeronics Division (Figure 1) represented a compromise between a completely functionalized organizational arrangement and one that was completely projectized. This was known as the *matrix* organization by Spaceage personnel. The marketing, finance, engineering, and manufacturing functions were on the same level of organizational responsibility and authority as the project groups. This matrix

---

[2] Prior to July 1965, contract definition was called *project definition phase*. The newer terminology is used in the Spaceage case series.

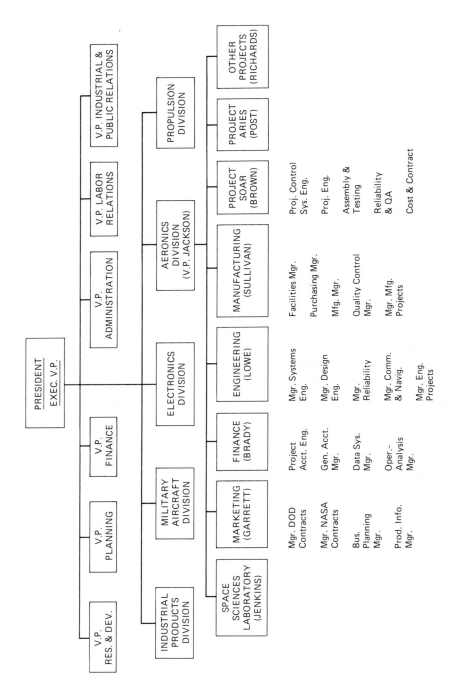

Figure 1. Spaceage, Inc. (A).

organizational arrangement had been in effect since the formation of the Aeronics Division. The general opinion of the Aeronics Division management team was that the matrix organization was the ideal solution for securing the most important advantages offered by both a functional and a project-type organization.

The three project groups (see Figure 1) in existence at the time of the meeting included Project SOAR, which was being directed by Pat Brown. SOAR, a NASA project which had been awarded Spaceage 18 months earlier, accounted for approximately two-thirds of the work currently in-house. The second project group, "Other" projects, directed by Dick Richards, accounted for the remaining third of the Aeronics Division's business. There were 20 of these smaller projects, all sponsored by the three military services and NASA. These 20 smaller projects ranged in contract size from $100,000 to $1 million. The third project group, ARIES, at the time of the meeting, was a major proposal group operating entirely on overhead.

The project groups had the responsibility for technical integration, preparing and maintaining project schedules and budgets, measuring performance against schedule and budget, maintaining technical surveillance of project status, and initiating any required action to solve actual or potential problems. In addition to a control section that maintained the PERT charts and handled work orders and budgets, the staff of the SOAR project group consisted of specialists in the areas of systems engineering, equipment engineering, project engineering, assembly and testing, reliability and quality assurance, and cost and contract administration. The job of the specialists was to maintain liaison with their counterparts in the various functional departments in order to closely monitor progress on the work being done by the departments. Approximately 15 percent of total personnel working on projects were assigned to the project group.

The Aeronics Division procedures required the project group to authorize work releases as well as approve funds distributed to the various departments for work performed on a project. If it became necessary for a department to expend more effort than planned to complete a project task, an agreement on the excess costs had to be worked out between a department and project group. In the final analysis, the department was responsible for locating a charge number for work performed. In the absence of an agreement to charge work to a project, the work could be charged to the department overhead account.

The Marketing Department was responsible for contract administration, proposal coordination, customer contact and development, and business planning. Engineering was responsible for systems, design, development, and reliability engineering. Manufacturing was responsible for facilities, purchasing tooling, fabrication, and quality control. The accounting and operations analysis functions were assigned to the Finance Department.

The departments would assign a project to an individual who was directly responsible for the project work performed within the department. This individual represented the department at project meetings and the project at department meetings. The department's project representative worked closely with the project group in selecting and scheduling personnel assigned to work on the project. However, all departmental personnel assigned to work on projects remained within the department for administrative purposes. The project group rated the performance of each employee who worked on the projects. This rating was given careful consideration by the department managers in the annual evaluation of each employee's performance. This evaluation determined employee promotions and their standing on the Spaceage pay scale.

February 4 Strategy Board Meeting

The strategy board had held regular Monday meetings since the beginning of the ARIES preproposal and proposal effort. When the need arose, additional meetings were scheduled. Indeed, the board met several times a week during most of the time the ARIES proposal was being prepared. As pointed out earlier, the competition evaluation chart (Table 2) had proved to be an effective vehicle for review, discussion, and planning at the strategy board meetings. After some preliminaries, Mr. Jackson, Vice-President of the Aeronics Division, turned to the chart to open the discussion.

"Well, Garrett," began Mr. Jackson, "I see from your chart that we have improved our score since the last meeting, but we still have to gain points if we are to be one of the firms selected for the Phase B competition."

"We can't expect to gain points on any of the technical factors," volunteered Mr. Post, ARIES project director. "We are 20 points below the maximum for overall design, but so are the other top contenders. The reason for this is that the customer has not firmly decided on a 'best' design at this stage. In fact, the purpose of the two-phased procurement is to hold off on detailed design specifications until the second phase of the competition. The same holds true for points on component design and development. The basis for the points shown on the technical side is the known related experience and technical effort that, in the opinion of the customer, indicate technical capability. By this time the customer's opinion on the technical factors is firm, so the scores shown on the chart for technical considerations are frozen."

"Your team has done a tremendous job in selling Spaceage's technical capability and understanding of the problem," said Mr. Jackson to Post. "Now we must concentrate on improving our standing for the management, production, and logistics factors. These considerations will clearly be decisive and unfortunately this is our area of greatest weakness. What can we do to increase our score?"

"There are 30 very attractive points available on management organization and approach," Mr. Post noted. "What about reorganizing the division, if that's what it will take for us to capture those points on organization? The 30 additional points would put us right at the top of the heap."

Mr. Brown, SOAR project director, commented:

"As far as I'm concerned, the present organization is operating perfectly. I don't feel an organization change at this time would be either necessary or wise. To reorganize in the middle of the project would be disruptive. We have established good working relationships with the functional departments, and we would like to keep it that way. We have experienced absolutely no difficulty in securing the full cooperation and support from the departments for the SOAR effort. Furthermore, the customer is completely satisfied with the organization as it is. In fact, the NASA representative commented on his last visit that he wasn't concerned with the details of the internal organization, as long as NASA had assurance of our ability to perform. Although we are still in the early phases of the SOAR program, our progress and performance for the 18 months work so far has satisfied NASA of our capability."

Mr. Richards, project director of other projects, said: "I tend to agree with Brown on this matter. Of course, we've experienced some problems on several of our projects. But I think the reason for that was poor estimating in the beginning. Things have been going much better for us the past six months."

At this point, Mr. Garrett of marketing spoke up:

"There are definite indications of a preference on the part of the customer for a vertical or project-type organization. I don't know if this is justified or not, but this is our general conclusion from the many discussions we have had with the customer. If you will take a look at the competitive evaluation chart, you will note that Dynamics, Inc., has the maximum number of points for organization. The reason for this is that Dynamics has established an entirely new division just for the ARIES project.

"As you know, the evaluation chart rates each company competing for the ARIES business according to the criteria and relative weights that the customer is likely to use for source selection. We keep the chart as current as our latest available market intelligence information. The ratings are our best judgment of the relative ranking of the companies responding to the RFP from the viewpoints of the individuals and groups in the customer organization likely to influence and make the final decision. We are reasonably confident that these numbers are a valid representation of the marketing situation we face. You will also note that it is not organization but cost control capability, as shown under the cost reliability column, that is Spaceage's most serious deficiency in the view of the customer."

Mr. Lowe of engineering commented: "I suppose Spaceage would have scored the maximum points for organization when the Space Division was formed to handle the PIONEER project. However, you can't very well organize a completely new division for each new project, can you? In fact, in our present situation, we could probably projectize the Space Division and not expect serious repercussions apart from the agony of fractionalizing and transferring all the department's function to the projects. But, if Spaceage gets the kind of new business that we are all plugging for, we simply will not have enough capable people to go around. A significant increase in business will stretch our organization, and it will be even more necessary than now to have the flexibility of scheduling our resources to the projects where they are needed most.

"It seems to me that functional departments are the only satisfactory way of maintaining the level of technical competence we need in the various specialties. And certainly, functional control is the only way to optimize the utilization of our specialized capabilities in order to effectively compete for new business."

Mr. Post, manager of the ARIES proposal effort, stated: "I was talking with a friend from the General Aircraft Company the other day about this organization question. Now, he told me General Aircraft's approach was to draw up organization charts for the proposal that showed the lines and boxes connected the way they thought the customer wanted them to look. In fact, however, a fictional 'organization' was superimposed on the regular organization, which continued to operate as it always had. As you know, General Aircraft has recently won a couple of real plums where this approach was utilized. Maybe we should do the same thing."

Mr. Brady of the Finance Department said: "What about the expense of completely projectizing the organization? It appears to me that it will be a costly proposition to have to duplicate all functions for each project. Under what circumstances is complete projectization justifiable? Just how far should an organization go in projectizing? Is the government willing to pay the added costs of projectization?"

"Maybe the answer is simply to state in our management proposal that we will establish whatever kind of organization the customer wants," said Mr. Post. "This demonstration of complete flexibility on our part should earn us the points. And it would certainly be evidence of our sincerity in wanting to cooperate to the fullest in meeting the desires of the customer."

To this, Mr. Sullivan from manufacturing responded: "Now just a minute there! Who's running this outfit anyway, we or the government? The government has no business sticking its nose into our internal affairs. The way we organize is our concern, not its. It may pressure us into bending a little here and there, but we shouldn't encourage it."

"Total projectization is no panacea," commented Mr. Richards. "the F.I.T. Corporation is almost totally projectized, and their manager for the Venus project, who is a friend of mine, gave me a typical example of one of his problems. For some reason, it become necessary to redesign the structure of Venus, which caused a delay in the downstream effort. So, all the electronics people who were assigned to the project just sat there twiddling their thumbs waiting for the structural design releases. Now, this seems to be a real waste of time and talent. However, I suppose the project managers there have the authority to push their people to work harder when they can start to make up for lost time. But I know some of the people assigned to projects at F.I.T. are not fully utilized on project work."

Looking at the competitive evaluation chart, Mr. Jackson said: "I notice our subcontractor and quality control programs also indicate some deficiencies. What is the reason for this, Garrett?"

Mr. Garrett responded: "The customer has some reservations about having the responsibility for subcontractor management located within the purchasing department. It tends to question the capability of most purchasing departments to cope with the tricky technical, interface, and control problems that are possible with subcontractors in this business. You will note that Dynamics, Inc., has the maximum points for subcontract management. This is because subcontract management will be directly under control of the project at Dynamics.

"Now, the customer seems to prefer an entirely separate organization for the quality control program, which reports directly to top management. The reasoning here, I suppose, is that it thinks an 'independent' quality check on the project work will provide a better overall management control system. You will note that Dynamics is again complying fully with the apparent desires of the customer on the quality control program."

"The most obvious area to pick up points is in the area of cost reliability," said Mr. Post. "We are operating under a severe handicap here because of the recent PIONEER experience. Of course, the government was more to blame for that abort than we were, but you can't very well sell that. They kept adding functions to the original specifications of the spacecraft, which caused the weight increase. Even so, the planned launch vehicle could have accepted the satellite weight additions; in fact, it is desirable to load the booster to maximum lift capability. Of course, we were really in an awkward position when the planned launch vehicle didn't materialize, and there were no available substitutes capable of lifting the PIONEER spacecraft with the weight additions. But, I don't buy that we were at fault technically in any way and that the schedule problems were caused by the changes introduced. However, we did experience serious cost overrun problems."

Mr. Jackson concluded: "We have approximately four more weeks to complete the ARIES management proposal. I have asked Mr. Garrett and Mr. Post to outline a proposed organization of the division and the ARIES project to be used in the management proposal. Take a copy of their suggestions with you (Figure 2, Table 3), and be prepared to discuss them at the next meeting. In the meantime, all of us should be thinking hard about what Spaceage can do to improve our standing on the competitive evaluation chart. We need that business."

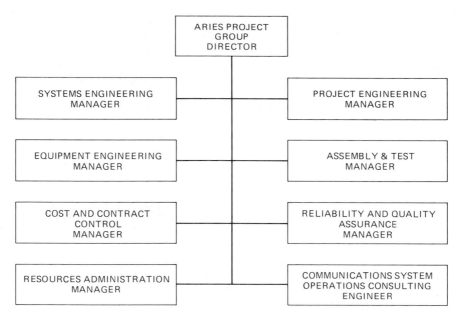

Figure 2.   Spaceage, Inc. (A).

DIRECTOR—ARIES

Responsible for obtaining and managing the required resources for the development, design, test, evaluation and production of the communication satellite system (Project

ARIES) in full accordance with contractual provisions for product performance, delivery schedules, and program cost.

MANAGER—Reliability and Quality Assurance

Responsible to prepare a reliability and quality assurance plan and provide for its implementation, which will give maximum assurance of meeting the performance, life and reliability objectives of the ARIES system. The reliability and quality assurance plan will include an approved materials and parts list, design, fabrication, assembly and test standards, which make optimum use of past experience as applied to the objectives of the ARIES program. Operate a failure reporting and analysis system. Provide for inspection of the various manufacturing, assembly, and test functions to assure compliance to approved designs, procedures, etc., keeping a complete record of all operations performed on deliverable hardware, such that the quality is known and acceptable per contract requirements.

MANAGER—Cost and Contract Control

Responsible to prepare and maintain the project budget, PERT/cost, and measure the performance of all activities and work against the budget. Interpret the contractual requirements and ensure that program plans, schedules, and budgets conform to the contract and that all work planned is properly covered by the contract before any expenditure of contract funds is made. Continuously evaluate the performance of all activities against project budgets, initiating required action to solve discrepancies. Support marketing in the preparation, presentation, and negotiation of proposals for contract amendments. Prepare and submit through marketing all required reports. Maintain a central file for the project including technical, schedule, and cost data, as well as the official contract documentation.

MANAGER—Assembly and Test

Responsible for final assembly and acceptance testing of all deliverable equipment in accordance with approved drawings, assembly, and test procedures. Provide test and assembly areas, facilities, tooling, and instrumentation required to accomplish assembly and checkout of the satellite, satellite dispenser, special tooling, handling, and special checkout equipment required to support ARIES objectives. Direct the above activities in accordance with project schedules and budgets.

MANAGER—Systems Engineering

Responsible to interpret the overall ARIES program system performance requirements and translate those requirements into performance specifications, including environmental conditions, for all flight, ground handling, and test, subsystem and equipment. Plan, accomplish, and evaluate analyses and development test programs to determine optimum ways and means of accomplishing required system performance and to allow proper tradeoffs of performance between the various subsystems and equipments to assure meeting performance objectives including life and reliability. Develop detailed system and subsystem acceptance test specifications and procedures to assure conformance of all delivered hardware to performance requirements. Organize and conduct periodic technical audits of the ARIES program, staffing the audit board with qualified specialists in the area under review. Continuously evaluate the predicted and measured system performance against specification requirements, initiating action required to solve discrepancies. Direct the above activities in conformance with program schedule and cost limitations.

MANAGER—Project Engineering

Responsible to prepare the ARIES program plan identifying all work elements necessary to successfully develop the ARIES system including the plan of how the required work will be accomplished. Prepare and maintain a project schedule, PERT/time, and provide measurement of performance against the schedule. Provide project material control, making sure that material, tools, equipment, and test facilities in proper quantities are available as needed to support the planned development, test, manufacturing and acceptance programs. Establish and maintain procedures for interchange of information with subcontractors, definition of subcontractor work plans and budgets, and measurement of performance by the subcontractor against the established plans and budgets. Continuously evaluate the performance of all activities against schedule requirements, initiating required action to solve real or potential schedule discrepancies. Provide for support of all field activities with competent personnel, equipment, facilities, and spare parts. Direct the above activities in accordance with program schedule and cost limitations.

MANAGER—Equipment Engineering

Responsible to provide the detailed design of all ARIES program hardware for flight, ground handling, and test. This includes the preparation and issuance of drawings in accordance with the stage release system, component design and test specifications and procedures, assembly procedures, instruction books, etc. Plan, accomplish, and evaluate component development programs to assure meeting specified performance requirements and to demonstrate capability in a logical development process from initial performance analysis through breadboard assembly and test, prototype and certification model testing. Provide direction and guidance to manufacturing, quality control, and the assembly and test operations to assure best equipment quality of all stages of the design and development process. Direct the above activities in conformance with program schedule and cost limitations.

MANAGER—Resources Administration

Responsible to obtain, maintain and dispose of office space and facilities in accordance with project needs. Keep a complete inventory of equipment and facilities assigned, making sure that duplication is eliminated, available equipment from other programs is utilized to the maximum extent possible, and space, equipment, and facilities are disposed of when the need is satisfied. Maintain a complete personnel inventory and assist operation managers in obtaining the people required to achieve program objectives.

CONSULTING ENGINEER—Communications System Operations

Prepare studies of communications system capabilities, and control utilizing repeater satellites to be sure that the satellite equipment requirements and characteristics are consistent with overall system operations plans and procedures. Prepare system operational checkout plans that will provide maximum information on communications capabilities with minimum expenditure of time and money.

Table 3.   Spaceage, Inc. (A).

Function of the Marketing Department with Respect to its Relationship with the ARIES Project Group

The Marketing Department is:

1. To provide supplemental USAF (SAMSO)[a] contact and customer access to Aeronics Division management, as desired by the customer.
2. Responsible for proposal preparation for any new projects except those for which a project group has been established. In those cases, the project director is responsible for proposal preparation for follow-on contracts.
3. To maintain and establish department policies for sales and contract administration.
4. To provide source of qualified sales and contract administration personnel for transfer to and from project groups as required by project directors.
5. To provide continuous resource allocation recommendations for allocation of personnel and physical facilities among the project sections and other sections to the Aeronics Division Vice President.

Function of the Engineering Department with Respect to its Relationship with the ARIES Project Group

The Engineering Department is:

1. To establish systems engineering standards and practices for the Aeronics Division. Maintain a staff of qualified design engineers who remain abreast of and lead the state of the art.
2. To establish design engineering standards and practices for the Aeronics Division. Maintain a staff of qualified design engineers who remain abreast of and lead the state of the art.
3. A source of qualified systems engineering personnel for transfer to and from project groups as required by project directors.
4. A source of qualified design engineers for transfer to and from project groups as required by project directors.
5. To provide systems engineering assistance to the ARIES project in the form of parttime effort of specialists on internal contracts as required by project directors.
6. To provide design engineering assistance to Project ARIES in the form of parttime effort of specialists on internal contracts as required by the project director.
7. Administrative home of project managers for those smaller engineering projects which are established at the subdepartmental level. Example—reliability contracts.

Table 3.   Continued

Function of the Manufacturing Department with Respect to its Relationship with the ARIES Project Group

The Manufacturing Department is:

1. To establish and maintain manufacturing standards for the Aeronics Division.
2. A source of qualified manufacturing personnel for transfer to and from project groups as required by project directors.
3. To provide manufacturing assistance in the form of parttime effort of specialists and short-term use of special tools, on internal contracts, as required by project directors.

Function of the Quality Maintenance & Test Department with Respect to its Relationship with the ARIES Project Group

The Quality Maintenance & Test Department is:

1. To establish and maintain quality control and test reliability standards, including long-life reliability in space, for the Aeronics Division.
2. A source of qualified quality control, reliability, and test personnel for transfer to and from project groups as required by project directors.
3. Provide quality control and test assistance in the form of effort of parttime specialists, on internal contracts, as required by project directors.
4. Performs design reviews as required by project directors.

Function of the Finance Department with Respect to its Relationship with the ARIES Project Group

The Finance Department is:

1. To establish and maintain financial procedures and standards for the Aeronics Division.
2. Support project directors by loan of full-time or parttime assistance as required by project directors. When full-time support is required, these personnel are physically located within the projects.

---

[a] The Space and Missile Systems Organization (SAMSO) of the Air Force Systems Command (ASFC) was formed in July 1967, merging the earlier Space Systems and Ballistic Systems Divisions (SSD and BSD) of AFSC. The ARIES system program office (SPO) was located at SSD; however, the new organization—SAMSO—will be referred to in the Spaceage case series.

SITUATION 19:   CAPITAL INDUSTRIES

In the summer of 1976, Capital Industries undertook a material development program to see if a hard plastic bumper could be developed for medium-sized cars. By January 1977 Project Bumper, as it was called by management, had developed a material that endured all preliminary laboratory testing.

One more step was required before full-scale laboratory testing: a three-dimensional stress analysis on bumper impact collisions. The decision to perform the stress analysis was the result of a concern on the behalf of the technical community that the bumper might not perform correctly under certain conditions. The cost of the analysis would require corporate funding over and above the original estimates. Because the current costs were identical to what was budgeted, the additional funding was a necessity.

Frank Allen, the project engineer in the Bumper Project office, was assigned control of the stress analysis. Frank met with the functional manager of the engineering analysis section as to the assignment of personnel to the task.

Functional Manager: "I'm going to assign Paul Troy to this project. He's a new man with a Ph.D. in structural analysis. I'm sure he'll do well."

Frank Allen: "This is a priority project. We need seasoned veterans, not new people, whether they have Ph.D.s or not. Why not use some other project as a testing ground for your new employee?"

Functional Manager: "You project people must accept part of the responsibility for on-the-job training. I might agree with you if we were talking about blue collar workers on an assembly line. But this is a college graduate, coming to us with good technical background."

Frank Allen: "He may have a good background, but he has no experience. He needs supervision. This is a one-man task. The responsibility will be yours if he fouls up.

Functional Manager: "I've already given him our book for cost estimates. I'm sure he'll do fine. I'll keep in close communication with him during the project."

Frank Allen met with Paul Troy to get an estimate for the job.

Paul Troy: "I estimate that 800 hours will be required."

Frank Allen: "Your estimate seems low. Most three-dimensional analyses require at least 1000 hours. Why is your number so low?"

Paul Troy: "Three-dimensional analysis? I thought that it would be a two-dimensional analysis. But no difference; the procedures are the same. I can handle it."

Frank Allen: "OK, I'll give you 1100 hours. But if you overrun it, we'll both be sorry."

Frank Allen followed the project closely. By the time the costs were 50 percent completed, performance was only 40 percent. A cost overrun seemed inevitable. The functional manager still asserted that he was tracking the job and that the difficulties were a result of the new material properties. His section had never worked with materials like these before.

Six months later Troy announced that the work would be completed in one week, two months later than planned. The two-month delay caused major problems in facility and equipment utilization. Project Bumper was still paying for employees who were waiting to begin full-scale testing.

On Monday mornings, the project office would receive the weekly labor monitor report for the previous week. This week the report indicated that the publications and graphic arts department had spent over 200 man-hours (last week) in preparation of the final report. Frank Allen was furious. He called a meeting with Paul Troy and the functional manager.

Frank Allen: "Who told you to prepare a formal report? All we wanted was a go-or-no-go decision as to structural failure."

Paul Troy: "I don't turn in any work unless it's professional. This report will be documented as a masterpiece."

Frank Allen: "Your 50 percent cost overrun will also be a masterpiece. I guess your estimating was a little off!"

Paul Troy: "Well, this was the first time that I had performed a three-dimensional stress analysis. And what's the big deal? I got the job done, didn't I?"

SITUATION 20: FACILITIES SCHEDULING AT MAYER MANUFACTURING

Eddie Turner was elated at the good news that he was being promoted to section supervisor in charge of scheduling all activities in the new engineering research laboratory. The new laboratory was a necessity for Mayer Manufacturing. The engineering, manufacturing, and quality control directorates were all in desperate need of a new testing facility. Upper-level management felt that this new facility would alleviate many of the problems that previously existed.

The new organizational structure (shown in Figure 3) required a change in policy over use of the laboratory. The new section supervisor, upon approval from his department manager, would have full authority for establishing priorities for the use of

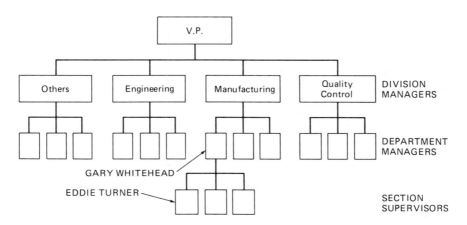

Figure 3. Mayer Manufacturing Organizational Structure.

the new facility. The new policy change was a necessity, because upper-level management felt there would be inevitable conflict among manufacturing, engineering and quality control.

After one month of operations, Eddie Turner was finding his job impossible. Eddie had a meeting with Gary Whitehead, his department manager.

Eddie: "I'm having a hell of a time trying to satisfy all the department managers. If I give engineering prime-time use of the facility, then quality control and manufacturing say I'm playing favorites. Imagine that! Even my own people say that I'm playing favorites with other directorates. I just can't satisfy everyone."

Gary: "Well, Eddie, you know that this problem comes with the job. You'll get the job done."

Eddie: "The problem is that I'm a section supervisor and have to work with department managers. These department managers look down on me as if I were their servant. If I were a department manager, then they'd show me some respect. What I'm really trying to say is that I would like you to send out the weekly memos to these department managers telling them of the new priorities. They wouldn't argue with you as they do with me. I can supply you with all the necessary information. All you'll have to do is to sign your name."

Gary: "Determining the priorities and scheduling the facilities is your job, not mine. This is a new position and I want you to handle it. I know you can because I selected you. I do not intend to interfere."

During the next two weeks, the conflicts grew progressively worse. Eddie felt unable to cope with the situation by himself. The department managers did not respect his authority delegated to him by his superiors. For the next two weeks, Eddie sent memos to Gary in the early part of the week asking whether or not Gary agreed with the priority list. There was no response to the two memos. Eddie then met with Gary to discuss the deteriorating situation.

Eddie: "Gary, I've sent you two memos to see if I'm doing anything wrong in establishing the weekly priorities and schedules. Did you get my memos?"

Gary: "Yes, I received your memos. But as I told you before, I have enough problems to worry about without doing your job for you. If you can't handle the work let me know and I'll find someone who can."

Eddie returned to his desk and contemplated his situation. Finally, he made a decision. Next week he was going to put a signature block under his for Gary to sign, with carbon copies for all division managers. "Now, let's see what happens," remarked Eddie.

SITUATION 21:   SMALL-PROJECT COST-ESTIMATING AT PERCY COMPANY

Paul graduated from college in June 1970 with a degree in industrial engineering. He accepted a job as a manufacturing engineer in the Manufacturing Division of Percy Company. His prime responsibility was performing estimates for the Manufacturing Division. Each estimate was then given to the appropriate project office for consideration. The estimation procedure history had shown the estimates to be valid.

In 1975, Paul was promoted to project engineer. His prime responsibility was the coordination of all estimates for work to be completed by all the divisions. For one full year Paul went by the book and did not do any estimating except for project office personnel manpower. After all, he was now in the Project Management Division, which contained job descriptions including such words as "coordinating and integrating."

In 1976 Paul was transferred to small-program project management. This was a new organization designed to perform low-cost projects. The problem was that these projects could not withstand the expenses needed for formal divisional cost estimates. For five projects, Paul's estimates were "right on the money." But the sixth project incurred a cost overrun of $20,000 in the Manufacturing Division.

In November, 1977, a meeting was called to resolve the question of "Why did the overrun occur?" The attendees included the general manager, all division managers and directors, the project manager, and Paul. Paul now began to worry about what he should say in his defense.

SITUATION 22:   THE MARKETING GROUP

Joe Walton wasn't sure if he would really like his new position of product manager. His job description stated that he would work with R&D in the development stages of the product and then he would have to "pick up the ball and run with it" through marketing, sales, advertising, finance, and manufacturing. The most difficult part of the job appeared to be the necessity for working with the diverse functional groups, none of which understood the total picture.

Joe would have to develop the "big picture" by obtaining reasonable estimates from the line groups and then integrating all the information into one viable plan. The functional group had the reputation of giving poor estimates and overinflating the time and manpower requirements so that there would be a sufficient cushion in case something went wrong. Joe was a little nervous as to how the line managers would react if he had to take the "fat" out of their estimates.

Joe was informed that engineering next month would be completing the R&D phase of a new product, and that the product would be ready for market introduction within the next 60 days. The vice-president for marketing then gave Joe the following instructions:

Joe, I'm going to give you a little bit of help on this project. Here is a checklist that includes the major items needed for new product introduction (see Table 4). I want you to determine, by yourself, the time needed for each element. Then, develop the work breakdown structure, the logic or arrow diagram, and the PERT/CPM. After you have identified the critical path, come on in and see me, and we'll discuss your major milestones, the end date, and how to convince line managers that your estimates are correct. Try to "marry" the work breakdown structure to the arrow diagram.

Table 4.

• Production layout	• Review plant costs
• Market testing	• Select distributors
• Analyze selling cost	• Layout artwork
• Analyze customer reaction	• Approve artwork
• Storage and shipping costs	• Introduce at trade show
• Select salesmen	• Distribute to salesmen
• Train salesmen	• Establish billing procedure
• Train distributors	• Establish credit procedure
• Literature to salesmen	• Revise cost of production
• Literature to distributors	• Revise selling cost
• Print literature	• Approvals[a]
• Sales promotion	• Review meetings[a]
• Sales manual	• Final specifications
• Trade advertising	• Material requisitions

[a] Approvals and review meetings can appear several times.

SITUATION 23: ESTABLISHING PLANNING PRIORITIES

The director of project management has just called you into his office and informed you that you are the project manager on a top-priority project requested by corporate headquarters. The director hands you two sheets of paper. On the first sheet, there is a brief description of the corporate request, together with a not-to-exceed funding limitation. On the second page, you find a list containing the names of four project office individuals the director has personally picked to make up your project office. You may negotiate for the functional employees of your choice with the functional managers in order to complete the project team.

The director informs you that he knows very little about the project except that it is a top-priority effort for corporate and that the other four project office members will be here in about 20 minutes to meet you and hear your first briefing on the project.

Despite your lack of information regarding the project, you must design a preliminary package of logical steps to manage the project. In Table 5 you will find a list of 26 activities for managing the project. Without discussing it with anyone, prioritize

Table 5.   Project Management Priority List.

Activity	Description	COLUMN 1: YOUR SEQUENCE	COLUMN 2: GROUP SEQUENCE	COLUMN 3: EXPERT'S SEQUENCE	COLUMN 4: DIFFERENCE BETWEEN 1&3	COLUMN 5: DIFFERENCE BETWEEN 2 & 3
1.	Develop linear responsibility chart					
2.	Negotiate for qualified functional personnel					
3.	Develop specifications					
4.	Determine means for measuring progress					
5.	Prepare final report					
6.	Authorize departments to begin work					
7.	Develop work breakdown structure					
8.	Close out functional work orders					
9.	Develop scope statement and set objectives,					
10.	Develop gross schedule					
11.	Develop priorities for each project element					
12.	Develop alternative courses of action					
13.	Develop PERT network					
14.	Develop detailed schedules					
15.	Establish functional personnel qualifications					
16.	Coordinate on-going activities					
17.	Determine resource requirements					
18.	Measure progress					

Table 5.   (Cont.)

Activity	Description	COLUMN 1: YOUR SEQUENCE	COLUMN 2: GROUP SEQUENCE	COLUMN 3: EXPERT'S SEQUENCE	COLUMN 4: DIFFERENCE BETWEEN 1 & 3	COLUMN 5: DIFFERENCE BETWEEN 2 & 3
19.	Decide upon basic course of action					
20.	Establish costs for each WBS element					
21.	Review WBS costs with each functional manager					
22.	Establish project plan					
23.	Establish cost variances for base case elements					
24.	Price out WBS					
25.	Establish logic network with check points					
26.	Review "base case" costs with director					
	TOTAL					

the list according to what you feel the proper sequence should be. Then, meet your team and determine the team's order.

SITUATION 24:   THE TWO-BOSS PROBLEM

On May 15, 1977 Brian Richards was assigned full time to Project Turnbolt by Fred Taylor, manager of the Thermodynamics Department. All work went smoothly for four and one-half of the five months necessary to complete this effort. During this period of successful performance, Brian Richards had good working relations with Edward Compton, the Turnbolt project engineer, and Fred Taylor.

Fred treated Brian as a Theory Y employee. Once a week Fred and Brian would chat about the status of Brian's work. Fred would always conclude their brief meeting with, "You're doing a fine job, Brian. Keep it up. Do anything you have to do to finish the project."

During the last month of the project Brian began receiving conflicting requests from the project office and the department manager as to the preparation of the final report. Compton told Brian Richards that the final report was to be assembled in viewgraph format (i.e., bullet charts) for presentation to the customer at the next technical interchange meeting. The project did not have the funding necessary for a comprehensive engineering report.

The Theromodynamics Department, on the other hand, had a policy that all engineering work done on new projects would be documented in a full and comprehensive report. This new policy was implemented about one year ago when Fred Taylor became department manager. The scuttlebutt had it that Fred wanted formal reports so that he could put his name on them and either publish or present them at technical meetings. All work performed in the Thermodynamics Department required Taylor's signature before it could be released to the project office as an official company position. Upper-level management did not want its people to publish and therefore did not maintain a large editorial or graphic arts department. Personnel desiring to publish had to get the department manager's approval and, upon approval, had to prepare the entire report themselves, without any "overhead" help. Since Taylor had taken over the reins as department head, he had presented three papers at technical meetings.

A meeting was held between Brian Richards, Fred Taylor, and Edward Compton.

Edward Compton: "I don't understand why we have a problem? All the project office wants is a simple summary of the results. Why should we have to pay for a report we don't want or need?"

Fred Taylor: "We have professional standards in this department. All work that goes out must be fully documented for future use. I purposely require that my signature be attached to all communications leaving this department. This way we obtain uniformity and standardization.

"You project people must understand that, although you can institute your own project policies and procedures within the constraints and limitations of company policies and procedures, we department personnel also have standards. Your work must be prepared within our standards and specifications."

Edward Compton: "The project office controls the purse strings. We [the project office] specified that only a survey report was necessary. Furthermore, if you want a more comprehensive report, then you had best do it on your own overhead account. The project office isn't going to foot the bill for your publications."

Fred Taylor: "The customary procedure is to specify in the program plan the type of report requested from the departments. Inasmuch as your program plan does not specify this, I used my own discretion as to what I thought you meant."

Edward Compton: "But I told Brian Richards what type of report I wanted. Didn't he tell you?"

Fred Taylor: "I guess I interpreted the request a little differently than you had intended. Perhaps we should establish a new policy that all program plans must specify reporting requirements. This would alleviate some of the misunderstandings, especially since my department has several projects going on at one time. In addition, I am going to establish a policy for my department that all requests for interim, status, or final reports be given to me directly. I'll take personal charge of all reports."

Edward Compton: "That's fine with me! And for your first request I'm giving you an order that I want a survey report, not a detailed effort."

Brian Richards: "Well, since the meeting is over, I guess I'll return to my office (and begin updating my résumé just in case)."

SITUATION 25: DEVELOPMENT OF A WORK BREAKDOWN STRUCTURE[1]

The Situation

There is no mystery about a WBS—people do it all the time!

Your Task

Assume you are going to take your family or some friends on a camping trip. Most of the things you do for this trip are first organized in your head. However, you feel the need to develop a WBS for this camping trip. Describe the uses to which this WBS can be put.

As a starter the following second-level work packages are indicated to get you into a frame of mind to do the rest of the work breakdown structuring for this trip:

- systems engineering
- meals
- car transportation
- equipment and clothing

Using these second-level work packages as a starter, develop the WBS down at least to the fourth level.

Here are some of the characteristics of a WBS:

1. The WBS divides the overall project into elements that represent assignable work units.
2. An individual is normally assigned responsibility to do the specialized work necessary to accomplish the work package.
3. Someone (a "work package manager") must be held accountable for each work package.
4. The work package manager is responsible for the specific objective, which should

---

[1] Paraphrased from Bertram N. Abramson and Robert D. Kennedy, *Managing Small Projects,* TRW Systems Group, Inc., 35–4961 (IM), July 1969.

be measurable; detailed task descriptions; specifications; scheduled task milestones; and a time-phased budget in dollars and manpower.

What other characteristics of a WBS can be identified?

An Additional Task

After you have developed the WBS for the camping trip, use it to construct a flow chart of the first day of the camping trip.

SITUATION 26: MANAGING THE PROJECT MANAGER'S TIME

The Situation

Time is one of the most valuable and scarcest resources of the project manager. An ideal project manager, who has ideal people on the project team, will probably have lots of time to sit back and reflect on how well the project is being managed. But most project managers are busy—sometimes frantically busy—trying to do all that has to be done.

Most project managers are imperfect, work with an imperfect team, have to work with an imperfect customer, and work for an imperfect management group. Such project managers are usually very busy trying to keep everything working and everyone happy. How can such project managers better manage their time?

A good way to start is to reach an understanding of how your time as a project manager can best be spent. For example, you might plan to allocate your time by working on project items as follows:[1]

1. A work—those items you do that will have a large influence on your project
2. B work—those items that have an effect proportional to the time they took
3. C work—those items that have little effect on the completion of the project on time and within budget

What's important is to be able to assess what's happening to your time as you work on the project. What are the factors that affect your time? Graphically speaking, A, B, and C work might be portrayed as in Figure 4.

Indicated below are some examples of typical project management work:

- Prepare project plan.
- Attend all project meetings to which you are invited.
- Hold review meetings in each work package.
- Build and maintain customer relations.
- Review text of project reports for errors.

---

[1] Paraphrased from Bertram N. Abramson and Robert D. Kennedy, *Managing Small Projects*, TRW Systems Group, Inc., 35-4961 (Im), July 1969.

- Respond to each crisis however small.
- Interview and select key team members.
- Attend customer review meetings.
- Evaluate each engineering change proposal.
- Check technical results.
- Act as consultant to other project managers in the company.
- Review major problems.
- Review significant results.
- Check contract for effect of significant project changes.
- Coordinate project-functional interfaces.
- Review *all* project correspondence.
- Become involved in detailed engineering problems.
- Participate in guided tours for important visitors who are not specifically interested in your project.
- Review first to fifth level work breakdown structure.
- Review work package schedule and costs at all levels.
- Set up project filing system.
- Write details of project plan.
- Attend "for info only" meetings.
- Attend project management seminar.
- Develop project planning and control system.
- Issue detailed instructions to each project team member.

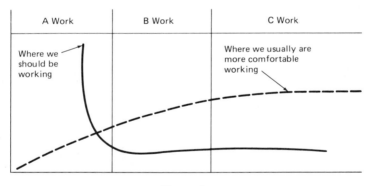

Figure 4.

Your Assignment

1. Put each of the above items of work in the appropriate category. Considering a typical project, have any items of A, B, or C work been left out?

2. Prepare an outline of your philosophy of how to organize and manage your time as a project manager. Develop a strategy of how this philosophy could be shared with the members of your project team.

Section VII
Permanent/International
Matrix Management.

The terms *matrix management* and *matrix organization* have come to be used to describe both project-driven, two-dimensional organizations and organizations that have "permanent" matrix forms. Although the project-driven matrix has been the prime focus in this casebook thus far, we wrap up the book with illustrations of "permanent" matrix forms. Permanent matrix forms include both the *product team* and the *international* matrix.

Product Team Management

Product team management is a generic phrase that describes a relatively permanent product-functional matrix in which business-results managers overlay a functional resource organization. A team of people is organized and charged with managing a product or product line serving specific market segments. Other names used to describe this form include *business boards, business committees,* and *business heads.*

A few examples will help to explain this kind of matrix.

A chemical company with sales of $2.3 billion had 24,000 employees in 26 countries. The company was organized into seven operating groups, each of which functioned as a separate company. But corporate controls were ineffective. Corporate management found that it lacked visibility in reviewing major projects, strategic programs, and other investment issues. Major expenditures contemplated by the group profit center managers were rarely challenged. To bring corporate visibility to the decentralized operations, several management improvements were undertaken:

---

[1] Portions of this section have been paraphrased from David I. Cleland and William R. King, *Systems Analysis and Project Management,* 3rd edition, McGraw-Hill Book Co., New York, 1983, pp. 71–72, and from the article, "Matrix Management: A Kaleidoscope of Organizational Systems," by David I. Cleland, published in *Management Review,* December 1981, pp. 48–56. Reproduced with permission.

1. A financial manager was placed at each plant and was assigned to report to both the plant manager and to the corporate controller—a form of matrix management.

2. A computer terminal, placed near the chief executive's office, gave daily, monthly, and quarterly sales data.

3. Sixteen executives were identified as business heads, (project team managers), each with responsibility for a group of products, to include product planning, investment, and product sourcing. These executives had no staffs of their own. They functioned as the eyes, ears, and legs of the chief operating officer and reported directly to him. Profit/loss responsibility rested with the business heads; functional managers retained cost center responsibility and provided services and technical support to the business heads.

The use of business head-functional support at this company has provided greater flexibility in establishing products or discontinuing them. Strategic programs are given a more thorough corporate review; senior management has been freed from involvement in short-range operations that had taken up much of the CEO's time. Truly strategic issues are resolved from a corporate portfolio business viewpoint.

The International Matrix

In the mid-1970s Chase Manhattan's corporate bank reshaped itself from a geographic form of organization into one that assembled officers into teams, each team organized to focus on a single industry, such as drugs or electronics. Chase at present is steadily moving toward a permanent/international matrix form of organization. According to *Fortune:*

> A short time ago, an organization chart of the bank's international department would have shown it almost entirely divided along geographical lines, with only merchant banking roped off and functioning more or less worldwide. Today the bank has several other cross-border operations, to which it may add still more, that give its structure an unmistakable matrix look: international institutions (which primarily means correspondent banks), export and trade financing, and private banking (for well-heeled individuals).[2]

Such structures are perhaps most visible in multinational corporations.

Multinational companies are usually organized to do business globally on a matrix system of management. In these companies, responsibility for strategic and key operating activities is divided among organizational elements as follows:

---

[2] "It's a Stronger Bank that David Rockefeller is Passing to his Successor," *Fortune,* January 14, 1980, p. 44.

Product.   Responsibility concentrated in produce or product line management with world wide perspective

Geography.   Responsibility concentrated within a specific territory, such as a country

Function.   Responsibility concentrated in an organization's functional specialty, such as finance, production, marketing, or research and development

In the international company, there are usually two coordinated avenues of strategic planning: product and geography. Such decisions are shared; accountability for results is also shared in terms of product and geographic profitability through profit centers. Financial visibility by product, function, and geography is the norm in the multinational company.

A basic factor in international management that is significantly affected by matrix management is the traditional concept of the profit center, with its delegation of authority to one manager who is held responsible for producing profitable results. To him, everything counts at the profit center level, everything is measured there, and people are rewarded accordingly. Certain key decisions, such as product pricing, product sourcing, product discrimination, human resources, facility management, and cash management, are traditionally considered the profit center manager's prerogative.

But in international matrix management, the profit center manager may share key decision making with others. Some managers, accustomed to making these decisions on their own, find sharing decision making with some other manager outside the parent hierarchy can be a culture shock. For example, in product pricing in the international market, the profit center manager will find it necessary to work with an in-country manager to establish price. Product sourcing decisions may be made by senior marketing executives at corporate headquarters, rather than by profit center manager. In practice, decision authority should be complementary. If the manager cannot reach agreement on these decisions, it may be necessary to refer the conflict to a common line supervisor for resolution.

Clearly, all this will not just happen in an organization by having someone order it into being. Such an approach requires day-to-day monitoring and new information and reporting methods. Communication and negotiating skills are required to operate successfully in any matrix management system.

Permanent/international matrix considerations are provided in the cases and situations that follow.

RELEVANT BIBLIOGRAPHY

Bartlett, Christopher A. "How Multinational Organizations Evolve." *The Journal of Business Strategy,* Fall 1983.

————. "MNCs: Get Off the Reorganization Merry-Go-Round." *Harvard Business Review,* March–April 1983, pp. 138–146.

Buss, Martin D. J. "Managing International Information Systems." *Harvard Business Review,* September–October 1982, pp. 153–162.

Cathey, Paul. "Matrix Managing is the Way to Go for International Control." *Iron Age,* January 22, 1982, pp. 3–5.

Cleland, David I. "Matrix Management (Part II): A Kaleidoscope of Organizational Systems." *Management Review,* December 1982, pp. 48–56.

"Corporate Culture." *Business Week,* October 27, 1980.

Davidson, William H., and Philippe Haspeslagh. "Shaping a Global Product Organization." *Harvard Business Review,* July–August 1982, pp. 125–132.

Davis, Stanley M. "Trends in the Organization of Multinational Corporations." *Columbia Journal of World Business,* Summer, 1976, pp. 59–71.

Doz, Yves L., and C. K. Prahalad. "Headquarters Influence and Strategic Control in MNCs." *Sloan Management Review,* Fall 1981, pp. 15–29.

Drake, Rodman L., and Lee M. Caudill. "Management of the Large Multinational: Trends and Future Challenges." *Business Horizons,* vol. 24, no. 3, May–June, 1981.

Eldin, Hamed K., and Ivar Avots. "Guidelines for Successful Management of Projects in the Middle East: The Client Point of View." *1978 Proceedings of the Project Management Institute, 10th Annual Symposium,* October 8–11, 1978, Los Angeles.

"Format Fears at Philips." *Management Today,* August 1978.

Harris, D. George, "How National Cultures Shape Management Styles." *Management Review,* July 1982, pp. 58–61.

Hout, Thomas, Michael E. Porter, and Eileen Rudden. "How Global Companies Win Out." *Harvard Business Review,* September–October 1982, pp. 98–108.

"How a New Chief is Turning Interbank Inside Out." *Business Week,* July 14, 1980, pp. 109, 111.

Hunsicker, J. Quincy. "The Matrix in Retreat." *Financial Times,* October 25, 1982.

"International Business." *Business Week,* September 8, 1980.

Janger, Allen R. *Organization of International Joint Ventures.* Conference Board Report no. 787, The Conference Board, Inc., New York, 1980, p. 14.

Killing, J. Peter. "How to Make a Global Joint Venture Work." *Harvard Business Review,* May–June 1982, pp. 120–127.

Levitt, Theodore. "Globalization of Markets." *Harvard Business Review,* May–June 1983, pp. 92–102.

Menzies, Hugh D. "Westinghouse Takes Aim at the World." *Fortune,* January 14, 1980.

"Philips—An Electronics Giant Rearms to Fight Japan." *Business Week,* March 30, 1981, pp. 86–97.

Prahalad, C. K. "Strategic Choices in Diversified MNCs." *Harvard Business Review,* July–August 1976, p. 72.

Seneker, Harold. "Mr. Nice Guy He Wasn't." *Forbes,* March 31, 1980.

CASE STUDY 35:   THE TRANSNATIONAL CORPORATION[1]

The Situation[2]

The Transnational Corporation realigned its strategy to accommodate an increased effort in its international markets. This realignment was undertaken in part to make the most of emerging project opportunities in these international markets. For many years this corporation had been organized on a decentralized product structure, with basic profit center responsibility resting at the departmental level. General managers, and key project managers, were rewarded on an individual incentive compensation system based on financial performance of their organization. Everything counted at the profit center, everything was measured there—and key strategic and operational decisions were made by the profit center manager with the counsel of a functional staff.

The communication challenge faced by the executives of this corporation centered on how to develop in key managerial personnel the knowledge, skills, and attitudes necessary to successfully manage an international matrix management system. Three key considerations were critical to the success of matrix management in this corporation: first, a dedication on the part of the key managers to make the matrix management system work; second, the design of management processes and procedures to bring about a sharing of decisions, accountability, and financial rewards; and third, basic cultural changes—attitudinal changes—supportive of "participative management," "consensus decision making," "team management," and such factors that emphasized team effort in the design and implementation of organizational strategies in a global market.

The corporation had a long history of profit center managers having equal authority and responsibility. In strategic matters these profit center managers established objectives, goals, and strategies. Product planning was carried out at the profit center level to include product technology, pricing, sourcing, configuration, and market support. Human resources, cash management, and investments also came under the profit center manager's jurisdiction. In short, these profit center managers ruled their fiefdoms where they called the strategic and operational moves. The general managers of the corporation had all been appointed because of their abilities as profit center managers.

It was within this cultural ambience that a decision was made to reorganize into an international matrix management system. Four basic organizational designs were incorporated into this matrix management system: *functions, products, geography, and projects.* The already existing functional and product areas were augmented by geographic and project organizations. Project managers were appointed to manage projects in foreign locations; these projects entailed the management of resources

---

[1] The name of the corporation has been changed at the request of the corporation president.
[2] Certain material in this case has been paraphrased from "The Role of Communications in Effecting Change to a Matrix Management System," by David I. Cleland, in a paper presented at PMI International meeting, Project Management Institute 1980 Proceedings, Phoenix, Arizona. Used by permission.

across product divisions, functions, and geographic structures. The philosophical cornerstones of this international matrix management system were:

- Shared decision making
- Shared accountability
- Shared financial results
- The fundamental concept that the "country" would be the primary building block of the international organization

A description of these cornerstones is rather simple compared with the awesome task of getting key people committed, intellectually and emotionally, to support the matrix management system—and this is where communication came into play. What follows is a description of the process of organizational change and communication used to implement a matrix management system in the transnational corporation.

The Organizational Change Process

Figure 1 depicts the strategic change process used as a framework to effect and communicate change in this corporation to an international matrix management system.

Six phases were identified in this change process. The change was designed to be evolutionary in nature, to be accomplished over two to three years, with maximum participation on the part of the managers responsible for the implementation of the change. A key concern of the chief operating officer was how to design and implement the change, keeping in mind the necessity for an ongoing dialogue on why the change was needed and how it was to be effected.

In Phase 1 the chief operating officer, working with his staff, developed a tentative statement of required organizational change to implement an international matrix management system. After this statement was developed, a task force was appointed to develop the data bases to support the organizational change (Phase 2). This task force, composed of approximately 45 people, represented different disciplines and different organizational levels. Over 300 key people were interviewed by the task force to develop data bases on everything from the strengths and weaknesses of the corporation in its international business to a comprehensive analysis of the market opportunities and the nature and intensity of the competition (Phase 3).

Several key weaknesses in the existing organizational approach came to light during this phase:

- There was no effective organizational mechanism to pull together a team from several profit centers to bid on large projects in the international market.
- Several product divisions were attempting to sell to the same overseas customers without any corporate coordination that would present a common market position.
- An effective system for evaluating competitors' weaknesses, strengths, and probable strategies did not exist.

- The strong prerogatives of the profit center manager in product planning—configuration, sourcing, pricing, and support services—often ignored key issues in geographic factors affecting market demand.
- Competitors were outperforming the corporation in virtually all markets.

In Phase 4, the task force assembled a mix of strategic alternatives for international matrix management, including an identification of alternative organizational approaches centered on various models of matrix management systems.

Phase 5 dealt with the strategic decision process of selecting organizational objectives, goals, and strategies for the matrix international organization. An international matrix organization was created on parity with the existing product-group structure. The matrix alignment of the international organization vis-à-vis the group-product structure is depicted in Figure 2. The sharing context implied in Figure 2 centered on the interfaces between product and geographic managers coming to focus in each country through the in-country subsidiary manager or project manager.

In Phase 6, the implementation strategies were designed, and implementation was started. Figure 3 depicts this process. A first step was the reoganization of the corpora-

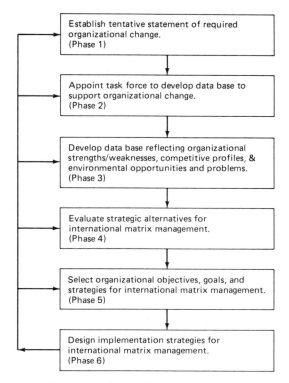

Figure 1.   Strategic Change Process.

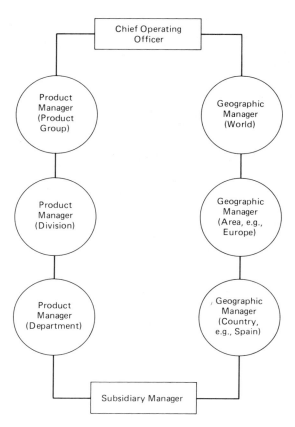

Figure 2. International Matrix Organization, Transnational Organization.

tion into a matrix structure to be complemented by support systems—information, accounting, personnel evaluation, budget, and so on. In Step 2, a consultant was engaged to conduct in-depth interviews with 30 key managers to gain their perceptions of some of the relevant problems/opportunities to be encountered in implementing matrix management in the corporation. These interviews were primarily nondirective in nature, conducted in the context of diplomatic immunity, and resulted in the development of a taxonomy of key manager perceptions about matrix management. The taxonomy developed in Step 3 consisted of the following:

- Corporate-expected cultural changes
- Degree of knowledge—matrix management
- Required executive attitude change
- Change required—incentive systems
- Strategic planning in the matrix context
- Education required in matrix management

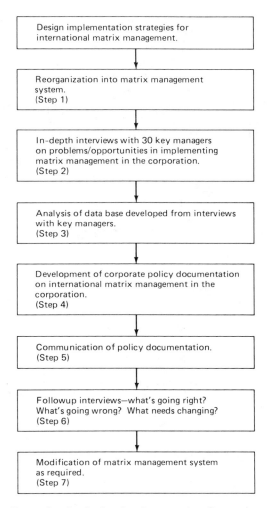

Figure 3. Designing Implementation Strategies.

- What not to do in the educational effort
- Current executive experience in matrix management
- Expected modus operandi—matrix management
- Role of the new international organization
- Degree of commitment to new international matrix management system

The interviews provided a basis for the continued development of an international matrix management system that would be acceptable to those people who had to grapple with the real-time elements of making it work. An evolutionary approach was selected to implement the system, starting first with the geographic area where the corporation had the most successful experience in the international marketplace.

In Step 4, corporate policy documentation was developed to portray the expected authority/responsibility/accountability of patterns of the matrix management system. This policy documentation was disseminated through corporate seminars and discussion groups in Step 5. This dissemination was accomplished in parallel with formal matrix management systems educational programs that emphasized the theoretical aspects of how matrix management should be done by drawing on the best book and periodical literature available. The educational programs consisted of three-day training sessions for all key managers in the corporation. The tutorial strategy for the training sessions involved a bare minimum of lectures, depending instead on small five- to six-person discussion groups exploring the meaning of matrix management. Actual existing and potential matrix management situations were drawn from corporate experience and written up to use in the small group sessions. An important output of the small group discussions was a series of recommendations on how certain aspects of matrix management could be implemented in the corporation. Some examples of these included:

- Project management organizational design in the international context
- How to define an international project
- Identification of corporate policy needs to implement matrix management
- Development of a work breakdown structure for an international project
- How to use a linear responsibility chart to identify authority/responsibility/accountability patterns in matrix management
- Project manager candidate specifications
- How to select an international project manager
- Some key problems/opportunities to be considered in making the international matrix system work

The educational program, combined with the use of organizational examples, provided an effective means for communicating corporate policy on how the new matrix management system was expected to operate. All the key executives, including general managers and key functional and matrix managers, became involved at some point in the design and implementation of the new system. Each person so involved had ample opportunity to influence—to assist in making the new management system work. Many long days, weeks, and months were spent in making sure that corporate purposes and intents were effectively communicated throughout the corporate community. Key executives became zealous missionaries to carry the gospel worldwide on the new corporate matrix management system.

Step 6 was accomplished by a consultant who conducted followup interviews with key people to get answers to such questions as: What's going right? What's going wrong? What needs to be changed? These interviews helped to identify and attack some of the problems that were impeding the development of the system. There were many problems identified and much "fine-tuning" had to be done to keep the system evolving, as depicted in Step 7 in Figure 3.

Several key characteristics of this corporation's approach facilitated the effective conversion to a matrix model of management. The common denominator of the organizational change was the candid and open communication that pervaded the organization from the top down during the period the change was underway. The openness of the organization was evident to people from the outside. Participative management, consensus decision making, the use of teams of executives, and the assistance of professionals to help in bringing about the change, all served to typify a cultural ambience of free and open communication in seeking, and finding, new organizational strategies.

Your Task

The experience of designing and developing an international matrix management system for the Transnational Corporation posed a real challenge for all concerned. Evaluate the approach taken by the senior executives of this corporation. Your evaluation should include, but not be restricted to, the following types of issues:

1. Assessment of the four basic organizational designs used as benchmarks for the international matrix organizational approach.
2. Gaining of an appreciation of how the profit-center decentralized organizational model would be affected by a realignment to the matrix design.
3. The value of using a task force in the company to evaluate the company's strengths and weaknesses in competing in a global marketplace.
4. The suitability of the "strategic change process" depicted in Figure 1.
5. The compatibility of the parallel product-group and geographic structures portrayed in Figure 2. In particular how does this structure relate to the following management concepts:
   a. unity of command
   b. parity of authority and responsibility
   c. "structure follows strategy"
6. What might have been done differently in the implementation process for the international matrix management system of the Transnational Corporation?

CASE STUDY 36: BOLIVIA RURAL ELECTRIFICATION: A CASE STUDY IN ORGANIZATIONAL STRUCTURE[1]

Introduction

The concept of rural electrification is nothing new. Its roots in the United States date back to the early 1930s. The procedures, both technical and administrative, have been developed and refined over the decades and are well known.

However, a rural electrification project can become a complex organizational prob-

---

[1] By David K. Johnson, Project Manager, International Division, Stanley Consultants, Inc., Muscatine, Iowa. From *Realities in Project Management,* Proceedings of the 1977 Project Management Institute International Seminar/Symposium. Used by permission.

lem when it takes place in a multiorganizational or multinational setting. This paper describes a project that is currently taking place in such a setting and examines the organizational structure developed to manage the project through the design and construction stages.

The paper is intended to be read as a case study. It is not the result of an exhaustive research effort, nor is the organizational structure described necessarily recommended for other situations. The organizational structure of this project is simply a real-world reaction to a real-world problem.

Project Description

The project consists of the first two phases of a nationwide rural electrification program currently underway in the Republic of Bolivia. The project, which has an estimated overall cost of $25 million, involves approximately 2,100 kilometers of primary distribution line (both 24.9 kilovolt and 10 kilovolt), 1,600 kilometers of secondary distribution line, 14 substations and switching stations, 41,000 customer services, and one office building.

The project was launched with feasibility studies jointly conducted by Bolivian authorities and the United States Agency for International Development. These studies identified several feasible rural electrification project areas, which, in turn, led to two separate loan agreements from the United States government to the government of the Republic of Bolivia (see figure 4). For both loans, the Bolivia Mission of the U.S. Agency for International Development (AID) is acting as the loan administrator on behalf of the United States government. The National Electricity Company (Empresa Nacional de Electricidad—ENDE) is acting as the loan administrator on behalf of the Government of Bolivia.

The National Electricity Company, ENDE, subloaned project funds to one distribution company and one distribution cooperative on the first loan (see Figure 5). The distribution entities, Cochabamba Electric Light and Power Company (ELFEC) and the Rural Electrification Cooperative of Santa Cruz (CRE), contracted for consulting engineering and construction management services for major equipment, hardware, miscellaneous materials, and construction services.

On the second loan, ENDE subloaned project funds to one government institute for rural electrification, two distribution companies, and one distribution cooperative (see Figure 6). The National Institute for Rural Electrification (INER) contracted for consulting engineering services and construction management, for major equipment, hardware, miscellaneous materials, and for construction services for its own subproject. ENDE directly contracted for these goods and services for the remaining three subprojects. The owners of the three remaining subprojects, Sucre Electric Cooperative (CESSA), the Potosi Electric Service (SEPSA), and the Tarija Electric Service (SETAR), were involved in this process in an advisory capacity only.

The consulting engineering and construction management services for all aspects of the project, with the exception of the subproject for the National Institute for Rural Electrification, were contracted with a consortium consisting of Stanley Consultants, Inc., of the United States; Energia y Desarrollo S.A. (EDESA) of Argentina; and Consultores Asociados CONSA S.R.L. of Boliva (see Figure 7). Stanley and

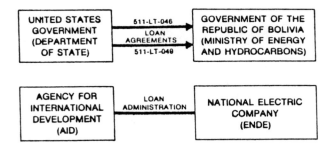

Figure 4.

EDESA are both well established firms of long-standing reputation in the consulting field. CONSA is a newly established Bolivian firm.

Other goods and services for the project have been procured through international competitive bidding from AID geographic Code 941 countries (selected Free World).

Poles, both concrete and wood, are coming from Bolivia and Chile. Conductors are being supplied from Costa Rica and Argentina. Power transformers are coming from Chile and Peru. Insulators, distribution transformers, metal-clad switchgear, automatic circuit reclosers, and vehicles are being supplied by the United States. Miscellaneous hardware and other minor items are being supplied from the United States, Bolivia, and other Latin American countries.

Construction services for two of the subprojects are being furnished by a contractor

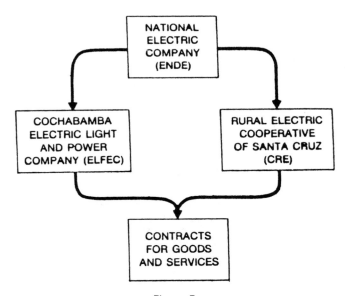

Figure 5.

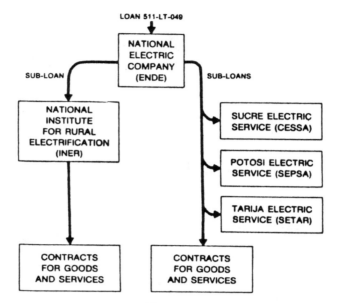

Figure 6.

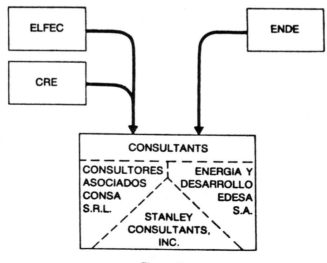

Figure 7.

with resources in Bolivia, Panama, and Peru. A joint venture, involving a U.S.-Puerto Rico contractor and a Bolivia contractor, is supplying the construction services for the remaining three subprojects.

Altogether, about one hundred contracts for goods and services have been let. Thus, it is indeed a complex management situation.

Logistics and communications also pose significant problems. Aside from the widely scattered sources of goods and services, the key organizations are remote from one another. The AID Mission to Bolivia is headquartered in La Paz in the Altiplano region of western Bolivia. ENDE headquarters is located in Cochabamba, about a hundred miles to the east as the condor flies. This is a 25-minute ride in a 727 jet or more than 12 hours by car. Telephone communication often required a full day to complete, before a microwave system was recently installed. Cables have been known to take as long as a week from one city to the other, and letter communication is equally unreliable.

One of the subborrowers, ELFEC, also has its headquarters in Cochabamba. This is also the site of the consultants' project office. The other four subborrowers are located in four different cities in central and southern Bolivia (Santa Cruz, Potosi, Sucre, and Tarija). Communications from these cities to Cochabama and La Paz is as difficult or worse than communications between Cochabamba and La Paz.

The home office of Stanley Consultants, Inc., is in Muscatine, Iowa. EDESA's home office is in Buenos Aires, and CONSA's home office is in La Paz. Telex communication is relatively fast and reliable between the United States, Bolivia, and Argentina. However, mail tends to be somewhat less reliable.

Organizational Structure

The project.   Excluding the construction contractors, the suppliers of goods and services, and the government institute's subproject, there are 10 separate entities involved in administration and control of the project. To control the flow of information and to establish lines of authority and responsibility, a formal project organization structure was developed as the first layer of the multilayered structure (see Figure 8).

This structure includes the U.S. Agency for International Development—AID (the loan administrator on behalf of the Department of State of the United States), the National Electricity Company—ENDE (the loan administrator on behalf of the Ministry of Energy and Hydrocarbons of the Republic of Bolivia), the five subborrowers, and the consultant.

The formal lines of communication and authority flow from AID through ENDE through the subborrowers to the consultant. The consultant, in turn, is authorized to deal directly with contractors and suppliers on behalf of the subborrowers and ENDE. Informal lines of communication connect the consultant to all parties.

The consultant.   The association of three independent architect/engineer consulting firms mobilized its combined project team in August, 1974, utilizing the organization structure shown in Figure 9. Since an association of three autonomous firms was involved, rather than a joint-venture combination, each firm retained administrative

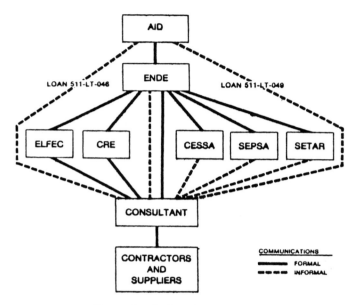

Figure 8. Project Organization.

control over its own employees. The result was a matrix relationship much like that which has been used internally by the U.S. firm, Stanley Consultants, for many years. An association form of interaction among the firms was chosen, rather than a new joint-venture firm, to avoid an additional organizational entity and to minimize costs for setting up and operating the consultants' organization.

The consultants' organization responds to this matrix of authority and responsibility through what is essentially a matrix organizational structure, as shown in Figure 9. A top-level administrative board was created to handle broad policy development and administration. Its activities include contract negotiations, contract changes, broad administrative policy, intercompany relations, top-level problem solving, and budgeting. Each company's representative on this board also maintains administrative control over his own company's staff assigned to the project.

A resident project manager has responsibility and authority for detailed administrative policy, operating procedures, scheduling, quality control of field services, and general conduct of the project. The resident project manager also has full authority to deal directly with the clients on all technical matters.

Stanley Consultants' staff includes a resident project manager with backup technical and administrative support from the home office staff, both in terms of services rendered at the home office and in terms of short field assignments of various engineering personnel.

The staff of EDESA consists of design and construction management engineering personnel plus home office support. CONSA, the Bolivian firm, provides some engi-

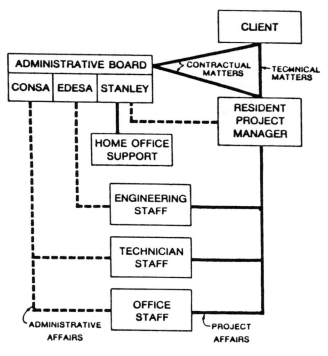

Figure 9.   Consultants Organization.

neering personnel together with technical support (surveyors, line stakers, and drafts-men) and office staff (secretaries, messengers, and accountants).

The U.S. A/E firm.   The organizational structure used by Stanley Consultants, as depicted in Figure 10, follows the firm's usual matrix configuration as used on several thousand projects over many years. The only unusual aspect was the blending of this layer into the other two layers, rather than into a project-level layer only. As can be seen from Figure 10, the resident project manager and a technical manager both report to Stanley's project manager. The project manager also is Stanley's repre-sentative on the consultant's administrative board. The resident project manager has reporting to him the staff assigned by the other two A/E firms. The technical manager, however, has the home office support staff reporting to him, including engineers and technicians from distribution design, substation design, structural design, specifica-tions, expediting, and cost-estimating departments.

Each member of the Stanley team continues to report to his assigned department, group, or division and participates in the project only when needed and to the extent needed. Even the resident project manager (or construction manager) reports for administrative purposes to the assistant head of International Division. For project purposes, he reports to the assigned project manager, even though the resident project

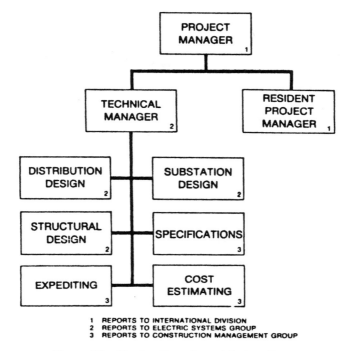

Figure 10.   Stanley Consultants' Project Team.

manager is assigned full-time to this one project and has no other responsibilities.

The project manager normally plays a prominent role on the Stanley project team, Figure 10. On this project, however, for purposes of blending this layer of organization into the foregoing layers, the project manager moved to a background role on the consultants' administrative board. The technical manager controls the design phase and normally has stature, responsibility, and authority equal to that of the resident project manager. In this case, however, he also moved to a background role to facilitate the blending of organization structural layers.

How the Structure Reacts

Formal versus informal.   Formal lines of communication were heavily relied upon during the early months of the design phase. However, it soon became evident that strong informal lines of communication needed to be established and recognized. As time went on, the informal lines of communication were used more and more to improve the reaction time of the entire structure to problems and changes. Much of the reaction time problem can be attributed to the normal bureaucracy within the various organizations and the logistical setting of the various subprojects.

The small problem.   The small daily problem is dealt with informally and directly by the individuals closest to the problem in the affected organizations, whether there are formal lines of communication between these organizations or not. Where operating procedures call for higher level approvals, these approvals are generally obtained after resolution of the problem. Occasionally, when the problem cannot be resolved, it proceeds up the ladder to the next rung. The important point is that the normal procedure is to handle minor problem solving at the lowest possible echelon, irrespective of formal communication channels. This keeps the formal channels from becoming clogged with trivia and free to handle more critical items.

A typical small problem might be the scheduling of a client-furnished vehicle for use by resident engineers and survey crews. Such a problem is generally resolved by the client's representative in the project office and the consultant's resident engineer or crew chief without involvement by management personnel.

The larger problem.   Changes in the scope of work and the resultant negotiation of contract amendments brings the formal lines of communication into play. Technical details are discussed, alternatives developed, and tentative agreements reached at lower echelon levels before formal negotiations between the consultant's administrative board and the client's management personnel began. Usually, only a few real issues remain at the "beginning" of the negotiation, and it is relatively easy for members of the administrative board and the client's organization to concentrate on the issues. Once agreements have been reached, the amendment proceeds through formal lines of communication for the proper approvals and signatures.

The largest problem.   The first bids for construction, labor, and materials under Loan 511-LT-046 came in at double the cost estimate and well above the available funds. It was the kind of thing that could render a project financially infeasible and kill it in its tracks. At first appearance, it seemed that only about 50 percent of the construction could be accomplished with the available funds. However, most major materials (conductor, insulators, poles, and transformers) had already been contracted for and at prices approximating the cost estimates.

The full project organizational structure immediately came into play at both formal and informal levels. Activities concentrated in two areas: (1) bid analysis, and (2) action alternatives. Input came from all sources within the structure. When ideas were sufficiently formulated, discussions were held along the formal channels in order to retain control over what might have become a chaotic situation.

Bid analysis and independent project cost re-estimates by the consultant, ENDE, and AID confirmed that the bids were extraordinarily high and that all bids should be rejected. In particular, prices for construction materials and hardware included in the bid packages seemed out of line.

A plan of action was formulated that involved rebidding all construction materials and hardware separate from construction labor. If labor still came in too high (many of the same contractors would be rebidding the construction labor, due to the project size and location), the project would then proceed under force account with a full construction management team. This decision was reached and approved through the formal channels of communication, from the grass-roots level on up.

The construction material and hardware bids came in close to the cost estimates and substantially under prices quoted by contractors in their first bids. Construction labor bids, although still above estimates, were in an acceptable range. Construction was delayed by the rebidding process; however, millions of dollars were saved, and, more important, project feasibility was retained. The multilayered organizational structure had worked well during this major crisis.

This major problem on the first loan occurred early enough in the process so that the pattern of splitting all construction materials and hardware from construction labor was followed from the beginning on the three subprojects under the second loan. This pattern also seemed to work very well on the second loan, as prices for goods and services came in close to the levels estimated.

Implementation Problems

The organizational structure has not functioned without problems. It was painfully slow in reacting at first, as everyone was carefully observing protocol, and the communication time delays were tremendous. As people became better acquainted, the informal lines of communication started functioning, and reaction time improved by leaps and bounds. It was a typical startup problem complicated by the three-layer organizational structure and communication delay problems.

Communication delays have been and, to some extent, continue to be frustrating and difficult to overcome. Fortunately, the normal operating procedures of the International Division of Stanley Consultants call for the logging in and out of numbered interoffice memos so that "missing" mail can be identified within a reasonable time period and replacement copies furnished.

Due to the relative reliability of this system, far too much reliance was placed on it in the beginning, as opposed to more expensive but much faster telex communication. The delays inherent in international mail systems led to more and more use of telex.

Precautions with telex also are necessary. Each telex is numbered, and a confirmation copy immediately mailed to verify the message. This has worked well and provided the reaction time needed to keep the small problems from growing into larger ones.

The organizational structure agreed upon among Stanley Consultants, CONSA, and EDESA meant the adoption of a matrix form of internal administration for this project by the Argentine and Bolivian firms. This was new to them and unfamiliar. Guidance and some patience by Stanley Consultants was necessary before the other firms released the proper degree of authority to the resident project manager. Fortunately, Stanley Consultants is accustomed to tutoring people (clients and new employees) on the values of the matrix organization structure and how well it can work if properly implemented. Still, the Latin American firms were stepping into unfamiliar water and even now occasionally release either too little or too much authority to the resident project manager. Their patience and willingness to adopt the matrix form has, however, been a key to the successful operation of the project team.

There have also been problems in the operation of the consultant's administrative board. The three board members are normally located in their respective home offices and meet only occasionally in Bolivia. On many occasions, only two of the board members are present. At times, consultation with other members has to be undertaken by letter or telex. Important decisions of this board are recorded and signed by all three members. Many "informal" decisions are reached, which have important impacts upon the operation of the project.

Conclusion

Management of projects involving more than a handful of different organizations scattered through several countries is always a challenge, even when the project itself is relatively simple. The Bolivia Rural Electrification Project certainly does not have the complexity of many contemporary undertakings, such as a modern military aircraft development project, but the multiorganizational and multinational aspects posed management problems similar to a more complex project.

Response to management problems required the formation of an organizational structure involving three very distinct layers. Each layer must function by itself and in harmony with the other two layers.

The three-layered organizational structure used on the Bolivia Rural Electrification Project has worked well because of two primary features: (1) it has a formal structure that recognizes each organization's role (i.e., responsibilities and authority) in the project and that provides continuity and stability; (2) it provides strong informal channels of communication to recognize efficient problem-solving techniques and provide fast reaction time.

A basically simple project made complex by its multiorganizational, multinational character was made manageable through a three-layered organizational structure.

CASE STUDY 37:   THE CARGO RAM PROJECT[1]

In January 1980 the Ford Motor Company received word that the Japanese were considering entering the medium duty truck market in Europe and the United States. Ford officials feared that if the Japanese were to enter the market with a low-priced product they could capture a large segment of the market, where Ford currently had a strong position.

Ford therefore began planning countermoves to offset the Japanese entrance into its market. In the U.S. medium-duty truck market, the cab-over-chassis design of truck was not popular. Most U.S. truck drivers preferred the Ram chassis, which allowed the engine to stick out in front of the driver. This chassis was durable and yet lightweight and was definitely superior to anything offered abroad. Europeans, on the other hand, preferred the cab-over-chassis design, which they called the *Cargo* model, for their medium-duty market. Ford, in attempting to design an international truck application, decided to join the U.S. Ram chassis with the Cargo model of truck offered in Europe. This project was entitled appropriately the Cargo Ram project.

In June 1982, Ford chose Brazil as the country where the manufacturing would take place. Ford constructed a facility during the fall of 1982, while contacting all

---

[1] The following case study, including names, events, and characteristics is fictitious.

suppliers who would be interested in supplying Ford with component parts for its Cargo Ram truck.

Lisor Corporation expressed an interest and was selected to supply Ford with all medium-duty axles for the Cargo Ram project in Brazil. Lisor was a domestic producer of light-, medium-, and heavy-duty truck axles for the U.S. truck manufacturers.

Because of Brazil's heavy local content laws, Ford was required to produce a truck that contained 90 percent domestic content by weight. (See Table 1 for additional information on Brazil.) Ford stressed this fact to all its suppliers, and, because of the weight of the axle in the truck, Lisor was encouraged very heavily to locate its production facility in Brazil.

Lisor currently had a service facility in Brazil with space available for expansion and, after a careful review, decided to expand this facility to meet the forecasted production schedule of 150,000 units annually.

Thus, Lisor's price quote to Ford was based upon 100 percent local content within this Brazilian-produced axle. This meant no imports at all from Lisor's U.S. facilities. As this was a critical contract, the price quote was substantially lower than normal in order for Lisor to obtain the contract.

Rich Schwartz: (Plant Manager)   Well, Sam, I think it is obvious from these final line production stats that we have a serious problem here. With a forecasted annual demand of 150,000 units, we have promised Ford almost 600 units per day on the

Table 1.   Mandatory Fringe Benefits and Other Social Costs.[a]

	% of base pay
Unworked time:	
Vacation	9.4
Sundays	18.8
Holidays	3.6
Subtotal	31.8
Additional wage costs:	
Sick pay	4.2
Thirteenth month bonus	10.8
Social Security	8.0
INPS on bonus	0.6
Family wage allowance	4.3
Workman's Compensation	4.5
Industrial social services	1.5
Industrial apprenticeship	1.0
Agricultural credit	2.5
Severance pay fund	8.0
Subtotal	45.4
TOTAL FRINGE BENEFIT COSTS	77.2

[a] Does not include employee contributions.

Table 1 (continued).   Profile of Key Labor Regulations.

Monthly Minimum Wage: Crll,928 (Cr134.44/$1) in San Paulo
                        Rio de Janeiro
Workweek: Maximum 48 hours—six days
            Office work 40–42 hours—five days
Overtime: Day @ 20% premium
            Nights @ 25% premium
            Sundays and holidays—twice the regular rate
Vacation: After one year: 30 days or up to 20 days in pay with no time off
            Annual bonus: 13th month salary paid at year end
Social Security: Medical care and hospitalization covered
                   Company contributes 10% of payroll
                   Worker contributions based on sliding scale
Pensions: 30 years of service or age 65 for men and age 60 for women—up to 80% of salary
Profit sharing: none
Other benefits: Employers must provide full pay for first 10 days of certified illness and 12
                  weeks full pay for maternity leave.

Table 1 (continued).   Labor Data as of 1980 Census.

Labor force	1980	1970
Industry	24%	18%
Commercial workers	9%	8%
Service Industries/Government	36%	19%
Farming and fishing	31%	55%

Total workforce 43.3 million

Roughly 80% earn the minimum monthly wage or above
Of this 80%:
    79% earn $275/month or 3 times the min. monthly salary
    28% "   1–2 times   "   "   "
    4% "   3–5 times   "   "   "
    3% "   10–20 times   "   "   "
    .014% "   more than 10 times "   "   "
Of the 20% receiving less than minimum wage:
    90% receive over half of the monthly minimum wage
    5.1% receive less than half of the minimum wage
    3.2% had no cash earnings

average. That's based upon 300 units per shift and two shifts per day. After our first three months of production, our daily average is only 375 units. As plant manager of the first Lisor production facility in Brazil, I hate to get a bad name this quickly.

Gompers: (Production Manager)   Granted, Rick, and I'm in the same boat as you with responsibility for production here. I'll tell you right now though that I don't think we will ever meet that 600-unit level of production.

Schwartz: What do you mean we'll never meet the 600-unit level of production?

Gompers: As I was saying, Rick, not only are the machines not running efficiently, you've also got problems with the gear sets you're putting into these axles.

Schwartz: Problems? Gear sets? What kind of problems?

Gompers: Well the gear sets being produced at this facility are not matching properly when we test them to see how they will run inside the axle.

Schwartz: What do you mean not matching properly?

Gompers: During the test many of the gears are not machined properly, and, because of the bad metals here, stress factors occur.

Schwartz: Absolutely wonderful! Why didn't someone tell me about this earlier?

Gompers: Well we tried, Rick, but you were always on your way out the door to the club. You wouldn't take the time to listen to us.

Schwartz: Well, you've got my attention now. What should we do?

Gompers: I suggest for the short term that we obtain gear sets from the U.S. where we can be assured of good quality.

Schwartz: Good idea, Sam, but with Brazil's domestic content law of 90 percent, we can't do that, especially since Ford created this model with our axle being 100 percent domestic content. A gear and pinion set that weighs 300 to 400 pounds might be enough to violate the 90 percent domestic weight content.

Gompers: Maybe we should ask Ford to change its domestic contents.

Schwartz: Are you crazy? We can't tell Ford we have a quality problem with gears and pinions. Somehow, we've got to get those gears and pinions down here from the U.S. without Ford knowing about it.

Gompers: We're already behind the eight ball, and I see no immediate relief. I'll contact some of the local gear companies and see if I can't arrange some type of outsourcing deal, since we can't import from the U.S.

Schwartz: You better do something. It is your responsibility to get the product out—no matter what!

Gomper's search for a company capable of producing gears was in vain. The only company he was certain had the capabilities was Elix Corp., located in the United States.

Gompers, realizing his job was at stake, in desperation, made an illegal business deal with a small gear manufacturer—Precision Gears do Brasil—and Elix. The deal agreed upon was outlined as follows:

1. Elix Corp. would ship the specified gears to Precision as "raw-bar stock."
2. Precision would buff out the electrolytically etched Elix identification and re-etch the gears with its own identification.

3. Precision would repackage the gears with its own shipping labels and then ship to Lisor.

Gompers figured out the angles of the deal in case he were to be investigated:

1. Currently Precision imports raw stock from Elix. Precision importing a few more boxes of "raw stock" should go unnoticed.
2. Kickback was needed to compensate for the risk involved: Precision was taking the most risk, so a 15 percent of cost kickback was offered. Elix benefits from the deal in increased sales.
3. Precision was given copies of Lisor's routing, blueprints, specifications, and other pertinent documentation relating to the gear production. Precision was also instructed to slightly modify all paperwork, so that it could not be recognized as Lisor's property.
4. Both Lisor and Ford were told of the need to outsource the gears in Brazil, at least temporarily, until Lisor could improve their gear-producing methods to meet requested demand.

The deal seemed to be moving smoothly—Ford was happy with the axles received from Lisor, Precision was happy with the 15 percent kickback profit, Elix was realizing additional sales, and the production manager at Lisor was no longer being pressured to get production out.

Meanwhile, the Brazilian government, in an effort to correct its imbalance of international payments, started a crackdown to keep cruzeiros in the country. A government inspector, Rosie Rodriguez, was assigned to investigate foreign-owned companies to ensure that they were complying with government regulations. Her responsibility included verifying material specifications, employment levels, imported and exported goods, financial reports, means of financing, tax rates, etc.

One of the companies to be reviewed was Ford, which was given a satisfactory report. Her next stop was Lisor, because Lisor had the largest outsource contract with Ford.

Upon entering Lisor, she found the plant manager was not available. He was performing his public relations responsibility at the country club. The next person in the chain of command was the production manager, Sam Gompers.

Rosie Rodriguez: I'm conducting a mandatory six-month review of transactions occurring in foreign-owned companies to ensure compliance with government regulations.

Gompers: What exactly can I do for you?

Rodriguez: Routine procedures outline an investigation of your business transactions, such as financial reports, methods of financing, subcontracting/contracting relationships, material specifications, goods being imported and/or exported, vendors' prices, costs of goods, employment levels, and the like.

Gompers: Let me contact our Accounting Department for the information you requested. While it's collecting the reports, I've time to take you on a tour of our production facilities.

Upon returning from the plant tour, they sit down to review the paperwork. On the surface, Lisor appears to adhere to specified government regulations.

Rodriguez: This report shows that Lisor has granted subcontracts to several companies. I guess my next stop is to investigate those companies. Thank you for your time. It looks like Lisor satisfies all government criteria.

The production manager, afraid that she might uncover the deal with Precision, offers to go along.

Gompers: I might as well go along with you. It's good policy to keep tabs on subcontractors, you know—find out how things are going, if they're encountering any problems, if we can be of any assistance—makes for good customer relations. I'll tell my secretary what my plans are, and then I'll be ready. Let's have lunch before making the rounds.

At the restaurant:

Gompers: So glad you could join me for lunch today, Rosie. I really feel that our decision to come to Brazil was a good one overall. And as a result of your visit, I feel that we are complying with everything that we should be.
  So, being a native of Brazil, do you have a lot of family in the area?

Rosie: Well, yes, I do as a matter of fact. I have 15 brothers and 2 sisters. My brothers all work in the banana fields within the area. And speaking of the area, what's the Precision Gear Company anyway? I see that it's a very big subcontractor of yours.

Gompers: It is merely being used as a subcontractor for us until we can get our quality problem resolved. It's just a short-term thing, and I really don't feel it will last long.

Rosie: Quality problem? What kind of quality problem?

Gompers: Well, it was really the fact that our machinists weren't working out well. I guess we need to train some new machinists soon.

Rosie: Well, I know where you can find 15 good machinists. I have 15 brothers who might work out well.

Gompers: Great, tell them to report to the personnel office Monday morning. I'm sure they'll do just fine.

Rosie: I'm sure, too. Well, I must get along now and fill out the necessary paperwork for Precision Gear Company. Since you've been over there and looked at everything, I'm sure that I have nothing to worry about. I can sense from the way we work together that there will be no problem.

Sam Gompers realized he had to come up with some legitimate reason for hiring these 15 people. Thus, on Friday afternoon, Sam Gompers developed a machinists training program. What appeared on paper to be a skilled machinists training program for the gear set problem was actually a clever way of accommodating the 15 brothers of Rosie Rodriguez.

First thing Monday morning, Rich Schwartz receives a telephone call from Joe Scara, the personnel director.

Joe Scara: Hey, Schwartz, do you know anything about some people starting work today in some kind of training program?

Schwartz: Training program you say? No, I don't. How many people are we talking about?

Scara: Fifteen, and there's something very strange about all of this.

Schwartz: What's that?

Scara: Well, first of all, their surnames are all Rodriguez.

Schwartz: That's not so unusual.

Scara: Well, they also all give the same home address and give Sam Gompers as a reference. Most of them are laid-off farm workers. When I ask them why they're here, they say, "Ask my seester, meester!"

Schwartz: Oh no! Today of all days for this to happen! I don't need this kind of pressure with my tennis club tournament starting this afternoon! I'll see what Sam Gompers has to say about all this, and I'll get back to you. In the meantime keep them occupied, and don't let them touch anything.

Rich Schwartz calls Sam Gompers, the production manager, into his office:

Schwartz: Gompers, do you recall telling anyone by the name of Rodriguez to start work today in some kind of training program?

Gompers: Hmmm. Rodriguez you say? The name sounds familiar.

Schwartz: Let me jog your memory. How does 15 Rodriguez family members sound?

Gompers: Oh! Those Rodriguezes. Well, it's a long story.

Schwartz: Well, start talking! I have two hours before I have to be at the club for my tournaments.

Gompers: It all started with our not being able to meet production because of the poor-quality gears we were producing here. According to our records, Precision Gears do Brasil is producing our gears for us when in reality, we are importing them from the U.S., labeled as "bar stock."

We got into a bind when Ms. Rodriquez, the government inspector came in to do her check on our compliance with the 90 percent local content law. She wanted to visit our vendors, and any rookie can tell by the way Precision is set up that there is no way they could be producing our gears.

Hiring her family was all I could do to get her to overlook some details of her audit. It was the lesser of three evils, the third one being to make her a middle-class suburban housewife. I'm not ready for that yet.

Schwartz: So I guess this story partially explains this memo from sales, which is asking us to review with Ford a request to increase our bid price. According to Financial, our costs have risen dramatically. I want you to get together with them and give them the whole story. Tomorrow, I want a full report on the factors behind our not being able to sell these axles to Ford at our original price.

The next day, a staff meeting was called to discuss the rising cost of sales.

Gompers: So, I guess we can all agree then that this outline we have here shows why we have to go to Ford and ask for an increase in our bid price over and above the increases allowed for Brazil's high inflation rate.
As all of you can see here,

1. We initially underbid in order to obtain the contract, thinking the inflation price increases would pull us out.
2. Our breakdown in quality, and our having to buy the gear from Elix in the U.S. costs a great deal more than our budget shows as costs for producing them here in Brazil, for material and labor alone.
3. On top of buying the gears from Elix and paying additional repackaging charges, we have incurred import duties on the "raw bar stock."
4. We pay gratuities to Precision Gears do Brazil for use of its name and facilities.
5. The cost of our in-house training program has increased dramatically due to several reasons. Two specific reasons are:
   a. Retraining employees who were put out of work when the gear line shut down. In the States, we would have just laid these people off.
   b. Hiring the Rodriguez clan in order to keep our deal with Precision under wraps. Just from their first two days in the program, we can see that they have no intention of working, that they're just using us.
6. Precision Gears do Brazil is asking more for the gears coming from the U.S. due to the devaluation of the cruziero, which is being passed on to us.

At this point in time, we have no other choice other than to ask Ford if we can raise our price due to these increased costs. Of course we cannot tell Ford all the reasoning behind our rising costs. We will simplify it and just state that we had to outsource our gears to Precision Gears do Brazil, who is the sole Brazilian supplier, and Precision is price gouging.

The following memo was received from Ford regarding the request for a price increase.
After careful review of your request for a price increase, we feel we cannot oblige. We at Ford have to control our own costs to remain competitive on the world market. We feel you at Lisor will have to look internally to reduce your costs.
Meanwhile, back in the United States, a high Ford executive calls a friend who happens to be his counterpart at the Lisor Corporation.

Mike: Hello, Freddy? Wanted to give you a call and see if you wanted to get together after work to have a drink? I felt we could get together and catch up on things.

Freddy: Sure Mike, sounds like a great idea. I've been under the gun lately. A couple of our projects are giving us some concern.

Mike: Well, Freddy, I hope you have gotten your Brazilian quality problem under control. We both know that your career and reputation ride upon that project.

Freddy: Quality problem? What kind of quality problem are you talking about?

Mike: Freddy, another call is coming in. I have to go. About that drink, lets have it some other night. I think you'll have to work late tonight.

Freddy: Edith (the secretary), I want you to gather all the reports you have concerning Lisor's Brazilian project. Also, call everyone involved for a 7:00 A.M. meeting tomorrow. I'm going to get to the bottom of this little problem.

Three weeks later. Freddy and 12 other top Lisor executives still could not come up with all the problems concerning the Brazil Project. Dr. Kay, a staff troubleshooter, was assigned to fact-find the problem.

As Dr. Kay headed to South America, he began to formulate his plan. Dr. Kay decided that the main plan of analysis would begin with:

- Talking to employees;
- Looking into the training program;
- Verify reports, routings, methods, etc.;
- Find out why more people were needed for the project;
- Investigate Precision. He had a gut feeling that something was amiss.

Dr. Kay was met at the airport by Rick Schwartz and Sam Gompers. On the ride to Lisor, the problems of the plant were discussed.

Dr. Kay: From what I've read, it appears that the quality problem with gears has snowballed into a major production and cost problem!

Schwartz: The quality problem has given us some problems, but the production and cost figures given to Ford were much too optimistic.

Gompers: That's right! The production schedule would have been difficult to meet even without the small quality problem.

Dr. Kay: Be that as it may, we can't afford to have poor-quality axles going out of this plant at any cost. When we get to the plant, I want to look into your training programs for the machinists. We need to get the production of gears back in-house so we can control quality!

Gompers: Well the training program has been a little slow to get going, but what we really need is someone to talk to Ford and renegotiate the contract; we just can't meet the schedule!

Three days later at the Lisor plant:

Dr. Kay: Gompers, what's going on here? I've been watching your machinist trainees. I saw a couple of them sweeping, and they were the busy ones! When I checked with the personnel director, he said all these trainees were hired on the same day with your specific authorization.

Gompers: Since this was a crash program, I personally expedited the hiring. I knew we had to get this program going.

Dr. Kay: Bull! How about if I told you that all the trainees gave the same home address, and they all gave the government inspector and you as references.

Gompers: I thought we could get a little favor from her if we used a government agency to hire these people. That's all there is to it.

Dr. Kay: Why then did all the machinists list her as a relative? Sam, something stinks here, and I want to know about it right now!

Gompers: OK, we had a problem with Precision, our supplier of gears. It was a small problem associated with quality, but we didn't want the government to find out! So Rosie agreed not to be too nosey if we hired her relatives. This kind of thing happens all the time here. It's a fact of life. It's a small price to pay to keep her off our back for a while.

At Precision the next day:

Dr. Kay: Schwartz, this is a strange operation here, isn't it? This bar stock is too small to make our gears. The only gears I see here are finished. Where is the rest of the operation?

Schwartz: You're right! This is difficult to believe. Maybe Precision has another plant. I haven't had a chance to catch up on this problem. I had a big tennis tournament last weekend; came in first. Do you play tennis?

Dr. Kay: Look at this cost breakdown. It includes only bar stock receiving, etching of serial numbers, and shipping costs. It was signed off by Gompers.

Next day at Lisor:

Dr. Kay: Schwartz, I want an entire accuracy audit of the bill of material to include all our local suppliers. We need to get a realistic picture of the costs.

Schwartz: Sounds good to me!

Dr. Kay: Also, suppose I told you I had a couple of finished axles disassembled this morning. Some of the gears are marked with Elix U.S. numbers. Some of the other gears were obviously altered!

Schwartz: You're kidding!

Dr. Kay: Call Gompers in here.

Gompers: How are you this morning?

Dr. Kay: Gompers, we found out that Precision isn't making our gears and couldn't if it wanted to. What's up?

Gompers: Well Dr. Kay, it's like this. It all started because these lazy Brazilian machinists weren't good enough. . . .

CASE STUDY 38: DORI INTERNATIONAL

In 1957, three Israeli engineers formed Dori International Corporation. These three engineers had vast experience in electronics, especially military applications. By 1982, Dori had grown to a $40 million (U.S.) corporation involved in military R&D, weapons production, electronic communications equipment, and guidance equipment.

In 1982, Dori received permission from the Israeli government to undertake a joint venture R&D agreement with an American corporation. As part of the agreement with the American Corporation, a joint U.S.–Israeli military R&D project would be undertaken by the two companies, with the Israelis performing the first portion. Furthermore, an American project manager would be assigned to Dori Corporation for the duration of the 12-month, first phase of the R&D project. The American project manager was 35-year-old Richard Klein, a man whom Dori Corporation hoped would decide to stay in Israel after the termination of the joint venture. The decision to use an American project manager was made by Myron Jacobs, Vice-President of Engineering for Dori. The second phase of the project was to be performed in the United States.

At the end of the first phase, which was entirely an Israeli function, the American project manager would return to the United States to head the second phase, provided that both the Israelis and Americans agreed upon the success of the first stage. As part of the agreement, either party could cancel the project at any time. The Americans would not be required to attend any meetings, but would be kept informed of the project status through both Myron Jacobs and Richard Klein. If status was unacceptable, a follow-on contract could be awarded to repeat the first stage of the project, but toward different objectives and specifications.

Jacobs: Richard, I should explain to you why I wanted an American to run this project. We are trying to Americanize our methodology for managing projects, and, as you know, that requires organizational change. For years, all our projects have been controlled by our line managers, even though only a small portion of the effort was accomplished within their line groups. To be compatible with American companies, we have created a project manager division, which also reports to me, and which contains eight full-time project managers. You will be attached to that group.

Klein: How long has this organizational change been in effect?

Jacobs: About two months. The problem is that our line managers are resisting the change and refuse to cooperate fully with our project managers. The line managers feel as though they have lost power and have been demoted. Of course, this is not true.

Let me tell you a little bit about Dori Corporation, Richard. We run the company like an overbooked hotel; that is, overbooked with work instead of people. As a result, we lack sufficient resources. Management refuses to let us hire additional people so we continuously play the priority game. I'm sure it is the same way in the States. Our universities do not turn out a great many engineers and, as a result, the good engineers are hired quickly. All new Israeli engineers, regardless of capabilities, eventually receive employment. We've tried to get engineers from the States, but I think all Israel gets only 2,000 families a year from abroad, and only a small percent are engineers.

If you have an average or below-average group of people on your project, it won't matter how you orchestrate the people; the same poor music will appear. You must motivate the people. In time of war, our people are probably more productive than any people on earth. Rank is unimportant, even in the military. You must get the respect of the people. You'll have your hands full since your project is only one year.

For the next two months, Richard battled his way through the blocks of resistance created by the line managers. Richard had weekly meetings with Myron Jacobs to discuss project status.

Klein: Your line managers appear to be resisting me more than I anticipated. I don't think that it's a personality problem. It must be something else.

Jacobs: That's expected because you're not an Israeli. They want you to prove yourself worthy of working with them. I anticipated that problem. You'll just have to cope the best you can.

Klein: Your line managers keep telling me that they cannot do what I've asked because this is Israel, not America, and I don't understand the Israeli culture.

Jacobs: Look, Richard! Our line managers are good employees, dedicated and committed to the success of our company. The Israeli culture is one of conflict and disagreement. Two Israelis, when attacking a problem will always take opposing views and argue. But in the end, they always get the job done.

Klein: Getting the job done doesn't help me unless it is completed within the time, cost, and performance constraints. From all indications it appears as though we're going to have trouble meeting the time constraints.

Jacobs: Put the people on overtime. We cannot withstand a schedule slippage. All payments from the military are based upon completed milestones and, with an Israeli inflation rate of 120 percent, a schedule slippage of one month could cause a 10 percent cost overrun on the project. On your project, time is more important than cost or performance.

Klein: OK, I'll try it. But I hope I can get better productivity out of the employees.

Jacobs: Any other problems, Richard?

Klein: I'm having trouble understanding these "risk factors" that your people have assigned to the R&D logic flow.

Jacobs: That's easy to explain. The risk factors are actually levels of uncertainty. Level 1 is expertise that exists in Dori Corporation. Level 2 is expertise outside Dori, but within Israel; it exists and is readily obtainable. Level 3 is expertise that must be either purchased from abroad or researched. Level 4 is advanced state-of-the-art expertise that may take years to develop.

Projects in the Level 1 and 2 categories are usually the easiest to schedule. Unfortunately, we have a lot of R&D projects that contain Level 3 and 4 categories. And, of course, these are the projects that our military people have given us impossible deadlines for. We always end up having to "crash" project activities, and sometimes we succeed. You are fortunate in that your project contains only one Level 3 task; everything else is Level 1 or Level 2.

By the end of the fourth month, the project was on schedule, but costs were 5 percent over budget. Several of the employees were questioning whether the final performance specifications could ever be achieved. Klein met Jacobs at the beginning of the fifth month to discuss status.

Klein: Working overtime sure has helped. You know, in the States people are less productive on overtime. But here in Israel, productivity increases. Why is that?

Jacobs: The problem is one of facilities and working conditions. Our people are so crammed together that they spend a lot of time simply talking to one another. On overtime, when most of the people leave, the employees get down to business.

Klein: Why not build better facilities?

Jacobs: Easier said than done. In the States, you can build a large facility in two years. Here in Israel, it may take three to four years simply to get the permits and authorization to build.

Klein: During construction, can't you work out a deal with the construction labor unions to work overtime?

Jacobs: We don't have construction labor unions here as you have in the States. A lot of our laborers are Arabs, and they work when they want to.

Klein: Are there any unions here?

Jacobs: Some of our Israeli companies have so-called unions, such as engineering unions, which regulate the salary of engineers. In such cases, salaries are based upon longevity rather than capabilities or experience. You can even become a manager based upon longevity, even if you have absolutely no management qualifications. That's a problem.

By the end of the seventh month, work appeared to be proceeding on schedule, but the employees were still questioning whether the final specifications could be met. To stay with the original schedule, Klein asked the line managers to work their people 55 rather than 45 hours a week. The following day, Klein was told to report to Jacobs for a meeting.

Jacobs: Richard, I understand that you're scheduling overtime during the next two months.

Klein: Yes, we'll need it to stay on schedule. I see no other way.

Jacobs: You know, Richard, that our people have been complaining about the overtime requirements on your project. You're creating a problem.

Klein: I don't see a problem! The people are getting paid for the overtime, aren't they?

Jacobs: When our people work overtime, it is usually for the dedication to the project, rather than for the money. Most Israeli families have two working parents. According to our tax structure, when one of the two working parents works overtime, they take home only a small fraction of what they earn on overtime.

Klein: I didn't know that!

Jacobs: There's more. The next two months are July and August, and the children are out of school. Most people like to be home with their families during these months rather than working overtime. Let's schedule the overtime after September 1.

Klein: I've been told by two of my key employees that you have authorized them to go on vacation to Europe for part of the summer. That's going to hurt my project.

Jacobs: Vacation is the wrong word. Each pay period, our employees contribute 2.5 percent of their salary to a travel/education fund, and the company contributes 5 percent. Every three years or so, our employees go abroad to take courses and see how other companies function. It is an educational process, not a vacation. Most Israeli corporations have similar tax-free benefits. You'll just have to cope with the situation.

Klein: I don't feel that our people are as dedicated as they should be to the project or performance specifications. That bothers me.

Jacobs: Look, Richard! Our people have compulsory military service for nearly 40 years of their lives. The people designing and manufacturing the equipment know that they, themselves, are the eventual users while they serve on active duty. Believe me when I tell you the dedication is there!

During the summer months, the schedule began to slip to the point where Klein was beginning to wonder whether or not performance would ever be achieved. The raw materials that were so desparately needed had not yet arrived. Klein attributed most of this problem to the procurement function being extremely low in the organizational hierarchy. Furthermore, the customer was demanding more and more status reports, especially charts and schedules, showing the work to be done in the second phase of the project. The frustration was that Dori did not have a computerized cost and control system, and that all artwork had to be performed manually. Furthermore, the work to be performed in the final 60 days had not yet been defined.

During August, Jacobs went on vacation to Europe for three weeks. Although there was an acting vice-president of engineering in the absence of Jacobs, Klein felt reluctant to talk to anyone else.

September was the 10th month of the project, and a local critical design review meeting was scheduled between Dori, Israeli Army representatives, and the Israeli government. Although Klein had conducted such meetings previously, this one would be different, because senior people would be present from military and government. Furthermore, Klein was told that all information in this meeting should be presented in Hebrew. As a result of this request, Jacobs decided to take complete control of the project until after the September 20th meeting.

For the first two weeks in September, virtually all work on the project stopped because almost all employees were busy preparing handouts for the two-day meeting. Klein felt rather helpless during this time because he did not understand Hebrew and wasn't sure what information was going to be presented. Klein told the employees, in English, what to present on the viewgraphs.

The meeting went off according to plan, Klein was puzzled because, during his initial introduction to the people and again during breaks and mealtimes, it became obvious that the attendees all spoke English fairly well. Klein was later informed by Jacobs that the attendees speak and understand "conversational" English, but not "technological" English. Therefore, the meeting had to be conducted in Hebrew.

For Klein's benefit, an Army spokesman summarized the results of the meeting in English:

- The project appears to be approximately two months behind schedule, without even considering the material procurement problems.
- Performance appears to be only 75 percent of specification requirements and to offer little hope that 100 percent of specification requirements can be achieved, even with a follow-on contract.
- The problems appear to be the result of the rigid, advanced, state-of-the-art requirements, rather than faulty management.
- Unless major improvements occur in the next six weeks, the second phase will be cancelled.

Klein recognized that he had only six weeks of work left before the final report had to be prepared. During this six weeks, Klein eagerly tried to obtain better performance results. Unfortunately, even with overtime, the project was completed at only 75 percent of the specification requirements.

During the last month of the project, Klein worked closely with the employees preparing the final report. Klein was getting anxious to return to the States and begin working on another project. However, he was somewhat worried about how his American management would view the results of the project and whether or not it would be a direct reflection upon him.

With only three weeks to go before the closeout date of the project, Klein was summoned to see Jacobs.

Jacobs: Richard, the Army has reconsidered its position. It feels that the project does show some potential and that a follow-on contract will be awarded to us next month. The follow-on contract will replace the second phase. If the follow-on is successful, there will be additional follow-ons. I've told our American counterpart about this, and he's happy with the outcome. You've done a good job, Richard.

The Army wants you to manage the follow-on contract and so do I. I called your company and it said that the entire decision would be up to you. How would you feel about managing another 12-month project here in Israel?

CASE STUDY 39:   THE RED DRAGON PROJECT

"I don't see how we can stay in business, throwing money down the tubes developing projects that will never get off the ground. Top-level managers better wake up or a lot of people are going to tell them to stuff it. This treadmill crap is for the birds. I've just wasted a year of effort!" Fred Bland was waiting for his meeting with the director of engineering following the departure of the Chinese from the United States.

Background

Microchip Division was approached in early 1980 regarding what was essentially a turnkey venture to produce printed circuit boards in the PRC (the People's Republic of China). In addition to having a manufacturing plant, the Chinese also indicated an interest in vertical integration to allow them to produce all end products eventually. The division had to formulate a long-term strategy that considered such factors as its market position in the Far East, the PRC's motivation for requesting construction of a plant, and the alternatives available to each party.

At the time the PRC approached Microchip Division, an agreement had just been reached with Japan's Banzai Computer Co. for a joint venture to construct a production facility on Japanese soil. Construction of a plant using the most modern technology was to begin that summer.

Microchip Division began negotiating with Banzai Computer to better position itself in the Far East market. Of the five small Japanese computer equipment producers, two were exporting to the United States and were believed to be formulating plans to build U.S. operating facilities. The announcement of the joint venture agreement had the desired effect of postponing expanded exporting and U.S. production plans as the Japanese raced to cover themselves at home.

Although it appeared that the PRC had not contacted any Japanese competitors for similar proposals, Microchip Division was aware that it had held preliminary discussions with a small, low-quality East German manufacturing company. This contact was not particularly worrisome, since there could be no question that the division was recognized as the world leader in microchip technology. The only problem was to reach a financially feasible agreement that would preclude the involvement of National Corporation, the largest competitor worldwide. The division's strategy was to provide itself with a long-term position in a potentially huge market and thereby shut out the competition, while protecting the division's proprietary technology at the same time.

The motivations of the Chinese were less clear. Since the 1970s, the PRC had imported few raw materials, preferring instead to purchase its circuit boards. The division's interpretation of this policy was that Chinese technology was not sufficiently advanced for them to attempt to produce the end item themselves. They operate a very small plant in the industrial city of Benxi, located in Liaoning Province (Manchuria). The plant was built in the 1950s, using Russian technology. In addition to having operated for 30 years without technical improvements, the plant would be capable of producing 500 circuit boards each year, if technology improvements were made.

When the Chinese first approached the division, they said that the circuit boards would be consumed internally to expand the domestic communications industry. This explanation seemed reasonable because the 1 billion Chinese own only 1 million television sets, and the Chinese made it clear that there was a great desire to expand the broadcasting of government programming (propaganda). In reality, they had a strong desire to export the product also, in order to bring in much needed foreign currency.

Initial Interaction

George Miassi, Director of Strategic Planning, recalled a conversation he'd had with Chauncey Alcott, Microchip Division's Director of Engineering in May of 1980. They had been discussing the initial moves in the negotiation with the Chinese for a project that had been code named *Red Dragon*.

Miassi: Chauncey, we've got to get a team over there as soon as possible to get this thing rolling.

Alcott: I agree. I think you and I have got to be in on it. You're the only one they've any contact with so far, and I've got to size up the situation before I can assign a project leader. We should take Fred Bland with us. He's a good solid technical engineer.

Miassi: Sounds good. This could be a great opportunity for you and your department to gain some positive visibility. At the same time, we can really corner the potential of the Far East market before the competition moves in.

The resulting trip took place in July of the same year. The team spent two weeks going through the Benxi plant compiling data for an initial feasibility study. As mentioned before, the plant was hopelessly outdated. The engineers' first impression was that the plant should be abandoned and completely rebuilt. There appeared to be no way to salvage the existing facility.

The Americans worked with several Chinese during this period. Huan Cho, Director of the Benxi Industrial Works, consisting of 12 plants manufacturing various products, had the overall responsibility for updating the production facility. His personal goal was to finish the project before his retirement in 1983.

One of the engineers in the plant, Gung Ho, attempted to answer the technical questions asked by the Microchip Division engineers. Unfortunately, none of the Chinese plant personnel spoke English. All communications were carried on through a young translator, Mi Lai, attached to the Ministry of Foreign Trade. Since Mr. Mi Lai did not work for the plants, he had no technical background. A great deal of frustration was experienced on both sides because of the inadequacy of the translation.

The Project Begins

Back at division headquarters, the two department heads discussed the next step.

Miassi: Chauncey, where do we go from here? You're the expert.

Alcott: We don't use project management here, but I think it makes sense in this case. A project team that works separately from the rest of the engineering jobs, that mainly concern plant expansions and renovations, is essential. I want to appoint Fred Bland as the project leader. He worked well with the Chinese. They respected his knowledge. I think he's a good man for this job.

Later:

Alcott: Fred, what would you think about heading up the Chinese project? You seemed to have developed a rapport with the Chinese. This could be a good project to open up some opportunities for you. George and I will give you all the support and guidance you need.

Bland: It sounds challenging. As long as I can call on you when I need help, I think I can handle this.

Alcott: OK. Let's get started. The Chinese want a proposal for a 100,000-unit-per-year-plant. Why don't you pick out the people you think you need and get started on it?

Bland: Hold on, Chauncey. I had the impression that there might be some problems with funding. A 100,000-unit plant is an expensive proposition. Their goals are so open-ended. I think they're counting on us to make a proposal that will meet their capacity needs and also not break them financially.

Alcott: That's not our concern. They requested a 100,000-unit plant, and that's what we'll propose.

The Proposal Is Developed

For the next 12 months, Fred Bland and one assistant worked feverishly on this proposal. The final product was presented to Chauncey Alcott for his review. Alcott was clearly impressed with the proposal. It was evident that the two people had put in effort beyond the call of duty to produce such a well thought-out product. The proposal clearly delineated the division's terms and was able to accomplish its goal of solidifying market position with minimal responsibility once the plant was completed. In August of 1981, Miassi, as the project sponsor, submitted Bland's proposal to the Chinese; it stated the following objectives:

- PRC Benefits:
    expanded market
    minimum capital costs
    higher production yields
    improved quality
- Division Benefits:
    long-term position in PRC
    no financial risk
    all selling rights for exports
    protection of proprietary technology
- PRC Contributions:
    capital improvement
    labor
    material installation
- Division Contributions:
    technology, know-how
    training, at cost
    engineering and technical support, at cost

The initial cost estimate was for $125 million. Shock was the Chinese reaction. They had no comprehension of why a plant would be so expensive. The division first discovered during that meeting that capital investment could be approved in Benxi up to only $1 million. The ministry in Liaoning Province could approve an additional $4 million. Anything over that had to go before the ministry in Beijing for a two-to-three-year approval period, which the Chinese vehemently wished to avoid. There was some discussion then of a scaled-down proposal aimed at upgrading the existing facility, rather than building a new one.

At the same meeting, George Miassi invited Huan Cho, Gung Ho, Mi Lai, and Loi Ro-Ring, a high ranking minister of foreign trade, to visit the division's newest, most modern plant in Phoenix, Arizona. The consensus at the division was that only by seeing this country and the level of technology in Phoenix could the Chinese ever understand what they were up against and the costs involved.

The visit took place early in February 1982. One outcome was to strengthen the positive feelings between the two groups, because the Chinese were very pleased with the people and cities they visited. In addition, the original objective of the visit was achieved as the Chinese compared the Phoenix plant to Benxi. As they were leaving, they admitted to Miassi that a new plant was beyond their reach at present and asked that a new proposal be submitted to upgrade their existing facility only.

The Confrontation

Alcott: Well, Fred, it's back to the drawing board. The Chinese have rejected your proposal. They want you to start working on a new one to upgrade the Benxi plant.

Bland: Wait a minute! I don't believe this. I warned you over a year ago that they couldn't afford this plant. We squandered resources that could have been better used on the Japanese joint venture, which obviously had the higher priority. And now you tell me you want me to start all over again. You wouldn't believe how difficult those Chinese are to work with. They are incredibly stubborn once they get an idea into their heads. I talk and talk. They smile and nod, and an hour later I'm still trying to convince them that the same thing won't work.

  The other big problem is that no one can make decisions. Everything has to be referred higher up. They kept pushing us to finish the proposal faster, but they couldn't get any responses back to me. Loi Ro-Ring actually has ultimate say on the project, and he knows nothing about chip production. He's a politician. Mi Lai can barely translate fifth grade grammar, let alone get across technical intricacies of the state-of-the-art operation. On their own, they can't possibly run a plant that will produce a quality product that they can export to any technically sophisticated market.

  And what the hell are they going to pay us with? Rice? They have been pushing for a trade compensation agreement from the first.

Alcott: Fred, why didn't you tell me you were having all these problems?

Bland: Jesus, Chauncey! Every time I tried to get in to see you, you were either in Japan or too busy. All that guidance and support you promised was diverted to the joint venture. I've been pissing in the wind for a year . . .

Alcott: (*interrupting*) I can see why you might feel this way. But, let me assure you that the corporate objectives are being met. The redirection won't change that. Your progress has been noted by upper management, and your contribution has been recognized.

Bland: Well, that's reassuring. I've put my heart into this project, and I'd hate to think the effort was wasted.

Later that day, Alcott received the following memo:

INTERNAL
MEMORANDUM

Date   March 1, 1982

To   Max E. Schott, Group V.-P., Corporate

From   George B. Miassi, Director of Strategic Planning, Microchip Division

Subject STATUS REPORT: RED DRAGON PROJECT

Project Red Dragon is an outstanding success to date. Since our first contact two years ago, we have continued to be the only chip producer actively negotiating with the PRC. Alcott has effectively prevented any realistic proposals from being developed, while building excellent rapport with key Chinese.

With this venture, we have elbowed out all the Japanese producers, the Germans, and, best of all—National Corporation. I am confident we can stonewall for up to another year before committing to any serious proposal. (AND, two or three more years will be required for the Chinese to authorize expense.)

Best of all, we're doing all this at minimal cost. Alcott assigned a dead-end engineer to coordinate the project and has those Chinese tangled up in their shorts. Max, we can easily carry this on for at least another three years.

GBM:ccp

cc: C. Z. Alcott

SITUATION 27: INDUSTRY/CONSTRUCTION PROJECTS DIVISION (I/CPD)[1]

The Situation

The Industry/Construction Projects Division (I/CPD) was formed to enhance Westinghouse's capabilities in competing for projects business in the industry products province. Since commercial operations began in April 1979, I/CPD has made an impact in the marketplace, with demonstrated success in winning international orders.

I/CPD is a Westinghouse Business Unit reporting to the Vice-President of Marketing, Industry Products. Division headquarters are at 2040 Ardmore Boulevard, Pittsburgh.

The general manager of I/CPD, said, "We go after the jobs that require project management, package pricing, and risk evaluation, and those that could include non-Westinghouse apparatus and services in the package. Above all, we emphasize teamwork between the Westinghouse divisions that produce the products, the various sales organizations, and our own staff."

This division is chartered to handle projects:

- Of $1 million or more in the industry products province
- With products from two or more divisions
- Managed under one contract
- Either domestic or international
- Having no other appropriate lead division

---

[1] The following description of this division is taken from Ⓦ *International News,* vol. 2, no. 1, February–March, 1981, pp. 8–9. Used by permission.

As shown in Figure 11, a successful projects capability requires coordination of a number of important functions. Those on the left are provided by I/CPD and include negotiation leadership, project management, proposal and contract capability, engineering, installation, and non-Westinghouse product. Functions handled by other organizations are shown on the right. Field Sales maintains responsibility for sales representation and business development leadership. I/CPD relies on the other divisions to provide competitive products and on Treasury for financing.

Geographically, a two-thirds portion (67 percent) of the I/CPD projects business won to date has been in the United States. The other third is divided between Saudi Arabia (17 percent), other Middle East countries (7 percent), and Latin America (9 percent).

More significantly, the percentage of international quotations has risen substantially during the past six months. Of approximately $200 million in outstanding quotations, over 85 percent is for international projects.

Some examples of international projects won and being managed by I/CPD are described here.

Gementos Tolteca.   The first international project won by I/CPD was originally quoted by Field Sales before I/CPD entered the marketplace. The customer, F. L. Smidth, a cement OEM, informed Westinghouse that a competitor was favored because "we could not offer the necessary project management to coordinate between U.S.- and Mexican-supplied apparatus," the general manager said. "It was at this point that our division was brought into the picture."

By establishing an acceptable project management organization, together with

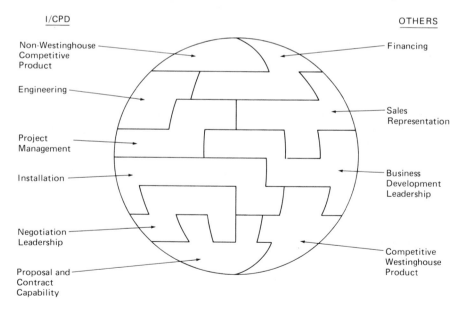

Figure 11.   Successful Project Capability.

successful customer visits to the Mexican supplier and continuous Field Sales selling leadership, Westinghouse was able to convert this lost project into a $6 million order, of which $4 million is for transformers, switchgear, medium voltage starters, motor control centers, and drives supplied by IEM, a Westinghouse licensee in Mexico.

During the management of this project, the customer has increased the scope of this order by more than $2 million.

The $200 million plant, which will have a production capacity of 1 million tons of cement per year, will belong to Cementos Tolteca, a Mexican company owned by Blue Circle Industries of London.

AEG-Telefunken.   In cooperation with Industry Products Marketing International, the I/C Projects Division achieved a breakthrough in the international construction market by winning an order valued at more than $1 million from AEG-Telefunken in Essen, West Germany, for electrical distribution and control equipment for the new Jeddah International Airport in Saudi Arabia. The Westinghouse equipment will be used to distribute electrical power and to control AC induction motors for the airport wet utilities, including irrigation, potable water, sewage, and fire pump facilities. AEG is the electrical installation contractor for this phase of the project.

This order resulted from the coordinated efforts of several groups within the Westinghouse organization. The international salesmen in Dusseldorf identified the project and maintained the appropriate customer relationships. The International Support Zone (ISZ), Pittsburgh-Ardmore, worked with the division marketing personnel to develop technical data and assemble an initial quotation. When this bid proved commercially unacceptable, I/CPD entered the negotiation to evaluate the risks and propose an appropriate commercial package. Quality performance thus far has been rewarded by an add-on order valued at more than $100,000.

Deliveries began in August 1980 and continued through January 1981. Installation will be completed this year.

Badger/ARAMCO.   An outstanding team effort between Industry Products sales personnel in the Netherlands and Saudi Arabia and I/CPD personnel in Pittsburgh was instrumental in securing a $750,000 order for supplying equipment for an ethane facility being built for ARAMCO at Yanbu industrial city in Saudi Arabia. The order, negotiated with the Badger Company in the Hague, Netherlands, was placed with Westinghouse by Algosaibi Engineering in Saudi Arabia. The Westinghouse sales team included sales people from ISZ, IPMI in Brussels, and I/CPD, Pittsburgh.

To get this project off to a good start, last December I/CPD personnel accompanied Badger personnel on visits to all company divisions supplying apparatus.

Arabian Gulf Oil Company.   I/CPD is managing the efforts of eight Westinghouse divisions and four outside suppliers in providing electrical equipment valued at more than $5 million for a crude oil gathering, conditioning, and pipeline system for the Arabian Gulf Oil Company (AGOCO) in Libya. Williams Brothers in Tulsa, Oklahoma, is engineering the project.

The negotiation involved a coordinated sales effort from Tulsa to Benghazi. During final negotiations in Benghazi, people from the Westinghouse Canada Office provided valuable assistance to the I/CPD project sales manager and the I/CPD contracts manager, and a senior application engineer from Dallas, was instrumental in supporting the project engineering requirements.

In November 1980, I/CPD was host to eight AGOCO employes enrolled in the International Human Resources Development Corporation's Petroleum Technology Program. During their visit they attended a presentation at the Westinghouse R&D Center and toured the East Pittsburgh plant, where they saw the AGOCO equipment being built.

Centromin del Pero.   In a project of substantial importance to Peru's economy, electrical distribution equipment valued at nearly $800,000 is being supplied to Centromin del Peru for a new transmission line to supply power for the Cobriza I and II copper mines.

The successful sales effort was handled by ISZ and a Westinghouse representative in San Diego, Chile. I/CPD is providing the necessary project management and engineering to coordinate the equipment supply among the seven divisions involved.

Saudi Arabian Royal Commission.   Electrical distribution equipment valued at some $2 million for a desalination plant for the Yanbu industrial city in Saudi Arabia will be manufactured at WESCOSA's plant in Dammam, Saudi Arabia. The WESCOSA portion is part of an $8 million order awarded to I/CPD by the Saudi Arabian Royal Commission for Yanbu and Jubail. The order was obtained through the combined efforts of I/CPD, WESCOSA, and ISZ. To meet the critical delivery requirements of the order, I/CPD will charter a 747 aircraft to deliver the U.S.-made equipment that must be installed first.

Following a trip to the Kingdom in November to bid this project, the I/CPD representative returned to Saudi Arabia in December for final negotiations and signing of a letter of intent with the Saudi Royal Commission.

Your Task

1. Evaluate the strategic rationale for the organizational design of the Industry/Construction Projects Division within the Westinghouse Corporation.

2. Determine what changes would probably be required in the cultural ambience of this corporation to facilitate the successful operation of this new division.

3. I/CPD is described as a "Westinghouse Business Unit." What does this mean?

4. Are there any other functions that you would add to Figure 11?

5. What future strategies might the senior executives of this business unit be concerned about?

6. How might this division's charter change over the next five years?

SITUATION 28:   THE CULTURAL EFFECT OF MATRIX MANAGEMENT

The Situation

Culture is a set of refined behaviors that people strive toward in their society. It includes the whole complex of a society—knowledge, beliefs, art, ethics, morals, law, custom, and other habits and attitudes acquired by the individual as a member of society. Anthropologists have used the concept of culture in describing primitive societies. Modern-day sociologists have borrowed this anthropological usage to describe a way of life of a people. Borrowing from the sociologists, the term *culture* is used to describe the synergistic set of shared ideas and beliefs that are associated with a way of life in an organization. The cultural ambience of the project-driven matrix organization is unique in many respects.

The matrix design is a compromise between a bureaucratic approach that is too rigid and a simple unit structure that is too centralized. The design is fluid: personnel assignments, authority basis, and interpersonal relationships are constantly shifting. It lends a sense of democracy to a bureaucratic context.

From an organizational design viewpoint, the entire organization must be psychologically tuned to the accomplishments within the organization that support higher-level organizational objectives, goals, and strategies. The purpose of a matrix design is not only to get the best from its strong project and functional approaches, but to complement these facets with a strong unit of command at the senior level and ensure that the balance of power is maintained in the organization.

In some companies only one or, at most, a few divisions may benefit from a realignment to the project-driven matrix form; the others can remain in the pyramidal, hierarchical format. Indeed, a single organization chart cannot realistically portray the maze of relationships that exist inside a large organization, because some units select project management, others opt for the conventional line-staff design, and others choose a hybrid form.

A company engaged in the core business of designing, building, installing, and startup of computer-based information systems has recently realigned its organizational structure to emphasize the management of projects to support its core business. Recently several key customers have asked the question: "Who in your organization is designated to act as a focal point for the management of our project?"

At a recent meeting, the senior executives of the firm recalled some of the reasons that had been used to realign part of the firm into a project-driven matrix design:

- There is a need to design, develop, and produce a complex information system on an ad hoc basis to satisfy a specific customer need.
- Customers desire that their projects be managed from a focal point as a relatively independent organizational unit within the vendor's organization.
- Numerous components, subsystems, and systems must be developed in parallel across/outside the organization to complete the project.
- Close planning and control of cost, schedule, and technical performance of each project are required.
- Need exists to share scarce specialty resources with other units of the organization.
- Emerging market strategy dictates the use of project management to remain competitive in the marketplace.
- Profit-center decentralization to product-groups could be further decentralized to project profit centers.
- Other alternative organizational designs (functional, process, geographic, etc.) that were evaluated did not seem to fit the need.

The senior managers of the functional organizations in this company were concerned about how the new matrix design might impinge on their prerogatives of maintaining autonomy of their organizational units. Another concern was how matrix management might impact on the operation of their function, i.e., if matrix management as it currently exists in their function continues, what impact will it have in the way they conduct their business? What would the function do differently? What cultural changes might be expected? What attitudinal changes might be required on the part of the key managers and professionals in the functional organization?

One of the senior functional managers had had some experience in matrix management, having served on a project team in his previous company. This executive stated at one of the management council meetings of the company:

> When matrix management is introduced into an organization, a series of cultural and organizational changes are set in motion. One of the first visible changes is the change in organizational structure. As a result of the structural change, managerial and professional roles change as well. Indeed, the realignment into a matrix structure sets in motion a "system of effects," which are often not considered when matrix management is initially introduced. The ultimate success of matrix management often depends on how supportive these accommodating systems have been and how the organizational culture supports the new matrix design. For example, the existing information systems have to be modified to provide information to matrix managers and matrix teams, as well as to the functional and general managers.

This executive further stated that the key managers and professionals should take time to fully understand the "systems" and "cultural" changes that matrix management might have on the company.

After a lively debate it was decided that no one in the company had sufficient knowledge and skills to assess the potential matrix management changes that the company faced. Accordingly, it was decided to try to find a consultant from a local university who might help the company adapt to the evolving project management system.

Your Task

Assume that you are a consultant whose field of expertise is matrix management. What would you advise these executives to do?

SITUATION 29: ACCELERATION OF AN INTERNATIONAL MATRIX MANAGEMENT SYSTEM

The Situation

The international organization of the Transnational Corporation has been in existence for some time. During a recent management council meeting, a matrix responsibility model of the product-group in-country matrix interface was shown, as reflected in

Table 2.   International Matrix Management Responsibility Chart. [a]

Business Unit Lead Responsibility	Shared Responsibility	Country Management Lead Responsibility
World product strategic planning and implementation	• Defining the nature of in-country presence (investments, local manufacture, licensing, etc.)	• In-country strategic planning and implementation
World product sourcing World pricing (export)	• In-country subsidiary management: Objectives, goals, & strategies Investment levels In-country pricing	• In-country marketing: Sales channels & organizations Distribution policies Special sales representatives
Product technology: Research Design/development Manufacturing	• Product support • Project management	• Support services • Corporate representation: Government relations Public relations
Human resources	• Human resources: Key personnel: Selection Development Compensation	• Human resources

[a] Source: Ricketts, John F., "Matrix Management in a Transnational Mode," *Matrix Management Systems Handbook,* David I. Cleland (ed.), Van Nostrand Reinhold Co., New York, 1983.

Table 2. A senior executive of the international organization described the four cornerstones of the new international matrix management system as:

- Shared decisions
- Shared accountability
- Shared results
- The fundamental concept that the country would be a primary building block of the international organization

Key managers present at the management council meeting accepted the premise of the shared context of matrix management. There was, however, speculation about how this style of management could be assimilated into the corporation's culture at a faster rate.

Your Task

Develop a summary strategy of how the operation of this corporation's international matrix management system could be accelerated. In developing this strategy you might wish to consider the following:

- How to get the emotional involvement of the product-group executive vice presidents,
- Identify criteria that product groups should use to establish priorities where acceleration could be applied,
- What *not* to do in this acceleration effort,
- Leverage that could be applied by senior corporate executives in motivating this acceleration by involved parties.

Prepare a summary briefing to share your ideas with the other people evaluating this case.

SITUATION 30: RESPONSIBILITY-SHARING IN THE INTERNATIONAL MATRIX

Introduction

Multinational companies are usually organized to do business globally on a matrix system of management. In these companies, responsibility for strategic and key operating activities is divided among organizational elements as follows:

Product.   Responsibility concentrated in product or product line management with worldwide perspective.

Geography.   Responsibility concentrated within a specific territory, such as a country.

Function.   Responsibility concentrated in an organization's functional specialty, such as finance, production, marketing, or research and development.

In the international company there is usually two coordinated avenues of strategic planning: product and geographic. Because decisions are shared, accountability for results is also shared in terms of product and geographic profitability through profit centers. Financial visibility by product, function, and geography is the norm in the multinational company.

A basic factor in international management that is significantly affected by matrix management is the traditional concept of the profit center, with its delegation of authority to one manager who is held responsible for producing profitable results. To him, everything counts at the profit-center level, everything is measured there, and people are rewarded accordingly. Certain key decisions, such as product pricing, product sourcing, product discrimination, human resources, facility management, and cash management, are traditionally considered the profit center manager's prerogative.

But in international matrix management, the profit center manager may share key decision making with others. Some managers, accustomed to making these decisions on their own, find that sharing decision making with some other manager outside the parent hierarchy can be a cultural shock. For example, in product pricing in the international market, the profit center manager will find it necessary to work with an in-country manager to establish price. Product sourcing decisions may be made by senior marketing executives at corporate headquarters, rather than by the profit center manager. In practice, decision authority should be complementary. If the managers cannot reach agreement on these decisions, it may be necessary to refer the conflict to a common line supervisor for resolution.

The Situation

The senior executives of a large international corporation decided that a basic policy document was needed that would portray the relative responsibility of the product group and geographic managers. A senior executive at the corporate staff level suggested that something like the international matrix management responsibility chart in Figure 12 was a good way to start.

Your Task

Evaluate the probable relevance of the international matrix management responsibility chart to a company competing in the international marketplace. In particular, evaluate the following:

1. What would you recommend be done to further evaluate this document in the company?
2. If there is a conflict between the two managers who are operating under this policy document, who should resolve that conflict?
3. What do you think is meant by the notion of "shared responsibility?"

BUSINESS UNIT LEAD RESPONSIBILITY	SHARED RESPONSIBILITY	COUNTRY MANAGEMENT LEAD RESPONSIBILITY
• World Product Strategic Planning & Implementation	• Nature In-Country Presence (Investment, Licensing, etc.)	• In-Country Strategic Planning & Implementation
• World Product Sourcing (Single Trader)	• In-Country Subsidiary Management	• Marketing
• World Pricing (Export)	—Obj/Goals/Strategies	—Sales Reps.
• Product Technology	—Investment	—Distribution
—Research	—Pricing (In-Country)	—Special Sales Reps.
—Design/Development	• Product Support	• Support Services
—Manufacturing	• Project Management	• Corporate Representation
• Human Resources	• Human Resources Key Personnel	—Gov't. Relations
	—Selection	—Public Relations
	—Development	• Human Resources
	—Compensation	

Figure 12.   International Matrix Responsibility Chart. (John F. Ricketts, "Matrix Management in a Transnational Mode," *Matrix Management Systems Handbook,* David I. Cleland (Ed.), Van Nostrand Reinhold Co., New York, 1983.

4. What official in the corporation should be responsible for seeing that the policy in this document is carried out?
5. What might be some of the problems growing out of the implementation of this policy?
6. How would you fix responsibility for profit center profit and loss in this organization if the company were operating under this policy?
7. Do you have any suggestions for improving this policy document?

SITUATION 31:   THE MULTINATIONAL CORPORATION

The Situation

In the late 1970s the senior executives of a large U.S. corporation, the Multinational Corporation (MNC) became concerned about its ability to compete adequately in the international marketplace. A task force of approximately 45 people was set up to investigate and develop data bases to analyze just where MNC stood in terms of its ability to compete in the international arena. This task force was composed of people from different disciplines and different organizational levels in the corporation. During the course of the task force's deliberations, over 300 key people were interviewed by the task force to develop data bases on everything from the strengths and weaknesses of MNC in its international business to a comprehensive analysis of the market opportunities and the nature and intensity of the competition.

One of the panels (called the *organization panel*) of the task force was assigned the mission of studying and evaluating other large diversified multinational companies to determine how they were organized to do business internationally, and the approaches they used to penetrate the international marketplace. The purpose of this panel's investigation was to develop insights that could be used to influence the strategic and organizational decisions the MNC would have to make to design and implement strategy in the international marketplace.

The approach taken by the organization panel of the task force consisted of several modules:

1. The selection of successful multiproduct/multinational companies for analysis
2. The determination of how such companies were organized and how they managed their international activities
3. The determination of the rationale behind each company's organization and management of their international business
4. The comparison of various company approaches to the international marketing and management taken by the corporations
5. The development of organizational patterns or methods of operation that appear to be common to successful international companies, and the evaluation of the methods of operation accomplished by the corporations

Following agreement on the strategy for the organizational panel to begin its work, the members agreed on the specific areas of investigation of the international companies that would be carried out:

1. Overall corporate objectives, policies, organizational philosophy, and the general philosophy concerning international business and how such business fits into the overall corporate objectives
2. International organization and the relationship with the domestic structure, in particular the relative influence of product, function, and geographic responsibility
3. Organization of international marketing and sales—how organized—reporting lines, and responsibilities
4. Approach to international sales—export, in-country, manufacturing, licensing, joint venture, etc.
5. International strategic and marketing planning
6. International staff services, personnel policies
7. Miscellaneous—turnkey projects, countertrade, barter, etc.

After the task force was organized and the strategy decided for its operation, the members began a period of several weeks of extensive travel, visiting and talking with senior executives in the largest and most successful companies in international business. Table 3 presents a summary of the companies that were interviewed, the levels of the people interviewed, and the length of the interviews.

After the mass of data was gathered and analyzed, the panel prepared Figure 13

Table 3. Summary of Companies Interviewed.

Companies	Level of Person Interviewed	Length of Interview, Hours
1	Staff-World Trade Corporation	4
2	Staff Vice-President/Consultant	10
3	Group Vice-President	4
4	CEO and Various Staff	12
5	Manager of Overseas Operations	2
6	V.-P.—Power Systems International	6
7	Three Vice-Presidents	4
8	V.-P. International/Staff Dept. Manager	5
9	Group V.-P. & Staff/Manager of Spain	4
10	Vice-President of Finance	3
11	President, International	3
12	Vice-President of Corporate Staff	3
13	CEO & Board Director	8
14	V.-P. Planning & Overseas/Other	16
15	Vice-President of International	3
16	Vice-President of International	2
17	Vice-President of Marketing & Staff	7
18	Vice-President of International	2
19	Line & Staff Vice-Presidents	12
20	Vice-President of Operations	2
21	Various Levels of Administration and Operational Groups	14

MULTINATIONAL
CORPORATION
(MNC)

P – % of influence concentrated in product
    or product line management with
    worldwide responsibility

G – % of influence concentrated within
    national boundaries independent of
    "P" and "F"

F – % of influence concentrated in
    corporate functional specialities (mfg.,
    eng., mktg., finance, planning)

-50%
-% International
Sales

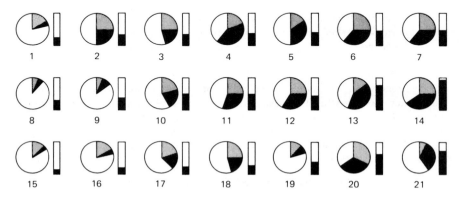

Figure 13.   Organizational Influences: Product–Geography–Function.

to portray the organizational influences found in the international organizations interviewed.

In addition, the panel members put together a briefing chart for each company
interviewed that contained summary information organized as follows: corporate overview; organizational strategy; key philosophies supporting organizational strategy;
international thrust; unique characteristics; and product, geographic, and functional
influence. These briefing charts, along with a summary chart, shown in Table 4,
were presented to the senior management of the company during one of the top-
level review sessions of the task force activities.

Your Assignment

Assume you are a senior member of the corporate management council and have
just heard the organization panel present its report. As you reflect on what the panel
members presented, you wonder what this all might mean in terms of a potential
realignment of the MNC corporate organizational structure and management philosophy. At the next meeting of the management council, you know that you will be
expected to state your opinion of what all this might mean to the corporation. What
will you say?

Table 4. General Conclusions.

1. There are as many organizational variations as there are companies, but all include some interrelationship of the three basic organizational elements—product, function and geography.

2. Product is the dominant (vertical) organizational element in almost all organizations; there is a high degree of correlation between a company's "internationalism" (international sales, overseas employees, and so forth) and the extent of horizontal coordination of matrix structure in the organization.

3. Matrix structures (dual solid-line reporting) and split-pricing responsibility (and reporting) are becoming increasingly common in large international companies.

4. The use of in-country managers is a common mechanism in most European companies to provide geographic coordination; in-country manufacturing divisions and sales operations report in some way to both their product group and the in-country manager.

5. The international companies (particularly in Europe and Japan) emphasize group performance and coordination in their organizations, rather than individual performance and responsibility; this is reflected in their compensation policies.

6. In international companies use of nationals in high-level management positions in overseas operations is an important part of overseas strategy—as in a general policy of mixing nationals with senior home office managers on assignment (using such assignments as a means of training key executives with high potential).

7. The necessity for having a capability for handling large multiproduct projects is recognized as increasingly important by all companies—primarily for penetrating developing country markets. It is handled "with difficulty" by most companies except where they have an A&E organization that is, by charter, given responsibility for such projects.

8. What other companies do organizationally must be viewed with the realization that companies outside the United States are more growth- than profit-oriented and are more interested in their companies as national assets, sources of jobs, etc., than in their stockholders.

9. Financial visibility by both product and geography is the norm among international corporations (whose international sales are more than 40% of total sales), as is centralized handling of foreign currency exposure.

10. International corporations almost universally have two coordinated avenues of strategic planning—planning by product and planning by geography.

SITUATION 32: IMPLEMENTING INTERNATIONAL MATRIX MANAGEMENT

The Situation

A large U.S. corporation elected to reorganize its corporate structure to create an international company reporting to the chief executive. This company was set up as a profit center and reported at the same level as five other profit center companies. Because the international company was to function primarily as a marketing organization, it was necessary to create an international matrix form of reporting relationship with the rest of the corporation. Under this form of matrix arrangement, it was assumed that decisions, resources, and results would be shared between the product-line, geographic, and functional managers in the company.

The first step in establishing this international management system within the company was to develop new organization charts and to begin the organization of supporting systems for the new structure: information, accounting, personnel evaluation, strategic planning, and so on. At about this time there began to develop a deep concern on the part of the senior executives that there would be some difficulties in implementing fully the new matrix management system. It was decided that a consultant should be hired to do some in-depth interviewing of the senior executives of the corporation to determine the perceptions these people had concerning the probable success of implementing the new approach.

Accordingly a consultant was engaged to conduct in-depth interviews with 30 top managers, to gain their perceptions of some of the relevant problems or opportunities to be encountered in implementing matrix management in the corporation. These interviews, primarily nondirective in nature, and conducted in the context of diplomatic immunity, provided a profile of how the 30 top people perceived the introduction of matrix management into the corporation.

The consultant conducted the interviews and then organized the results into a report that he forwarded to the top decision makers in the company. The essence of the report submitted by the consultant is contained below, where the findings developed during the interviews are presented by topic. The comments cited under each topic are representative of the total comments made by the interviewees.

1. Expected Cultural Changes.   The matrix management system will be most difficult to manage. A cultural factor has to be changed—namely, the profit center concept. Everything counts at the profit center level, and everything is measured there.

The process should not be started without addressing two critical questions: (1) how will the results be measured, and (2) how are the rewards going to be passed out, beyond the profit center concept, on some team basis, or whatever?

The crux of the whole matter is shared decisions, shared accountability, and shared results.

There are three things that have to be done to make matrix management successful: (1) a dedication on the part of the corporation managers to make matrix management work; (2) the sharing of awards and the scorekeeping has to be changed from the single profit center idea currently in practice; and (3) basic cultural changes, attitudinal changes, have to come about.

We must consider the cultural changes that will result from matrix management, such as matrix accounting, and matrix scorekeeping.

There's a basic change needed in the top management style and in the culture of the corporation.

The biggest problem in the corporation's cultural ambience is the direct line responsibility of the profit center manager.

Biggest problem in education is to change our culture. We have operated for 30 years with the idea that the profit center manager has equal authority and responsibility. This has to be redefined. Now we are moving to a period of joint decision making.

2. Degree of Knowledge.   By far our biggest problem at the present time is the uncertainty of matrix management and what it means. We should concentrate on getting roles defined in terms of specific authority and responsibility as soon as possible. Faith and trust are also problems. We should remember that we're all on the same team and that we have to operate in such a way.

Most key people don't know what matrix management means. They're used to the bottom line, solid line mentality. This includes executive vice-presidents, group vice-presidents, and division managers.

How will the international organization work? This is really what has to be clarified. The use of dotted lines versus solid lines isn't going to give us the answer.

Matrix is a big unknown for many people. They fear what it means to them.

I tend to "blur the interfaces" in matrix management. By blurring the interfaces, this forces people to get together and try to sort out what has to be done by way of shared decisions. This tends to lower many of the attitudinal barriers.

3. Attitude Change.   Our senior people really don't understand what matrix management means or accept what it might do to their territory. They just can't accept the notion of some of their people having two bosses. I urge you as an urgent first step to deal with the attitudinal question of matrix management and then to deal with the methodological aspects of it.

People must develop the attitude that they are willing to sit down and talk in the matrix business: There must be an ambience of faith and trust that this is what it's all about.

The last prerogative that I will give up is price control. Do I have to share this with somebody else?

The biggest problem of all is the matter of attitude. How are we really going to divide the territory?

Emphasize that it (matrix) can work only through people, that it has to work through the willingness of the people to be committed, that this is the direction we should go in.

If you create the attitude that everything should be kicked upstairs in matrix management for resolution, you will kill the idea. The resolution has to be done at the lowest possible level. Only extraordinary items should be kicked up to the executive vice-president or president and on into the management committee.

The biggest problem will be in getting people to understand the division of responsibility in the matrix organization.

The problems in matrix organizations are matters of the balance of power.

Attitudinally, people will fear and be apprehensive of the matrix organization. It is countercultural. We should develop something along these lines.

An attitudinal factor: How are you going to deal with the feeling the business unit has that it is giving up some of its territory?

The attitudinal question may be the most difficult of all.

There are "walls of autonomy" that have to be torn down. These are paper walls. People stand on their territory and won't let anyone come in.

The executive vice-presidents have the greatest resistance to change in this respect. There are a lot of "bull mooses"; yet these people are the ones who have to make the top interfaces work. I think we will have less trouble with the division and subsidiary kind of interfaces.

Average line managers can't accept the matrix idea. They cannot accept that they may have to report to more than one person.

4. Compensation System/Incentive System.   Both product managers and country managers have to become involved in a joint reward system. This is absolutely vital.

How are the rewards and punishment systems going to work in the new international activities?

How are we going to measure and reward managers in the matrix environment? This is different from what most of us are used to.

There is a great need to revamp the compensation system, if we are going to go to matrix management. The management committee should be concerned about this.

We must get involved in looking very critically at our current incentive system and possibly redesign it to something like a group incentive system.

5. Strategic Planning.   Major decision areas and the basis on which they will be shared have to be delineated in such areas as subsidiaries, profit objectives, strategic planning, and so forth.

Another strategic issue is product differentiation, which has to be dealt with in terms of the strategic planning issue. Maybe we don't do country-by-country planning, but rather a modified type of product planning.

How is strategic planning going to be accomplished in the matrix organization? And how is the plan to be generated?

How do we get the business units to work together in strategic planning? A strategic plan should be based upon country and business unit dimensions. This all has to be dealt with in the matrix concept. Perhaps a strategic plan will have to be signed off by both parties.

There is a need for education in how we are to do our strategic planning, particularly how the product, geographic, and business unit managers share responsibility in the development of goals.

Strategic planning processes have to be changed. Country strategic planning management has to fit in logically and completely with the business units and various presidents' expectations.

6. Education of Management Council.   The trouble will start when the first decision comes along and is kicked up to the management council for resolution. This is when the best training for the management council will come about.

The management council has operated as a team for some time. It doesn't need education in matrix management, except in the sense of dealing with strategic issues and opportunities arising out of the international operation.

The management council must grapple with some strategic issues, such as dual accounts: who pays, and who keeps the change? Dual reward systems, dual objective setting, how to handle strategic expenses, how to do strategic planning, how to measure cost and incremental effect, how to manage facilities, human resource decisions, cash management, credit, and collection—these are all strategic issues that the management council has to face up to sometime or other.

In successful matrix management, it is necessary that you get disputed decisions up to the management council for resolution before the decisions become polarized.

7. *Function of In-Country Managers.*   We need to develop a profile of the function of the in-country manager.

8. *Educational Techniques—Shared Decisions—Matrix Responsibility Chart.*   Procedures must be developed on an orderly basis as to who has to be consulted and who participates in the shared decisions.

We must be concerned about the decision making in the matrix context, and how that will be shared on a consensus basis. Some of these strategic issues are sharing the budget, sharing the incentives, and so forth.

The joint decisions of matrix management is a tough one, and this is really the key problem—cultural problem—within the corporation. The decision context will be difficult. We can't get two people to agree on a decision; therefore, you'll have no decision. Rather, we have to develop the opportunity where we have a dialogue, with ultimately somebody taking the lead.

The second issue lies more heavily in the operating sphere (although it can invade strategy-making also), and that is what you call *interface,* which I think is a better shirt sleeve term than *matrix.* We want to be competent in joint or shared decision making. Our cultural impediment is 25 years of decentralized, "independent," autonomous profit center management.

In the educational effort, emphasize some of the shared decisions, such as planning process, strategic planning, evaluation of key people, choice of key people, selection of strategies, development plan for key people, the building of what product and where, the actual sales effort, and so forth.

Use some matrix responsibility chart that ultimately can delineate who's responsible for what.

The real issue in matrix management is the decision making and how that is going to operate.

How are bookings, billings, adjustments, investments, and so forth handled?

What's the process for resolving conflict?

Shared responsibility and authority—that's really what it is all about.

A strategic issue that has to be dealt with is the financial aspect. How is this to be handled? Both sides have to make this work. It has to deal with processes as well as performance standards. Human resources is another area in which it can be used.

Some of the shared decisions that the key managers are going to have to deal with include product sourcing, product pricing, terms and conditions, limit of authority, cash management, capital investment, subsidiary profit and loss statement management.

Don't walk away from the word *matrix;* it is consistent with interface, but it does keep in front of us all that we have to share the division with somebody else.

9. *Modus Operandi.*   We must deal soon and completely in developing a clear definition of responsibility and authority.

There will be many decisions that have to be worked through the interfaces. These have to be understood.

I emphasize again that the interfaces have to be developed by the executive vice-presidental level.

The matrix manager has to know where the power is, and he gains this power by working through the interfaces involved.

The international organization must never forget that it is there to work with and support the line-operating people, and that its success will be only as successful as the line manager wants it to be.

How is the international organization going to mesh with the rest of the corporation?

There will be a tremendous need for communication.

A real concern is the question of how to know if matrix management is successful. This can be done only in the context of establishing the appropriate objectives, goals, and so forth.

What are we going to do to the division manager's freedom to roam the world and sell his product? Is this going to be hampered by the international organization?

How are we going to share the profit/loss monthly review meetings? Can the international people attend these with us?

Matrix management puts more on management cost, which is probably true, but what's the cost of not doing this?

The international organization should be aware of the need to make long-range decisions.

10. Examples of Matrix Management.   There is a misconception that the controller's organization is managed on a matrix basis within a corporation. This is not true. A division manager has little choice in many vital financial decisions. These decisions are based on corporate policy. There can be little ground for negotiation.

We structured an incentive program to award two or more people on a project basis. We spent time explaining how this would operate, and then we set up teams. In setting up these teams, we had a dialogue on what each really does. We sat down and went through the development of a work breakdown structure and dealt with the question of shared decisions.

Matrix management exists in many contexts. For example, in the business unit manager's sharing of labor relations with someone else, his sharing of financial policies; in addition, the business unit manager has little to say about how his debt inequity will be worked. They (the business unit managers) are really not completely in charge and never have been. Field sales is another place in which matrix management has been practiced, for example, in the choice of distribution channels and in pricing.

Your Task

What insight do these key managers' perceptions give of the problems and opportunities of implementing matrix management in this company?

What strategy would you recomend in implementing matrix management in this corporation?

What problems do you see that might arise while matrix management is being implemented in this company?

What might be done to preclude the emergence and development of such problems?

Be prepared to defend your answers to these questions.